Dear Rookie—

I'd never have gotten through Mr. K's chemistry class without you. Distillation of Wood! Boyle's Law! You're the best and I adore you, as in an ALL-CAPS sort of way, as in LOWERCASE LOVE. Can't go back to lowercase with you, been through too much. Stay sweet, stay you.

Carrie "Brownie" Brownstein

You are too true to be good !!! May your summer be filled with a surplus of serotonin and sun (sorsun). xoxo deedee

S0-ATV-172

Silverton School Library
1160 Snowden
Box 128
Silverton, CO 81433

ROOKiE,
←me   you→

Thank you for being so nice to me this year.

♥, Gillian Jacobs

DEAR ROOKiE,
I'LL ALWAYS REMEMBER:
• SLURPEES IN THE GRAVEYARD
• DISNEYLAND W/ DYLAN T.R. & OLIVIA B.
• WAKING UP IN HISTORY IN A POOL OF DROOL
• DRESSIN LIKE FREAKS AND LOVIN iT
gnome shoes
DON'T EVR CHANGe! SERIOUSLY.
LOVE YA! ♥ KING TUFFY
P.S. U R A TRUE INSPIRATION!

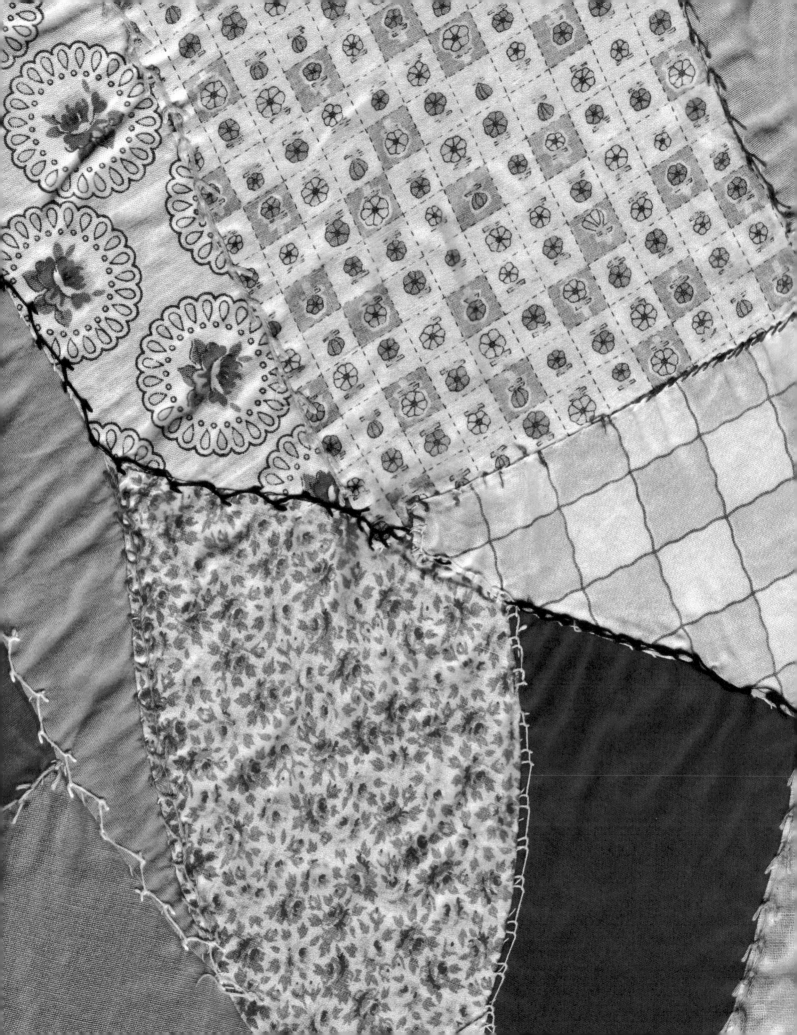

ROOKIE

YEARBOOK TWO

EDITED BY TAVI GEVINSON

RAZORBILL
AN IMPRINT OF PENGUIN GROUP (USA)

Editor-in-Chief: Tavi Gevinson

Editorial Director: Anaheed Alani

Art Director: Tavi Gevinson

Designer: Tracy Hurren

Managing Editor: Lauren Redding

Deputy Editor: Phoebe Reilly

Story Editors: Anaheed Alani & Phoebe Reilly

Production Manager: Tracy Hurren

Production Assistant: Marie-Jade Menni

Publisher: Chris Oliveros

Associate Publisher: Peggy Burns

◆ ◇ ◆

Cover design: Tavi Gevinson & Tracy Hurren

Cover art:

Olivia Bee

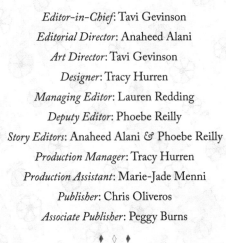

razor bill

A division of Penguin Young Readers Group
Published by the Penguin Group
Penguin Group (USA) LLC
345 Hudson Street
New York, New York 10014

USA / Canada / UK / Ireland / Australia / New Zealand / India / South Africa / China
Penguin.com
A Penguin Random House Company

ISBN: 9781595148278

Printed in the United States of America
Originally Published by Drawn & Quarterly

1 3 5 7 9 10 8 6 4 2

CONTENTS

CONTRIBUTORS

Sonja Ahlers
Ruby Aitken
Anaheed Alani
Maude Apatow
Ava Asaadi
Olivia Bee
Jaclyn Bethany
Esme Blegvad
Judy Blume
Ruby Book
Krista Burton
Rebekah Campbell
Elvia Carreon
Pixie Casey
Naomi Christina
Hazel Cills
Petra Collins
Joe Coscarelli
Emma Dajska
Shae Daspin
Katherine Denney
Zaid Díaz

Sady Doyle
Lena Dunham
Karen Elson
Anna Fitzpatrick
Sarah Sophie Flicker
Tyler Ford
Stacey May Fowles
Britney Franco
Meagan Fredette
Cindy Gallop
Laia Garcia
Roxane Gay
Tavi Gevinson
Ben Giles
Minna Gilligan
Emily V. Gordon
Gabi Gregg
Grimes
María Inés Gul
Eleanor Hardwick
Danielle Henderson
Beth Hoeckel

Jessica Hopper
Mindy Kaling
Etgar Keret
Mirren Kessling
Shanzeh Khurram
Nao Koyabu
Stephanie Kuehnert
Ginette Lapalme
Allegra Lockstadt
Marie Lodi
Lisa Maione
Jane Marie
María Fernanda Molins
Alexandra Moon-Age
Brooke Nechvatel
Gabby Noone
Clara Pathé
Chelsea Peacock
Lola Pellegrino
Lauren Poor
Marlena Pope
Rachael Prokop

María Rangel Isas
Phoebe Reilly
Rodarte
Dylan Tupper Rupert
Erica Segovia
M. Sharkey
Julianne Escobedo Shepherd
Miriam Shlesinger
Alex Simms
Beth Siveyer
Amy Rose Spiegel
Elizabeth Spiridakis
Hattie Stewart
Emma Straub
Maggie Thrash
Chrissie White
Jamia Wilson
Leanna Wright
Suzy X.
Kendra Yee
Allyssa Yohana
Jenny Zhang

ACKNOWLEDGMENTS

Thank you to…

Our incredible staff of writers, illustrators, and photographers for sharing pieces of themselves to make all of this. I marvel multiple times every day at how badly I lucked out to even know such people.

Anaheed Alani, Lauren Redding, and Phoebe Reilly for editing, managing, and shaping this beast.

Everyone at Drawn & Quarterly for publishing this book and making it look good: Emily Belanger, Peggy Burns, Tom Devlin, Tracy Hurren, Marie-Jade Menni, Chris Oliveros, and Julia Pohl-Miranda.

Sonja Ahlers for working her collage magic for us again this year with those beautiful monthly opening spreads.

Kelly Abeln, Leeay Aikawa, Ruby Aitken, Esme Blegvad, Emma Dajska, Minna Gilligan, Caitlin Hazell, Beth Hoeckel, Allegra Lockstadt, Leanna Wright, and Kendra Yee for making us such rad stickers.

Minna Gilligan, María Inés Gul, Allegra Lockstadt, Brooke Nechvatel, Suzy X., and Kendra Yee for creating new illustrations just for this book.

Sonja Ahlers for lettering titles for September and December, María Inés Gul for lettering titles and drawing Björk for January, Lisa Maione for lettering titles for January and May, and Brooke Nechvatel for creating watercolor titles for June, February, and April.

Cynthia Merhej for lettering the Rookie logo and cover.

Olivia Bee for taking that striking cover photo, and the teenagers in it for cutting their hair at just the right time.

Hattie Stewart for letting us raid her bountiful library of doodles to decorate the month of May.

Genevieve Champagne of (Found)erie in Montreal for letting us borrow clothes from her lovely shop to decorate these pages.

Ginette Lapalme for making us that no-fail cootie catcher.

Chris Ware for letting us use his wonderful self-portrait.

Claire Boucher aka Grimes for letting us show off her fantastic illustrations.

Judy Blume for writing such a thoughtful letter to our readers.

Mindy Kaling for answering all of our questions, in her interview and letter.

Lena Dunham for conducting that brilliant interview with Mindy, making us all feel like their best friends.

Judd Apatow, Mike Birbiglia, Carrie Brownstein, Katie and Allison Crutchfield, Autumn and Arrow de Wilde, Dana Falconberry, Eleanor Friedberger, Gillian Jacobs, Julie Klausner, Kate and Laura Mulleavy of Rodarte, Kate Nash, Dee Dee Penny of Dum Dum Girls, Winona Ryder, Kyle Thomas of King Tuff, Chris Ware, and Xenia for writing Rookie such nice end-of-the-year messages for our inside covers.

All of these people for making so much other work that inspires us. We encourage our readers to have a look-see.

Claire, Grace, and Hunter; Mom, Dad, Miriam, and Rivkah.

Anaheed for everything everything everything.

Our readers for reading us, supporting us, sharing with us, and being the all-around best.

WELCOME

Hi, Rookies! How nice to see you here again. Or, if this is your first time picking up a Rookie Yearbook, hello, and anything you don't like is definitely just an inside joke that should be overlooked.

Rookie started as a website two years ago and a print anthology one year ago, making this book the best of the best of our sophomore year online. My own sophomore year of high school (which coincided with Rookie's freshman one) consisted of an unfortunate Old Spice phase (prompted by a search for a deodorant that did not try to make me smell like rain) and a bunch of feelings that were either too strong or too disaffected—rarely anything in between. HORMONES SUCK. But being a young person doesn't always. When I interviewed Sofia Coppola for the site, she said she's consistently drawn to teenage characters when writing films because they have time to be introspective, a luxury that adult lives tend to get too crowded for. In some ways it feels like a curse that we have to both feel everything extra strongly (hormones, first times, etc.) and be so habitually bored that we dwell on it all. But this time in one's life can also be terribly special. Rookie tries to make the realistic best of it.

Thinking about my sophomore year in relation to my freshman one feels like comparing apples and oranges, or whatever—I changed a lot, I knew new things, my social circle and interests shifted. It wasn't better or worse, just different.

I like to think of this book's relationship to our first one the same way. Let that cover image of seminal teenage transition via haircut signify this change, and let the spirit of the following pages give voice to all the parts of all of us that *never* really change. Throughout high school, I have always found solace in episodes of *Parks and Rec*; throughout Rookie, we have always promoted pizza and good vibes. (AND WE ALWAYS WILL.)

While I have your attention, please pay extra attention to the acknowledgments on the previous page, especially that last one about all you guys.

And please, please enjoy!

Love,
♡ Tavi

JUNE 2012: *Paradise*

HELLO ROOKIES I CANNOT EVEN GREET YOU PROPERLY BECAUSE I'M SO EXCITED I HOPE I HAVE YOUR ATTENTION.

Happy freaking June! Summer is here! Time to start counting down to 7-Eleven's Free Slurpee Day!

I'm pleased to say, however, that this summer will bring more than free chemical sugar sludge. I know, I didn't think it could ever get better than that either, but then we put together a plan for a Rookie Road Trip, and now it feels like chemical sugar sludge times a zillion!

The Rookie Road Trip, presented by Rookie, The Ardorous, and Urban Outfitters, will start in New York City in late June and end in Los Angeles a month later. We're gonna drive across the country in an odor-ridden van, stopping along the way to meet up with you guys and do stuff like get ice cream and make zines and talk about our feelings and re-enact the heart-to-heart in *The Breakfast Club* and also brainwash you all into becoming our friends wait what? Maybe we'll just get ice cream and make zines and talk, and get other kinds of chemical sugar sludge, and try other DIYs, and, oh gosh, between your brains and ours, the possibilities are ENDLESS. It's really fun and special to have an online community in which we can talk about the things we're thinking about, but it'll be more fun and special for all of that thinking and sharing to take place in person. I may even jab some of you with my finger to make sure you're real. TEENAGE GIRLS: Now in 3D!

We would love to meet you along the way! If you live somewhere along our route, send us a note and let us know about your favorite local places to hang out that you think would be suited for an afternoon field trip of Rookies. This means restaurants, stores, markets, parks, arcades, ice cream parlors, bowling alleys, swimming holes, forest trails, and/or other places that are safe and don't show *Two and a Half Men* on a TV in the corner.

Once we get to L.A., Petra and I will create an installation at Urban Outfitters' Space 15 Twenty, where we'll set up camp for a week, hosting a bunch of events: There'll be zine making and other DIYs, live readings by our contributors and friends, dancepartyfuntimes, and lots of chemical sugar sludge. We'll also be building a giant shrine, so if you come to one of the meetups along our route, bring some kind of souvenir of your teenagerhood that might be at home in a giant Rookie shrine—a journal, bracelet, photo, tape, or any weird thing, so long as it is not dangerous and/or *Two and a Half Men* memorabilia, and you are OK with never getting it back, 'cause we'll need them for keeps. (It's less shady than it sounds, we swear.)

June's theme is Paradise, and it is basically a love letter to our final destination of Los Angeles. Expect lots of Beach Boys, *Weetzie Bat*, and Joan Didion, and a ton of writing about what happens when you realize that the whole idea of a paradise is kind of a myth, and about how to construct your own paradise, since adolescence can kind of suck, and I know it gets better, but you need to make yourself happy in the meantime, you know?

And so, in the meantime, ROAD TRIP. We hope to see you there.

Love,
Tavi

Come to the Sunshine

Delightfully eerie and eerily delightful.
By Lauren P.

Thanks to Allyssa, Hilda, Jake, Jessica O., Jessica G., and Ocean for modeling, and Jaclyn Bethany for styling. Vintage dresses from Audrey Grace Boutique; new dresses by girl. by Band of Outsiders and Zoe Twitt. Sunglasses by Linda Farrow for Jeremy Scott, beads from Kate Spade, crowns by Kelsey Genna and Lauren.

Secret Wounds

Admitting that you need help is the most powerful thing you can do.
Writing by Stephanie, collage by Sonja.

In the spring of seventh grade, I had a terrible falling out with my friend Becky.* I can't even remember how it started—she spread a rumor about me or maybe blabbed one of my secrets—but it came to a head when she had her mom call our principal to tell him that I was going to kill myself.

The principal called my parents on a Friday night when I was sleeping over at another friend's house. My mom, knowing that I was having problems with Becky and not wanting to embarrass me in front of my other friends, managed to remain calm and waited until I got home the next morning to ask me about it. When I walked into the house and saw the looks of concern on my parents' faces, I felt completely humiliated. They asked me why Becky would say such a thing, and I mumbled something about being unfairly stereotyped on account of my all-black wardrobe.

The following Monday my parents and I had a meeting with the school principal, Becky, and her parents. My one vivid memory from that meeting was when the principal mentioned that on the night of Becky's mom's phone call, "as it turned out, Stephanie was at a slumber party, probably enjoying some fresh-baked blueberry muffins!" (*Fresh-baked blueberry muffins? WTF? I thought.*)

---

*All names have been changed.

The principal forced me to have a few sessions with the school guidance counselor anyway. Those consisted of a lot of fake smiling and insisting that really I was fine, just having a dumb argument with a dumb friend. The counselor also had me decorate T-shirts with puffy paint. Seriously. And the school put me on suicide watch.

The truth is that I wasn't suicidal, but I did hate my life. I'd endured three years of bullying at the hands of girls at my elementary school because I wore the wrong clothes and got good grades. In junior high, the boys joined in, taunting me for being flat-chested and ugly. I'd also just found out that my best friend—my only close friend at the time—was moving away. I floated around my junior high like a dark cloud, always on the verge of either bursting into tears or lashing out in anger. Which didn't really help with my suicide-watch status.

One afternoon at stage crew, I was too busy stewing about my various problems to pay attention to what I was doing, and I snagged my arm on a nail sticking out of the wall in the tool room. I almost screamed, but I gritted my teeth and stopped myself. Then I realized that I felt strangely calm. I hurt so much inside that hurting myself on the outside was like opening up a pressure valve. Instead of telling one of the supervisors, who I was sure would make a big deal

out of it, I put on a flannel shirt to hide the little cut. Later that week when I was feeling crappy again, I went back to the nail and accidentally-on-purpose ran my arm across it.

From the end of seventh grade on, I continued to cut whenever I was feeling anxious, angry, or sad. I cut in secret, locking the door to my bedroom or the bathroom, carefully hiding the evidence, and feeling fortunate that it was the early '90s and I wasn't the only one who had a flannel or a beat-up army jacket on at all times.

I didn't tell anyone what I was doing for a long time. I was a perfectionist; I felt like any problems I had were flaws that I didn't want my parents or teachers to see any more than I wanted to get a B on my report card. I wouldn't confide in any adults at school for the same reason. As for friends, I was so stung by Juliet's moving and Becky's betrayal that I stopped confiding in anyone I might consider a peer. Plus, I knew that most people wouldn't understand my new method of coping, and might set me up for another meeting with the principal.

Then, sophomore year, while hanging out at the park, I befriended a group of neighborhood kids who "got it." Acacia became my new best friend. She kept a razor blade in the wallet that was chained to her jeans. I don't remember her telling me this or talking about the cuts on her arms, but I know I took off my long sleeves around her and started carrying a razor blade in my chain wallet, too. My sort-of-not-really boyfriend discovered my cuts when were making out. My face got hot, but then he said, "That's cool," and showed me his.

I didn't think it was cool, though. It was a relief, after spending much of my life feeling like a freak for various reasons, to find a group of friends who understood me so well that I didn't have to hide my scars, figurative or literal, from them, but I was not *proud* of my cutting, any more than a junkie is proud of their habit. When a film crew from some news outlet came by the park to talk to us about self-harm, Acacia and I scrammed. To us, cutting went along with smoking cigarettes in terms of stress relief: Deep down, you know it's not good for you, but it calms you down in the moment, and once you start, quitting is hard. Late at night on the phone, or maybe one-on-one outside of Denny's after someone noticed someone else's fresh cut, there were whispered conversations that started: "I wish you would stop…and I wish I could stop, too." Sometimes we talked about our reasons for cutting, but often there weren't words for that black pit of depression or anger that lived in your gut and threatened to swallow you whole. On top of that, we were dealing with things that we had no clue how to handle on our own, and we distrusted the rest of the world too much to seek help for our problems—like Acacia's violent situation at home, or what I was going through my junior year, when my cutting got really bad.

I'd just broken up with the first guy I'd ever slept with. While we were dating, he isolated me from my friends and insisted on reading my journal. When I talked to the wrong person, wore something he deemed "slutty," or refused his sexual advances, he punished me with the silent treatment, destroyed my things, and threatened suicide. It took me six months to realize that this behavior was not normal—it was abusive. It took me years to realize that I didn't deserve it.

He'd basically rewired my brain so I blamed myself for all the things he did to me. Cutting became both relief and punishment. I was going to the bathroom at school and running out on my friends at Denny's to do it. It scared some of them. One begged me to stop with tears in his eyes. I started to realize that cutting was a dangerous addiction that had spiraled out of control, but I was too stressed to stop.

Then, one night in early November, I got into a car accident. It wasn't really a big deal. I made a left turn, miscalculating how fast the guy coming up the street was going, and he clipped the back corner of my car, ripping the bumper off. No one got hurt—a lucky break, since my two passengers weren't wearing seatbelts.

My parents didn't even raise their voices at me, but I had never been angrier at myself. The rage and self-loathing festered while I sat in the living room waiting for them to finish inspecting the car, and when they came inside I completely lost control and ripped away the thin shield that had kept my deepest secret hidden for almost four years. I threw my army jacket on the floor and displayed my arms, which were crisscrossed with bright red cuts, fading pink scabs, and tons of little white scars.

"I cannot handle any of this anymore. I am fucking crazy. You need to check me into Riveredge right now," I told them, referring to the mental institution that some of my friends had been sent to when their parents were sick of their behavior. Still rather obsessed with *The Bell Jar* and *Girl, Interrupted*, I thought the sanatorium might be a nice little break. I kind of hoped I was crazy enough to stay forever, just so that I would never have to deal with real life again. I imagined that a padded white room would be like a safe little cocoon compared with the outside world.

I honestly don't remember much of the rest of our conversation that night. I know that my parents went very pale upon seeing my arms. I assume that my mother cried. No one yelled, except for me as I begged them to commit me so my problems would go away.

It was decided that I would see my mother's therapist instead. Mom also insisted that I stay home from school the next day. She told me that whenever I didn't feel like I could handle things, I could call her and she would pick me up from school and we'd talk about it or watch soap operas or read or do whatever I needed to do. She helped me begin to find healthy releases.

Frightening as it had been to reveal my secret to my parents, in the end, it was incredibly liberating. Oddly enough, the sense of release that I got from it was quite similar to how I'd felt back when I'd first snagged my arm on that nail, but it was better, because now I was actually *taking control*. It wasn't until I let go of my secret that I realized how all-consuming it had been: hiding my cuts from my parents and the friends who didn't know, worrying that a sleeve might come up or someone would grab my arm and I'd flinch, revealing all of my vulnerabilities. Not to mention, cutting had become the *only* way I knew how to deal with any sort of stress. If something upsetting happened and I wasn't able to sneak away with something sharp, I felt completely powerless. As with many addictions, what had initially seemed helpful ended up becoming such a crutch that I forgot how to take care of myself.

I don't have a last cutting memory like I have a first cutting memory, because quitting was a process that lasted until I was 24 or 25. After I told my parents my secret, I stopped viewing cutting as helpful. I felt guilty every time I did it, which sometimes led to more cutting, but more often than not it led to me reaching out to my mom or to friends who were making a serious effort to kick the habit. This healing period was intense and incredibly difficult, and there were setbacks. But every time I managed to put down something sharp and pick up either the phone to call someone or a pen to write in my journal, I felt stronger and more proud than ever.

My desire to cut lessened a great deal after I went back to college at 21 to pursue a creative writing degree and started finally opening up to my therapist. Since then, writing has been my healthiest form of catharsis. For me, cutting was never a "cry for help" or a bid for attention, but a way to suffer in silence. I couldn't begin to heal until I cried out loud. ✿

ME AND YOU AND EVERYONE WE KNOW

Screwing the gender binary while looking soooo cuuuute. Photos by M. Sharkey. Interviews by Sady. Styling by Shea Daspin. Makeup by Jonathan Young for Dior Cosmetics. Hair by Allison Woodruff for Marie Robinson Salon. Thanks to Angel, Hari, Christian, Faye, Lily, Liam, Mars, Marck, Eleet, and Mitchell for modeling.

ANGEL, 20. Sweater: Jeremy Scott.

CHRISTIAN, 23 (left) "I've been questioning gender for as long as I can remember. I always felt like there was social injustice towards women. I've always questioned why men have to behave one way and women have to behave another."

HARI, 19 (right) "I identify a lot with both sides of the gender binary, and I think it's fun to put that into my physical appearance. It also just throws people off and scares them and upsets them, and I like that. It's fun. But I also feel like it's accurate."

MITCHELL, 20 "I identify as a gay male, because I'm a boy and I like boys. I never actually had to come out. When I told my father, he was like, 'Whatever.' I'm not really guarded, and I discuss things that are going on in my life, whether or not people are going to find issues with them. It is kind of like, whatever, fuck you, I don't give a shit. If you don't want to let me in, I'll go to the next place." Necklace and ring: nOir.

MARCK, 22

FAYE, 21 "I identify as a woman. But I think there's a lot of preconceived notions as to what feminine means, and what a female is supposed to look like. Sometimes I identify as queer in the sense that gender is not super-relevant to me. It's just not a priority. I'm not happy that the gender binaries are so apparent. It ostracizes people and makes them feel bad about themselves, or [feel] that they're not normal. I think this strict patriarchal society is slanderous, and it's dangerous, and it hurts people."

LILY, 18 "I'm not a gay girl who happens to be an artist who happens to be named Lily. I'm Lily, who is an artist, who happens to be gay. When I was 13, I came out to my entire grade during this assembly where they had an open mic, where people were saying a lot of really inspirational things about their personal lives. And so I went up and told them that I was gay. At first they cheered. I was surprised, and I was so happy. Then after a few days I started to get all the hate, and that was really hard. After I moved to New York, things got easier. I never get mistaken here for a boy, because it's very open and people can tell. But in my hometown, it wasn't as common for a girl to have short hair, for a girl to dress like a boy, for a girl to look like they have no chest. And so I remember being in McDonald's, and they would say, 'Can I help you, sir?' At first I was a little offended, but then I realized, *I'm presenting myself in a way where they actually can't really tell. And I do look like maybe a 12-year-old boy.* And I started to realize that it wasn't such a bad thing."

LIAM, 19 "It started to become clear to me that I liked women in fourth grade, when I had a crush on Jasmine from *Aladdin*. It felt natural, and I didn't feel weird about it, but people would act weird about it. I didn't like the word *lesbian* to describe me. Now I identify as a queer transmasculine person. I'm on the masculine spectrum, but don't identify as male in the way that society would identify me as such. So, like, when it comes to my junk, the way I do relationships with people, and the way I interact with my environment, I don't really think I'm a man in that way. So I was like, *Well, I think I can be a man in my own way.*"

"I tell everyone. I try to be out to as many people as I can, because I want there to be more trans* visibility. I want to go to law school, because I want to do advocacy law for specifically trans* people. And I really want to dismantle the system of legal gender in America."

MARS, 18 "I think I started realizing [I was different] in 10th grade. I went to an all-girls Catholic school; it's a little hard not being a girl there. I think the problem now is that other guys don't see me as a guy. I'm not particularly masculine, and I don't really try to be."

ELEET, 20 "I identify as a transgender female. My family could always tell: the way I talked, the way I walked, the way I moved, the way I socialized with my peers and my family members. They always said that I had 'a little fruit in [my] tank.' But hey, you either love it or you hate it. Honest to say, my upbringing was a little hard for me. But everything I've experienced in my life is what made me stronger, and it made me the person that I am today. And it made me want to reach out to my community, and let someone know: Don't give up. Go for what you want in life." Necklace: nOir.

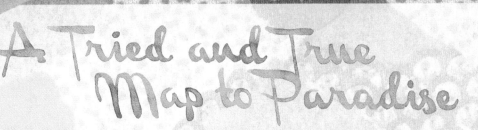

A Tried and True Map to Paradise

Notes from the passport office on how you will never get your act together, and that might be a good thing.
By Sarah Sophie Flicker. Playlist lettering by Tavi.

This may be a bit of a harried piece. Which stinks, because Rookie is my favorite magazine, and I was really hoping to impress you guys. I was hoping to sing down like a sage from a mountain high, inspiring you all with my hard-won wisdom and "grown-up" nuggets of truth.

But here is the real truth. I'm writing this on my cellphone, sitting in the passport office, as my five-year-old daughter is slumped next to me, wailing from boredom. We found ourselves here because her passport has expired and we leave in 48 hours on our big "girl trip." First stop is a wedding where she is the premier flower girl. Not only have we been practicing flower tosses and slow, graceful walks in the hallway for two months, but also the darn wedding is nearly in a palace and she gets to wear a very fluffy princess dress. Needless to say, she is living for this and I can't mess it up. In my attempt at a segue, we are embarking on a trip that is her version of paradise.

I have spent my whole life believing that at some point I would get things perfectly right. That at some magical point in maturity I would gain some clarity and know all the right answers—or fully know who I am. I now realize that this will never happen. And this is a good thing!

When I was a teenager, my idea of pure, unadulterated happiness was childhood—that time before hierarchies and complicated relationships developed, before our stories were told and retold by us and by others until we became false characters fossilized inside of them. To my daughter, bedtime, bath time, and the end of playtime qualify as real-life drama, but I beg to differ. She hasn't yet begun to regulate herself based on what she believes other

people think of her—and that seems to me like a version of paradise. My goal lately is to try to get back to that place as often as I can.

I'm writing this piece to implore you, reader, to please go easy on yourself. I'm writing this to say that everything you're going through right now—the awkwardness, the discomfort, the introspection, the clumsy grappling—is really the road to Arcadia. You don't get to experience paradise without a lot of hard work—you know that already. What you might not know yet, because you maybe haven't been there yet, is that once you reach the Promised Land, staying there is impossible. You come and go. You lose the map and have to be reminded of important landmarks. You forget altogether that it exists. And you have to work all over again to find it. Which you will, again and again.

What I'm getting at is that paradise is an island called YOU. Meaning you are the captain of your own ship, the master of your destiny, the keeper of your flame. Paradise exists in those fleeting moments when you are deeply in your own skin, when you've sunk down to the bottom of who you are and allowed yourself to rest there for a while. It's when you feel close to someone you love. Paradise is feeling understood, heard, open, and vulnerable. Paradise is feeling good and making someone else feel good. It's the muse whispering in your ear, it's doing something you love and excelling at it, it's friends, community, love. Paradise is all these things, but it is ever fleeting.

You can't wait around for good things to transpire. A lot of times you have to manifest the goodness. I thought of this

nifty little story by the great science fiction author Ray Bradbury. He loved cartoons and science fiction as a child. Kids made fun of him and said that no one was interested in "the future," so he tore up all his favorite comic strips and started to cry. He asked himself, "Why am I weeping? Who died? The answer was me. I had allowed these fools to kill me, and to kill the future." He decided never again to pay heed to negative people. "I've learned that by doing things, things get done," he said. "We ensure the future by doing it." I extend that idea to happiness: We ensure our own happiness by creating it for ourselves. It doesn't always work, but it's better than not trying at all.

Once I hit my teens, happiness became purely aspirational—it was never palpable in the present. Even today, I find myself looking forward to old age, to some fantasy of my "golden years," when I won't expect so much of myself, when I'll feel like I've done everything I need to do and can just settle down and enjoy what's left of the ride. But the truth is that that day will never come. Every stage brings its own disappointments, and its own struggle to find paradise. As you become more comfortable in one area of your life—friendship, dating, school, whatever—you enter a new phase that is equally hard and scary. That cold, damp, lost-in-the-dark-woods feeling of your teens never really leaves you. Now that I'm an adult and a mom, I'm faced with completely new scary questions that I don't know the answers to every day!

What I've learned is that it's OK to say "I don't know." I tell my kids that all the time when they ask me something—it's important for them to know that I don't know everything. And I'm officially a grownup! If I don't have the answers all the time, they certainly can't be expected to!

Another thing: Happiness and confidence take practice. You sort of have to train your brain to think more positively. For me, it was as silly as telling myself to "stop it" when I start to feel negative or self-defeating. I may have to tell myself to "stop it" 100 times a day. But it gets easier, and eventually it's less than 100 times a day, and finally your thoughts automatically go to greener pastures!

Oh and also, don't compare yourself with your friends or with other people you do or don't know. We are all born with different levels of confidence and coping skills, no one is perfect, and no one's life is perfect. I have to remind myself of this all the time.

Here's the point: Paradise doesn't exist. What's exciting about being human is that we get to learn…forever! With each new chapter in our lives, we have a new learning curve. Life is exciting when you look at it this way, 'cause there's no pressure to know how to do things, there's only the pressure to learn and do your best.

P.S. Oh my gosh, one more thing…I can't even believe I'm writing this, because it's so so so uncool and, to be honest, it comes from a selfish place. But here it goes: Talk to your parents. I say this because I am one. Now that I am a parent I know how much I love my kids. I can't think of anything I wouldn't do for them. I love them so much it hurts. I love them in ways that didn't seem possible before they existed. Most of your parents do, too. Sometimes we parental types mess up or put our wishes for you first, but the truth is, we really really really really want the best for you. So give communicating with us a chance. And if your parents fail you wildly, which we are apt to do at times, talk to another grownup who has their act together or a good, trustworthy friend. Just talking about our troubles and insecurities is magic. Even when no solution is reached. OK, sorry, just had to say that! ❀

VM3—

California Dreamin' By Rodarte
1. These Arms of Mine — Otis Redding
2. Left Of the Dial — the Replacements
3. Tell Me When It's Over — Dream Syndicate
4. The Unheard Music — X
5. California Dreamin' — the Mamas & the Papas
6. Crying — Waylon Jennings
7. Blue Moon — Elvis Presley
8. Blue Thunder — Galaxie 500
9. Regulate (ft. Nate Dogg) — Warren G.
10. Sad Mood — Sam Cooke
11. Parties in the U.S.A. — Jonathan Richman
12. Free Fallin' — Tom Petty

PO
DOM
1 C
FOR
2 GE

SUMMER IS READY WHEN YOU ARE

Now is the time to go all out in whatever acid-trip-mermaid getup your heart desires.
By Eleanor

Styled by Alexandra Moon-Age using clothes and accessories from Mary Benson, Pick N Mix, Beyond Retro, American Apparel, We Are Handsome, Swash, Ashish, Miss Selfridge, Blitz Vintage Department Store, Roberto Piqueras, Studio Dagda, Sara Sboul, Topshop, ASOS, KTZ, Nova Chiu, Office, New Look, Melissa, Claire's Accessories, Tatty Devine, Lucy Folk, Funky Bling, Fenton, Jennifer Behre, Shourouk, A-morir, Moutoncollet, and Tabio. Hair and makeup by Christina Corway at See Management. Thanks to Bonnie, Kay, Maeve, and Sophie for modeling, to Sara Sboul for assisting, and to Saltdean Lido for letting us shoot at their pool.

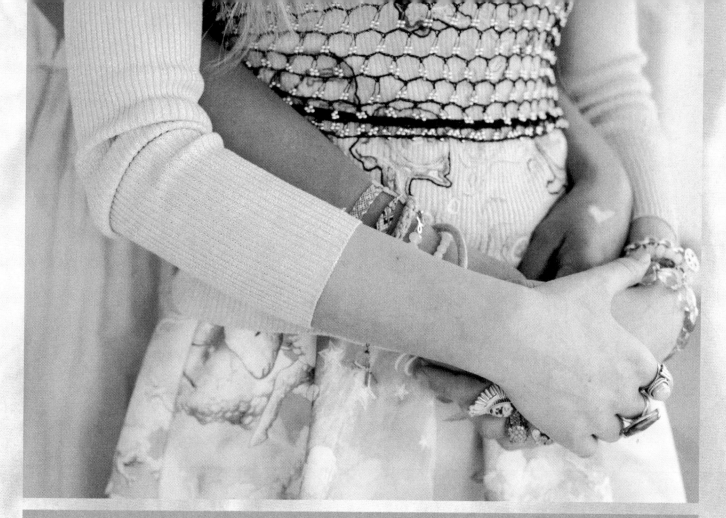

JULY 2012: FREEDOM

Hi! Welcome to July, or month ELEVEN of Rookie, or FREEDOM. This month made sense to me when I figured out it was possible for Rookie to have a monthly theme that is not about the '50s, '60s, or '70s. Technically a lot of the things that make up this month are from the '90s, but I'd like to think it's not a DECADE month; it's just that all of the images and stories that make me think of freedom were well captured during that era, but are also pretty constant throughout teenagerhood: sleepovers, sneaking out, endless bike rides, parking lot hangouts, dirty suburbs, etc. This month is about the freedom you find when you're not really an adult yet, but have a vague sense of the responsibilities that await, and a desperate desire to defer them for as long as possible.

And I am REALLY REALLY excited about this last thing: **Rookie is finally going to be in print!** Our first annual print edition, *Rookie Yearbook One*, will be on sale in September.

So happy freedom, happy sleepovers, happy *Rookie Yearbook One*, all that.

Thank you for existing.

love,
tavi

SCHOOL'S OUT FOR SUMMER

BEASTIE BOYS

NO AGE

ARCADE FIRE

BLACK FLAG

Sonic Youth

ROOKIE

PAVEMENT

I JUST WANNA GET ALONG

And skateboard and sleep and some other stuff.
By Eleanor

Thanks to Coco for modeling, Sara Sboul for embroidering these jackets, and Jenkin Van Zyl for making a lovely patch.

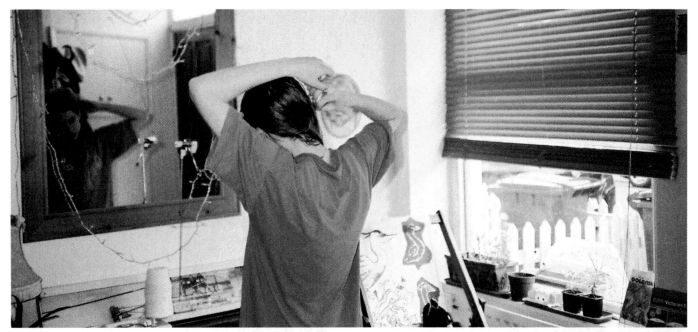

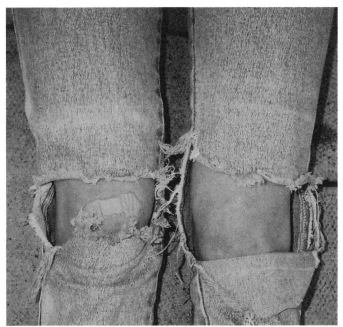

I DIDN'T REALIZE I COULD BE THIS LOUD AND HEARD SO FAR AWAY:
an interview with
CARRIE BROWNSTEIN

In which we learn how to be a rock star, writer, comedian, and all-around gift to humanity.
Interview by Tavi and Anaheed, illustration by Suzy.

Carrie Brownstein is a rock star (most recently with Wild Flag, before that with Excuse 17, Sleater-Kinney, and the Spells), a writer (formerly on Monitor Mix, her NPR music blog; currently on the sketch show *Portlandia*, which she created with Fred Armisen; and future-ly of a memoir), and an actor (in a few movies, including Miranda July's *Getting Stronger Every Day*, and of course on *Portlandia*).

She grew up all over Washington State, starting in Seattle and making her way through Redmond and Olympia before winding up in Portland, where we met up with her on our road trip. We talked while we ate a gigantic breakfast (and Tavi experienced an important milestone in life; more on that later). Carrie was incredibly generous with her time and her knowledge, and we thank her for that.

ANAHEED When did you tell your parents that you wanted to be a musician for a living, and how did they react?

CARRIE When I was 15 or 16, I decided that I wanted to get a guitar. By then I had gone through a lot of phases, just like any teenager. My interests were constantly changing, and I think my parents, very

wisely, thought that investing in musical equipment wasn't the best way to spend their money. So they asked me to buy my guitar myself. There's something about when you're asked to do something on your own that changes your relationship to it. Because then you have something to prove—which is a really good motivator for any art or creativity. That's actually the hardest thing to maintain, I think, the more you do something—always resetting yourself to having something to prove. Playing guitar was the first thing where I had something to prove to my parents, but mostly to myself. Like, *I can stick with this.*

I didn't think of it as a career or a job until probably my first or second year of college, when I remember telling my dad that I was going to take a spring quarter off to tour. That was really the first thing that seemed threatening to my parents, like it was going to veer me away from what they perceived as the proper course of action: You go to college, you graduate. I guess sometime in the middle of college I thought, about music, *This is actually what I care about. This is the most healthy version of myself, the most dynamic version of myself.* I'd never felt that way in connection to other pursuits. But I think my parents continued

to think of it as a hobby for much longer than I did.

I think it's scary to imagine yourself doing something creative as a job for a lot of people. There's this volatility to it, whereas other careers—even though it's an illusion—seem like they might be more stable, even though really nothing now is stable! But I did finish college.

ANAHEED What were you studying in college?

CARRIE I was doing sociolinguistics, which was highly esoteric subject matter. [*Laughs*] It's basically the relationship between language and society. I was doing a lot of discourse analysis—studying computer-mediated discourse, the way that people communicate online and how that changes power dynamics. It was pretty interesting.

TAVI Do you think studying that kind of communication helped you with writing for *Portlandia*?

CARRIE I think so. I've always had an interest in the minutiae of social dynamics and how people perform at relationships—the way couples kind of perform at be-

THIS IS ACTUALLY WHAT I CARE ABOUT... THIS IS THE MOST HEALTHY VERSION OF MYSELF, THE MOST DYNAMIC VERSION OF MYSELF...

you might as well study something you already love, because then you have a really interesting lens through which to see everything else

guitar seemed like a very good tool for angst

ing couples for an audience, or even to themselves. There's who they are, and then there's who they imagine themselves to be, which will sometimes manifest itself in conversations. Like when you hear people talking a little bit louder, and you realize, *Oh, this is a performance.* Studying the way people talk manifested itself in *Portlandia* a lot, because a lot of what Fred and I do is to look at the ways people communicate and try to get down to the most essential but also the most absurd part of that.

TAVI Many of the girls we've met on the road trip are about to go to college, and a lot of them want to study something that they're interested in, but that isn't directly related to a job of some kind. But I feel like that is still helpful.

CARRIE I really think it is, because, first of all, studying something that you're interested in—that's what you're going to retain. I think of all the subjects that I wasn't interested in, and I haven't retained hardly any information from those classes. I think everyone feels this way—they can't believe how much they know about movies and records and actors and fashion, but then they can't recall poems or historical facts nearly as well. So you might as well study something that you already love, because then you have a really interesting lens through which to see everything else. And that's going to stick with you a lot longer than trying to force yourself to study something that you don't feel passionate about.

ANAHEED How did you choose guitar as your instrument?

CARRIE I had taken piano lessons when I was very young, but it didn't feel that expressive to me—even though now I listen to piano music and think it's very expressive. I just didn't relate to it. Guitar seemed like a very good

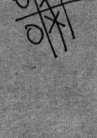

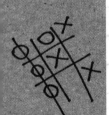

tool for angst. It has this flexibility and bendability to it, and it can take a lot of abuse. It also has a fragility; you can vacillate between something being very sweet and something being very angular and gritty, just within a matter of seconds. Also, I really like distortion. And, as a young person, I liked the way it amplified—it was exciting to have *volume* in my life. To play something loud, to fill a room—and then that room just gets bigger and bigger as you start to play out—that's very exciting. I just thought, *Oh, I didn't realize I could be this loud, and heard so far away.* That's a really great feeling.

ANAHEED A lot of our readers are interested in being in bands but don't know where to start looking for bandmates.

CARRIE I think the best way is to play music with your friends. If you have a friend that you love and you love spending time with and you think that they're smart or cool or funny, or there's just something about them that you want to be around, just ask. Ask them to learn how to play, if they don't already know. Because there's so much of [being in] a band that's about being in a kind of relationship—people see the worst side of you and the best side of you. And it's nice to go through that with someone that you care about.

But if your friends don't want to play music and refuse to learn—which is, you know, fine—then it's so easy to make recordings of your stuff, or go to shows in your town and figure out who lives around you whose music you like. That's what happened with Corin [Tucker] and Sleater-Kinney. I loved her band [Heavens to Betsy], and when that band was ending I just said to her, "I love your music." I think it's nice to be a fan of the people you play music with. Figure out who you love music-wise, then go pursue them.

Right now is a great time to be in a band. You could put out your record by yourself, or have a small label put it out, and you have a pretty good chance of getting heard. With word-of-mouth and blogs and everything—if it's good, your music will get out there. I've never thought that as much as now. It's almost harder to be undiscovered now than to be discovered. [*Laughs*]

TAVI I feel like a lot of people in bands don't want to be big, or think that being ambitious or thinking of their band like a business would feel like some kind of creative compromise…

CARRIE Well, in Olympia, ambition was like a dirty word for a long time. I think in very idyllic and idealistic communities, people want everything to be very even and democratic. And that's wonderful for supporting one another, but I don't think it's antithetical to being a supportive member of a community to aspire to do well, and to feel proud about things. I think it's OK to have wants and needs that might be at odds with what your friends' bands are doing, or what the community's doing. You don't want to undermine yourself, and to feel like for every step forward you have to justify why you want to do it. If you want success, especially for girls and women, there's this overly apologetic sensibility, like you have to justify or overexplain why you're going for it. That shouldn't exist. But yeah, I definitely came from that.

Miranda July and I have known each other since we were 19, and we both came from Olympia, so we've talked about this a lot. We both really wanted things for ourselves. We wanted people to hear our music, and she wanted people to see her performance art and see her films—and that's not a betrayal, I think. That's the trick—not feeling like you're betraying other people. If you have friends who are making you feel that way, that's not the right community for you. It's good to find people that are encouraging you, not undermining your efforts or making them seem shallow. Because I think for most people it's actually not about being rich or famous; it's about being able to support yourself doing what you love. And I think if you can support yourself doing what you love, no one should criticize that.

ANAHEED Is there a reason you do so many different kinds of things? Would you get bored otherwise?

CARRIE Being creative is, to me, one of the only ways that I can really be vulnerable, and to connect with other people in ways that are uninhibited and meaningful. The more of those things I have, the more dynamic my friendships are, and the more that I feel like I'm communicating with people—whereas in noncreative outlets I feel much more critical of myself, and just closed off. I think that for a lot of people their creative outlets are the ways that they are able to express most clearly who they are and what they're feeling. So I guess that just expanded the way that I'm able to communicate, or my way of using language—because I'm a hermit, otherwise, a little bit.

TAVI Being in a band, and doing *Portlandia*—those things involve collaboration. But you also did writing for a while, which is so much more solitary…

CARRIE Collaboration is difficult, but it's when I'm at my best, and most open to other people. I really like the way that an idea improves through the input of someone else, especially someone that you start to share a similar language with—whether it's a sonic language in a band, or a comedic sensibility like I have with Fred. We add to each other's ideas, and what we stumble upon together is ultimately better than what we might have come up with alone. Sometimes someone brings a certain part out in you that you didn't know you had.

But working alone is a good test for oneself. I like writing as a way to remind myself that I am capable on my own. I really want to finish a book, so I've had to prove to myself that I don't really need someone's help.

TAVI Guys, sorry to interrupt, but I just had bacon for the first time.

ANAHEED What?!

CARRIE You loved it!

ANAHEED Wait, you've never had bacon before? You totally did it the right way: You didn't pre-announce that you were about eat bacon for the first time.

CARRIE Because then we would've been watching you. And now there's bacon on everything else we ordered, so.

ANAHEED Um, where were we…you're working on a book?

CARRIE Yeah. It's mostly like kind of a music memoir. [Writing] is a much more isolating experience, I will say. But I think it's good.

ANAHEED I don't know if this is an insulting question to ask, but I feel like it might be OK because I'm older than you. Do you think about getting older in rock music with dignity? It seems so hard to do.

CARRIE This is like a landmine question for me, because when Wild Flag started, I was in my early 30s. That still feels pretty young. I'm the same age, roughly, as Jack White, Britt Daniel from Spoon, James Mercer from the Shins. Sufjan Stevens is a year younger than me. There are a lot of people who are right at my age. It's a nice age. But when Wild Flag started, the adjectives being applied to me were like *veteran*, and it felt very diminishing. I was really angry, because it feels like it happens in music especially. There are a lot of females on television, like Kristen Wiig, Amy Poehler, Tina Fey—they're right there at 40, and they're fine.

ANAHEED But they get a lot of shit, too.

CARRIE Yeah, they do. I think it's just very difficult to butt up against sexism and ageism, especially where they intersect. The optimist in me wants to think that they don't exist; and then I'm like, *Oh my god—no one ever talks about Jack White like he is over the hill, or a "veteran."* In the *New York Times* review of a Wild Flag show they said something like I was "still wiry," or "still agile," and I'm like, what am I, 80 years old?! Like, hobbling out onstage? It was awful. I was very angry about it.

I've been thinking about Frank Ocean, and how he came out. A lot of the way it was written about was that it was a very welcome expansion of what maleness is. Which is great. But I was thinking about how when women add identifiers to their personhood, whether it's a job thing or a sexual thing, or *anything*, the conversation becomes about whether they are *less female* now. Maleness, or the masculine perception, is like a synonym for humankind, you know what I mean? Why is it that any time there are these steps forward, or me getting older and playing music— why can't this be furthering what it means to be female?

ANAHEED No one ever asks, "Can men really have it all?" In interviews men are never asked, "How do you balance your career *and* fatherhood?"

CARRIE If a man is able to have a job and take care of a kid, that's expanding the notion of what a man can be; and when a woman wants to have a job and have a kid, it's *lessening* how much of a woman she's seen as.

TAVI She's "special."

CARRIE It's just so strange. Every time I want things to be transcendent and not have to do with gender dynamic or sexism, those things just rear their ugly head. It's hard to divorce yourself from that conversation.

ANAHEED Does it feel more welcoming to be working in comedy? Do you not get talked about in that way?

CARRIE Yeah. I was surprised that that was happening with music, because it wasn't happening with *Portlandia* at all. Fred and I went on a live tour, and no one ever commented about age. It's interesting how much freer you feel as a person and a creator when other people aren't tossing undermining adjectives at you! I guess that's a privilege that some people have all the time, but most female artists don't have the privilege to not be constantly undermined.

TAVI If you are a girl and you make things, you are evaluated as a Girl Who Makes Things and not a person who makes things. And then you have to think about it that way, and think about what you're saying as a Girl Making Things. Like, I obviously love being a girl, and I love girly things; but I also wish that I could think about things as just a person more often.

CARRIE Sometimes you feel like you're not allowed these multitudes. People would ask me, years ago, "What does it feel like to be a woman playing music?" And I said, "Being asked this question is what it feels like. It's become part of the experience." The fact that we're having this conversation, that extra explanation, has become part of the experience of being an artist. It's so exhausting!

TAVI That's such a weird question, because it makes me imagine, like, playing guitar while sipping tea. I don't know what it's supposed to "feel like" to be a woman playing music.

CARRIE I did an interview at the end of 2011, and they asked, "What was the best female record of 2011?" and I said Bon Iver. [*Laughs*] But you should be able to answer like that, because it should be about…

TAVI Identity.

CARRIE Yeah. And [Justin Vernon] wouldn't care. He'd just be like, "Yeah, I put out the best female record of last year." And he did! He's so sensitive and wonderful in that way.

ANAHEED Last time we talked to you, you introduced our readers to Eleanor Friedberger and the Unibroz. Are there any young new bands that you're listening to now?

CARRIE There's this band called Deep Time. Their album just came out on Hardly Art, which is a subsidiary of Sub Pop. It's a guy and a girl from Austin, Texas. It's really cool angular melodies and catchy sounds. I recommend it. ✱

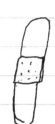

BODY CONSCIOUS

I'm done getting down on myself when I'm getting down.
Writing by Amy Rose, photo by Alex Simms. Playlist lettering by Tavi, photo by María Fernanda.

When I entered middle school, I was horrified to learn that I was expected to change in front of other people in the locker room. I wasn't really worried about what my specific classmates thought—I was simply crippled by an overwhelming fear of ANYONE seeing my body, which to me was imperfect to an embarrassing degree. With that in mind, can you imagine how terrifying it was to get undressed in romantic scenarios just a few years later? Every sexual encounter was potentially devastating—or so I thought. It took me a long time to learn how to focus on my own fun-having instead of the way my butt was/wasn't jiggling in the mirror hanging from someone's closet door.

I talked to some of the other Rookie writers about this insecurity and found out that many of them had experienced the same thing when they became sexually active. As always, they were mad wise and shared a million ways in which they figured out how to be more comfortable with their bodies—in a sexual context, but also the rest of the time.

Here's some of what I learned—and I wish these wisdoms had been jackhammered into my brain back when I was just starting to get naked with other people, 'cause I probably would have enjoyed sex and all its related activities a lot more!

1. PEOPLE ARE PRETTY MUCH ALWAYS STOKED TO SEE OTHER PEOPLE WITHOUT CLOTHES ON.

What, you think people have sex in order to mentally critique each other's imperfections? No! They do it because they think the other person is hot! As Jamie said, "When you see someone else naked, you aren't like, 'Wow, this person has really bizarre nipples.' You're just like, 'OH COOL, I'M SEEING SOMEONE NAKED.'"

2. BANISH "THE OTHER WOMAN."

For a lot of us, a specter hung over our first sexual experiences: an image of an IDEAL PARTNER against whom we were always comparing ourselves. We were afraid our partners were doing the same. Leeann geniusly described this imaginary person as "the other woman."

When I was a teenager, the other woman, whom I will call Linda, was always in my head, making me feel bad about myself. Linda changed a lot, usually taking on the attributes of whomever I envisioned my partners wanting more than me on any particular day. Sometimes she was a blond indie musician or a sexy actress or the girl with whom I shared a class. She was basically everyone but me. Whenever my partner closed his eyes for a second, I would panic that he was imagining Linda. I was so focused on all the ways I couldn't compete with her that I would work myself into a lather of self-loathing (the least sexy kind of lather, probably) and totally lose interest in what was going on physically.

"When I feel the other woman creeping into my head, my little mantra is 'It's just us in here,'" said Leeann. Hopefully her words can help you forget about your Linda. Because she's not real, people. Linda is just not real.

3. THAT DISTINCTIVE FEATURE THAT MAKES YOU NERVOUS ISN'T AS BIG A DEAL AS YOU THINK.

Maybe teenage you, unlike teenage me, isn't concerned about your whole entire body and all of the ways it is sub-ideal—but maybe there's one part of your physical self that you feel weird about and don't like to expose. It might be your ass or your boobs or your "excess" elbow meat. For Jenny it was a birthmark on her back. Eventually she discovered a way of thinking about it that made her feel a lot better: "I was so scared of showing it to anyone that when I first had sex, I had to sit my boyfriend down and be like, 'OH GOD, THERE'S SOMETHING I HAVE TO TELL YOU.' And then I told him that I had a birthmark the SIZE OF ASIA on my back. Later, after we had gotten it on, he was like, 'Wait, so where is this thing you were talking about?' That was the first time I realized that my body was not deformed. I stopped warning guys about my birthmark after that. And one time when I was 18, a guy asked me about it, in a totally neutral way, after we'd had sex. I realized that I was attracted to all kind of boys and that some of them had bodies I had never experienced before and that sometimes I wanted to talk about it, not in a LET ME GAWK AT YR WEIRDNESS kind of way, but more of a 'I feel so comfortable with you and you must know that I think you are so hot and so perfect that I feel like I could ask you anything' type of way. And that made me feel a lot better about myself, too."

4. DANCE.

Can we all agree that dancing helps us focus on feeling good, and stop worrying about *looking* good? Jamia said that dancing makes her feel "embodied," which is an idea I like a lot. I think it means that you are fully occupying your own physicality, and you're using all your powers to make it feel AWESOME. By dancing.

Jamia suggested taking some fun classes to get started. "When you are in a class full of other people with beautiful asses and jiggling bellies, the insecurity just melts off." Doesn't this sound sublime?

But dancing alone can be just as awesome and body-affirming. As Naomi said, "It doesn't matter what you look like in your bedroom! All that matters is how you *feeeeel*."

5. LOVE YOUR UNDERWEAR!

"I think owning lingerie that doesn't make you feel like you are *performing* sexiness, but that actually makes you feel sexy on a personal level, is important," said Jamie. I concur! For some people that might mean black lace; for others, boxer briefs. You definitely don't have to go gangbusters at Victoria's Secret. My lucky (wink) pair of underwear isn't lacy or see-through or backless, but it does make me feel like my butt is an amazing gift unto the world. Even on days when you're not expecting anyone else to see them, it can be spirit-lifting to slip into some racy underthings. Fact: Looking hot for YOU is the first and foremost way to feel sexy.

6. DO IT YOURSELF.

"Self-love is a really fun way to get to know your body, figure out what feels good, and banish all the noise," Rose pointed out. "Before you try to tell someone how to make you feel comfortable and sexy, it's good to be able to go there alone."

Masturbation helps you demystify your own body and appreciate what's unique and glorious about it, and it builds a close personal relationship between you and your sexuality. "Knowing your body makes sex with other people a lot more pleasant, because you can communicate what you like and what you don't like," added Arabelle. "Being able to take charge of your desires is so, so important."

7. PEOPLE ARE, LIKE, BEAUTIFUL, MAN.

Have you ever felt that if you just spent enough time with any person on earth, asked them the right questions, and really gave yourself a chance to *discover* them, you would absolutely be able to love them deeply, no matter who they were? I feel that way all the time. And the more I talk about this feeling, the more common I find it is, which makes me feel a very special connectivity with the world.

"If I look at anyone long enough," said Tavi, "I will fall in love with them. I only want friends and romantic partners who are the same way, because people are beautiful and that's why life is interesting. Even though I believe in evolution, I think there's something holy about the fact that what it's resulted in is human consciousness and the ability to make and appreciate art and appreciate each other, so I feel like we should all be doing that more, and that means appreciating parts of each other that are weird and hairy and smelly."

Jenny feels the same way: "I feel like I'm falling in love all the time," she said. "I just want to be in love every second with everyone. I am genuinely attracted to people who have the kind of bodies that are conventionally considered flawed. And never once have I thought of their bodies as 'flawed.' And if I think that way of them, can't they think that way of me?" Yes! If everyone I asked about this feeling told me that duh, of course they feel that way too, then I think we can assume that the kinds of people we want to be intimate with share our attitude—and if you do, too, you can assume the same of your partners. So finding someone's body sexually beautiful and having them feel the same way about yours is basically guaranteed.

I think something Leeann said fits in nicely here: "You have to remind yourself that you have the right to give and receive pleasure no matter what you look like." You deserve to enjoy your sexuality and that of others. If you can give love freely, then it will come back to you, regardless of your insecurities.

8. DON'T HAVE SEX WITH ASSHOLES.

Don't let people jerk you around. If the person you're considering fooling around with is cajoling you into doing something by putting you down, or cajoling you in general, DO NOT HAVE SEX WITH THAT PERSON.

Sometimes flirting involves gently teasing another person with good intentions. But there's a difference between that and someone being negative about your hair or body or clothing or friends or WHATEVER. Guess what? They most likely won't be any nicer to you when you're not wearing clothes. There are jackholes who think that a good way to get someone to be with them is to lower that person's self-esteem. They hope that, in doing so, they will make themselves seem superior. So terrible. Avoid those jackholes, seriously.

Arabelle was especially adamant about this. "Don't fuck people who make comments about your body other than how beautiful it is," she said. "Actually, don't even hang out with them. Your friends should make you feel beautiful, and the same goes for the people who see you naked— ESPECIALLY THOSE PEOPLE, because you are exposing yourself to them, and it is a gift that they shouldn't take for granted."

9. TAKE A BREAK.

Sometimes getting caught up in the whole idea of how you relate to sex can be an utter mindfuck, especially if you're figuring these things out for the first time. If you feel yourself becoming overwhelmed by feelings of sexual insecurity or unattractiveness, it can be useful to bow out for a little bit. Taking a vacation from sexual activity can help you regain your confidence as a person by reminding you that your worth comes from all different parts of yourself.

"I decided to be totally celibate for a year when I was about 19 or 20 to reclaim a confidence and power I wasn't sure I ever felt in the first place," Jessica remembered. "It was amazingly helpful. I didn't quantify my charm according to whether someone wanted me in a particular way, and it was fully empowering, even though I only made it eight months. I haven't sweated my appearance, attractiveness, or body confidence since."

10. FEMINISM IS MEANT TO MAKE US FEEL BETTER ABOUT OUR BODIES, NOT WORSE.

If you identify as a feminist, you may know about the body-acceptance movement, which is all about loving and celebrating your physical person, no matter what size or shape your body is. For those of us who fervently believe in this idea, myself included, it can lead to moments of intense self-criticism, because HOW could you be feeling insecure and still believe passionately in the movement? When this happens to me, my thinking goes like this: "I SAY that everyone is beautiful as they are, so how come I can apply those feelings to everyone except myself? How come I'm still ragging on myself for not looking Photoshopped? Why are there Lean Cuisines in my freezer? I AM A FRAUD! A SHAM, I TELL YOU!!!"

"It's easy to get down on yourself even more for being down on yourself to begin with," said Tavi, "like, 'I must be such a hypocrite, preaching body acceptance but not living it!' But living it is HARD, and it's an every-day thing, and some days are bad, so let's all just chill out and hug ourselves for like two seconds." You're not a "bad feminist" for occasionally feeling self-doubt. You're just a human being, and we're all uncertain at some time or another. Also, body acceptance is a process. You can identify with and strive for it and still have moments of insecurity.

11. FILL IN THE BLANKS: "I FEEL _____, SO I NEED _____."

Once you learn to fill in the blanks of that sentence with your partner, you're basically set. Sex is a MUTUAL thing. You aren't there just to make sure someone else gets off; they have to extend you the same courtesy, and make you feel respected and appreciated while doing so. If you're feeling uncomfortable, try Leeann's technique: "I'm a big fan of letting people know what I'm thinking when I'm insecure. I just say, 'I'm feeling super insecure about my body right now, and it would help if we turned off the light,' or slowed down for a minute,

or whatever I think might help. Knowing that my partner is willing to change things so that I'm more comfortable reminds me that I'm in control of the situation, that this is a loving exchange between two people, and that we can do whatever we need to do to make it work for us both."

Having good sex, and feeling GOOD about sex, it turns out, isn't about being Linda. It's about being YOU, and making it work in a way that's respectful and fun for you and your partner(s). I spent SO LONG trying to please others and worrying that I was doing it wrong, and I let my own pleasure fall by the wayside as a result. Don't do that! Speak up, dance, and don't fuck idiots. Most important, have a great time. ♛

4. RAIN ON LAKE I'M SWIMMING I' – LIGHTNING BOLT

5. REVIVAL OF THE SHITTIEST (TRACK TWO) – GANG GANG DANCE

6. STREET SAUCE – SONIC YOUTH

7. ROTATION – DEERHUNTER

8. THE KÖNER EXPERIMENT (TRACK ONE) EXPERIMENTAL AUDIO RESEARCH

9. THE SAILOR – TERRESTRIAL TONES

10. DELONG SONG – SUN CITY GIRLS

11. FOREST GOSPEL – ANIMAL COLLECTIVE

12. SWEET LOVE FOR PLANET EARTH – FUCK BUTTONS

13. SKYWINNOWING – KRÍA BREKKAN

14. LIBRA, THE MIRROR'S MINOR SELF – BROADCAST AND THE FOCUS GROUP

15. DELIA'S THEME – DELIA DERBYSHIRE

"I WAS ALWAYS VERY IMPRESSED BY DRONING WASHING MACHINES HEARD THROUGH THE FLOOR ON THOSE SICK DAYS IN BED [HOME] FROM SCHOOL, AND MORE SO BY THE SYMPHONY OF SUMMER MOWERS IN SUBURBIA, ACCOMPANIED BY VARIOUS PLANES"

— SONIC BOOM (SPACEMAN 3, EXPERIMENTAL AUDIO RESEARCH)

THIS INSPIRED THIS MIX

SOUNDSCAPING
BY ELEANOR

1. KRANKENDUDEL — ERIC COPELAND

2. MAGICAL POWER MAKO (TRACK TWO) — MAGICAL POWER MAKO

3. SYNTHESIZER GUIDE BOOK ON FIRE — BOREDOMS

SNEAKING AROUND

Sometimes you just push open a door and let yourself out.

By Jenny

I knew a girl, Feng,* who ran away from home for a few weeks. She was a year older than me and took her piano lessons right after mine. When I emerged from my lesson she was always there, sitting on the teacher's couch, stone-faced and unreadable, waiting her turn.

"She plays magnificently because she practices three hours a day," the piano teacher told me when I screwed up "Für Elise" for the fourth week in a row.

My mom told me Feng's father, who was a famous piano player in China but completely unknown in America, stood over her when she practiced and slapped her fingers with a ruler when she made a mistake. My parents reminded me how hard her father was on her whenever I complained about how hard *they* were on *me*.

My parents thought that by making me learn an instrument, they were offering me a world of privileges that were never offered to them. I was supposed to be thankful that they didn't stand over me with a ruler, that my knuckles were soft and loved instead of cracked and bleeding. One day, after bitterly banging on the piano till there were tears in my eyes,

*All names have been changed.

I volleyed the missile I had been aiming at my parents ever since I figured out what my piano lessons meant for them: "I can't live out your dreams. You can't make me."

"Oh, but we can," were their exact words.

One afternoon when I was in middle school, Feng came over to my house for a few hours. She wouldn't accept anything I offered her. Soda? Chips? Candy? "No, thank you," she said.

"Fine," I replied. *Be perfect*, I thought. *Do what your parents tell you to and never question it.*

But I was wrong about Feng. She ran away from her parents when she was 14 and came back with an inked-up boyfriend and piercings that her father threatened to rip out. Where did she go, I wondered, and what did she see while she was out there?

Once, when I was seven, I went to school with a low-grade fever. I tried calling my neighbor's nanny to pick me up from school, but she told me she didn't know how to get there. The secretary in the main office said I had to return to the classroom if no one was coming to retrieve me.

I walked out, my forehead burning. When I rounded the corner, instead of turning right to go back to my classroom, I turned left and ran in the direction of the

closed double doors that I had believed to be an airtight barrier keeping me from the outside world during the weekday hours between 7:30 AM and 2:30 PM. I heaved myself against them, and realized something so extraordinary that I still remind myself of it every day—sometimes you can just push open a door and let yourself out.

☆ ✧ ✱

The next time I made a break for it wasn't till almost nine years later. I was 16 and miserable. My life was ruled by rules: *Don't go outside. Don't talk to boys. Don't think you're different from everyone else. Don't think you can grow up and be a writer. Don't bother with extracurricular activities. Don't try to get out of weekend SAT prep classes. Don't ask if you can go to the movies. Don't, don't, don't.*

My house in high school was at the dead end of a street, and the symbolism was not lost on me. Behind it was the elementary school field. In order to get there you had to trespass on a short, fenced-off path. Someone had ripped a giant hole in the fence, making it possible to slip through to the other side. I knew that dark path and grassy field behind my house extremely

well, because they constituted my primary escape route.

The summer after my sophomore year, I was rifling through the kitchen cabinets when I found a key that was marked DECK. I kept it in my desk drawer, hidden under a stack of envelopes, for months, plotting and seething in my head.

"Stop dreaming and start acting," my parents told me all the time. In a sense, they were right. At the start of junior year, I begged them to let me go to a local hard-core show at a music venue a few towns over. They said no way, and I stayed up all night writing them a letter about all the ways in which they were hurting me, all the ways in which I tried so hard to please them, but how, if they were going to force me into a box that was too small for me, pretty soon they wouldn't have a daughter to boss around anymore.

I put the letter on my father's pillow. The next day they told me I could go to the show, but had to be back by 9:30—and also not to ask again, because this was the one and only time they would ever say yes. I said I didn't want to go if I wouldn't ever get another chance.

"Then don't," my mother said.

"You might wake up one day and I'll just be gone," I shouted, embarrassed that I had spilled my guts out in the letter. "I might run away like Feng, and then you'll be so sorry for everything you made me do."

"Try to fend for yourself out there," my parents said. "We'll see how long you last."

That was the last time I tried to reason with them. That was the last time I included them in my plans for adventure, the last time I ever asked them if it was OK to go out into the world and hitch a ride to a punk show or sit on the hood of someone's car in a parking lot late at night. I wanted the chance to do these things before I became an adult and had to do adult things. I had a key to our deck doors. I was going to use it.

In order to sneak out, I had to wait until I heard my father snoring, which usually happened around 10:30. Then I would put my stuffed animals and dolls underneath my sheets to make it look like there was a sleeping body in there, in case my mom

came in to check on me (did she?) and make my way down the first flight of stairs to the kitchen, down the second flight to the landing, and then tiptoe across to the back door that led to the deck. Like a cat burglar, I'd press my body against the side of my house, terrified that any moment my parents' bedroom lights might suddenly turn on, and I would see my mother's face at the window, looking down at me, needing no more reason to destroy me than all the ones I had already given her. I would slowly inch my way around the side of my house, careful not to knock over the trash or trip over the garden hose, and then, when I finally reached the driveway, I would make a run for it. I would sprint across the six or so feet between my driveway and the fence that was my portal to the beyond.

I would stumble up the dark path, press my lips together to avoid spider webs, brush bugs and branches out of the way, and look for the parked car that, in just a few moments, would take me away. I would make my way across the field, adjusting my skirt and pulling up my tights. For a hot second, I would allow myself to imagine that where I was going tonight was going to change me forever. Then I would open the door, climb in, and say, "Thanks for getting me," like it was nothing at all.

The first time it was this 15-year-old Polish boy, Stan, who lived just a few blocks away and actually only had a bike. He had dreads down to his shoulders that he washed with dog shampoo, and he lived for moments when people physically recoiled from the sight of him.

He told me he liked to bike all around town in the middle of the night and that he once took a brick and smashed in the driver's-side window of the most expensive car he saw parked along the side of the road. "You can come with me sometime," he said.

I didn't know if what I wanted was to go with him specifically, or if I just wanted to go somewhere with someone, anyone. I wanted to meet these boys that my parents warned me against, boys that they claimed would drag me down the dark and swift road to teenage pregnancy and straight on

into Junkie City, because that was the sheer power of bad influences.

Stan waited for me that first night. I jumped on his handlebars and put my hands over his while he pedaled us all across town.

"Fuck your parents," he said. "Don't fucking give them the time of day." I wanted to say, "Wait, I actually kind of understand where they're coming from."

Later, lying on the grass with him, I knew that in an hour I would get up and ask him to take me home. I would sprint across the field to get to my house and I would shakily let myself in through the deck doors and sleep for an hour or two before waking up to go to school, and I would walk into my first-period class feeling just a tiny bit less angry and sad.

Other than Stan, most of the boys who were willing to wait until midnight to see me, who were willing to drive their cars at that hour to pick me up, who didn't try to get my parents' permission to see me, were not boys at all, but older men.

I knew these two college dropouts in their early 20s who were friends of friends of friends. They shared a two-bedroom apartment in town and got into fistfights over which one of them was the "true fucking king of *Tony Hawk*." One of them constantly reassured me that he wasn't dumb, just sick of the jerks and scumbags he met at community college, and that he was planning to apply to a couple of very competitive universities next year. The other was a self-taught "Buddhist" who was very interested in my "culture."

"Do you want to watch me attempt some calligraphy?" he asked me. "I have a sick collection of bootlegged kung-fu movies, although you've probably seen a bunch of them. By the way, have you read the *I Ching*?"

I hadn't read the *I Ching*, and I liked watching kung-fu movies about as much as I liked to pull pubic hairs out of the drain, but I never said anything. I wasn't ready to escape from my escape.

It thrilled me to see two grown men who didn't have their shit together, who weren't doing much of anything with their lives. I felt like I was being courted and desired in

I didn't know if what I wanted was to go with him specifically, or if I just wanted to go somewhere with someone, anyone.

"you can come with me," he said. "sometime,"

I felt like I was being courted and desired in a way that was both scary and manageable, because deep down I knew that I wasn't going to live in this town forever.

a way that was both scary and manageable, because deep down I knew that I wasn't going to live in this town forever. I knew I could return home before morning. As easy as it was to let myself out, I could also let myself back in.

I also knew a 28-year-old English doctoral candidate at Columbia University, and we would send each other long emails about our lives, and sometimes I would call him late at night and he would tell me that I was a genius and that I was the most extraordinary girl he had ever met and that he hated the popular kids who were cruel to me in middle school and that he had fantasized about beating the snot out of them to avenge my honor.

I met up with him once in his car, which he had driven all the way from Manhattan to Long Island. He apologized for being out of shape, and I apologized for being shy. I was afraid he would touch me, and I was also afraid he wouldn't. In the end, we just sat there, trying to re-create the electric sexual tension that hovered over our late-night telephone conversations. Maybe it was there for him, but for me, as soon as I made the choice to sneak out to see him in the flesh, the fantasy of our romance was shattered, never to be recovered.

I kept it up for almost two years, from the beginning of my junior year until I went away to college. I snuck out to go on long drives with friends of friends of my friend's older brother. I snuck out to skinny-dip in the pool of a dude I met at the community center where I volunteered. I snuck out to the hotel room of a band that had traveled all the way from Louisville, Kentucky, to play a show at that same community center. The drummer laid his head on my knee, and the bassist made me a ring out of dead flowers and twine and gave me his handkerchief with a note that said "Alien princess from another world, take me to your land!" Sometimes I snuck out just to be alone, to lie down on the grassy field behind my house, to listen to *Sunny Day Real Estate* on my CD player and wonder what it would feel like not to have to hide anything from anyone. The more I snuck out, the more convinced I became that I could get away with everything.

It's true that I wasn't ever caught, and it's true that I never felt unsafe, but in the end, that stuff was just luck. In the end, I felt lonelier than ever, partitioning my life into segments. My parents didn't know this midnight world, and the dudes I snuck out to see didn't know what my life was like in the morning. These boys and men meant everything to me for the time they were in my life, but at some point I needed my life to include other people, other kinds of interaction. I didn't really want to deny my parents the privilege of knowing me. I wanted the privilege of being understood by others. And I really, really needed to get some sleep.

☆ / ★

Was it hard for Feng to come back, because she saw how good it was out there? Or was it hard because she saw how bad it was?

I ran out every night, but I came back every night, too. Maybe my parents knew all along, and let me have my nights away. Maybe I underestimated their beneficence. I don't know, but I do know this: My parents were not the ones who took away my paradise. I was. I pushed open that door so many times that the thrill of breaking free became the stuff of daily routine.

At some point, I knew I no longer wanted to go back to that parking lot. But I'm not sorry I let myself out. Once I realized that the pleasures of being wild and careless were just as flawed and fleeting as everything else on this earth, I continued on with my life, fearful that I had used up my quota for adventure, that I would be forever hardened by disillusionment. But it was not so. The love and the freedom and the heartbreak that were still in store for me, that *are* still in store for me, continue to pull me in the direction of all that is unknown. I feel as I've always felt—like I want to know everyone, and I want everyone to know me. ☆

SUNNY DAY REAL ESTATE

What would it feel like not to have to hide anything from anyone?

care*less
CINNAMON SUGAR FREE GUM

"Alien princess from another world, take me to your land!"

EATING: a manifesto

Stick this on the fridge. By Krista.

It would happen at least twice a day: I'd be wiping the counter at the coffee shop, pulling espresso shots, making new drip coffee—and I'd *feel* it. It was always a different woman, but always the same scene: a woman in her mid-30s to mid-60s, hovering over the glass pastry case, *staring* at the brownies. I'd head over to help her, wiping my hands on my apron.

"Can I getcha something?"

I could predict where we were going with my eyes closed.

"Oh. Well. No," the woman would say quickly.

"OK." I'd turn around, put cookies on a plate, put the plate into the pastry case.

"Well…"

I was waiting for it. Here it came.

She'd lean over the counter and say, "Those raspberry brownies sure look good."

"They're delicious," I'd say.

"They *look* delicious."

"Yes."

"And fat-free, too, right? Hahaha."

"Ha."

"You know, I *have* been good," she'd say, with a faintly creepy, conspiratorial we're-just-two-girls-in-this-together-right-honey tone.

"Mm-hm."

"You know, I could maybe *split* a brownie, they're really too big for one person, don't you think? Maybe I'll just have half."

"We don't sell half-pastries."

"You don't? Really? Seems like you could do brisk business with, y'know, women—hahahaha!—who just want a little *bite*. It's so big, really, I'm not sure I could eat that much. Hmm. All right. I mean, I'm gonna be kicking myself for this later, but sometimes a girl just needs a snack, you know what I mean?"

And there would be a line backing up out the door of the coffee shop and she'd still be dithering and I'd want to like rip my hair out and scream, "JUST EAT THE FUCKING BROWNIE OMG YOU DON'T NEED MY PERMISSION AND YOU DON'T NEED TO FEEL GUILTY ABOUT WANTING SOMETHING HOLY SHIT."

I mean, if you feel guilty about just eating a *brownie* that you want, *what else in your life do you want that you're not expressing?*

Girls and women of the world, *could we stop apologizing for wanting and eating food?* Because this is one of the most ridiculous things that we do collectively as lady-people, and not only does it annoy the shit out of me personally, but it is also INCREDIBLY SAD. Could we stop feeling "guilty" for wanting an effing brownie? Or a plate of fries? Could we stop actively seeking permission from our friends to go ahead and "be bad" and order the cheesecake? Could we all just go ahead and order whatever it is that we feel like eating, instead of saying, "Oh, I feel like a pig, you guys are just getting salads"?

Because—now I know this will come as a shock—WOMEN EAT. We get hungry. We get hungry for pizzas and Double Stuf Oreos and nachos and ice cream and giant french-toast breakfasts, and you know what? WE DON'T NEED TO FEEL BAD ABOUT THAT.

Here I am making a vast and sweeping gender stereotype, but do you ever, ever hear dudes say "I just want a little bite" or "This is so bad, you guys, but I totally ate a whole pint of Ben & Jerry's last night"? No! Because it's OK for men to eat! Men get hongray! Men need frozen dinners called "Hungry-Man"! Men need Manwich! Boys are allowed to grow into men, but "attractive" women in our culture are expected to stay at pretty much an eternal pre-adolescent weight. What's society's current ideal man look like? Fit. Big muscles. What's society's current ideal woman look like? Thin. *Really* thin. No hips. No belly. Hairless except for the head. Basically a 10-year-old girl with added boobs for sex appeal.

You see it everywhere—every café, every restaurant, every kitchen across the country. Women bargaining with waiters and friends about whether or not they should get a side salad or fries with their entrée. Women making demeaning jokes to one another about their desire for food, like "Once on the lips, forever on the hips" and "Well, it's midnight, so technically your body doesn't know whether it's today or tomorrow, so the calories zero themselves out, hahaha" and women *bonding with one another* over their shared guilt! You're being *bad* and getting the chocolate cake? Ooh, now that you're doing it, let's both be *really* bad, and I'll order the key lime pie and we won't tell a *soul*, will we? It's just us girls!

Why are we apologizing for wanting food? What the hell? BODIES NEED FOOD. WE DIE WITHOUT IT. Food tastes good! And we're programmed to crave it! Sure, some food is healthier than other food, but what is up with punishing ourselves for wanting pickle chips? Why is it acceptable—nay! encouraged!—in our culture for women to feel guilty and publicly "admit" our guilt for wanting to eat a cookie? Why are we rationalizing our "bad behavior"—you know, our EATING—with statements like "I've been really good lately" or "I'm gonna need to walk this off later"?

It makes me furious.

I want this to end.

I want women to allow themselves to want food. I want women to be hungry and ask for what they want to eat without apologizing. I want women to stop looking for permission from others before they eat something that is not a carrot or spinach. I want my friends to get the chili fries if they want the chili fries, and not say something like, "It all goes straight to my ___" (hips, thighs, butt, etc.). I want to see a girl sink her teeth into a *huge* cheeseburger and fries and not cut the burger in half to save some for later. I want my mother to allow herself more than one small square of dark chocolate per day. I want women to take pleasure in food, without punishing ourselves for wanting it.

Hear me, womenfolk: I want all of us, everywhere, to stop apologizing, stop rationalizing our behavior, *and just eat the damn brownie already.* ☆

DRUGSTORE COWGIRL

Friends, gas station food, lava lamp heels—all good things. By Erica and Chelsea Peacock. Thanks to Amanda, Beth, Justin, and Sara for modeling.

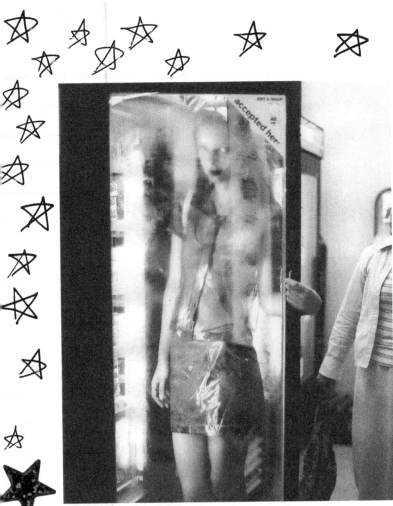

THIS IS HOW IT FEELS TO BE FREE

Feminism can be a prison if it's all about the anger.
Writing by Jessica, collage by Beth.

When I was younger, maybe 10 or 12, I used to say I hated men. I probably did. My feminism was born of anger—at men and at a world in which they seemed too powerful, and all too happy to take advantage of other people's powerlessness. Second in line for my feminist wrath were women who I thought made it harder for other women by giving in to men in order to borrow a piece of their power.

As I got older, I continued to judge women for being "complicit." I judged them according to my definition of what being a woman with a full life meant. I judged moms who were "just" homemakers. I judged women who married young. I judged girls I knew who didn't have any hobbies and just hung around watching boys play video games. I thought that since feminism had bum-rushed the patriarchy, every woman should be striving and fighting and aspiring, and that being a feminist meant you had to be at the frontlines of protest, doing clinic defense and giving your male friends a public browbeating if they made a remark that was less than PC. I used feminism as a yardstick to measure whether everyone else was right or wrong. And most of the time, they were wrong.

I believed that the one true way to be a feminist was to always be fighting. In some ways I still believe that, though mainly I believe that feminism is an act of resisting a world that tells me women are shit (as are children, the poor, anyone who isn't white and American, etc.). But the thing about constantly fighting is that, after a while, it's incredibly exhausting. You constantly feel vulnerable, forever poised to defend yourself against attacks. Being that person isn't very fun, and being around her not particularly pleasant.

About eight years ago, at the tail end of a bell hooks tear, I read her just-released book *The Will to Change: Men, Masculinity, and Love*. There was a line in the introduction where she wrote about subconsciously *waiting for men to die* in order to feel like women could live a free life. The line took my breath away. I just started sobbing. I had spent so much time and energy reinforcing this idea in my head that men were my enemy, and it had made me so bitter and mistrusting of them and of any woman I felt was "on their side." I had so much pain and anger wrapped up in my politics. I knew I couldn't continue like this any longer.

The rest of the book was a real awakening. It helped me realize that for my feminism to sustain me, it needed to be based in love. I had to love men and accept that feminism was not just about liberating women from oppressive roles, but also about liberating men and boys from a society that tells them to be straight and tough and have money and big dicks and to never feel or complain. I also needed to love women and understand that everyone has their struggles, and even if I couldn't see them, I needed to appreciate them. I needed to be inclusive, because it doesn't do the cause or women any good to constantly label things "not feminist enough." Just because you aren't out busting through glass ceilings and spitting on cops doesn't mean that you aren't "properly feminist." If I meet a girl who feels inspired and empowered by Taylor Swift, why not include her definition of girl power in mine? Why not seek solidarity with her instead of pointing out all the ways in which Taylor Swift is not a fucking riot grrrl, you know? Why zealously call out other feminist books/bands/Tumblogs for not being *perfect enough*?

The most embarrassing thing about having had an ultra-dogmatic vision of how a feminist should look/act/sing/write was that it *wasn't very feminist of me*. In fact, it was rather *macho* to be constantly ranking people according to my internalized hierarchy. The thing we as feminists know to be true is that women and girls (and brothers-in-struggle and other non-female allies) need our support, not our constant policing.

I can't pinpoint the moment that I started to rearrange my feminism, but I remember how that change took root: I saw my male roommates, friends, and bandmates as people with their own struggles, rather than dismissing them as variations on a stereotype. I hadn't even considered that they might be as burdened by what the world expected of them as I was by what it demanded of me. I stopped assuming motives: "He just wants to sleep with me," "He is only helping me because he thinks I am stupid." I had empathy.

This change didn't mean I stopped viewing the world with a critical eye—it actually made it easier to see the world clearly, since I was no longer blindly angry and at war with everything. My heart was still vulnerable to injustice and sadness, but so much more connected to the peace and power that came from having solidarity with other women, and other feminists. I was no longer waiting for anyone to die so I could live. I was free. ☺

EMBRACE YOUR IGNORANCE:
AN INTERVIEW WITH NEIL DEGRASSE TYSON

We talk to our favorite astrophysicist about the mystery of the universe. Interview by Hazel, photo by Olivia.

Neil deGrasse Tyson is an astrophysicist, a writer of many books, an excellent Twitterer, and an unofficial spokesperson for the universe. He's even had an asteroid named in his honor. Do you have an asteroid named after you? Yeah, I didn't think so. I called him up to talk about extremely intelligent aliens, accepting the unknown, and why dark matter is so terrifying.

HAZEL The Kepler spaceship has spotted 2,740 potential planets in our galaxy so far, and at least 10 of those are potentially habitable. Do you think there are life forms as developed as humans living on those planets?

NEIL DEGRASSE TYSON Well, that assumes that humans are some measure of development. It may be that we're actually quite primitive compared with other species out there.

That's true.

In fact, you could argue that the reason we haven't been visited is that [aliens] have already observed us and concluded there's no sign of intelligent life here. If you have a spaceship that can cross the galaxy, you're way smarter than us, because we have nothing that remotely approximates that. So why would we assume that we would be interesting enough that they would want to study us? That's just humorous. How interested are you when you walk past a worm crawling on the ground? Do you ever say, "Hey, I wonder what that worm is thinking?" You might have even just stepped on the worm. So imagine a species with that intelligence gap interacting with us. They could not come up with a thought stupid enough to fit inside of our brains. [*Laughs*] Just think about it!

Can you explain to me what dark matter is?

Five sixths of all the gravity we measure in the universe has no known origin. It's a mystery. We can track the black holes, the gas clouds, the planets and stars, and all the atoms, and that accounts for one sixth of all the gravity in the cosmos. We don't know what's causing the rest of the gravity, so we're calling it "dark matter." But we don't even know if it's matter—that's just a placeholder term. And then there's another mystery: a pressure in the vacuum of space that's operating against the wishes of gravity and making the universe accelerate in its expansion—we call that "dark energy." But we don't even know if it's energy. We don't know *what* it is. If you add up dark matter and dark energy, it comes to 96 percent of everything that drives the universe.

That's so scary!

It is completely spooky scary. If you look at a pie chart of what we know and understand in the universe, it's a four percent slice of the pie. That other 96 percent is completely mysterious to us.

Why is science so dominated by men?

That's not true in the biological sciences. The number of women in college majoring in biology might be 50 percent by now. Veterinary medicine is almost 100 percent women. It's true that women are still underrepresented in the deep physical sciences, like physics and astrophysics. There are a lot of people thinking about this [gender inequity] problem, and there's still more progress to be made.

But I also think that you shouldn't always presume that you need to have a woman be the role model for a girl. Because that presupposes that a woman had to have occupied a profession that you're interested in before you could ever be interested in it. That's limiting your possibilities rather than expanding them. If you require a role model who is your gender, you will never enter a field where there aren't any women. I think we're far enough along with girls that they can see a male scientist who loves his work and not say, *Oh he's a man—I can't do that. They'll say, Oh, he loves what he does, and I want to do that too.*

When I grew up I wanted to be an astrophysicist. If I tried to find a role model who grew up in the Bronx with my skin color who was an astrophysicist, I would never have become an astrophysicist. I assembled my role models à la carte.

Do you ever get really overwhelmed by the universe? How do you cope with not knowing everything about it?

I don't get overwhelmed, because I don't think about what I don't know as oppressive to me. If you think of it as oppressive, or if you have a measure of your ego that's larger than nature provides for you, then it's possible that you could end up quite depressed, seeing how small we are on Earth, [orbiting] around an ordinary star in an undistinguished corner of our galaxy between a hundred billion other galaxies. But if you come in with a humble enough ego, all of this is kind of enlightening instead of depressing.

The not knowing is the actual attraction of it. So many people only want answers. To be a scientist you have to learn to love the questions. You'll learn that some of the greatest mysteries of the universe remain unanswered, and that's the fun part. That's the part that gets you awake in the morning and running to the office, because there's a problem awaiting your attention that you might just solve that day. You have to embrace the unknown and embrace your own ignorance. ♛

→ WAY OUT WEST
By DYLAN

5. To BE YOUNG (IS TO BE SAD, IS TO BE HIGH) — RYAN ADAMS

6. GREENFUZ — THE CRAMPS

7. WAY OUT WEST — BIG STAR

8. RIDE INTO THE SUN — THE VELVET UNDERGROUND

9. A SILVER SONG — CONSPIRACY OF OWLS

10. California STARS — BILLY BRAGG & WILCO

11. LODI — CREEDENCE CLEARWATER REVIVAL

NEIL YOUNG & CRAZY HORSE — THIS IS NOWHERE

12. EVERYBODY KNOWS THIS IS NOWHERE

13. IF NOT FOR YOU — GEORGE HARRISON

14. HAPPINESS/THE GONDOLA MAN — ELLIOTT SMITH

15. EVERYONE — VAN MORRISON

16. WEST COAST CALAMITIES — ARIEL PINK'S HAUNTED GRAFFITI

4. OBVIOUSLY FIVE BELIEVERS — BOB DYLAN

3. SWEET HEAD — DAVID BOWIE

2. DANNY SAYS — THE RAMONES

1. FREE & EASY, TAKE 2 — THE BRIAN JONESTOWN MASSACRE

PARK MOTEL

AUGUST 2012: On the ROAD

When I left for the Rookie Road Trip in June, I expected our van to be filled with bearded musicians from the '70s and for all billboards to suddenly show classily designed Coke ads instead of any for Attorney Peter Francis Geraci. Imagine my surprise when I realized that not everything looks like an old movie!

Of course, the scenery did end up being beautiful, and my fellow road-trippers were much better companions than any of the dudes from *Almost Famous* would've been, and I kind of got used to ignoring the billboards. But the memories that are most prominent to me now, the moments that most strongly satisfied the curiosity with which we faced this GREAT NATION OF OURS, are the ones that were just about the people we came across every day—be they kindred spirits, or people with lives very different from our own, or not people at all, but DOGS. (The dogs were SO CUTE.) Staying with Olivia's boyfriend's family in Portland, with Joey and Mark in Omaha, and with Ira's sister Randi in San Francisco; having dinner at Dylan's mom's house in Seattle, and with a family in Big Sur; a woman at a restaurant in northern California talking about the tiger she was planning to purchase and train; the family at a gas station in Nebraska that played a prank on Petra's boyfriend; and obviously, all our meetups with our readers. It was comforting to find that no matter where we were in the country, there were people who made it feel like home, and that no matter how far we'd traveled and how many people we talked to, there were always people unlike any I'd encountered thus far. This country is very big and very small at the same time, and scary in all the right ways.

In that sense, this month isn't really about being physically *on the road*; it's about meeting strangers and hearing their stories, about memories and keepsakes, and about the kinds of secret discoveries that lie along the way to a final goal or destination. I couldn't wait to get to California, but there were pockets of beauty and weirdness along the way that I found myself thankful we sought out.

I'm taking this chunk of space in my own damn editor's letter to thank those who could make it to our events. Thanks to Urban Outfitters and Space 15 Twenty for their collaboration, for supporting our vision for the meetups and the teen-bedroom replica we created in their gallery, for understanding why we needed a whole collection of *Sweet Valley High* books for the installation, and for miraculously finding them. During this summer's events, Rookie felt like a real presence in the world, not just in a corner of the internet. And that whole humans-connecting thing? That happened! Thank you again.

LOVE,
Tavi

QUEENS

NEIGHBORHOOD

Just a rad girl gang with rad DIY'd jackets.
By Eleanor

Urban Outfitters jackets customized
by Eleanor, Mirren, and Ava.

DEEP
END

DEPTH OF FEET

Queens of the Neighborhood: A TUTORIAL

A denim-jacket DIY. By Eleanor, Mirren Kessling, and Ava Asaadi. Playlist lettering by Sonja.

I love turning a denim jacket from just a really useful item of clothing that I can wear with anything, to all that plus a wearable method of expressing something about myself. I use my jackets as a canvas for screaming: "HEY GUYS THIS IS EVERYTHING I AM/LOVE/BELIEVE IN." And thus complete strangers can take one glance at me and instantly know what I'm all about. A custom jacket is of course also a key component in any badass gang: the Pink Ladies, the Man-Eaters, the Pin Pals—what would they be without their jackets?

My own mini girl gang (we currently refer to ourselves as Mermaid Tears) includes, but is not always limited to, me, Ava, and Mirren. (We adopted Sasha for the shoot.) For this fun-packed extravaganza, we each got our hands on an Urban Outfitters vintage denim jacket and brainstormed about ten thousand ideas for materials, techniques, and imagery so that we could show the world we mean business. We hope we inspire you to think of ten thousand ways to customize your own jean jacket.

We started off by working on what we've dubbed our "homework sheets"—photocopied templates that can be colored in and bejeweled in preparation for making your dream jacket.

ELEANOR'S JACKET
First, I tie-dyed my jacket. I should note that I tie-dye all the time, and by now I usually just make it up as I go along. If you're a beginner, it's probably a good idea to follow the instructions that come with the dyes.

You will need:
- A spray bottle filled with diluted bleach (be careful when handling!).
- Fiber-reactive dyes in your desired colors. (Tie-dye kits come with dyes, and craft stores carry a wide variety of hues.) I used Dylon brand.
- Salt
- Plastic tubs (I used ice cream containers)—one for each dye color you're using.
- Spooooooonssss
- Newspaper (to protect the floor/table/

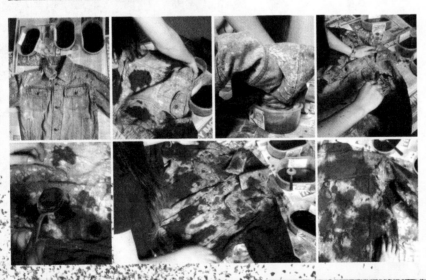

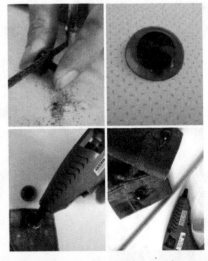

surface where you're working and make your parents happy).

1. Cover your work surface with newspaper. Then fill an empty spray bottle with watered-down bleach, and spray the jacket all over to lighten it up. The ratio of bleach to water is completely variable. Start with a lot of water and a little bit of bleach, and slowly add more bleach if you feel the fabric is not getting light enough. You don't want to immediately overdo it, as too much bleach can eat away at the fabric. Do this outside or in a well-ventilated space, as the fumes don't smell great, and working with bleach is not 100 percent risk free. Give the bleach a short while to set (I waited about 30 minutes), and then put the jacket in a cool, gentle wash.

2. Once your jacket has dried, you can get to the tie-dyeing. I decided to use pink, orange, and purple dyes. I poured about four ounces of dye into each tub, along with 2–3 gallons of very hot water. Then I added two tablespoons of salt to each tub. (The more salt you mix in and the hotter the water, the less likely the dye is to fade. If you want a faded look, you can put in a little less salt, use cooler water, or wait a shorter amount of time for the dye to set before washing.) I dipped various areas of the jacket into the tubs, and sprinkled some dye mixture onto other parts. Sprinkling salt on the jacket at this stage can make a nice speckled effect. I

recommend wearing gloves, which I did not do (and consequently I had red hands for days afterwards, which raised eyebrows in my place of work). I let the jacket dry overnight before hand-washing it in cold water and allowing it to dry again. Washing is important, as it ensures that you won't start leaking rainbows in the rain, and it fades the color a little so it looks more subtle.

3. I found a gorgeous vintage belt at a market stall and stitched it to the collar of my jacket. You can easily find pieces like this at markets, in boutiques, or online. You could also use fabric, trimmings, and/or other embellishments. If you want to make your collar detachable (so you can mix and match it with other jackets and outfits), you can attach it with safety pins instead of sewing it on.

4. For the back, I found a flower ribbon in a local craft shop, and I cut out the flowers to appliqué onto my jacket. You can cut shapes out of any printed fabric, or make your own shapes. I used anti-fray glue on the edges of the flowers before sewing them on. Then, to complement the mirrored collar, I bought some mirrors (you can get these from a lot of craft stores), which I stitched into the center of each flower.

5. After seeing Meadham Kirchhoff's Fall 2012 collection, I was inspired to make my own googly-eye buttons for the cuffs of

my jacket. I bought a pair of stuffed-animal eyes from a craft store. These normally can be simply punched through fabric, but as the buttons on denim jackets are hard to remove, I decided to saw the backs of the eyes off, using a small hacksaw on a cutting board. **Be careful if you do this! I had my parents help me with this part!** Then I super-glued the eyes over the original buttons.

MIRREN'S JACKET

I was inspired by Elsa Schiaparelli, the 20th century surrealist designer, to make silk roses to sew onto the shoulders of my jacket. I made the roses out of a variety of pink silks. I used a cross-stitch fabric as my base, which I cut to form a circle (any thick fabric, like felt, will do). I then cut a piece of the silk in a petal shape, gathered it, and sewed it onto the thick fabric vertically to make the central bud of the rose. I wrapped a different pink around the rest of the circle horizontally to make the rose, sewing it in place as I went. Then I ironed the rose flat. I found that if I used a slightly too-hot iron in different parts, it discolored the silk a bit to give it a more aged look. Finally, I sewed my roses onto the jacket, being careful not to make the stitches too obvious.

On a recent trip to the Wallace Collection in London, I was inspired by the 18th century painter François Boucher to paint a Rococo-style scene on the back of my jacket. I discovered that it is possible to paint denim with acrylic paint—AND IT STAYS! (I even tested this for you by washing my jacket in a quick wash at a high temperature.)

You can paint the denim jacket just like you would paint a canvas. If you're going to have a go at painting a sky and you want it to look realistic, imagine the position of the sun and the direction its rays are coming from. On my jacket, I imagined the sun being in the top left-hand corner, so the top left-hand clouds are white, while the bottom right-hand ones are the darkest.

Finally, I safety-pinned some patches I had made to the front of jacket. Flip back one page to see the one I made (the photo on the top right) by scanning and printing a drawing, then transferring it to fabric using Dylon Image Maker. (You could also use iron-on transfers.) I then appliquéd this to a backing fabric and added trim. Finished!

AVA'S JACKET

First, I embroidered a piece of tie-dyed fabric and affixed it to the back of my jacket with safety pins. For the tie-dye, I twisted the fabric into a coil and cinched it with elastic bands. Then I just followed the instructions on the dye packet.

Once the fabric was dry, I drew my rocking-horse design on it in pencil. From here on it helps to have embroidery experience, but the backstitch is pretty easy to learn (search for "backstitch" on YouTube). I used it to create a continuous line, and I added details like sequin flowers to the hair. The embroidery hoop you see below helped keep the fabric taut while I sewed.

For the collar I used some lace fabric that I bought at a thrift store. Fabric stores often have discount baskets for smaller swatches; otherwise, I recommend doilies or table-cloths. I cut the lace in half and pinned it to the jacket collar. (Pin before you stitch to prevent mistakes.) For detail, I sewed an assortment of sequins into the lace. I did the same for the inside of the cuff.

I bought a couple of coin purses from the junk shop and made them into elbow pads by turning them inside out, unpicking the stitches, and cutting them into the right shape.

All done! ❀

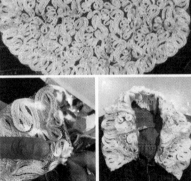

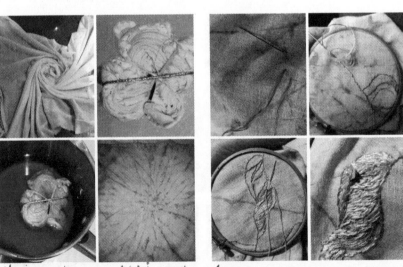

THAT SUMMER SUNSET   By the Rookie STAFF

1. HOT FUN in the SUMMERTIME-SLY & The FAMILY STONE   2. EMPIRE STATE OF MIND-JAY-Z and ALICIA KEYS

3. BULLFIGHTER JACKET-MINIATURE TIGERS   4. SUMMER LOVE-JUSTIN TIMBERLAKE   5. HAPPINESS-ALEXIS JORDAN

6. MAKE SUMMER LAST FOREVER-LOU CHRISTIE   7. MY BODY'S A ZOMBIE FOR YOU-DEAD MAN'S BONES

8. LUNA Y SOL-MANU CHAO   9. SOUL LOVE-DAVID BOWIE   10. OPHELIA-THE BAND   11. PATA PATA-MIRIAM MAKEBA

12. GIVE IT A REST-SHE ROCKERS   13. CONTINUOUS THUNDER-JAPANDROIDS   14. SO DESTROYED-PRINCE RAMA

15. BI KAFFEH-SAFAR BARLIK   16. LET'S SAVE TONY ORLANDO'S HOUSE-YO LA TENGO   17. GOING TO CALIFORNIA-LED ZEPPELIN

18. AFTER the GOLD RUSH-NEIL YOUNG   19. SUMMER...IT'S GONE-GRANDADDY   20. SIX WHITE HORSES-GILLIAN WELCH

21. WICHITA LINEMAN-GLEN CAMPBELL   22. THAT SUMMER SUNSET-SKEETER DAVIS   23. SUMMERTIME SADNESS-LANA DEL REY

24. DON'T KISS ME GOODBYE-ULTRA ORANGE & EMMANUELLE   25. MASSIVE NIGHTS-THE HOLD STEADY

26. CRUEL SUMMER-SUPERCHUNK   27. 4 A.M.-BABASÓNICOS   28. THERE'S AN END-HOLLY GOLIGHTLY

29. IT'S OVER-E.L.O.   30. THE THRILL IS GONE-B.B. KING   31. THE LAST DAY OF SUMMER-The CURE

32. SEPTEMBER'S NOT SO FAR AWAY-The FIELD MICE

33. ALL TOMORROW'S PARTIES-
The VELVET UNDERGROUND

Parking

Verkamp's
Souvenirs

SUMMER OF Love

A road diary from our cross-country trip this summer.
By Petra. Playlist by Petra, lettering by Sonja.

THE ROOKIE ROADTRIP SOUNDTRACK
1. DARK WAS the NIGHT - RY COODER   2. SWEET THANG - SHUGGIE OTIS

3. DOWN IN MEXICO — The COASTERS
4. THE LOVE YOU SAVE (MAY BE YOUR OWN) — JOE TEX   5. MURDER — The TRAMPS

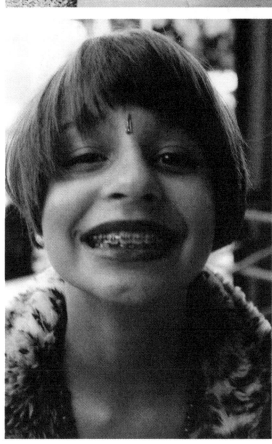 

6. THESE BOOTS ARE MADE FOR WALKING - NANCY SINATRA   7. DEVIL GOT MY WOMAN -
                                                              SKIP JAMES
FUNNEL OF LOVE - WANDA JACKSON 9. SON OF A PREACHER MAN - DUSTY SPRINGFIELD

10. SWEET EMOTION - AEROSMITH   11. WASN'T BORN TO FOLLOW - THE BYRDS
12. EMMYLOU - FIRST AID KIT   13. RING OF FIRE - JOHNNY CASH

14. BANG BANG - NANCY SINATRA   15. SUMMERTIME SADNESS - LANA DEL REY

16. THE LONG BLACK VEIL - JOHNNY CASH   17. OBLIVION - GRIMES

WHERE your book BEGINS

Journaling 101.
By Emma D.

I've always organized my life in notebooks. I keep all of these things simultaneously: a few sketchbooks, a planner, a personal dream book, and separate notepads for things like to-do lists, overheard conversations, and meaningful quotations.

I've found that all those notebooks express more of myself than the regular diary I kept until high school. My diary was random, depressing, extremely dramatic, and rather boring. It was a great way to vent frustration, but writing in it didn't feel constructive. I gave up on it and, under the huge influence of *Ghost World*, switched to a visual diary. Finally, I could express feelings too complicated or too intimidating to put into words. I discovered that I'm just better at drawing than I am at writing—my sketchbook was actually helping me figure things out!

I believe keeping some kind of record, visual or written, is good for you. It helps you to clear your mind, develop your ideas, and know yourself better. It allows you to be emotional and honest as well as grumpy and pathetic. But if you feel thwarted in this process, like I did, or if you're just looking for new ways to express yourself, let me share with you a couple of ideas and technical tricks that will help make your journal fun to create and to look at.

MEDIUM

First, you need to find the medium that suits you. Some options:

Pick the perfect notebook. Indulge in a fancy notebook. A good-looking book reminds you that you keep it for your pleasure. Also, it's inviting, so it might motivate you not to give up on journaling.

Or: Turn an ordinary notebook into the perfect one. The truth is, pretty and expensive notebooks never work for me. I'm so scared of ruining their pristine sheets with my shaky handwriting and messy drawings that I literally can't put pen to paper! I always end up buying a cheap notebook and customizing the cover with some stickers or collages made from cut-out pictures or old maps or whatever, just to break the ice. With some loose sheets you can even sew/glue a notebook on your own, or turn a planner or an empty photo album into one.

If a white sheet of paper still triggers nothing but writer's block for you, try boosting your artistic spirit with a "creative workbook" like *Wreck This Journal* or *The*

Scribble Diary. They're like coloring books for teenagers—in a good way.

If you don't like writing/drawing on paper, just stick to your screen. I won't be talking about blogs, Twitter, Pinterest, etc., because, despite their many similarities to personal journals, speaking to the public usually brings a different quality to your work. Still, there are lots of apps and sites devoted to journaling, list making, mind mapping, and all kinds of thought organizers that can be an inspiration for your journaling routine.

METHOD

Next, consider your approach. A few things to remember:

You don't have to be a perfectionist. Don't judge yourself for poor handwriting or clumsy drawings—your diary is a space for trial and error, a secret place where pretentious poems and anatomically incorrect portraits of Harry Potter are equally welcome.

You don't have to be organized. Sometimes there's just too much going on to keep your journal consistent, and that's OK. You don't have to write or draw in it every single day, nor do you have to stick to certain lengths or just one method of expression—I highly recommend trying different literary or drawing styles according to your mood and the amount of time you have for journaling. However, if you need order to be able to express your thoughts, divide your journal into sections or keep a couple of notebooks for different things.

Find a good hiding place…unless you live alone and have absolutely no secrets. I was raised with respect for privacy, but I'm a middle child, so I know the reality of siblings' curiosity. Sometimes it's best if your family doesn't know you keep a journal at all—this eliminates the temptation for them to find it. You can wrap your journal with the dust jacket of a normal book and keep it on the second row of a bookshelf. (I tried hiding my journal between folded T-shirts in my wardrobe, but nosy siblings

also have a habit of borrowing clothes without asking.) If "privacy" is a flexible concept in your home, be clever. Maybe invest in a padlock.

IDEAS

Now it's time to actually start filling your journal with your thoughts and ideas and emotions. Of course, there are standard diary entries, poetry, and creative writing, but the following ideas, a cocktail of drawing, writing, and mind-mapping concepts, should help anyone who feels unsure about what exactly you want your journal to be. I've tried all of these and adjusted them to my needs. Some have become a part of my routine for good.

Writing. Let's begin with something easy and probably closest to the common idea of journaling. Try writing about events as though they were a movie, or imagine them as photos and describe those. Write down overheard conversations. Make up backstories for people you see on the street. These exercises in observation and description can be a good start to a more experimental approach.

Comics. Cartooning is time-consuming, but I find it really rewarding. Don't be scared, I'm not talking about elaborate graphics or complex autobiography in the spirit of *Persepolis* or *Fun Home*. Try depicting ordinary objects and everyday events; sketch out thoughts or conversations. You don't need to use frames or speech bubbles; no one's gonna see these but you, after all, so there are no one else's expectations pressuring you to conform.

Sketchbooks. If comics seem too complex, try another kind of sketching diary. It doesn't have to be narrative at all—you can think of your sketchbook as a collage, letting concert tickets, Post-it notes, and postcards fill your personal mini-museum. Abstract compositions, like many of Minna's and Caitlin's Dear Diary entries on Rookie, carry as much emotion as detailed written accounts do. Rookie's María Inés fills her sketchbooks with clouds of song lyrics and doodles.

Daily activities. The simple practice of drawing (or photographing) everyday activities—what you ate/wore/bought/etc.—has caught fire on the internet over the past couple of years, for good reason. You won't know why something like this is addictive until you try it yourself.

Graphs, lists, mind maps. There's a chapter in Jennifer Egan's book *A Visit From the Goon Squad* that's meant to be a 12-year-old girl's diary—and it's written entirely in PowerPoint. The character used seemingly impersonal and corporate graphs and charts to depict the changing relationships between members of her family in few words but with great accuracy. Creating hand-drawn infographics about your life can be more entertaining than solving a sudoku. Not to mention lists. There can be a list for everything (as demonstrated in Nick Hornby's novel *High Fidelity*), and lists can be funny.

Everything else. So, there are some ideas to get your started. After you've been journaling for a few months you'll probably have heaps of your own ideas. A diary told through playlists? Moodboards? Agent Cooper–style voice recordings? Since journaling is all about expressing yourself, there are as many possibilities as you have moods. So add, multiply, experiment, and have fun! ✄

Lone RIDER

A fictional story mapped by pit stops and junk food.
By Pixie

Capri Sun, Prescott City public school bus, September 8, 1999

Laurel swears that Capri Sun was invented by a child psychologist: "There's nobody else who would take such pleasure in watching kids consistently fuck up and get pissed off in the noble pursuit of juice." Laurel's parents, it should be said, are both child psychologists, which explains why our teacher, Mrs. Kimball, had to refer to her as "Eraser" in kindergarten. "My mother thought it was a brave statement on 're-capturing my own identity,' and my father was worried that it meant that I wanted to make other people disappear," she says, laughing. "I just thought it sounded good. I was like five."

She was Eraser when I met her on the school bus during one of our first rides home. I had a Capri Sun left over from snack time, a lukewarm strawberry something-or-other that I'd been too afraid to drink in class for fear of having to use the school bathroom. I was struggling, as always, to open it by myself, the straw bending just as it met the spaceman packaging.

"You have to stab it," the girl across the aisle from me said, extending her hand. Within two seconds, she'd shoved the straw into the pouch. "My mom doesn't let me have these," she said, handing it back to me.

"You can have this one," I offered.

There are certain irreplaceable feelings in life. One of them is the act of sharing when you're a kid, when you've just mas-

tered the concept, when you realize what kindness means, before you're old enough to put a filter on it and manipulate it for your own good. The other is meeting your first best friend.

"I'm Libby Campbell," I told her as she gulped down the juice.

"I'm Eraser Bunch," she said. "But you can call me Laurel."

McDonald's french fries, passenger seat, '07 Hyundai Elantra, somewhere along I-94, October 11, 2010

I stopped listening after she said "early admission." It didn't matter anyway. Everything that came out of her mouth after that just sounded like *gone, gone, gone.*

Auntie Anne's cinnamon sugar pretzel, O'Hare International Airport, November 19, 2010

"Stand up straight, Elizabeth," my mother says. There must be a sad kind of pamphlet sent to high school moms every year, alongside the ones about teenage pregnancy and bath salts, titled *So You Think Your Daughter Is Slouching.*

We're in line for Flight 8917 to Boston to visit my aunt Kathryn and at least five colleges—two that I can definitely get into, one that I *might* be able to get into, and two that we're really only going to so we can buy the T-shirts and I can further my parents' delusions. My father has brought several application packets with him; the

ones with the kids who look like Hogwarts rejects on the front are the ones with the most fingerprints.

Right before we board the plane, Laurel sends me a series of texts from the homecoming dance that I'm missing:

my mother dropped me off and screamed "don't feel pressured to conform to mating rituals and strict gender roles" so that was great

liam looks like a stalk of corn with teeth you are totally right i love you

rihanna has too many songs

made out with k #yolo #neveragaintho #breathmint

miss u too much nothing is fun w/o u

Gingerbread latte, driver's seat, '09 Honda Civic, somewhere along I-94, December 18, 2010

This time we talk about our Christmas lists: She says she wants surfing lessons, and I say that I want a new winter coat, and then we don't really say anything at all.

Pepperoni Pizza Combos, Campbell family caravan, Myrtle Beach, South Carolina, February 18, 2011

Laurel believes that Pepperoni Pizza Combos are "the only acceptable road-trip food." Her mother hates the smell of them, which is why she can only eat them when she's on vacation with my family. We go to Myrtle Beach every year; Laurel has been coming for the last seven or so. Her parents relented after my father, a biology professor, promised that he'd always make the trip educational in some way. Last summer, he had us hold an informal debate at Cap'n Joe's Fish Pot: Laurel was pro fried shrimp, and I was pro fried clam.

We're in the way, way back of the van. Our bags are loaded in the middle seat, giving us a wall of privacy from my parents, who are nodding their heads in time to something by the Eagles.

"All I want on this earth is a Cone-A-Rama Big Wheel," Laurel says, referring to a disgustingly huge waffle cone that we both attempt to eat every year. If you finish it, you get your picture on the wall. She's been trying—and failing—since she was 10. My father overhears and yells, "Is this the year you make the wall?"

"I've got a good feeling," Laurel says.

"Don't make yourself sick," my mother says, annoyed. "Your mother would kill me if she knew I let you eat that thing every year."

"This is gonna be the year," Laurel says, wrapping an inflatable pillow around her neck and shoving her empty bag of Combos under the seat. "I'm feeling like a champion."

I take mental pictures of every exit by blinking my eyes. Next year, we'll both be in different classrooms, staring out at different landscapes, with different voices surrounding us. I know why she wants her picture on the wall—because she's not sure when she'll get back, and somebody has to leave proof that for years and years we came, we saw, and she eventually conquered.

Sugar-free Red Bull, driver's seat, '09 Honda Civic, somewhere along I-94, March 31, 2011

If I go to sleep it will be tomorrow if I go to sleep it will be tomorrow if I go to sleep it will be tomorrow if I go to sleep it will be tomorrow stay awake stay awake stay awake…

Celebration cake, dining room table, my house, April 1, 2011

Everyone is wearing red sweatshirts and smiling. "I knew you could do it," my father says, waving around my acceptance packet. Ten points for faux-Gryffindor, I guess.

Later, Laurel asks me if I'm surprised, and I tell her of course, of course I'm surprised, my SAT math score was a giant turd, and I thought I had no chance at all. I don't tell her that I've suddenly become an expert on time and distance, that maybe I should major in cartography, that I know every possible path from Massachusetts to California and that all of them take too long.

Downstairs, our parents laugh together, eating cake, drinking wine, and celebrating their daughters. Over the years, our weirdo mothers have become best friends. We've never bothered asking who their best friends were before their daughters met on the bus.

Menthol cigarette, passenger seat, '07 Hyundai Elantra, somewhere along I-94, May 28, 2011

"If you're smoking that to piss me off," she says, "it's working."

"My entire life," I tell her, "does not revolve around you." I don't know how to hold the cigarette. I try to flick off some ash and it lands in my lap.

"You have to tap it," she says, extending her hand.

I offer her the cigarette, and she throws it out the window.

"My mother doesn't let me have those," she says, staring at the lights ahead of us.

Sour Patch Kids, back porch swing, Bunch family home, June 30, 2011

Our parents have noticed: We are not ourselves, they say. We are especially not ourselves when we are together. They mention winter break, spring break, summer break, anything to make the word "break" sound remotely positive.

I don't know why I tell her. She smiles the sad, knowing smile of someone who

has always scored a little higher on every test and says something about *other ways*.

We swing back and forth in the humid air, taking turns sticking our fingers into the candy bag and licking the sour sugar from our skin. All around us are crickets, the internationally renowned orchestra for the speechless.

DQ Oreo Blizzard, backseat, Campbell family caravan, somewhere along the Massachusetts Turnpike, August 23, 2011

Everything I own is packed into plastic bins, surrounding me on all sides. My parents are—once again—wearing their red sweatshirts. "This is so exciting," my mother says, her left leg shaking up and down. She turns back to glance at me. "Elizabeth," she says, "sit up straight."

Kettle corn, Ferris wheel car 18, the Big E/Eastern States Exposition fairgrounds, W. Springfield, Massachusetts, September 14, 2011

We're here on a "bonding expedition," according to our RA. We've each been given 10 tickets, and I've decided to use eight of them on the Ferris wheel, because I just want to sit down for a while. Alex and Meg, who started dating during, like, the first hour of school, are sitting in the car in front of me, kissing as they elevate.

"Lone rider?" the man running the wheel asks me as I settle in with my kettle corn. I shrug, and he locks the door, and soon I'm flying above everyone on the ground, little specks, tiny strangers, thousands of people I might be lucky enough to meet. ❦

the MAGIC hour

A dusky photo album.
By Olivia

Thanks to Anna, Candace, Hadley, Lillie, and Meadow for modeling and to Cooper for assisting.

SEPTEMBER 2012: *Drama*

Hello, Rookies!

HAPPY ANNIVERSARY! In two days, this website will be one year old. I can't believe it! So much love has gone into this collection of pixels, so thank you to our AMAZING staff of editors, writers, illustrators, and photographers for all that you do. Much of this love comes from you readers as well, so THANK YOU LOTS. We would not exist if you didn't read us, and we would not be as good if you didn't tell us what you'd like to see, or send us your work (both of which we encourage you to do more!). Honestly, nothing has ever made me as happy as seeing the Rookie community come together and watching you people find each other, online and in person at our road trip meetups. That is not an exaggeration. Like, for as much as I act like I hate people when I'm at school or in line at Potbelly, I'm actually maybe the #1 fan of humans and of humans relating to one another and of humans relating to things other humans make. I think it's kind of the best, and it happens with Rookie because you help make it such a welcoming community, and for that I want to buy you all the thank-you cards at Walgreens and make them into a mosaic of your face.

Thank you for being with us, whether it's been a year or a day. Thank you wonderful staffers, thank you wonderful guests, EVERYONE IS AWESOME YIPPEE.

Love,
Tavi

I'm Falling Apart

Being diagnosed with mental illness was scary, but it was what I needed to get well.

By Sady

The week after my 30th birthday, my best friend had me committed to a psych ward. Two days later, I emerged with a life-changing diagnosis. The hard part hadn't even started yet.

I deserved to be committed. I needed it. For a long time, I had been in a dark, painful mood, a mood that had steadily transitioned into my personality. When I felt anger, I felt it so intensely that it took over my whole body. I would go to the grocery store with a carefully composed list, walk through the aisles fuming, and then leave so furious that I completely forgot to buy any food. The anger—which could have been over anything from a fight with a friend to a political issue—often lasted for weeks. Also, I was tired—always, always bone tired. I was so exhausted that it was a huge physical effort to sit at my desk and type, except for rare weeks of nonstop energy in which I came up with an idea, worked to make it happen, watched it happen, and then treated it like a toy I'd gotten bored with. I could always get my paying work done, but anything outside of that was subject to my ever-fluctuating energy levels. My emotions seemed remote, flat, hard to discern, as if I were trying to see them through dirty glass. What little I could feel felt bad. I pulled away from people. I was determined not to trust anyone. I was depressed, in other words, except for those strangely productive weeks and long, terrifying rushes of anger.

About a month before my birthday, this took a bizarre turn. Not only did I distrust people, I suspected many of them were only *pretending* to be my friends. I was convinced they were plotting against me. And I realized something: I deserved it. I was acting like a terrible monster, even if I didn't know exactly why. I would find a friend with whom I'd had a fight, for example, and apologize for calling them a name that they had in fact called me. I was saying I'd done or said things that had never hap-

pened. But I wasn't entirely sure that I *hadn't* slapped a man with whom I'd had an argument about WikiLeaks. (I hadn't, people were there, they saw an absence of slapping.) But if I hadn't, how could I know that any of my other memories were valid? The real and the imaginary were starting to feel the same. I was sending people rambling Gchats talking about what a bad person I was, and if the conversation topic shifted, I couldn't keep up. I seemed to be talking mostly to myself.

When my friend came over to my house, the night before I went in, she hadn't seen me in a month. I hadn't bathed in weeks. I was dressed in a mismatched, nonsensical collection of clothes I'd picked up off the floor. I had lost about 20 pounds; bones were sticking out of my face and wrists. (I had stopped eating.) People told me I couldn't make eye contact. I also couldn't speak above a whisper or in a complete sentence. I had been up for at least 24 hours, and I couldn't sleep. I would lie down, then start back up again to wander around the apartment. My friend stayed up all night watching this, and in the morning she took me to the psych ward of a New York hospital that accepts walk-ins. Nurses took my blood pressure and asked us both a few questions about my behavior and thoughts. A doctor took my friend into a different room and asked her to describe what she'd seen of my behavior. Once they'd talked to her, they handed her my bag and my coat and told her to leave. They told me I would be staying.

I'm describing this because I want you to see how it sneaked up on me. Mental illness is like this. It doesn't always show up suddenly and dramatically. I had been diagnosed in the past with depression and generalized anxiety disorder, both of which are common illnesses, and which together I thought explained my problems. I would have been insulted if you'd suggested I had anything more "serious."

I was just joyless, I was just angry, I was just lonely. By the time I was unwashed, incoherent, and skeletal, I had gotten so used to being unhappy that I almost didn't see the difference. (Note: If you start to feel bad for long periods of time, if your thought patterns or personality start to change in odd ways, *go to a doctor*. It could be a bad mood. It could also be something much more dangerous.)

What the doctors at the hospital finally decided was that I had bipolar II disorder, which is a scary diagnosis. It has a high suicide rate and can be very painful and destructive to your life if you don't get it treated. It basically means alternating between two phases: overconfidence and recklessness (and/or anger), and deep shame when you crash down into depression and see the mess you've made. The diagnosis made sense of most of my worst times and emotions. My boyfriend had noticed phases where I couldn't say no to anything, and then corresponding periods of isolation and darkness when I could barely function socially. But before I could get this alarming news, I had to deal with the other scary thing, which was being in the hospital in the first place.

Since I had not checked myself in, my stay was marked as "involuntary." The hospital would have one doctor give a potential diagnosis, then keep me for 24 hours of observation. After that, another doctor would look at me, and if he agreed that I needed to stay, they could keep me for up to 72 hours, and then move me to a hospital for a longer stay if they thought it was advisable. My consent was not necessary for any of this. I couldn't have left if I'd wanted to. My future was entirely in the hands of these strangers.

Let me tell you: If you already think people are monitoring you and you're already worried that people are plotting against you, being locked up against your will by people who actually do want to monitor your thoughts feels like literally the worst thing that can possibly ever happen. It feels like all your fears are coming true. You are away from home, there is nothing to do, and strangers are dictating your every move—when you eat, what you eat, when you sleep, when you wake up, when you take a shower.

I was scared, I was homesick, and I was very, very angry. Imagine, if you will, a feminist blogger surrounded by men who tell her daily that they don't think she's competent to make her own decisions. While I was there, several patients flipped out and yelled at the doctor. This was assumed to be a sign of illness, but actually it's a pretty normal reaction. I wanted to yell for most of the time I was there.

I got through it for two reasons. First, my boyfriend visited me every day, so I stayed connected to my real life. Second, I asked for some paper and a marker. (They would not let patients have pens, because we might use them to hurt ourselves.) When I was scared or angry, I wrote that down, and because I had a place to express my emotions, I was able to stay calm enough to get myself home within 48 hours.

"The only reason we're letting her out so early," one doctor told my mother, "is that she has a very good support system." This was true. I seemed to get more phone calls than most patients. I was one of only two people to be visited by a partner, and he came both days. My mother called more than once, and she took my calls. I had been taken to the psych ward by a friend.

And this was important for me to remember, because in the wake of the diagnosis, all of those caring, loving people drove me right back out of my mind again. For a while, all of them were convinced that every emotion I had, and everything I did, was somehow related to my illness. One of the symptoms of hypomania (the small upswings that were responsible for my weeks of productivity) is "irritability," so if I got irritated, I was clearly manic. If I was sad, I was "depressed." If I stayed up late to work because I liked the quiet, that was "sleeplessness." Everyone agreed that I had probably gotten sick because I worked too much, so if I pushed myself, my moth-er would declare that I was doing "exactly what put [me] in the hospital."

"I'm doing what got me the health insurance that was the only reason I could go to the hospital," I snapped once. By this point, being told to be quiet, never get irritated, work less, and sleep all the time had started to feel very *Yellow Wallpaper*. And yet, all of this was good for me. If you are sick in a way that disturbs your thought patterns, you need to have people you can trust to keep track of how you're thinking. This is scary, because it means opening up to at least a few people about your illness. One of the things that disability activists often protest, which had never bothered me before, is how often people use "crazy" to mean "bad." This can send the message that having a mental illness means *you* are bad, and that mental illness is therefore a shameful secret you have to keep. Which is the opposite of healthy. I'd never noticed it until I was recovering, at which point "crazy" seemed to be everywhere. And at first, it did hurt. If "crazy" could be used to write off a woman who's upset even when she has no history of illness, it could definitely be used to write off a woman who'd spent two days in the hospital. But I still use it myself, and here's why: If you're rowdy and funny at a party, you're so "crazy." If someone is nasty and passive-aggressive, that drives you "crazy." If you go over to that person's house and place a bag of flaming dog poop on their doorstep, you're acting "crazy." (Also, don't.) But if you have to go to the hospital because people think you might die, then you're *ill*. Ill people are not to be dismissed, mocked, or insulted by being called crazy—*that* is an insensitive misuse of the word. And anyone who makes fun of someone for being ill is an asshole, and what assholes think fundamentally does not matter. That's why you're reading a magazine called Rookie, and not WhatSomeAssholesThink.com.

And it is really, really important to remember that. Because if you are diagnosed with a mental illness, even something as common as depression, you will probably have to live with that diagnosis for a long time. It will change you. Before my diagnosis, I couldn't use a birth control pill, because I could never remember to take the pills on time. Now I have to be a very organized person who takes her medications as if her life depends on it, which it does. Before this, anything and everything was a good reason to put off sleep. Now I monitor how many hours of sleep I get per night, to make sure that I'm not getting sick. And before this, I was someone who didn't have to worry what people might think if I told them how my brain worked. Now I do worry. I knew depression was dangerous, but it was common enough that mentioning it wouldn't freak people out. Bipolar disorder has a much more intense ring to it. I have to worry about employers, friends, and, potentially, future dates finding out. Because of this article, you'll always be able to Google me and find out that I have this sickness. You'll know how bad it got.

And I'm telling you anyway. Because here's the part of the story that matters: Once I got the diagnosis, got the pills, and got in touch with a therapist I really liked, I woke up in the morning. And I was happy, genuinely happy, for the first time in a very long time. That's what matters about my nervous breakdown—or yours, or anyone's. When I got the help I needed, I was able to recover.

I'm lucky. I know that. That's why I say that having my breakdown and going to the hospital was the easy part. Everyone I spoke to after the fact who had any experience at all with serious illness told me that dealing with the diagnosis would be a lifelong project: There would be more doctors, different medicines, and the long, hard work of taking care of myself. Plenty of people have received diagnoses, struggled with them for years, and still died from their illnesses. But plenty of other people never receive a diagnosis, nor the care they need to get better. They spend their lives trying to move forward, knowing something is wrong and blaming themselves for falling apart—or being blamed by the people who love them. No matter how scary it was to be hospitalized and diagnosed with a mental illness, it was also a blessing. Because it gave me what I needed to get well. ♦

TEN RULES FOR WRITERS

Not even rules, more like hidden truths.
By Etgar Keret

1. MAKE SURE YOU ENJOY WRITING.

Writers always like to say how hard the writing process is and how much suffering it causes. They're lying. People don't like to admit they make a living from something they genuinely enjoy.

Writing is a way to live another life. Many other lives. The lives of countless people whom you've never been, but who are completely *you*. Every time you sit down and face a page and try—even if you don't succeed—be grateful for the opportunity to expand the scope of your life. It's fun. It's groovy. It's dandy. And don't let anyone tell you otherwise.

2. LOVE YOUR CHARACTERS.

For a character to be real, there has to be at least one person in this world capable of loving it and understanding it, whether they like what the character does or not. You're the mother and the father of the characters you create. If you can't love them, nobody can.

3. WHEN YOU'RE WRITING, YOU DON'T OWE ANYTHING TO ANYONE.

In real life, if you don't behave yourself, you'll wind up in jail or in an institution, but in writing, anything goes. If there's a character in your story who appeals to you, kiss it. If there's a carpet in your story that you hate, set fire to it right in the middle of the living room. When it comes to writing, you can destroy entire planets and eradicate whole civilizations with the click of a key, and an hour later, when the old lady from the floor below sees you in the hallway, she'll still say hello.

4. START AT THE MIDDLE.

The beginning is like the scorched edge of a cake that's touched the cake pan. You may need it just to get going, but it isn't really edible.

5. TRY NOT TO KNOW HOW IT ENDS.

Curiosity is a powerful force. Don't let go of it. When you're about to write a story or a chapter, take control of the situation and of your characters' motives, but always let yourself be surprised by the twists in the plot.

6. DON'T USE ANYTHING JUST BECAUSE "THAT'S HOW IT ALWAYS IS."

Paragraphing, quotation marks, characters that still go by the same name even though you've turned the page: All those are just conventions that exist to serve you. If they don't work, forget about them. The fact that a particular rule applies in every book you've ever read doesn't mean it has to apply in your book too.

7. WRITE LIKE YOURSELF.

If you try to write like Nabokov, there will always be at least one person (whose name is Nabokov) who'll do it better than you. But when it comes to writing the way you do, you'll always be the *world champion at being yourself.*

8. MAKE SURE YOU'RE ALL ALONE IN THE ROOM WHEN YOU WRITE.

Even if writing in cafés sounds romantic, having other people around you is likely to make you conform, whether you realize it or not. When there's nobody around, you can talk to yourself or pick your nose without even being aware of it. Writing can be a kind of nose-picking, and when there are people around, the task may become less natural.

9. LET PEOPLE WHO LIKE WHAT YOU WRITE ENCOURAGE YOU.

And try to ignore all the others. Whatever you've written is simply not for them. Never mind. There are plenty of other writers in the world. If they look hard enough, they're bound to find one who meets their expectations.

10. HEAR WHAT EVERYONE HAS TO SAY, BUT DON'T LISTEN TO ANYONE (EXCEPT ME).

Writing is the most private territory in the world. Just as nobody can really teach you how you like your coffee, nobody can really teach you how to write. If someone gives you a piece of advice that sounds right and feels right, use it. If someone gives you a piece of advice that sounds right and feels wrong, don't waste so much as a single second on it. It may be fine for someone else, but not for you. ♦

Translated by Miriam Shlesinger.

HOW TO GET REJECTED FROM COLLEGE

Didn't get into the school of your dreams? You're in good company.

By Hazel

I recently got rejected from my dream college, a college that will remain anonymous (though it shouldn't be hard to figure out, seeing as how it is pretty much everyone in America's dream school). I applied early decision and worked my ass off on my essays. My extracurriculars were unique and representative of my personality and my future major. I had shining recommendations from some of the most revered teachers at my school. My GPA and my SAT scores, however, were not so sparkling. But the university's admissions committee assured me they would look at "the full package." One day during first period I got an email telling me I was rejected. Well, there went my day. I left school and then my dad took me to out to breakfast. NO TEARS.

After that rejection, I got rejected from a lot of the other schools on my list. Fortunately, I was eventually accepted into one school, which is where I go now, and it is awesome. But I know how it feels to get rejection letter after rejection letter.

Maybe you got rejected from a college. Maybe it was your dream school. Maybe it was your safety school! Maybe it was EVERY SCHOOL ON YOUR LIST. If so, you probably feel like you're spiraling into a tunnel of doom that continues forever and ever into the fiery depths of misery. I'm here to tell you that it's going to be OK! This guide isn't meant to teach you how to get rejected from a school (that's really easy to do, because colleges love making kids cry), but rather to give you some tips on dealing with that rejection.

1. NEVER BE TOO SURE OF YOURSELF.

The worst college rejections are the ones that you are sure are going to be acceptances. I had friends who were legacies, whose families had school wings dedicated in their names, and who had their college

interviewers tell them, "There's no way you won't be accepted." They were all rejected.

I told myself I definitely wasn't getting into any of the schools I applied to. This doesn't mean I didn't put all of my effort into my applications; but it eased the blow of getting rejected. When I was rejected, it didn't turn my world upside down. My low expectations made it easier to handle.

I've seen a lot of my friends expect to be accepted to places that rejected them, and they inevitably felt really shitty about it. So I think my method isn't a bad idea. Don't sit around expecting acceptances, because nothing is ever certain! NOTHING!

2. "EVERYTHING HAPPENS FOR A REASON" IS ACTUALLY SORT OF TRUE.

You will hear this phrase a lot when you get rejected from a college, especially if it's the one you really wanted to go to. I hated this phrase when this happened to me, because at the time I didn't really understand what the "reason" was. I thought it was just "to make Hazel feel inadequate." But my first rejection led me to apply to the school I'm attending now. I love it here, and I never would have even applied if I hadn't been rejected from my former dream school.

This story is so common: Kid meets dream school, kid gets rejected from dream school, kid gets into another school, kid lives happily ever after (for four years, at least) at that other school.

3. OWN YOUR REJECTION.

When a friend of mine got rejected from his top choice, he immediately posted about it on Facebook. He knew that all his friends were waiting to hear whether he got in, so making a blanket announcement saved him the trouble of breaking the news to each and every one of them individually. It

was also a really cool move, in my opinion. My high school was extremely competitive about college admissions, so most of the kids there kept their searches private. My friend's post was something like "Yeah, I got rejected; whatever, I'm alive." When I got rejected I did the same thing.

Getting rejected is nothing to be ashamed of! So many smart and talented people get rejected from multiple colleges. You know more kids who have been rejected than you think, because kids lie. They might say, "Oh, I'm not interested in that school anymore," even though they were obsessed with it when they applied. Sharing your own rejection might make 10 people who are secretly in the same boat feel less shitty about themselves.

4. YOU'RE ALLOWED TO FEEL REALLY, REALLY SAD (OR PISSED OFF) ABOUT BEING REJECTED.

Not everyone wants to go to college, and that's totally cool. But if you do want to go, you're allowed to get upset if the process doesn't go the way you planned. Sure, some people are all blasé about being rejected; but for others it can be devastating. That's not stupid or lame. Your sadness shouldn't consume your life (I doubt it will), but if you want to take a few days off from school, or burn your college sweatshirts in a fiery blaze, or even just cry about it, it's OK.

5. TRANSFERRING ISN'T OUT OF THE QUESTION!

People act like transferring is impossible, but it's not! Yes, the idea of applying to college all over again can be daunting, but if you are crazy in love with a school and you truly believe you are destined to go there but got rejected the first time around, try transferring in after your first semester, or your first year. If you had shitty grades in high school, kill it your first year in college and then reapply. You have nothing to lose, because you're already in college.

6. YOU ARE NOT YOUR APPLICATION.

Unfortunately, it's really hard for a college to get to know you through the application process, but your app (and *maybe* an interview) is all they have to decide if you're in or out. I don't care what your essays are about or what your GPA is, the college application will never truly represent you. I sincerely doubt your high school GPA and SAT scores are indicative of your work ethic, talents, and personality! Therefore, if/when you get rejected, please don't take it personally. If a college rejects you, they're rejecting your application (aka your high school grades, a standardized test score, essays, and an electronic form), not *you* as a person. You are way bigger and better than your application!

7. YOU'RE TOTALLY GOING TO LOOK BACK ON THAT TIME YOU GOT REJECTED FROM COLLEGE AND LOL.

The college-application process seems so important, and it can definitely be nerve-racking, but when you look back on it you'll think, *Why did I waste so much time and energy feeling bad about this?* And hopefully you'll laugh.

When another friend of mine got rejected from college, he wrote a really funny letter back to the university, rejecting their rejection of his application. I published it in my high school newspaper, and everyone thought it was hilarious, because almost all of us had gotten rejected from at least one school! This annoying period of disappointment will end, and those freakouts (if you haven't had at least one, you will) are going to seem crazy funny. Just you wait.

◆ ◆ ◆

Applying to college is infinitely awful in all respects, and being rejected is the worst part. But if you keep these seven points in mind, your future (or past) college rejection will be a lot less horrible. I wish you luck, young college-applying student! ◊

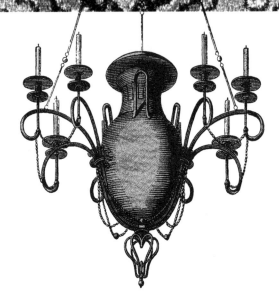

NO SHAME IN YOUR GAME

Sexism in gaming culture: a rant.
By Emily G.

I'm a female with a podcast about video games, so I am frequently asked tough questions: "How do I get my girlfriend to like video games?" "Are you a 'real' nerd?" "How do we fix sexism in the gaming world?"

My answers to those questions are, in order: "Start with two-player platformers," "What?" and "I wish I knew."

Gaming culture has traditionally been a male-dominated arena, and as women have entered and taken up space there more and more, there have been many ugly instances of sexual harassment. In February, on a live-streamed Capcom fighting-game reality show called *Cross Assault*, a female player named Miranda's own coach made so many disgusting comments to her and about her that people calling in to the show started questioning his behavior. The coach, Aris, didn't back down—instead he insisted that sexism was just part of the fighting-game community, and that it was "ethically unjust" for people to tell him to stop. Miranda ended up forfeiting every match in protest, but luckily she hasn't given up on the fighting community.

In June, when Anita Sarkeesian of the blog Feminist Frequency announced a Kickstarter for a video series she wanted to make exploring tropes of women in video games, the tirade of hatred released on her was staggering. People left threatening comments on the YouTube video for the project and altered her Wikipedia so that it was continually filled with insults and pornographic images. Gamer trolls were furious with her. The good news: Even more people were furious with those trolls. Anita was looking for $6,000 for her project; she ended up with $158,922.

Anita started out just wanting to look at sexism within games themselves, but clearly the issue goes beyond female characters in fighting games being dressed inappropriately for the match. It's a big problematic cocktail of young men who haven't yet learned how to interact with (and compete against) females, sexist portrayals of women in games, and the anonymity of the online community. I don't play a lot of video games against strangers online, partially because the people who do tend to spray hatred like champagne on New Year's, but I do often appear in YouTube videos that are video game–related. Some comments under those videos say I'm funny, but most of them refer to my appearance, something my male co-host does not experience. On my podcast, there are occasional calls for me to be replaced by someone "who knows what **he's** talking about," and here's another curious thing we've noticed: Whenever anyone says anything emotional on the show, it is almost always attributed to me instead of the dude who said it. Other than that, I mainly encounter surprise—surprise that I'm buying games for myself at the store; surprise that I, and not the dude I'm with, want to play the demo games at PAX.

I don't know how to fix sexism in gaming, but I have a few thoughts on how I personally handle sexism, as I've been a girl my whole life and a gamer for most of it. In no way do I speak for "all women" here—just myself—and in no way am I implying that the way I handle things *should* be the way that other girls or women handle themselves. Judging women for the way we deal with being harassed or assaulted heaps another layer of "your fault" on us.

I think about power a lot, and the way it shifts among people. I am acquaintances with mostly men—more specifically male comedians—and the signal that they accepted me was when they finally started making fun of me (constantly). My huge, weird laugh, my bad jokes, the runs in my tights—nothing is off-limits to these guys. But as harsh as their jokes can get, never once have I felt threatened. The power differential between me and my friends is that I am a woman and they are men, and the golden rule of giving people shit is that the person with more power does not exploit what gives them that power when joking with a person with less power. (Not very catchy, I know.) If you are about to say, "But me and my closest friends make fun of each others' genders, ethnicities, or

weird deformities!"—let me stop you there. I do that too, and it's awesome, but that's something you save for people you're very comfortable with—not acquaintances, and certainly not strangers.

In the gaming world, I see sexual harassment as both a power issue and a product of pure laziness. Some dudes are threatened by girls who play video games and are too lazy to come up with actual insults based on how you're playing, so they say disgusting things based on your gender instead. These guys may protest that they're just trash-talking, and to them I say that *if you need to try to intimidate a girl to beat her at a game, you should get better at video games* (and at trash talk). Side note: If you find yourself fighting for the right to sexually harass another human being, take a step back and really look at yourself. You've missed a step along the way.

But I digress. What concerns me, besides these guys' behavior, is when their harassment works. I'm not saying that gross, callous, sexist remarks shouldn't hurt, but it'd be a good idea for us to recognize that a sexist remark is, at its core, an attempt to shift the power differential. And we cannot let it stop us.

Ladygamers, we cannot stop gaming because of these dudes. Yes, the gaming culture should change, but it cannot change without our involvement. We have to be there, front and center, letting morons know that their behavior is not OK, but also that it's not going to stop us. Not letting a sexual harasser's words affect you doesn't mean that you condone their behavior, it just means that you refuse to let some d-bag have the authority to stop you from doing what you want. Acknowledge harassment as an attempt to take some of your power away from you, and then tell it "no thank you" or "FUCK OFF," depending on how you're feeling. Never stay in a situation where you feel physically unsafe or miserable, obviously, but online, we need to get in there, stretch out, take up some space, and let everyone know we're not going anywhere. If we treat sexual harassment like a big deal, it grows in potency and takes up more room in our minds and our fears—more room than it deserves.

Now, sexual harassment is, of course, a really big deal. So how do you shrink down its influence? This is a double-edged sword. When we're sexually harassed and we try to laugh it off or ignore it, that's used as evidence that we like it or at least that we know it's all just fun and games; and when we are bothered and speak up about it, that's used as evidence that women are too sensitive. Both accounts are wrong: We are laughing because we're uncomfortable but still trying not to embarrass your dumb, unfunny ass; and we're not too sensitive, you're just too dense to realize how threatened you are by us. You're also not realizing what it feels like to be a female, to have to consistently monitor your own safety, to have to be judged based on your appearance every day, and now, to have to put up with your "hilarious" comments.

When I am confronted with sexual harassment while gaming, I tend to go with a few sarcastic lines that I hope let the person know that they're being stupid and that I'm not affected by stupidity. I usually start with: "Nice one, real original," then proceed to "Shut up and focus," and finally, if they won't shut up, I put these words in their mouths: "Ooooh, you're different from me and I don't know how to express myself." (Bonus points if you're kicking ass in Halo Firefight at the time.)

These tend to work for me. The last line often results in a dude's calling me an asshole, which I see as a victory, because "asshole" is a pretty ungendered insult!

I said I wouldn't speak for all ladies, but I may try to here: It's not that we want to be treated like porcelain creatures, fragile and easily upset. We certainly don't. We also don't want to be sexually threatened just for existing. There must be some middle ground here: How about treating us as equals?

Giving up something you enjoy because of someone else's attempt to make you feel small is giving that person some of your power. If you experience sexism while gaming, you don't have a responsibility to stay and take the abuse. You have a right to advocate for yourself, and you have a right to game however you want. Let's keep our power and our controllers. ♦

All Dressed Up &
Nowhere to go

Just some inspiration for putting tinsel around your cotton candy beehive.
By Erica, Chelsea Peacock, and Rebekah Campbell.

Thanks to Sara, Halle, and Lydia for modeling, and to Recollection Vintage for lending us these beautiful clothes.

Saving Yourself

How to not let other people's drama bring you down.
By Jenny

For as long as I can remember, my family, my super-close friends, my kinda close friends, my not-so-close friends, and sometimes total strangers have come to me with their problems. My friends constantly tell me that I'm like a "big sister" to them. One of them once said, "You just have a listener's face; it makes people want to vomit their feelings at you." If I go to a drugstore and stand in the shampoo aisle long enough, it's all but inevitable that some elderly lady will come up to me and ask for assistance and then end up telling me about her life. When I took a 50-hour Greyhound from Iowa City to San Francisco, I sat next to a woman who was fleeing her abusive husband; I listened tearfully to her story of how she sold her possessions and bought a bus ticket to Sacramento. Sometimes when I sign on to Gchat and see which of my friends are online, I get this fearful feeling in the pit of my stomach and the horrible, heartless, calculating troll heart inside my regular heart takes over and starts thumping real fast, telling my brain, "Sign off before he/she starts talking about how depressed he/she is and how everything is awful and there is only despair to be felt!"

In the past several months, I've spent hours on the phone and on chat and in person talking to depressed friends. I've spent entire nights talking people out of suicide. I recently went on the National Suicide Hotline website, not because I was feeling suicidal, but because I had been the confidant to so many people's suicidal thoughts that I started to feel like I needed some support in order to support others. At first it seemed indulgent to feel this way, like I was trivializing other people's real problems and making it all about ME—how exhausting it was for ME to be everyone's confidant, how awful it was for ME to always have to be around people who were deeply, deeply depressed—but after the fifth night of sleeping three hours because I had stayed up until two in the morning persuading someone not to hurt themselves and to see that they had a lot to live for, and then getting off the phone, crying into my pillow until I was dry heaving, and turning on my computer and finishing an essay that I had neglected all day to work on, I realized that I wasn't making it about me *enough*, that I needed to make things *more* about ME, because the ME that my friends relied on when they were feeling desperate, the ME that my friends believed to be strong and cheerful and resilient, was getting weaker and darker and more fragile with each passing second that I was neglecting to look out for myself.

How do we take care of ourselves when other people need us to take care of them? How do we create space and time to nurture and love ourselves without feeling like we are abandoning the ones we love, people who need our support? I haven't totally figured it out yet, but perhaps the following tips can at least get us all on the right track.

IT'S OK TO NOT BE OK.

When I was a teenager, I felt like the adults in my life were constantly telling me that I was really lucky and that my problems were trivial and that in 20 years I would see how good I had it. I hated that, because who wants to wait 20 years to be able to say MY PROBLEMS WERE AND ARE STILL REAL? Let's just get this over with now: YOUR PROBLEMS ARE REAL. It doesn't matter if people say you "don't seem like the kind of person who gets depressed," because there is no "kind of person" who gets depressed. There isn't a category of people who have sole proprietary rights to depression.

Not being OK can look a million different ways. There are some very visible warning signs of not being OK, but there are also lots of ways in which a person's pain can be invisible. My friends who are cutters or public criers, my friends who write poetry about their blood and guts or who regularly abuse alcohol and drugs—their pain has always been so, so visible. But don't be fooled into thinking that your pain isn't legit if you're the one who is listening to your friend's sad poetry or holding her hair back when she pukes. Pain can be dramatic and obvious, but it can also be nuanced and inconspicuous.

In college, I had a "spot" that I would go to every night to cry. No one knew about it. One night when I was feeling particularly sad, a good friend told me, "This is really weird. You're normally so cheerful. I never thought I would see you in a bad mood." I realized that I hadn't been honest with her. I had been tightly controlling how much of me I allowed her to see, so my problems were invisible to her.

MAKE YOUR NEEDS VISIBLE TO OTHERS. TELL SOMEONE YOU'RE NOT OK.

My little brother has severe OCD, and two years ago, when his illness was really spiraling out of control, we would talk every night before bed. One night he came to talk to me and found me crying on my bed. I wanted to pull myself together so I could help him, but I felt too sad and weak. I thought he might be freaked out by my crying, but to my surprise he walked over to me and asked if I was all right. Instead of saying "I'm fine" like I usually did, I said, "I'm not OK. My boyfriend broke up with me and my heart is broken and I feel like I can't live."

And you know what? My baby brother, who was born on Christmas nine years after I was born on Christmas, who used to snuggle with me in my little twin bed when I was in high school and he was in elementary school, who used to pee into jars that I had to hold between my legs in the car on long road trips, whom I have taken care of since he was born, whom, prior to that moment, I had never once considered confiding in, *helped me*. He asked me about my relationship and listened to me and told me, "I wouldn't grovel and beg someone to take me back, because, uh, I have too much self-respect, and no one is really worth that," which turned out to be the most calming thing anyone could have said to me at that exact moment.

Don't underestimate the people in your life—that younger sibling or that friend who always seems so needy may surprise you by being there for you in all the ways that you have been there for them.

CREATE THE EXPECTATION THAT YOUR FRIENDSHIPS SHOULD BE MUTUALLY SUPPORTIVE.

No relationship is truly equal—there will always be someone who is more of a talker and someone who is more of a listener. There will be times when one person is needier than the other. But no matter what, there has to be room for elasticity, for your role in a friendship to change and evolve. If you feel like you are constantly listening to your friend's problems but she never listens to yours, that is not a balanced friendship. It might even be a toxic one.

I had a friend I talked to almost every day. We had been friends for more than 10 years, and because I cared about her and loved her and also because 10-plus years of friendship breeds a particular kind of loyalty, I used to spend hours listening to her problems and giving her advice. If it wasn't relationship problems, then it was problems with her job, and if it wasn't problems with her job, then it was problems with her family, and if it wasn't problems with her family, then it was problems with her medications, and if it wasn't that, then it was it was something else. There was always *something*. Whenever we talked she would ask me, "How are you?" and I would say, "I'm doing OK, I guess," and then she would launch right into whatever horrible problem she was currently experiencing. I still love this girl a lot, and I'm rooting for her, but at some point I had to be honest about our friendship—it was completely one-sided and completely unhealthy and unfair to me.

IT IS NOT YOUR RESPONSIBILITY TO SAVE EVERYONE.

This past summer I spent five hours a day on Facebook chat with my brother, while Gchatting with a friend who was dealing with a scary episode of psychosis, while fielding calls from several different people in my life who were contemplating suicide, while also dealing with a vengeful ex-boyfriend, while also dealing with being uninsured and having a fancy set of health problems, while also working full time, writing full time, helping my parents move into a new house, and starting a new romantic relationship with someone who was also working through a lot of mental health issues, while also *trying to be a person*. It didn't work out so great. I was not a person. I was just this weird deflated bag of nothing that took in everyone else's problems, and what happens when you are everyone's confidant and no one is your confidant is that eventually you explode. And sometimes you explode all over the people who love you the most.

For me, it was my mom. I'd go home for the weekend after a long week of DRAMA DRAMA DRAMA, and my mom would knock on my door with a bowl of freshly sliced fruit, and, apropos of nothing, I'd lose my temper and be the pissy, ungrateful brat I always turn into when I don't have a regular outlet for my feelings. It's not OK to do that to your family or your partner or your best friend, and it's not OK to do that to yourself. Do what you have to do—go invisible on Gchat if you're finding it impossible to check your email without getting into a huge conversation with your friend about their latest horrible life decision. Make a vacation auto-reply that says "I will be away from email from X date to X date," and don't explain yourself. Put your phone on silent. Don't be afraid to write back to texts with a simple "Hey, there's a lot going on right now—call you in a couple days?" Get off Facebook, get off Twitter, get off Instagram, get off all of it, and take a mental health day. Take a mental health week or month, or however long you need. Be a bad listener, zone out, and then acknowledge that you just can't be a good listener today. At times I've had to say, "I'm so sorry. I've

been crying all day and haven't slept in three days, and I feel awful because I can't focus on what you're saying right now, and I feel like I should try to lie down. Can we talk in a few days? I really want to hear about this thing that is happening with you." Be explicit about your needs, because guess what? Ain't no one gonna guess them for you.

AND SOMETIMES, YOU JUST CAN'T.

You are just one person. You cannot carry the weight of someone else's life on your shoulders. Of course, if a friend is in immediate danger of hurting themselves, do whatever you have to do to be there for them. When you feel like they are safe, encourage them to seek professional help. Talk to your friend and find out who else they trust and can go to for support. Encourage them to reach out to others, then reach out to their support network yourself—let them know what is going on with your mutual friend so that you are not the sole person responsible for their safety. Once you've seen to that, it's time to step back and see to yourself.

Be honest about what is realistic and healthy for you. If a lot of people are relying on you for support, assure them that you very much *want* to be there for them, but that you *need* to be there for yourself as well—not just as well but *first*. Don't feel guilty for needing time away from other people's problems. Make room for people who make you happy and hold you up. Spend time with your favorite books and records and movies. Listen to "Just Fine" by Mary J. Blige on repeat until you're flying through the streets of your happiest dreams.

It can be uncomfortable to talk about the toll it takes on us to be there for others. We all want to be the most patient, kind, and generous friend/girlfriend/sister/daughter we can be to the people we love. But you have to remember to take care of yourself—after all, you can't be there for your loved ones if you're falling apart. When you feel overwhelmed, say, "I'm sorry, but I can't right now," so that later, when you can, you will be whole and strong, and really, that's all that any of us can ever hope to be. ♦

OCTOBER 2012: PLAY

GREETINGS, ROOKIES! IF YOU DARE, I mean. (Imagine that said in the SPOOKY VOICE of a CARTOON GOBLIN of some sort.)

This month's theme is PLAY, and we will be talking about all things playful: HALLOWEEN, comedy, sports, pop music, comics, cartoons, board games, candy, etc. I'm really excited, because after a middle school identity crisis's worth of believing that liking anything made purely for entertainment value was a compromise of my intelligence, I feel such a RUSH when I listen to One Direction while walking to class. My demeanor would have you believe I'm listening to black metal mashed up with puppies crying, but I swear it's just my inability to control my face. Inside, I am smiling like the baby sun in *Teletubbies*.

Liking things is fun; wasting time and energy figuring out what your taste says about your personality is not. I think that if you can differentiate between taking everything with a grain of salt, and just plain snobby hating, you will live a life full of all the joy that Netflix has to offer. (This is not even a Netflix ad, it's just very much my best friend.)

Oh man I'm so ready for this month. Here's a playlist I've been enjoying lately, just 'cause.

Slime Time

1. We Are Never Ever Getting Back Together - Taylor Swift
2. Teenage Kicks - The Undertones
3. Sweetie - Carly Rae Jepsen
4. Johnny, Are You Queer? - Josie Cotton
5. You Take Time - Bleached
6. Civilian Stripes - Divine Fits
7. Forced to Drive - Breeders
8. Forrest Gump - Frank Ocean
9. Genesis - Grimes
10. Ego - Beyoncé
11. Super Trouper - ABBA
12. Unusual World - King Tuff
13. This Must Be the Place - Talking Heads

LOVE,
TAVI

CREATURE FEAR

Just a batch of delight, this one. Photos by Eleanor, collage by Ben Giles. Styled by Nao Koyabu with clothes, lingerie, and accessories from Meadham Kirchhoff, Vinti Andrews, the Little Vicious, Beyond Retro, American Apparel, Sophia Webster, the Pocket Library, Molly Goddard, and Charlotte Olympia, and stickers from John Lewis. Thanks to Arvida Byström for modeling.

RISK-Y BUSINESS

How a friendship was destroyed…by a board game.

Writing by Maggie, illustration by Ruby A. Playlist by Anna F., art by Minna.

This is a tale of how the board game Risk 2210 A.D. destroyed one of my most treasured friendships. In retrospect I realize that the friendship was already doomed, and would have ended anyway. But if we'd never played Risk, it might not have ended so horribly.

Josiah was from Alaska, and one summer he invited my friend Nico and me to come live with his cool hippie parents in Fairbanks. Nico was the one I officially considered my best friend. But it was Josiah who could make me laugh like no one else in my entire life. He had a bizarre sense of humor; it was very pun-centric and spazzy and rambunctious. Nico, on the other hand, had a calm, Swedish demeanor that perfectly rounded out our trio. A typical scene would find Josiah and me rolling around on the floor in hysterics while Nico quietly read a book about heirloom tomatoes. The three of us hung out all the time. We even went on a cruise together. I imagined that after college we would live together forever.

Before I talk about the game that fractured this halcyon trio, it's important to establish that Josiah had a very serious, longstanding crush on me. I was aware of this at the time, but I chose to take no action. This wasn't because I didn't like him. I did like him, *a lot*. But I also liked things the way they were. I liked being in a state of suspended enamorment—a crush that lasts forever but goes nowhere. I think it was a precautionary measure—I knew the two of us were going to blow up one day. I just didn't expect it to be over a game.

It's been five years since our summer of Risk, a summer we both mentally buried as soon as it was over. But I emailed him for this story, and he emailed me back, and now we're finally, *finally* going to hash out what we did to each other, and whether we can ever play Risk again.

THE GAME

Josiah, Nico, and I had played tons of games before—card games, board games, video games—and we'd never once fought or had problems. But Risk 2210 was different.

Risk 2210 A.D. is a futuristic version of the classic board game Risk. In classic Risk, the board is a political map of the world, and the goal is to dominate territory and eliminate all other players. Risk 2210 uses the same basic format, but it's set in the future and contains Command Cards that open the game to a wider range of moves (there's an Invade Earth card, for example, that allows you to attack your opponent from the moon, dramatically altering the balance of power in a single play). The game involves complex strategy, diplomacy/dealmaking between players, and, potentially, ruthless backstabbing. A single game can go on for days. It can take over your life.

The trouble started when Josiah invited his childhood friend Shanti to play a game with us. Shanti was a very sweet, noncompetitive guy. No one expected him to be a major player. But here's what happened: Shanti did whatever Josiah told him to do. In one crucial turn (which I documented obsessively in my journal), Shanti refused to attack Josiah's forces in the Pacific, even though they were weak and wide open. Instead, Josiah persuaded him to attack me in South America, even though that made no tactical sense. Shanti was so sweet and trusting that he did whatever Josiah wanted, which gave Josiah an immense advantage over Nico and me. In retaliation, Nico and I started strategizing moves together to take Josiah down. And that's where our friendship began to deteriorate.

MAGGIE So this was the beginning of the end. You shamelessly used Shanti to target me and Nico, which I considered to be cheating.

JOSIAH It was *not* cheating. I was merely playing my opponents' weaknesses.

MAGGIE And there's our basic conflict: Sneaky vs. Stickler. You liked to bend the rules, and I didn't. All your moves were "technically" legal, which drove me insane. Nico wanted to stay out of it and remain neutral, but I made that pretty hard for him.

JOSIAH You were BFFs, so yes, it seemed he was implicitly on your side. Heck, I probably would have been on your side if I had to share a room with you every night, for fear that I'd wake up with a pen in my jugular!

MAGGIE I was so furious, I didn't even want to speak to you. And that's pretty awkward, giving the silent treatment to the person whose house you're living in. I was refusing to go upstairs because you were there, so I forced Nico to hang out with me in the basement. It must have been really weird for you, being excluded by your friends in your own house.

JOSIAH Being left out sucked. I can't think of any more mature word to use than *sucked*, but that's appropriate, as it was a very immature situation. We were 20-somethings acting like 0-somethings. I remember you and Nico would dress up and play Monopoly loudly while I was trying to sleep. I don't know how you managed to make Monopoly loud, but you did.

MAGGIE Oh, I remember that. We would dress up like billionaires and play these theatrical characters.

JOSIAH And I was never invited to join you. Whenever I went to the basement I felt like an intruder in my own house. I tried to navigate your anti-Josiah or Josiah-indifferent moods by letting you come to me. The problem was that I was OB-SESSED with you and wanted to hang out constantly, *"just youuuuu and IIIIIIII…"* So I was battling this irrational desire to be around you with the rational thought that I'd just be making things worse by being around you. The irrational side usually won.

THE CHAPERONE

At this point Nico was winning almost every game because Josiah and I were busy brutally sabotaging each other. Nico's calming presence kept the tension at a manageable level for a while. But around mid-July the games had gotten so intense that Josiah's dad started playing with us, with the unspoken understanding that he was there to keep us from fighting too horribly.

MAGGIE This is where it starts to get em-barrassing. We were so out of control that we needed a *parent* to referee our behavior.

JOSIAH Fighting in front of my dad was *so* awkward, and I think this is one of the reasons your she-who-yells-loudest style of argument bothered me so much.

MAGGIE THIS IS THE NATURAL REG-ISTER OF MY VOICE. I can't believe we're having this argument again. You always think I'm yelling at you, but that is just how my voice sounds!

JOSIAH But I was worried that my dad would think you were way cray cray angray (which you probably were anyway).

MAGGIE Well yeah, I was definitely angray. My entire journal from that summer is like a catalogue of your every obnoxious move: "Josiah showed his Nuclear Command Card to everyone but me. I despise him." "Josiah used his Frequency Jam just to spite me. I despise him more than ever." "If Josiah knew how much I hate They Might Be Giants he would probably play them in-cessantly because he's that much of a brat."

JOSIAH I was definitely turning my unre-quited nonstop infatuation into tabletop rage. I just wanted to *decimate* you.

MAGGIE I remember getting in these bitter fights. Like, the kind of fights that should have ended in us pushing the game over and furiously, passionately making out.

JOSIAH If only… Basically every second of every day that summer I wanted to spend passionately making out with you, espe-cially during the bad times.

MAGGIE What the hell was wrong with us? Why didn't we just stop playing Risk and start making out?

JOSIAH Well, it would have been awkward with my dad there.

MAGGIE True. It also would have required one of us to set down our precious pride for five seconds in order to make the first move. And that was never going to happen.

THE GAME OF STRATEGIC CONQUEST

DOWNWARD SPIRAL

I'd always known that Josiah and I were fundamentally incompatible. We shared a sense of humor, but we also shared a lot of not-so-humorous qualities. We were both stubborn, prideful, and, at the time, pret-ty immature. Risk brought out all those qualities and turned them up to the max. To this day, I wish Josiah and I could go back to our pre-Risk days, when we would just goof off and hold hands and be flirta-tious pals. But Risk brought out the worst in both of us.

JOSIAH I knew that we could/should nev-er be officially boyfriend and girlfriend. I was far too self-centered back then, and an acceptable girlfriend would have had to praise my every farce and be uncondi-tionally adoring. Your violent streak also frightened me a bit, but it also intrigued me—something about playing with fire comes to mind. Your fun-loving side was what kept me around, though. Fun > danger any day.

MAGGIE Which is exactly how I feel about Risk. It's dangerous, and it's brutal, but it's *so fun*. We played Risk constantly, obsessively, even though it was turning us into monsters. It didn't help that we were living on top of each other, that Nico and I were 4,000 miles away from home, and that there's nothing to do in Fairbanks but play Risk and slowly go insane.

JOSIAH I remember losing sleep at night preplanning my moves. "If she takes the Northwest Oil Emirate, I'll counterattack her South American troops with my naval stronghold in New Atlantis!"

MAGGIE And you played *rough*. You never once gave me a break. Every game was a constant struggle against your relentless onslaughts. It made me hate you, but it also sort of made me love you. I loved that we played as equals, that there was zero faux-gentlemanly "let her win" stuff.

JOSIAH No way. Board game chivalry is for shmucks. I knew you *liked* to be given no quarter, to be treated like the hardcore contender you are. Perhaps I was hoping to build up to the aforementioned makeout-fest climax, but that moment never came…and this pent-up feeling lasted for days, because the games would last for days!

SCORCHED EARTH
Partway through August, Josiah and I each hit a new low. We'd been playing a particular round of Risk for four days. Josiah had conquered the moon and most of the Western Hemisphere. He was going to win, and I couldn't stand it. So while he was asleep one night, I purposefully wrecked the board. Then I lied about it. I think I tried to blame it on the dog. When I emailed Josiah about doing this interview, I finally admitted to him that I'd sabotaged his game. What he wrote back really shocked me.

JOSIAH Yeah, that was a true low. As low, perhaps, as when I secretly read your journal where you admitted the dastardly deed.

MAGGIE You…you *read my journal*. Wow. *That* is low.

JOSIAH Yes, I read your journal. The entry where you admitted to wrecking the game board was just a bonus, as I basically already knew you had, and now I knew that you had lied about it as well.

MAGGIE I've always felt bad about wrecking the board—that was low even for me—but now I'd say we're even.

JOSIAH I think you left the journal in the living room one night while you and Nico were asleep. It was like dangling bread in front of a starving child. Plus, I felt like you were super angry with me already, so what more was there to lose by taking a peek?

MAGGIE So…what did you find?

JOSIAH Well, most of what I read was rather dry, because you were just objectively documenting what you did day to day. I remember the tone started to change near the end, and the ink flowed thick with Josiah loathing. I don't remember specifics, just that the language became surprisingly vitriolic. I was a bit taken aback by how passionately you expressed your hatred of me. While I had occasionally become annoyed with you that summer, I never felt even close to the level of blind rage you were expressing in the journal.

MAGGIE I needed to go home. I definitely needed to stop playing Risk.

JOSIAH I think Risk was just a PIECE in the GAME of our twisted relationship.

MAGGIE I slammed you for your sneaky, dishonorable Risk moves, but I made some real-life moves that were just as twisted. I think I just wanted to see how far I could push you. Pretty damn far, as it turns out! I can't believe you still liked me after the way I acted, and the things you read in my journal. Your crush was indestructible.

JOSIAH The Josiah-bashing in the journal didn't even bother me that much. What did bother me was the glaring absence of Josiah-crushing! We had a lot of sneaky-fun-smoochy-times that summer, especially early on, but I don't remember finding a single instance where you wrote about them, or if you did it was just like a factual report, no "and my heart went all a-flutter" annotations.

MAGGIE My crush on you would resurface every once in a while, and I'd remember why I came to spend the summer with you in the first place. But those moments kind of got lost amid all the bile and tension.

JOSIAH Not for me, they didn't. My heart would explode every time you laughed at some stupid joke that came out of my mouth. I was head over heels for this girl who would be toasting my heartmallow to a nice gooey golden brown one moment, then plunging it into the fire the next.

MAGGIE I was very cruel, I acknowledge that now. I knew I had all the power in our friendship. I knew you were infatuated with me, and that I could be as cruel as I wanted. And as annoying as you could be, you never deserved that.

JOSIAH Reading your journal, it seemed my fears were confirmed, that I like-liked you much more than you like-liked me. So yeah, don't open Pandora's Book, guys—you'll just be left feeling like a sorry sap.

MAGGIE And also don't wreck a board game just because you're not winning. You'll only feel like even more of a loser.

JOSIAH It's funny…friendship-shattering drama aside, this conversation has chiefly reminded me what an awesomely addictive game Risk 2210 was.

MAGGIE I'd like to think that we could handle it now, and possibly handle each other too.

JOSIAH Care to roll the dice again? ⑭

HANGING OUT WITH: LISA SIMPSON

1. HOT TOPIC – LE TIGRE
2. BAKER STREET – GERRY RAFFERTY
3. ZERO (LIVE) – SMASHING PUMPKINS
4. PROUD MARY – TINA TURNER
5. MEAT IS MURDER – THE SMITHS
6. MAYBE I'M AMAZED – PAUL McCARTNEY
7. STEP BY STEP – NEW KIDS ON THE BLOCK
8. BLOWIN' IN THE WIND – BOB DYLAN
9. YOU DON'T OWN ME – LESLEY GORE
10. JAZZMAN – LISA SIMPSON & BLEEDING GUMS MURPHY

LITERALLY THE BEST THING EVER: M.I.A

Let me count the reasons.

Writing by Jenny, illustration by Suzy.

Over the past two weeks, I have tried and tried and tried to write this article. I have been trying to write this article since before I even knew I would be writing this article. I started to write about how when I was in college, I had one group of friends who were ARTISTS and another group who were ACTIVISTS, and the two didn't mix at all. If you loved art, that meant you were frivolous and wild and funny and irreverent and provocative but in a way that was solely about the making and creating and consuming of art; and if you were an activist, you were serious and angry and you liked reading boring, constipated, jargon-y academic books about ISSUES like RACISM and SEXISM and QUEERNESS and OPPRESSION, and there was no time for the frivolous, superficial world of art— even though in my heart I knew that the two had to go together, that it's impossible to make meaningful art without being interested in the world beyond the one you know, and part of wanting more humanity in the world is deciding that art is meaningful and that all people should have the right to access and create it.

I tried to write about when I first heard of M.I.A.'s music. How I was in my last semester of college and reading about Operation Babylift, and I learned that many of the 4,000 children and infants who were "rescued" from Vietnam during the final days of the Vietnam War were not in fact orphans at all, and that that meant entire families were separated under the guise of "humanitarian aid," and that most of those families were very poor and lacked the resources to later track down their children who were now living as adoptees in America. How in the middle of reading about all that and feeling sick to my stomach because it was another example in a long history of white folks trying to "save" brown and yellow and black folks, my boyfriend at the time barged into my dorm room with a copy of M.I.A.'s first album, *Arular*, and he was like, "You're gonna love her. She raps like a demented middle-school delinquent, and her father was a

Tamil Tiger," referring to the Liberation Tigers of Tamil Eelam, a militant separatist group that fought for an independent state for the Tamil minority in Sri Lanka. That assertion turned out not to be true, although it was true that her father, Arular, left the family when M.I.A., or Maya Arulpragasam, was two months old to train with the Palestinian Liberation Organization and to later form the Eelam Revolutionary Organisation of Students, a group that also fought for Tamil independence.

I tried to write about how it felt the time I had a dance party in my dorm room and I was playing *Arular* on my computer and at one point I looked around and realized that most of my friends were people of color, and we were dancing to music by a radical woman of color. We were dancing to songs with lyrics like "Pull up the people, pull up the poor" and "Somewhere in the Amazon / They're holding me ransom." And the sad truth was that M.I.A. was the first brown woman I had ever seen on television NOT in the context of some PBS documentary about global poverty or village life in war-torn Southeast Asia. When she started appearing on the covers of magazines like *Rolling Stone* and *Spin*, I realized that I had never seen a Southeast Asian woman on the cover of a major magazine that wasn't *National Geographic*, that it was the first time I had seen a brown woman looking so PUNK and so FLY, like the kind of badass who flips you the middle finger just to say hi before embarrassing you in a dance-off. I can't even tell you what it meant to me to FINALLY see a photo of a brown woman who wasn't dressed in "native" or "indigenous" garb, talking about being a Tamil refugee from Sri Lanka and the brutal, systematic, state-sponsored violence waged against her people—in a mainstream magazine read by people like you and me who knew next to nothing about the struggle of the Tamil people, because major news outlets were barely reporting about it. I can't begin to explain how moved I was to see a refugee being the protagonist of her own story, refusing to be the object of a white, Western gaze, who insisted on being her own sub-

ject, whose visibility signaled a refusal to be mere background scenery, who sang catchy, weird, danceable songs about bombs and tanks and guerilla warfare and poverty and refugee camps and racial profiling and police and military brutality.

I have started and stopped and gone back and erased everything and started again because I want to get this right.

Because when I was growing up, I never thought there would come a day when a radical woman of color would be making music that people loved, while advocating for the right of her people to take up an armed struggle for independence and self-determination. Because M.I.A. has always made it clear that she cares about politics, and not just politics, but the people who are impacted by politics, those whose lives are most affected by policies made by people who have the power to tell or silence the lives and histories of entire groups of people.

Because women and people of color have always been shamed for being too "emotional," for daring to bring the personal into the political. Because the political is the personal. Because when you are a refugee who cannot go home because your own country is no longer safe to live in, how can you be any other way but emotional? When civil war has torn your country apart, when civilians in your country are taken hostage and killed in the crossfire, when you are the target of police brutality and racial profiling, when your very existence is criminalized and threatened because of your race or ethnicity or gender or sexuality, how can you take it any other way except personally?

Because I don't think I was the only teenage girl or am the only adult woman who was and is afraid to speak out about my beliefs because people tell you that if you even try to do that, you'd better be prepared to spend all of your time fighting injustice and being the most educated, informed, serious person in the entire world, and you can NEVER EVER EVER care about superficial things. Because only people who are politically apathetic can get away with being superficial. We reward people for their political apathy or silence

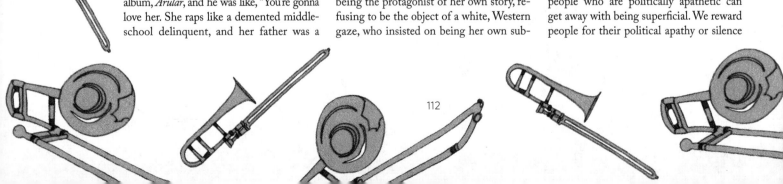

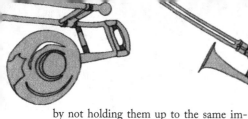

by not holding them up to the same impossibly high standards to which we hold people who might care about politics, even those who are just learning about them.

Because M.I.A. has always rejected all of that nonsense. Because she once said in an interview for *Clash* magazine, "People reckon that I need a political degree in order to go, 'My school got bombed and I remember it 'cause I was 10 years old'... I think removing individual voices and not letting Tamil people just go 'This happened to me' is really dangerous."

Because political activism is for everyone—flawed people, self-absorbed people, immature people, mature people, artists and philistines and intellectuals and sensualists and materialists. People who do good in the world are not saints, and it's bullshit to believe that political activism is something only incredibly serious and morally upright people do—that kind of thinking not only makes it very unattractive to be politically active, but it also excuses the rest of us from any obligation to educate ourselves or take action. It elevates the notion of "political activism" to something reserved for the saintly, the extraordinarily gifted, the spectacularly selfless and devoted, like Martin Luther King or Gandhi, both of whom have been mythologized into angelic warriors, leaving the rest of us to think: *Well, of course I can't be expected to sacrifice on* that *level.* M.I.A. is not an angelic warrior or a political pundit or an academic or an intellectual, but she cares about politics and she cares about having FUN and she makes a call to action fun to dance to. And seeing her publicly eviscerated for not having sophisticated or even consistent politics only makes me more determined to help create a space where young people who are just learning what their political beliefs are can do so without fear of being shamed.

Because M.I.A. will tweet "FUCK NEW YORK TIMES! DO YOU THINK YOU NEED TO GO HERE ON VACATION!" and "HERE IS THE LUSH COASTLINE THEY ARE TALKING ABOUT" with a very disturbing and graphic photo of dead Tamil civilians in response to an article in the newspaper's travel section called "The 31

Places to Go in 2010" in which Sri Lanka was listed as one of the top tourist destinations a year after the long and bloody civil war ended. That was the first time I had seen a pop star publically criticize the tourism industry and point out that people who have the privilege to travel also have a responsibility to educate themselves, and she did it in a way that was emotional and unafraid.

Because M.I.A. isn't always articulate or eloquent, and her moments of inarticulateness and ineloquence have given me the courage to not be so hard on my own moments of inarticulateness and ineloquence and to accept and love my bad teenage poetry and my attempts to speak and write about issues I was and am still learning about.

Because she is a brat, and unapologetically so. When the journalist Lynn Hirschberg tried to make M.I.A. come off like a shallow, privileged provocateur who ate fancy truffle fries while talking about wanting to be an "outsider" in a *New York Times Magazine* profile, M.I.A. retaliated by tweeting Hirschberg's cell phone number and posting an audio clip that she had secretly recorded of the interview, revealing that it was, in fact, Hirschberg who had ordered the fries. This move was widely viewed as unethical and immature, but I ate it up. And when M.I.A. flipped America the middle finger at the Super Bowl, my heart beamed and soared like a shooting star. Because I'm all for antics; I'm all for juvenile gestures.

Because M.I.A. got me into London dubstep and grime and Jamaican dancehall and the funk carioca and baile funk that came from the favelas of Rio de Janeiro. Because her music makes patois cool and beautiful in a world where those who deviate from "standard" English are often assumed to be uneducated and ignorant. Because "Paper Planes" saved me in 2007 when I was living in Iowa City and dealing with some next-level racism. Because M.I.A. filmed the video for "Paper Planes" in Bed-Stuy, Brooklyn, where she lived for a year, where she once filmed an incidence of police brutality from her apartment window and posted it on YouTube. Because she

performed "Swagga Like Us" with Jay-Z, Kanye, Lil Wayne, and T.I. at the Grammys ON HER BABY'S DUE DATE, and was having contractions while being magnificent and magnetic and killing it.

Because her first mixtape, *Piracy Funds Terrorism*, is the only thing that can make me feel better in the dead of winter when it seems like daylight disappears an hour after I wake up. Because when she was first blowing up and people were attributing her success to the DJ/producer Diplo, a white dude from Philly who was going around taking credit for M.I.A.'s sound, she wasn't afraid to stand up and be like, HEY I CREATED THIS AND YOU AREN'T GOING TO TAKE THIS AWAY FROM ME. Because that happens to female artists, and especially female artists of color, ALL THE TIME. "I find it kind of insulting," she told Pitchfork, "that I can't have any ideas on my own because I'm a female, or that people from undeveloped countries can't have ideas of their own unless it's backed up by someone who's blond-haired and blue-eyed."

Because M.I.A. is literally the best thing ever to have happened to pop culture and pop music in my lifetime, and like Le Tigre said in their song "Hot Topic": "I can't live if you stop." Because she's the queen of my world. Because somewhere there is a T-shirt that says "If I can't dance, then I don't want to be part of your revolution," and here in my little Brooklyn apartment, I'm dancing to M.I.A. and wanting all the rest of you to join me. ☻

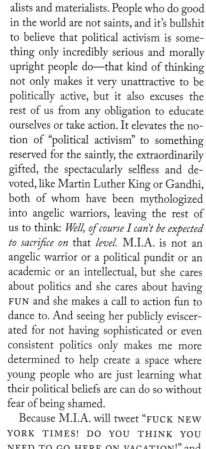

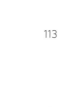

SCARY MOVIE

Kiss the boys and make them die.
By Petra

Thanks to Teshaunna, Tyneesha, Fox, and Raevv'n for modeling,
and to American Apparel for lending us clothes.

A GUIDE TO GHOST HUNTING

It's almost Halloween. Go freak yourself out.
Writing by Rachael. Playlist by Anna F., art by Minna.

October is the best month to get really and truly scared. Sure, you could go on some wimpy hayride and get chased by "ghosts" in period clothing and white makeup—or you could look for a *real* ghost. 'Tis the season for ghost hunting, because even your skeptical friends can be persuaded to indulge on the grounds that it makes for some harmless Halloween fun.

I've always been fascinated by ghosts and creepy phenomena. As a child, I firmly believed there was more to the world than what was immediately visible—and I desperately wanted to be able to truthfully say, "I see dead people." Many years later, I can say…I've seen weird shit. I can't say for sure whether I believe in ghosts, but I've experienced some things I can't explain.

I don't do a ton of ghost hunting myself. I don't have to—most of the crazy things I've seen were in my own house. But after years of meticulous internet research and close viewing of ghost-hunting reality shows, I know a thing or two about how to go about it. Here's a primer to help you get started:

1. FIND A GOOD LOCATION.

Ghosts can be anywhere—which is great, because it means everyone has a chance to find one. But to up your odds, you'll want to pick a place that's known for weird happenings—whether it's a house, a cemetery, or a historic location. Even if you live in the country and don't have a handy brochure of haunted locations, you're still certain to have a few local legends. In my rural county alone, we have a haunted bridge, a haunted opera house, and a haunted intersection. If you're in a city, your local haunted places are probably well known, and perhaps they are featured in year-round ghost tours.

The tours can be cheesy, but you never know what you'll see. My first and best tour was in Fredericksburg, Virginia, a town where the walls still have holes from Civil War cannons. We visited an old church whose history I no longer remember, but I'll never forget how, when the guide spoke, the closed doors on the old-fashioned box pew quietly swung open behind us. And every picture I took of that church was full of orbs, each one with a pinkish light cutting off a corner. (And yes, I know there are a ton of scientific explanations for photographic anomalies. More on that later.)

Was there an unsolved crime or tragic disaster in your area? Those ghosts might have the incentive to communicate. Now, if this is a recent tragedy, or if it happened on private property, be respectful of the living—if someone who knew the deceased could conceivably walk into your ghost hunt, don't do it. But the sites of unfortunate events are a reasonably good place to begin your search. It seems to be understood, from horror movies and folklore, that souls tend to hang around if they have suffered sudden, violent deaths, or if they have unfinished business (like identifying their murderer!).

Sometimes ghosts can be found even closer to home—alarmingly close. When I was seven years old, we moved into a new house with a tragic backstory: The first woman to live there had died in the basement fighting an electrical fire. I just *knew* she had to be haunting the place, and it was confirmed at a sleepover I had for my birthday. A gaggle of girls were asleep in my living room, which has several large windows overlooking the gardens. I was one of the first to fall asleep, but at some point in the middle of the night my friends woke me up in a panic, saying that there was someone in the window. They pointed at a round shape looking in, a small head with its chin resting on the windowsill. "It's just a shadow," I grumbled. Then it waved at us in a creepy, disjointed motion, like its arm was passing behind its head. There was screaming and running, but the shadow-person seemed content to stare and wave, and eventually we were able to close the curtains and go back to sleep.

Of course, we didn't get a good look. All I know is that the shape and movement of that shadow could not have been from a living person, and there was nothing in front of the window that could have accounted for it. But ever since that day, I've always kept my eyes—and my mind—open.

2. ONCE YOU'VE CHOSEN A LOCATION, LEARN MORE ABOUT THE GHOST OR HAUNTING ASSOCIATED WITH IT, AND COME UP WITH A GAME PLAN.

Are there any specific legends attached to this place? Does the ghost show up at a certain time, or under some strangely specific condition? At the opera house in my hometown, the story was that the ghost would show herself only to people with the same last name as the original owners: Kline. But the staff soon discovered that patrons with the last name Small were seeing the ghost too! (The German word *klein* means small.)

Be careful! Keep in mind that a lot of cemeteries are closed at night. Don't let

"Some Pumpki

GREAT!

your adventure end with your getting arrested (unless that's a risk you are willing to take in pursuit of THE TRUTH). You can still encounter ghostly activity during normal business hours. Case in point: There's a Toys "R" Us in Sunnyvale, California, that's famously haunted by a ghost named Johnson, who used to be a ranch hand on the property. If you can find a ghost in a Toys "R" Us, you can find one anywhere.

3. GATHER YOUR SUPPLIES.

If you bring only one thing, let it be a camera. You'll want your highest-resolution one (i.e., not your cellphone), so you won't have to try to pick ghosts out of pixels later. If you want to go a step further, bring something else to record video or sound. A tape recorder is great if you suspect your house is haunted—leave it on overnight in an empty room, and see if it picks up any voices or other sounds that shouldn't be there. And if you want to get *really* fancy, grab some sort of room thermometer to test for cold spots. Professionals have ridiculously expensive equipment for this, but until you commit to ghost hunting full time, I think a simple thermometer is worth a shot. I've never tried anything other than a camera, partly because recording technology wasn't as user-friendly back in the early naughts, when I lived in that haunted house, but mostly because I didn't think I'd ever sleep again if I actually heard a ghost's voice IN MY HOUSE.

If you do bring a tape recorder, keep it on the whole time—you never know when a ghost might decide to join in on the conversation! Ghostly sound recordings are called "electronic voice phenomena," or EVP. Most of the ones I've heard online sound like someone's reading too much into static, but sometimes you get some spooky voices. Try asking your ghost some friendly questions, like their name or how they died, and then play back the sound later to see if you hear any answers.

4. TAKE LOTS OF PICTURES.

Look for things in the photos that your naked eye didn't pick up: orbs, lights, weird shadows, or other anomalies. A lot of "ghost photos" have very reasonable explanations: reflections, the camera's flash, someone's thumb in front of the lens. You know you've got a good photo when no one can tell you why it's *not* real.

5. BE OBSERVANT.

There is no surefire formula for ghost hunting. Mostly, you just have to be observant. Everyone wants to see floating furniture and old-fashioned ladies in flowing dresses, but most hauntings are less dramatic.

Listen for weird sounds. I don't put much stock in footsteps or creaking—all buildings make those noises. But some sounds are harder to explain. At my house, we would sometimes hear a crashing noise from our kitchen, but when we investigated, nothing would be out of place. Once, one of my family members heard voices coming from the living room in the middle of the night, while everyone was fast asleep.

In my experience, weird things happen on reflective surfaces, so keep an eye on mirrors, shiny screens, and windows. When you take pictures of these things, keep your flash off.

When I was a teenager, I walked out of a hallway entrance facing the sliding glass door that opened to our patio. While I was standing RIGHT BY THE DOOR, I saw a reflection that I thought was my mother standing in the kitchen. I turned around to say hi, and *no one was there*. I quickly turned back, and there was a clear reflection of a brunette woman wearing white. I looked back and forth several times, but no matter how often I checked, the only people in the room were me (in blue) and the reflection. I ran out of there to find my mother, who turned out to be in a completely different part of the house, wearing bright pink.

Despite how much I love ghosts in theory, I was TERRIFIED. It's one thing to go out looking for ghosts, prepared with friends and tools, but when something seemingly impossible happens in your own home, with no one else around? I eventually recovered and started basking in the knowledge that I finally had a true ghost story, but to this day, when I'm visiting my parents and have to walk past that door alone, I avert my eyes.

6. LAST WORDS OF WARNING.

It might be tempting to bring the ghost to you rather than going to find it. Do so at your own risk. Many ghost hunters will tell you not to use a Ouija board to make contact, because you're opening a door to a psychic plane, and you don't know what's going to come through. (In my opinion, participants are probably subconsciously moving the planchette anyway, so it's a suspect tool.)

I recommend that you always go ghost hunting with friends. Not only will you feel safer that way, but should you find a ghost, you'll also have someone to back up your story.

Good luck, have fun, and remember to watch out for what might be behind you. Right. This. Very. Minute. 👻

...DON'T BE AFRAID OF THE ...DARK!

1. DON'T BE AFRAID OF THE DARK – SONICS
2. CAN'T SEEM TO MAKE YOU MINE – THE SEEDS
3. ONLY SEVENTEEN – THE BEATLE-ETTES
4. LIVE – THE MERRY-GO-ROUND 5. ARE YOU GONNA BE THERE (AT THE LOVE IN?) – THE CHOCOLATE WATCH BAND
6. MELVIN – THE BELLES 7. PSYCHOTIC REACTION – COUNT FIVE
8. QUITE A REPUTATION – THE CHYMES
9. (I'VE GOT) NOWHERE TO RUN – THE MORE-TISHANS
10. BABY THAT'S ME – THE CAKE
11. PUTTY – JENNY & THE STATESIDERS
12. I'M FEELING OK – THE FIVE AMERYKANS
13. LOUIE LOUIE – THE KINGSMEN

GARBAGE

Just some casual amazingness.
Photos by Lauren P., styling by Laia.

Clothing from H&M, Eleven Objects, Sobotka, and Zana Bayne. Makeup assistance from Nicole Poor. Thanks to Cecilia, Cleo, Dom, Elona, Lilly, and Grace for modeling.

PAIL KIDS

IT TAKES A LOT TO LAUGH

Using humor to deal with racism.

By Jenny

Three years ago, when I was going to grad school in Iowa City, I went to see Melt-Banana, a Japanese noise rock band, and while we were waiting for the band to set up, this drunk girl grabbed my arm and asked me, "So, are you with the band?" Maybe she didn't mean anything by it. Maybe it was just a harmless, drunk question. Maybe I didn't need to read anything into it. And maybe the time when my friend E., who is Taiwanese-American, visited me in Iowa City and we started to get this really creepy feeling like everyone who saw us walking down the street together thought we were either foreign exchange students or related to each other—maybe that time I was just being paranoid as well. And maybe the time when I took a shuttle van to the Cedar Rapids airport and was subjected to 30 minutes of questioning by my driver on what it was like to have grown up in "Communist China," those were innocent questions, even though I had explained to him that I actually grew up in Queens, and that I left China when I was four and a half. And maybe when he insisted that I was "in America now and shouldn't be afraid of speaking freely," he was honestly trying to help. And maybe all the times that I walked into a store and, apropos of nothing, was asked by someone, "So where are you originally from—China or Japan?" those were just sincere inquiries with regard to my heritage.

Or maybe other people didn't have to put up with this stuff, and maybe I didn't want to, either. Maybe it wasn't an innocent coincidence that at a concert where a Japanese band was headlining, some drunk girl decided to come up to me, the only Asian person she saw at the show, single me out, and ask me if I was in the band.

"I'm not in the band," I said.

She looked at me askance and said, "C'mon, what instrument do you play? Are you the singer?"

And maybe at that point, it was OK that I started to feel like shit and turned to my boyfriend and said, "That girl just asked me what instrument I play in the band because I'm Asian."

"Wait, but you are in the band, aren't you?" he joked. "Why else would you be here?" And we laughed, because it feels good to laugh when you are dealing with racism. We laughed because it feels good to laugh when someone makes you feel small and powerless.

In middle school, I had a classmate whose mom would sometimes drive me home from school; once, when we were stuck in traffic, she yelled out, "Move!" to the car in front of us, and then muttered, "Chinks," to her daughter, who started giggling. When I lived in France, every single day, random strangers would pretend to karate-chop their way to me on the street. Whenever I went outside, men would shout out all the Asian-language words they knew, which were usually some combination of *ni hao*, *arigato*, and *konichiwa*.

And those are just the obvious, easy examples. There were less-obvious ones, too. I have known plenty of people who considered themselves properly socialized, tolerant, good people, who would never tell me that Chinese people have slits for eyes, or that our names sound like pots banging, but those same people still hurt me when they confessed that they honestly could not tell the difference between Chinese, Korean, and Japanese people. They still hurt me when they told me that the zongzi I brought for lunch every day smelled weird and grossed them out. They still hurt me when they laughed during the parts of movies when the broken-English-speaking Asian character showed up for comic relief.

This should go without saying, but I'll say it anyway: No one deserves to be hurt by racism. This seems like an easy statement to abide by, until you realize that racism is not

always intentional, and it's not always obvious, and sometimes people don't agree on what constitutes racism or even acknowledge that it exists. And for those reasons, sometimes it sucks to talk about it, it sucks to think about it, and it sucks to have to deal with it at all. But if you are a person of color, chances are at some point you are gonna have to deal with it, and for me, when I was first confronted with it, I went from feeling hurt to feeling active self-loathing to feeling full-on apeshit angry. All of it sucked.

Let me just say that it's *totally OK* to be apeshit angry. Don't let anyone ever shame you for feeling bad about racism or put you down or make you feel like you are over-reacting. THERE IS NO WAY TO OVER-REACT TO RACISM, BECAUSE RACISM IS A SYSTEMATIC DEVALUATION AND DEHUMANIZATION OF ENTIRE GROUPS OF PEOPLE. I repeat: RACISM IS A SYSTEMATIC DEVALUATION AND DEHUMANIZATION OF ENTIRE GROUPS OF PEOPLE, AND NOT REACTING TO IT ONLY HELPS PERPETUATE IT.

That said: At some point, when dealing with racism—especially casual, genteel racism that can be easily dismissed by others—being angry all the time is only going to deplete you. And very few people—whether they are high school kids, teeny tiny kids, grown-ass adults, or your friend's grandparent who still freely speaks in outmoded, endearingly antiquated racist phrases—are gonna stick around and listen to you explain why what they said was hurtful and wrong. Anyway, it's *exhausting* to always have to be the one to "teach" others how to recognize racism when it ain't something as obvious as calling someone by a racial slur or doing physical violence to someone because of their race or ethnicity.

As a person of color, I believe racism is a serious matter. But just because it has affected me in serious ways doesn't mean I can't or don't want to have joy and humor and *play* in my life. In fact, I want *more* of those things to balance out the moments when racism leaves me feeling joyless. Sometimes humor is your best defense—even if it means the only person laughing at the punch line is you. Stephen Colbert said in a 2007 interview in Parade Magazine, "Not living in fear is a great gift, because certainly these days we do it so much. And do you know what I like about comedy? You can't laugh and be afraid at the same time—of anything. If you're laughing, I defy you to be afraid."

Racism is scary. Being the target of racism, having to exist in a racist world, is scary. Feeling like you have no power to stop it is scary. Here's what you can try to do when you just want to laugh and not have to feel afraid:

USE HUMOR TO CALL PEOPLE OUT ON THEIR RACISM.

The always brilliant Wanda Sykes has this bit in her stand-up where she talks about her thoughts on white folks who claim that they are the targets of "reverse racism."

Her shutdown is simple and to the point. She says, "Isn't reverse racism—isn't that when a racist is nice to somebody else? That's reverse racism." And then she says, "What you afraid of is called *karma*." BOOM. ROASTED.

RE-APPROPRIATE RACIST LANGUAGE/IMAGERY/ STEREOTYPES.

This one can be tricky, and sometimes it can lead you down a bad path of self-lampooning and even self-loathing, and some people believe you shouldn't fuck with racist language and that it's best to just not use it, but DA-YAM is it satisfying to tell someone that my mother's maiden name is Ching Chong Chang and watch that person's face screw up in total confusion. When I took improv comedy classes at the UCB Theatre in New York, I once did a job-interview scene with a dude who addressed me as "Mrs. Chang," and the whole class laughed immediately, which made me uncomfortable because the Chinese last name was the entire joke, which basically meant that having a Chinese last

name is funny, which basically meant that *my* last name is funny, and I, for one, certainly don't bust out laughing every time I remember what my last name is. But I went with it. I replied that my hobbies were eating rice, catching flies with my chopstick, dressing like a geisha, being inscrutable, and practicing kung fu. That got an even bigger laugh, and I felt good, because I no longer felt like I was the butt of a racist joke; instead it felt like the whole class was laughing *at* racism and racist humor.

PRE-EMPT RACIST COMMENTS.

Again, sometimes this backfires, but when it works, it *works*. Once, some dude told me that the birthmark on my back looked "like Asia," which was ridiculous, so I started to tell people that I had named my birthmark "Asia" because I wanted to preemptively self-Orientalize before anyone else could do it to me. That particular joke usually prompted an uncomfortable silence coupled with a *WTF does that mean* look, which was fine with me, because at least it established a tone of *Yeah, racist jokes are uncomfortable for everyone, so don't do it, OK?*

Sometimes when I see an Asian person on TV I will tell my friends, "Oh yeah, that's my uncle," or when we go into a Chinese restaurant, I will say, "By the way, that waitress is my mom." It's a silly joke, and it's not even that funny, but it feels satisfying to make, because you're basically saying, YO, DON'T EVEN THINK ABOUT MAKING A "YOU ALL LOOK ALIKE" JOKE 'CAUSE I ALREADY HEARD IT ONE MILLION TIMES, SO SHUT YER MOUTH. For all the times that someone has asked me if I'm related to Jackie Chan, or if I know kung fu, or if Chinese people eat cats and dogs, or whatever the stereotype du jour happens to be, and made me feel powerless, I loved being able to say: HEY, MY DAD IS JACKIE CHAN, I HAVE A BLACK BELT IN MARTIAL ARTS, I JUST ATE FIVE CATS BECAUSE I'M CHINESE, AND I CAN'T OPEN MY EYES SO THAT'S WHY I BUMPED INTO YOU. WHAT ELSE HAVE YOU GOT?

Now, you have to be careful with this one, because the point of pre-empting racist comments is to show how inappropriate

and uncreative they are, NOT to give racists an opportunity to enjoy *The Self-Loathing Internalized Racism Comedy Hour*, if you know what I mean.

EXAGGERATE RACISM TO EXPOSE JUST HOW RIDICULOUS AND ABSURD AND ABOMINABLE IT REALLY IS.

I once had a friend tell me that his father told him that Asian women had sideways vaginas. He knew, of course, that it wasn't true, but he thought it was a pretty funny joke, and it made me feel humorless because I didn't think it was funny at all; in fact, it was the kind of thing that made me feel sad and sort of violated, so I wrote a poem about having a sideways vagina:*

YOU GO AWAY FOR A MONTH AND COME BACK A GADABOUT
me I stay a cynic
later becoming a stoic
later my friends point out I'm neither
you're a zen Buddhist, they say
and your skin has the texture of rice
oh right
my name is the sound of three pots clanging
against a tin garbage can
my family is related to lao tze
and my mother taught me filial piety
my vagina grows sideways
when a man wants to fuck
he gets at a right angle
a yi ayi a ya a ya a yaaaaaaaaaaaaaaaaaaa
and it's over.

It's a really fun poem to read aloud at a public reading. Usually no one laughs at the part where I list all of the ludicrous stereotypes I have had the misfortune of encountering in my fairly privileged and sheltered life, but I always feel relieved when I get to the end and everyone laughs and (hopefully) realizes that it *can* be funny to lampoon racism.

AND WHEN ALL ELSE FAILS, IT'S ALL RIGHT TO CRY.

Or scream, or write an angry rant in your journal, or throw your shoes at the door, or punch your bed, or whatever it is that you

---
* *This poem has been edited ever so slightly.*

need to do to let it out. It felt really good to laugh at the racist drunk girl at the Melt-Banana concert with my boyfriend, but that feeling was cut short when she grabbed me by the shoulders and said, "Are you calling me a fucking racist?" and then turned to her equally drunk friend and said, "This bitch just tried to call me a fucking racist."

My boyfriend tried to defuse the situation by explaining to these girls why what the first girl had said to me was indeed racist—but that only made things worse. The girl's friend tried to throw her drink in my face, and the original girl kept jostling me and punching me in the shoulder during the concert, shouting, "You're the fucking racist. You're the fucking racist. Don't you ever call me that again," even though I hadn't called her that, even though she *was* that, and even though I wished I had been brave enough to tell her so.

I ended up fleeing the show and crying in a bathroom stall. That night I lay in bed with my boyfriend, still crying, still shaking. He cried too.

"I'm sorry this happened to you. I'm sorry it's ever happened to you. I'm sorry it might happen to you again. I'm sorry I can't protect you from it."

"It's OK," I said. "It's OK and it's not OK."

That night I went to bed feeling like I was born sad.

The next morning, I woke up feeling much better. I went to brunch with my friends and told them, "You will *not* believe what happened to me yesterday. This drunk girl wandered into the Melt-Banana show and thought I was with the band because I'm Asian. And then she told me *I* was racist. It was not a fun night."

One of my friends joked, "You should have said, 'Konichiwa.'"

Another one said, "Or, like, 'Namaste,' just to confuse her."

It felt good to be with friends who had my back. It felt good to be in a safe environment, one where I felt comfortable enough to laugh. It felt good to exist without fear, even though I knew there would be another time when I wouldn't be able to laugh it off. But it felt good, that morning, to have some fucking fun. ♛

ON THE OUTSIDE LOOKING OUT

Being unpopular wasn't enough to make me cool.
Writing by Anna F. Playlist by Anaheed, art by Minna.

I did my most serious high school studying in the weeks before my freshman year had even begun. The morning after Labor Day, my bedroom floor was littered with the most recent issues of every teen magazine imaginable. I had mined them for tips on the clothes I was supposed to wear (miniskirts, Uggs) and the music I was supposed to listen to (Justin Timberlake). They promised me that all I had to do was consume the right products, and I would fit in. Hell, if I played my cards right, I could even be *popular*.

During the second period of my first day of high school, I had math class. I was ready for this—math was *my* subject. For middle school I went to a super competitive school in Ottawa, Canada. I spent every spare minute doing a lot of homework. There was very little time left for socializing, so I didn't. As a result, I had no idea what kids my age were into, only that everyone at my school held academics in high regard. Surely, I thought, the best way to earn the respect of my peers at this new place would be to sit as close to the front as possible, raise my hand for every question, and build a friendly rapport with my math teacher, right? I mean, who doesn't like an overachieving math nerd?

Everybody. Everybody dislikes an overachieving math nerd. I was not a hit with the popular kids. I was not a hit with anyone. The girls with matching blond highlights and denim miniskirts rolled their eyes at me as they passed me on their way out of the classroom.

The next day I moved to the other side of the room, near a girl with a flannel shirt and band patches on her backpack. I imagined the contempt she had for the girls with the highlights and figured I could seek refuge with her.

"Ugh, she's the *worst*," she whispered to her friend as I sat down behind them. It took me a second to realize that she meant me. This caught me off guard—I was expecting some bitchiness from the popular kids (I'd seen *The Breakfast Club*), but weren't all the outcasts supposed to band together? Couldn't we unite over our shared rejection and become best friends? The answer was clearly no. Flannel-shirt girl was disliked by the popular kids because she listened to the Stooges and wore thrifted clothing. I was disliked by the popular kids *and* by her because I was an eager student and a teacher's pet.

After a few months of eating lunch on my own, I eventually, totally by accident, fell in with a different crowd of "misfits," none of whom were in my math class. Some of them had gone to my elementary school. We got along really well, I finally learned to be myself, and everything ended up all right.

Ha ha ha, no, just kidding. While these new "misfits"—alternative kids, outcasts, whatever you want to call them—didn't care if you straightened your hair or wore Abercrombie, they still had their own unspoken code of conduct. They all instinctively knew what bands to listen to: Radiohead was cool, except for their first album, which was clearly super lame; Sonic Youth was cool, except for their latest album, which was even lamer than Radiohead's first one. They knew what clothes to wear: They all mocked the expensive Ugg boots that were in fashion while shelling out for Chuck Taylors.

Having people to hang out with after months of lonerdom made me so excited, I didn't care if we didn't have much in common. My new friends were never mean or cruel, but I started to intentionally distance myself from the things I liked, the better to blend in with them. Hanging out in my room once, a friend spotted a copy of *YM* with Hilary Duff on the cover. "Ugh, I can't believe people actually like her music," she said. I laughed in agreement, while secretly praying that she didn't go anywhere near my CD collection.

This became a pattern. I hid the fact that I was a Junior Achiever and made excuses for why I couldn't hang out on nights that I had meetings. I never mentioned that I tried out for the cheerleading squad, or that despite not making it, I still had massive respect for the sport. I hid or downplayed most of my own obsessions, like math and old *Simpsons* episodes. I never told my pals that most of the music they listened to just sounded like noise to me. (How could a band with a name as cute as the Pixies make music that angsty?)

Our hangouts consisted of me smiling and nodding silently during the conversations they had amongst themselves. I was terrified of what would happen the second they realized I wasn't a "badass" like them. They smoked cigarettes and got high. They hung out in parking lots at night and swore in front of adults. My dream Friday involved

renting new releases from Blockbuster and staying up past my bedtime, eating pizza, and maybe even having *two* sodas. I soon started faking stomachaches when I went out, finding reasons why I needed my parents to pick me up from whatever party we were at so I could just go home and watch TV.

Pop culture led me to believe there was a dichotomy between the cool kids and the outcasts. Shows like *Gossip Girl* treat popularity as aspirational; *Daria* tells us it's something to be reviled. My freshman year I was a neurotic mess, feeling like a freak no matter whom I was with, happiest when I was alone. I was neither a Cher Horowitz nor an Enid Coleslaw—both of whom seemed to be OK blowing off homework, which I just could not wrap my head around.

Sometimes I wonder what would happen if all my favorite pop-culture misfits were put in the same high school. Would any of them even get along? Daria would probably moralize about Enid's pranks, Enid would find Willow Rosenberg's nerdiness dull, and all of them would roll their eyes at Lindsay's friends in *Freaks and Geeks*.

For various reasons, I ended up going to several different high schools; each one had a different idea of what was and wasn't cool. When I started the 10th grade, I signed up for every extracurricular I could, whether they were considered dorky or not, both to meet new people and to challenge my perceptions of what I liked. I made the cheerleading squad this time around, and played rugby the following semester. (Neither were for me—turns out I hate sports.) I joined the improv team and learned there were people who thought my jokes were funny. I also tried to give the things I had once dismissed another try: I ended

up relistening to the "noisy" music my ninth grade friends had liked, and now it's most of what I listen to. (My 14-year-old self would scold me for risking hearing loss to see the Pixies when I was 19.)

There's a lot to be said for owning your interests and not trying to fit in with any one group in particular. It is fun and exciting to share obsessions with your friends, but that doesn't mean you're required to like all of the same things. It's OK to not like One Direction OR Grimes, just like it's OK to love both of them. Life is not a high school movie with clearly defined aesthetic boundaries, especially since most of the teenagers in high school movies—outcasts or otherwise—are played by conventionally beautiful, aggressively styled 28-year-olds with problems that never seem to relate to your own. Really, there's just no point in trying to force yourself into someone else's definition of cool. It just makes high school suck more than it needs to. ☺

JUST KIDDING

1. A COMPLICATED SONG – "WEIRD AL" YANKOVIC
2. MY HOPE – MOLLY LEWIS
3. NOBODY'S ASIAN IN THE MOVIES (COMMENTARY! THE MUSICAL) – MAURISSA TANCHAROEN
4. MEDIUM MAN SONG – MIKE BIRBIGLIA
5. THREW IT ON THE GROUND – THE LONELY ISLAND
6. SEX WITH DUCKS – GARFUNKEL & OATES
7. POOP SONG – SARAH SILVERMAN & LAURA MARANO
8. RE: YOUR BRAINS – JONATHAN COULTON
9. FRIDAY – JIMMY FALLON (FEAT STEPHEN COLBERT & TAYLOR HICKS)

ONE, TWO, SOMETHING'S COMING FOR YOU

Most uncanny.
By Olivia
T-shirts by Cooper Campbell. Thanks to Amani, Aysia, Chadena, and Jesse for modeling.

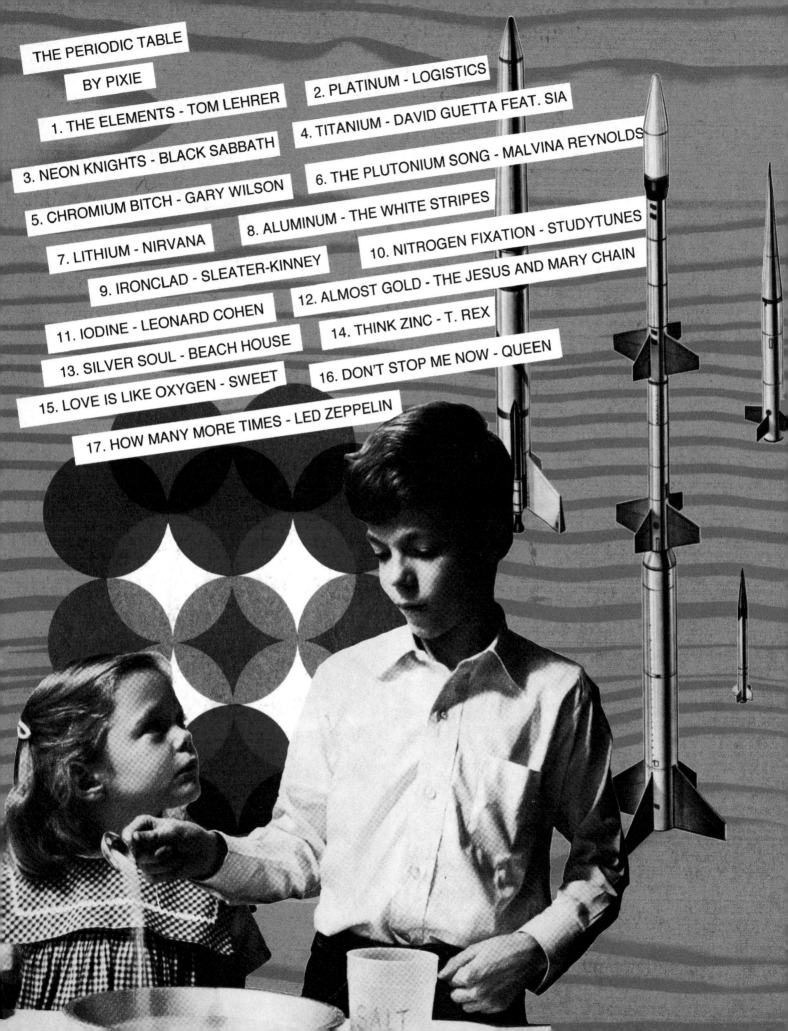

NOVEMBER 2012: INVENTION

Happy November! Happy colorful leaves and ginger smells and fuzzy sweaters!

Our theme this month is INVENTION: making things, making things up, lying, science, photography, more DIYs than usual, and paying respect to people who consistently churn out new stuff we love, from Beyoncé to Chris Ware. For some reason, the way people in the past imagined the future—now the present—has been on our minds, too, *Jetsons*-style. I'd like to think that those people of yore would be super impressed by all our technology, but I dunno if I myself would be that stoked about *Angry Birds* if I were expecting hovercrafts and robot maids. Wait: WHY DON'T WE HAVE HOVERCRAFTS AND ROBOT MAIDS? I am so disappointed in you, present day. I need more tools to enable my laziness! I need to be able to Facebook stalk from bed, guilt-free!

One thing the present day does offer is the ability to, um, run the website you're reading this on. Even better is when we get to bring this all to life, and everyone gets to meet one another and hang out in person. If you're in or near Los Angeles, we are hosting three Rookie events in your area this month. Join us, will you? I can't wait to see everyone who came to our Strange Magic events again, and to meet new Rookies, too!

Thank you for being here, and I hope school and friends and loved ones and life and things are going OK.

Love,
Tavi

Work Hard and Be Kind:
An Interview With Chris Ware

We talk to the cartoonist about his new book, being a teenager, and the reality of dreams.
Interview by Tavi, self-portrait by Chris Ware.

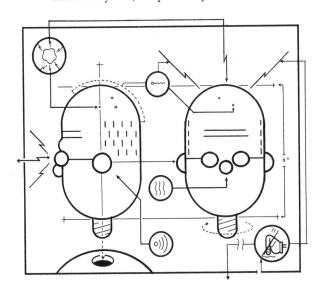

If I could ask all humans to read just one thing, it would be any of Chris Ware's books. They're not quite comic books or *graphic novels*; he's almost created his own medium. Sometimes his books have pages of satirical advertisements drawn by him. Sometimes there's no dialogue throughout an entire spread. Some panels look like complicated mazes but flow like streams of consciousness. The same characters pop up in different stories, the most overlooked details of everyday life get the most attention, and I always come away from it all feeling more connected to any person I may pass on the street and with a strong desire to create something of my own. That is, I believe, the best a person taking in a thing another person made can hope for.

Chris was gracious enough to answer some questions for us over email, and for that we are grateful and honored, and proud to publish his answers here for you.

TAVI What were you like as a teenager?

CHRIS WARE That's a complicated question, since I think I mutated every three months or so, but a general string of adjectives might be: insufferable, desperate, scrawny, bad-skinned, triangulating, self-doubting, self-conscious, crude, and unappealing. I spent a lot of time watching television and following a program of musical taste that one of my friends unintentionally curated for me (i.e., I copied everything he liked), and I tried to make my naturally buoyant hair look longer by straightening it with a hairdryer. I attended private school until 10th grade in Omaha, Nebraska, where I wore a "formal uniform" which I modified to express my true self via footwear or digital watches that weren't officially sanctioned by the Episcopalians. I was terminally unathletic and terrified at the thought that I might one day have to remove my shirt in public. To make up for this perceived deficiency, I stupidly

got into various experimental substances, a period which ended in a moment of self-realization after buying said substances while driving my grandmother's Oldsmobile Toronado—probably the dumbest, most shameful moment of my life—when I found myself thinking, *What if I'd gotten arrested? What would that have said about me, about her, and about my mother, who tried to raise me right?* Fortunately, I abandoned that particular path of inquiry.

What were your biggest influences at that time?

Because of this brief substances-experimenting I became "interested" in the idea of the 1960s (or whatever "the idea of the 1960s" meant to a Midwestern middle-class kid in the 1980s) and ended up buying a lot of so-called underground comics at head shops and out of the back room of the local comic book store from which I'd bought superhero comics as a middle-schooler. It was there, while hoping to find pornography, that I discovered *RAW* magazine, Robert Crumb, and Harvey Pekar, and somehow, through the example of these and other artists like Gary Panter and Charles Burns, came to the conclusion that the only thing I had any remote proclivity for—drawing—might possibly be employed in creating comics, which to me seemed like an untapped, slightly edgy world of expressive possibility and genuine honesty, and maybe even a way of meeting girls. (It wasn't.) In the 1980s, popular culture was so mired in falseness and compromise that comics seemed (and still seem to me, actually) an unpretentious potential vessel for solitary authenticity. It was Robert Crumb who amazed me first artistically, Harvey Pekar who made me realize that regular life itself could be written about, and Art Spiegelman who provided the first (and still the finest) example of how it all might be synthesized into a thoughtful, readable artistic medium.

When I saw you speak last month at Unity Temple in Oak Park, someone asked you what the ACT of drawing FEELS like, and you said it was just horrible. I also read somewhere that you can't look at any of your books because you'd notice only what's wrong with them. There's a page in *The Acme Novelty Library* with tips about being a cartoonist that make it sound miserable. If neither the process nor the product is satisfying to you, what drives you?

I don't know. I guess I'm motivated by actually finishing something—something that I know I've tried my absolute hardest at and have put every bit of myself into—while the tolerability of the actual creative experience remains a distant concern. There are also those rare moments while writing and drawing where something comes up completely unexpectedly on the page—like a gesture or a facial expression on a character—which suddenly reveals something about the story or the person I simply never would have thought of just sitting around thinking. In the best of these instances, I might also realize I've been lying to myself about

some part of my own personality for years, and that consequently there's something I need to change.

What advice would you give to someone who is in the early stages of that and possibly struggling?

To work as hard as possible, and then, when you think you're done, to work just a little bit harder. To know that if it feels "right" it may actually be completely wrong, and that if it feels "wrong" it may be completely right. There's no governing principle to any of this except that strange instinct and feeling within yourself that you simply have to learn to trust, but which is always unreliably changing. To create something for people who have not been born yet. To pay attention to how it actually feels to be alive, to the lies you tell yourself and others. Not to overreach—but also not to get too comfortable with your own work. To avoid giving in to either self-doubt or self-confidence, depending on your leaning, and especially to resist giving over your opinion of yourself to others—which means not to seek fame or recognition, which can restrain rather than open your possibility for artistic development. With all this in mind, not to expect anything and to be grateful for any true, non-exploitative opportunity that presents itself, however modest. And to understand that being able to say "I don't know what to do with my life" is an incredible privilege that 99 percent of the rest of the world will never enjoy.

So many of your stories—as you pointed out at that speaking event—are about people whose dreams have gone unrealized, or who are maybe creative but not necessarily talented, or who just never went after what they wanted, and now it's too late, and they carry with them a sadness about it. From where I stand, as an admirer of your work/a person who has seen only positive reviews of your last book (and all of your books) in prestigious publications, I would say you have found success in a creative field. What part of you consistently writes the story of someone who hasn't?

I feel extraordinarily lucky for any so-called success I've enjoyed, and I'm deeply grateful for every single kind word and generous sentiment I've received. It's a far cry from what I experienced as a kid, and not what I ever expected my adult life would bring, though I'm sure whatever counts as drive within me was forged in that crucible of self-doubt and fear-of-being-jumped-in-the-hallway I endured in my early adolescence. Beyond that, I believe that everyone has within them some urge to create something—whether it's a story, a picture, a song, or a child—but for one reason or another many of us simply aren't lucky enough to be able to. [That drive] comes of trying to understand and to feel and to empathize; it's the reason we have language and, in turn, art.

But to answer your question more directly: I went to art school, and while I did intend to write and draw comics, I also thought maybe I could become a more traditional fine artist—a painter or a sculptor or whatever. I didn't, and while in most ways I'm grateful for the directness and artistic freedom comics provides, sometimes I still feel as if I "gave up" on something.

Normally your books are quite carefully put together, and reading them can be like solving a maze—the order and arrangement of the panels is very purposeful and important. Your new book, *Building Stories*, is a box of books and pamphlets and broadsides and the like, but you've set no guidelines for where to start or finish. Why?

I wanted to make a book that had no beginning or end, and, despite the incredible pretentiousness of how that sounds, to try and get at the three-dimensionality of memories and stories—how we're able to tell them starting at this or that point depending on the circumstance, and to take them apart and put them back together, whether to actually try and make sense of our lives or simply to tell reassuring lies to ourselves. I also wanted to make a book that seemed fun to read, and the idea of a box of nonthreatening booklets has always appealed to me. Also, I had a dream about exactly such an object.

There's a quotation from Picasso on the inside cover of *Building Stories*: "Everything you can imagine is real." You said at Unity Temple that you can remember stories your grandmother told you and how they looked in your head more vividly than some events that actually occurred in your own life. There's that part in one of the booklets where one of the characters dreams that she finds an amazing book she wrote, and even though it only ever existed in her subconscious, it confirmed for her that she had that potential in her. I'd never considered giving so much validity to a reality that's so personal and in-your-head and fictionalized, and I found it very comforting. So, how did you figure that out on your own—that something that exists only in your mind could have a valid enough reality to be a comfort?

Well, really, our memories are all we have, and even those we think of as "real" are made up. Art can condense experience into something greater than reality, and it can also give us permission to do or think certain things that otherwise we've avoided or felt ashamed of. The imagination is where reality lives; it's the instant lie of backwash from the prow of that boat that we think of as cutting the present moment, everything following it becoming less and less "factual" but no less *real* than what we think of as having actually occurred.

Do you ever dream about any of your characters?

I do. Some of them have come to me fully formed, very vividly, in the same way that I can only really feel the presence of people who have died in my dreams. Sometimes I think [dreams are] how we sort through all of the day's new data and file it as ideas within the storylike structure of how we imagine and remember our lives.

Do you ever dream in the style of your drawings?

No—the way I draw is intended to be completely transparent, though maybe I'm the only person who sees it that way. I consider my drawing, for better or worse, to be a way of showing things translucently, the way typography is transparent on a page—intended to be read, but not really completely *seen*.

What would you like to tell the young, impressionable minds reading Rookie?

Well, that life is a lot more serious and shorter than it seems like it will be. And that you can easily waste it. And that happiness is overrated. Be kind. This said—and I can't talk about the rest of the world—but I'd say that you're a member of the first generation of modern Americans whom I consider genuine, ready-made citizens. And by that I mean America has essentially exited its protracted national adolescence (approximately the 1920s through the 1980s, with the 1960s being the apex and the baby-boomer presidencies of Clinton and Bush as the hangover) and as a nation we're at something of a deciding moment of anxious self-awareness, both as to where we've been drawing our resources, and from what and how we've been weaving our moral fabric.

I'm not blowing smoke here, but I'm overall quite impressed by the seriousness, intelligence, and maturity of the generation half my age, both on the larger scale of considering social issues without the giddy recklessness of the 1960s all the way down to the way I've seen children and teens treat each other one-on-one. My wife is a high school teacher in the Chicago Public Schools, and she regularly comes home with stories of kindness and empathy on the part of her students that I find absolutely unfamiliar to my own teen experience, which was marred by self-preservation, meanness, and insobriety. There appears to be a certain clearheadedness and sense-of-place-in-the-worldedness with "the youth today" that wasn't prevalent when I was a kid or a teen. I think there's a sense of direness or a certain kind of embarrassment if not plain disgust at the foolish reluctance my generation and my parents' generation might have enjoyed which you all seem to have refreshingly no time for at all, while also seeming to know how to have a fine time yet to know the relative value of fun versus what makes life important. In short, I think you're doing great, and I'm impressed, if not a little envious. ♦

FRANKEN-FOODS

Weird culinary inventions. By the Rookie staff.

It's been said that necessity is the mother of invention—we think weird cravings in the middle of the night are a way better motivator. Trying to come up with something resembling a meal using minimal effort and whatever is in the fridge leads to some inspired concoctions. Here's a roundup of some of our more edible results.

WAFFLE SANDWICHES

DILEMMA: You have peanut butter and jelly, but no bread on which to spread them. Do you forgo your lunch? Do you eat these condiments directly from the jar, the way the cavemen ate their peanut butter?! You're kind of freaking out over here. SOLUTION: Enter toaster waffles, the greatest invention since sliced bread. Instead of smothering them with syrup, use them as the foundation for your sandwich. My favorite combination is peanut butter with sliced peaches. Something tells me a waffle BLT won't be quite as magically delicious, but who knows? —Anna F.

FIE (AKA FAKE PIE)

One of the worst things in the world to crave is pie, because (a) who has pie lying around unless Paula Deen is your mom, (b) good pie is rare and delicious, and (c) even if you go to the store to get a frozen pie, it's still labor intensive and you'll forget all about your craving while the dang thing heats up in the oven. UNLESS YOU KNOW HOW TO MAKE FIE. Now pie is what? Buttery, sugary pastry and some sort of gooey fruit filling. So toast a slice of bread, butter it till it's dripping, put sugar and cinnamon all over it, and then open one of those cans of fruit in the back of your pantry: peaches, apples, pineapples, mangos, cherries, mandarin oranges—anything will work. Put several spoonfuls on your toast, put more sugar on top, and: FIE, Y'ALL. (In related news, if it's specifically pumpkin pie you're craving, you can make **Pumpkin Pie in a Can**: Open a can of pumpkin-pie mix, add milk and sugar, and stir.) —Krista

BREAKFASTGHETTI

One time, I really wanted to eat leftover pasta at 8 AM, but I felt like it wasn't breakfast-y enough. So I put the pasta and some sauce in a frying pan, cracked an egg into it, and scrambled it all together to make a spaghetti scramble, and it was so good that I make it on purpose now. If I have convinced you, make sure you put olive oil in your frying pan so the spaghetti doesn't stick. —Gabby

MEAT BANANA

The Meat Banana is my favorite snack. I don't know if I came up with it or my mom did, but it's pretty easy: You peel a banana, wrap a slice of bologna around it, and eat. Now that I'm "grown up" I don't eat bologna anymore; I use a piece of ham instead. Still the best. —Laia

POPCORN AND ICE CREAM

In "Slumber Party," my favorite episode of the original *Beverly Hills, 90210*, Donna Martin (Tori Spelling) reveals a deep, dark secret: She likes using popcorn as an ice cream topping. WHAT IN THE WHAT? When I first saw it, I was curiously hungry. So I had my own slumber party and made my friends try it—and it was delicious! It has that sweet-and-salty combo I really love. I used Orville Redenbacher and plain old vanilla, but really, the world is your oyster, only better than an oyster, because there's ice cream. —Marie

PEPPERONI CHIPS

My friend and I invented this new childhood classic: Put pepperonis in the microwave until they turn into crispy chips. —Lauren P.

CAKE WAFFLES

This is exactly what it sounds like. Put cake batter in a waffle iron and VOILÀ, YOU'RE DONE. It makes the task of cake-baking less daunting because you don't have to use the oven, and it's soooo much quicker. PLUS IT'S IN THE SHAPE OF A WAFFLE. I served these with ice cream and sundae toppings at my 16th birthday, and they truly made the night, convincing me that teen-movie moments can happen IRL. If there is one complaint I have about John Hughes, it's that Molly Ringwald never ate any cake waffles. —Tavi

MARSHMALLOW SOUP

Stick a few marshmallows in a bowl and microwave them for about 30 seconds. They'll get big and puffy and look like they're about to explode, and then they'll shrink back down as soon as you open the door. Stir them around with a spoon so they become a big, sticky, fluffy sludge. Add in Rice Krispies, Nutella, peanut butter, and anything else you might have lying around. Eat this one quickly, since marshmallows can harden as they dry out. Then make more. —Anna F.

CHOCOLATE AND CHEDDAR CHEESE POPCORN

One time I was alone at my friend's house because I was feeding her cats while she was on vacation and I was going through her pantry looking for snacks. She had nothing to eat. Literally nothing. *What does Danielle eat?* I wondered as I rooted through her cupboards. The only semi-edible things I found were some old "fun size" Hershey's chocolate bars, which actually crumbled when I bit into them, and some very stale cheddar cheese popcorn in a holiday tin. (It was July.) But no one here is a quitter, so I melted the dusty, crumbly bars in a bowl and drizzled the chocolate over the popcorn. AND IT WAS DELICIOUS. Melted chocolate and cheddar cheese popcorn. Do it. —Krista

PEANUT BUTTER AND CHEDDAR & SOUR CREAM RUFFLES SANDWICH

In junior high I came up with a lot of weird after-school snacks on the random. One of my favorites was a peanut butter sandwich with Cheddar & Sour Cream Ruffles. The idea for this combination probably happened accidentally, like I was eating a peanut butter sandwich and the chips separately, then had a WILD URGE to put them together. My mom used to buy Jif, but I'm curious to try it with my modern-day favorite, Peanut Butter & Co.'s White Chocolate Wonderful. —Marie

Now go forth and experiment! ◊

EXTRAORDINARY MACHINE

A robot finds love. By Eleanor.
Thanks to Fumie and Yoshiko
for modeling.

The Great Pretender

Telling the truth about lying.
By Jenny

I started kindergarten in China without a parent at home. My mother and father were in America, this place that the extended family I was staying with showed me on a map, and whose distance they tried to demonstrate by moving furniture around in the living room. When that didn't work, they took me outside to our garden, where we grew sour green grapes in the summer, and drew pictures for me in the dirt.

"We're here," my grandparents told me, pointing. "And your mommy and daddy are there."

But the "there" they showed me was something I could see and touch; the "there" where my parents were I could only see in the photos they sent to us, accompanied by letters filled with promises big and small: that they would bring me to America one day to live with them, that I would get an electric keyboard the very day I arrived, that they would buy me a necklace made of real pearls, that I would one day go on a plane and fly through clouds.

Before my father left, he read me picture books in bed every night, hoisted me on his shoulders when I couldn't sleep, and took me on long, wonderful walks at night through our neighborhood. One of the books he read me was about a young boy who goes on an adventure to India, where everything glitters with gold and princes ride through the streets on elephants. I was two and a half when he left. Three when my mother did.

It was soon after that that I started the Chinese equivalent of kindergarten. At home, my family spoke Mandarin—the country's official language—so I had trou-

ble keeping up with the other kids in my school in Shanghai, who spoke to one another in Shanghainese. I understood most of what they were saying, but whenever I tried to respond in their dialect, I sounded like someone with a speech impediment, stuttering and stammering and making weird O shapes with my mouth. I communicated in my own made-up patois that was one part mispronounced Shanghainese, three parts Mandarin.

"She's probably just stupid," I heard one kid say to another.

I wanted desperately for the other students to like me, to find me interesting, but nothing about me seemed interesting enough to impress anyone. So I came up with a new tactic.

"My parents live on a boat," I told some kid during lunch. "They keep whales as pets. My dad knows how to fly a plane. That's how he got to America. Once I touched lightning, but guess what? I didn't die."

It didn't work. No one believed me, and I had exactly zero friends.

Meanwhile, I told my aunts and uncles and grandparents that I was having the time of my freaking life at school. I told them that I was friends with everyone, that my best friend was the daughter of a judge and she brought me orange juice every morning. I told them that we learned new songs every day and that the teacher praised me for my singing in front of the entire class and that she told everyone that they should learn from me. I told my family that the teacher took us on field trips almost every day, to the zoo or the movies. When my grandfather picked me up from school in the afternoons, I'd ride on the back of his bicycle and from the moment he started pedaling, I'd begin to tell him all sorts of outrageous lies, like how once, at the zoo, I had been chosen to ride

on an elephant and I did it with such bravery that everyone clapped and the teacher had even cried because of how proud I had made her.

Eventually it got to the point where my auntie called up the teacher to thank her for all that she had done for me. She told my teacher that I had been going through some difficult times because my parents were living in America, and she had been worried that I might find it difficult to adjust to life without them on top of starting school, but that everyone at home was grateful to my teacher for filling my days with trips to the zoo and the movies.

"There was a pause," my auntie told me years and years later. "And then your teacher goes, 'Well, that does sound terrific. I wish I was that good of a teacher, but unfortunately, we've never done any of those things.' At first, I was puzzled when I realized you were lying to us. I thought to myself, *My niece isn't the kind of child who lies.* But then I realized you were being extraordinarily strong. You were protecting us. You knew we were worried about you, so you tried to save us from worrying by lying to us and telling us that you were flourishing."

"Mmn," I said, embarrassed by her theory that my lies were heroic acts and by my theory that I was just a loser kid who wanted attention.

When I moved to New York to live with my parents, I was five years old and I had to learn a whole new language. Learning a language when you are not a baby turns you into a baby. A baby with the face and body of a nonbaby. A baby who cannot articulate any of your feelings or needs or wants. A baby who cannot prove to the world that you are smart, that you are capable of complex thoughts, that you are more than the language you do not yet know. I pissed my pants the first time I needed to go to the bathroom, because even though my parents had taught me to raise my hand straight up in the air and say, "BATHROOM!" if I needed to pee, they hadn't taught me what "Go ahead" meant, which was what my teacher said to me. Not knowing what to do, I remained in my seat, praying I could hold it in for another few hours, and then suddenly, the entire class was shouting at me while I sat there pissing myself.

In my first year in America, I went to my babysitter's house every day after school. She watched over me and a few other children. When my mother picked me up, I told her that I was friends with every single kid at my babysitter's house. That they saved their chips from lunch and gave them to me. That they hugged me every hour because I was so cute. If my mother noticed that every time she came to pick me up, I was always alone in a corner, and that the other kids didn't wave goodbye to me like they did to one another—if she noticed, she never said a word. She was merciful that way.

When I learned English, I started to lie in two languages. In fourth grade, my best friend Hanzhi told me that there was a midget in his class who was like a foot smaller than everyone else, and I took that story and made it about me and told everyone in my class that I had a friend back in China who was so small that he could actually die from taking a dump unless someone held him up and prevented him from falling into the toilet and being flushed away. My father told me that he knew of some distant cousins who had eaten a cat, and so in seventh grade, when my biology teacher said, "You know, in some countries, people eat cats and dogs," I had the idea to blurt out, "That's true! I've eaten a cat! And it tastes like just chicken."

For the next two years of my life, I didn't go a day without hearing some kid say, "Break me off a piece of that kitty-cat bar!" or "Meow…yo, her mouth is watering because she thought she heard a cat!"

By the time I went to college, I was done inventing tall tales. I wasn't telling people that I had eaten a cat because I wanted

someone—anyone—to be interested in me, but I still didn't believe that telling the truth about myself would make anyone want to know more, so I continued lying, only my lies became a little more nuanced, and slightly more complicated. I had a boyfriend who wrote fiction and who told me that maybe, one day, I might be as good as him. Instead of saying what I actually thought, which was, *Hey asshole, more like one day you might be as good as me*, I said, "I really want that to happen." I pretended exuberance when what I really felt was irrepressible depression. When I couldn't contain my depression any longer and allowed a tiny, tiny part of myself to emerge, my friends would tell me that seeing me sad was unsettling for them. That I was supposed to be the rock, the stable one.

"You're never sad," one friend told me when I didn't laugh at her jokes one night.

"I know," I said, continuing to lie.

I laughed at jokes that were sexist and racist.

When I started having sex, I faked all of my orgasms, which, by the way, is not something that teenage boys whose previous exposure to sex has consisted mainly of internet porn are likely to pick up on. As I got older and my partners grew more experienced, I realized that I couldn't keep faking orgasms, so instead I faked apathy. I told every new boyfriend that I happened to be one of those women who prefer *giving* to *receiving*, which is pretty much the general narrative affirmed by most mainstream depictions of sex, so most dudes were like, "OK, cool." The one or two real orgasms I had took so long and required so much patience and trial and error on both my part and my partner's that I feared it would drive them away. I was certain that if I was too demanding, if I kept asking for things, someday someone would tell me, "No. You're not worth it."

When other people told me that I was a doll, that I was precious, that I was cute, that I was just so *nice*, I nodded and affirmed these little lies because I felt that the truth of my being was too monstrous to reveal. I *had* to lie. I had

to pass as a nice girl, a nonthreatening girl. I had to pass as the kind of girl who could hang with dudes and listen to their sexist tirades about how girls were such nags, that girls whined all the time, that girls always wanted dudes to spend money on them, that girls spent too much time putting on makeup that didn't even look good. I had to pass as the kind of girl who didn't take anything seriously, especially not the bigoted humor that I had been subjected to my entire life. I had to pass as all of those things because if my friends saw the real me—the me that was scarily angry, and who took things *very* seriously, and that was so, so far from nice—they would surely abandon me.

♦ ◊ ♦

Right at this moment, as I write this, I am fighting the urge to lie. I want very much to lie to you, my dear dear Rookie hearts, to give this article the happy resolution that my real life doesn't yet have. I want to say I've stopped lying, that I no longer feel the need to protect the people in my life from the parts of myself that are difficult to admit. I want to say I no longer fear that my loved ones will abandon me if they learn that I'm not a happy person, I'm not an easygoing person, I'm not a confident person, that I don't always feel attractive or particularly sexual, that I do things that I'm not proud of, that most of the time I feel wildly lost and confused and scared and angry and sad.

But I won't lie to you. I will be honest, even if honesty is not always charming, even if being honest means risking rejection, risking disgust. Let's start with this confession: When I attended the first Rookie party ever (!!!!) a year ago, when Rookie was just a fledgling

By Dylan

baby of a thing, I felt out of place and awkward and unable to think of anything, like literally *anything*, to say in conversations. Instead of enjoying myself, I panicked about every little thing: *Is there a circle forming and am I now outside of it? Wait, do I have anything funny related to gym teachers that I can say right now? Oh my god, people are talking about tampons! Tell your tampon sex story now before someone else jumps in. Oh god, you dummy, someone already jumped in!* I went to the bathroom so many times just because I didn't know what else to do with my body.

When it was all over, I felt like a failure of a social creature. And instead of owning up to that, I decided to publicly post on Facebook how I had met one of my idols, Miranda July, and that I could die happy now.

"Miranda July?????" my friends wrote me. "I'm jealous!"

I still laugh at jokes that I don't think are funny. I still don't speak up because I'm afraid to take up space. I still fear that my friends will abandon me if I am not completely entertaining and captivating and cheerful all the time. Recently, I was really let down by a friend, and instead of telling her that, I kept it inside, afraid that just by acknowledging my feelings, I might seem too demanding.

When I graduated from college and started working and paying my own bills, my mother asked me, "Do you miss being a teenager? Do you wish you could go back to high school?"

"Are you kidding me?" I cried. "I hated high school. Those were the worst years of my life." I felt smug, condescending, knowing my mother would not understand. How could she? My mother had always been happy. She had always been popular—she was president of her class through middle school and high school—and was still popular now, as an adult. Everyone who met her adored her; strangers routinely stopped her on the street to tell her how stunning she was. My mother once told me that she was a generally trusting, happy person and even though she knew deep down that it was impossible, she truly believed that she had never been lied to by

anyone, ever, in her entire life. My mother basically gleamed with health and well-adjustment with every waking breath, and could never figure out how her own flesh-and-blood daughter ended up so sulky and unlikeable as an adolescent. My mother could never, ever understand me—or so I thought.

"Me too," she said. "I hated high school. Those were the worst years of my life too."

That's when I realized that I wasn't the only one who made up stories to protect loved ones from the ugly truth. If my mom does it, everyone does. We hide behind these characters we've invented for ourselves—the happy partygoer, the "low-maintenance" girlfriend, etc.—because it seems easier than asking everyone all the time to confront the truth, which can be as boring as "I have nothing to say," or as simple as "I feel insecure." Even in this article, I have taken on the role of the Adult Who Has Some Hard-Won Advice That You Should Listen To, though I don't know why you should listen to me, and I don't know if what I have is advice so much as a story.

I wish I could say that I'm done lying, but I'm not. I'm not even done telling tall tales. I still make up shit all the time in my fiction and my poetry. But I can't keep making up stories about who I am, and playing this imaginary character who is never vulnerable, never disappointing, never difficult, never too much.

All I can say now is that I'm *trying* to stop lying. And that's not a lie. ◊

1. A Hard Rain's A-Gonna Fall - Bob Dylan

2. See the Sky About to Rain - Neil Young

3. Crucify Your Mind - Rodriguez

4. Blue Light - Mazzy Star

5. Dirty Rain - Ryan Adams

6. Sweet Thing - Van Morrison

7. Carey - Joni Mitchell

8. Sight, Flight - Wye Oak

9. I Am Trying to Break Your Heart - Wilco

10. Mercury Girl - Cleaners From Venus

11. Rhododendron - The Elephants

12. A Silver Song - Conspiracy of Owls

13. Hey Mr. Rain (version 1) - The Velvet Underground

14. Nine Million Rainy Days - The Jesus and Mary Chain

15. Rubber Traits - Why?

16. Cry for a Shadow - Beat Happening

17. Still in Love - Cat Power

18. Sycamore - Bill Callahan

19. Steady Rollin' - Two Gallants

20. A Distorted Reality Is Now a Necessity to Be Free - Elliott Smith

21. What's Going Ahn - Big Star

22. I Don't Believe in the Sun - The Magnetic Fields

23. Golden Age - Beck

HOW TO MAKE A COMPUTER

A DIY for the aspiring hacker.
By Maggie

What I'm about to show you is, no joke, the most exciting thing to happen in computing since the 1970s. Earlier this year, a small team of engineers in the UK who wanted to get kids interested in computer programming started making credit-card-size computers and selling them for $35 apiece (cheap enough that kids could buy them and not be afraid of breaking them). They thought they would sell 10,000 in the first year. Seven months later, they've sold half a million. Their invention, the Raspberry Pi, is way more than a tiny computer—it's the heart of a hacker movement.

If you were a teenager in 1975, a personal computer looked like the photo at the bottom left corner of this page. To make it do anything, you would need to add a keyboard, a power supply, a case, a TV, and tons of patience and know-how. Nowadays computers are everywhere and everyone uses them, but nobody seems to wonder why or how they work.

Most electronics today are what are called "black boxes." They are built to keep users out; the computer industry (dominated by Microsoft and Apple) doesn't really want us opening up their machines and messing around with their insides. They would much rather have us buy the newest, shiniest thing than let us know how to repair or modify old computer parts on our own. (The latest MacBook Pro, for example, might be the least hackable laptop ever made. They even use proprietary screws to make it almost impossible to get inside!) The big companies love compliant, unquestioning customers, and they treat us like children (with a lot of money). What they don't like is *hackers*.

A common misconception is that hacking = accessing other people's computers. (See: any movie or news story about "hacking.") But the true meaning of hacking is much broader—it's about problem solving, rejecting limits set by outside forces, curiosity, and a true DIY spirit. In tech terms, it includes reverse engineering (taking stuff apart to learn how it works) and modifying electronics to suit your own needs and to answer your own questions.

The Raspberry Pi (bottom right) can transport us to those fun days of the 1970s when a computer was just a circuit board and a central processing unit, and the rest was up to you. But unlike in the '70s, when these assembly-required computers cost hundreds if not thousands of dollars, the Raspberry Pi costs only 35 bucks.

Before I get into the technical how-to, I want to share some of the really cool stuff you can do with your soon-to-be computer. Of course you can do all the normal things that you're accustomed to doing on your Mac or PC, like watch *The X-Files* and write your novel. But with a Raspberry Pi, you can do so much more. You can use it as a robot brain, or a spy gadget. You can even put it in a balloon and send it into space. It can pretty much do whatever you design it to do, which is exactly what makes it so special.

I got mine this summer, and I've had a lot of time to tinker with it, so I put together this DIY to get you started. I know that at first, looking at these instructions might make you want to run for your life.

But don't panic! I assure you that you can do this. Don't worry about the technical language—those are just names of parts you'll gather and use to make your computer.

What you'll need (see top photo at right):

1. **Raspberry Pi, Model B:** $35. I got mine from Farnell.com, which ships all over the world. You can also buy one for slightly more at Limor Fried's website.
2. **A micro-USB power supply:** Under $10. If you have a generic (non-Apple) phone charger, that will do.
3. **A composite video cable (CVC):** You probably already have one of these—it's a cord with yellow, red, and white plugs. Just use the yellow part. If not, you can get a CVC for pennies. (If you have a newer TV or computer monitor you might need an HDMI cable instead. These are in the $5 range.)
4. **A USB keyboard and mouse:** These are the kind that attach to a computer with a USB cable, not the keyboard and trackpad on your laptop. You might already have these; if not they're about $15 each.
5. **An SD card:** 2GB minimum size, 8GB recommended; $6.50. This is a memory card that you'll need to start your home-made computer.
6. **An SD card reader/writer:** $1.20.
7. **An ethernet cable:** You probably have one—it's a cable whose ends look like old phone jacks. If not, you probably have $1.75.
8. **All kinds of other circuit boards, micro-controllers, wires, battery packs, LEDs, etc. (optional):** These are great if you are into using your Raspberry Pi to control lights, sensors, buttons, and even robots.
9. **A wireless USB adaptor (optional):** This tiny part will add Wi-Fi access to the Pi, eliminating the need for the ethernet cable.
10. **A powered USB hub (optional):** The Raspberry Pi has only two USB ports for connecting peripherals like printers, scanners, storage drives, and cameras, but you can add on many more with a hub.

You might also need/want :

- **A TV set:** If you don't own one, you can

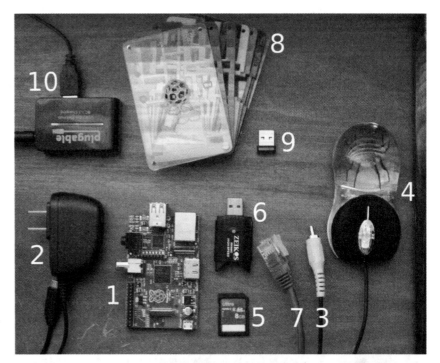

get one for $10 at a thrift store. Or you can use a computer monitor instead.

- **Access to another computer and the internet.**

Putting it all together (see bottom photo on preceding page for a visual of steps 1–6):

1. Take the SD card and the card reader and plug them into a computer with an internet connection. Then download and copy an operating system (OS) to the SD card. I suggest you start with Raspbian Wheezy, available at RaspberryPi.org. ELinux.org has instructions for putting the Mac or Windows OS on an SD card. If those instructions really freak you out, you can cheat and buy an SD card with the OS pre-loaded from eBay.

2. Insert the SD card into the slot on the bottom of the Pi.

3. Plug one end of the ethernet cord into your Pi and the other one into your modem or router (whatever you use to connect to the internet) to get internet access on your Pi.

4. Plug in your mouse and keyboard.

5. Plug your video cable into the Pi, and then into the TV or monitor.

6. Plug in your power cord first to the wall, and then to the Raspberry Pi. The Pi has no on/off button. If everything is set up right, you should be seeing a solid red light labeled PWR, and a flashing green light labeled OK. On the first boot, it might take a minute for anything to appear on the TV/monitor. The first thing you will see is something like this:

This is the kernel (the bridge between the computer's hardware and its interface) booting, and the computer reporting to you exactly what it's doing. Eventually it will stop and ask you to log in.

7. When asked for a username, type "pi" and hit enter. Then you'll be asked for a password; type "raspberry" and hit enter again. Type the password carefully; it won't display on screen. But if you get it wrong, the computer will let you try again. (You can change your username and password later.)

8. You will now see a configuration menu. This is where you set up your Raspberry Pi to recognize your keyboard, display the correct time, etc. Use the tab and arrow keys to move around, and the enter key to pick options. A couple things that might not be self-explanatory: There is an option to "expand root partition to fill SD card." You definitely want to enable this—it will allow you to save more software and files onto your SD card. There's another option to "start desktop on boot." If you want your Raspberry Pi to look like a Windows or Mac startup screen (otherwise known as the graphical user interface, or GUI) when you boot it, enable this one too. If you are using a TV (especially an older one) instead of a monitor with your Pi, enable the option called "change overscan" (if you're using a computer monitor, you'll probably want to disable this to fill the whole screen). If you need more help, there's a good configuration guide over at the eLinux.org Raspberry Pi forums.

9. If you are still in the command-line interface (where it looks like lots of lines of text on the screen, as in the picture at left), type "startx" and press enter to launch the GUI.

And that's it. Welcome to your new computer! At first, the system might feel a little strange to you. That's because you're in Linux, an operating system that you might not have seen before, but which is pretty simple to get the hang of. The Raspberry Pi can run a variety of Linux distributions, but the one I recommend, Raspbian Wheezy, is the best/easiest one to start

with. The great thing about Linux is that basically all the software made for it is free, and it's all open-source, which means everyone has access to the code, so anyone can mess around with how it works.

So, let's say you want a free alternative to Microsoft Word on your Raspberry Pi. You just open up the terminal and type:

```
sudo apt-get update [enter]
sudo apt-get install
libreoffice-writer [enter]
```

and the machine will download the source code from the internet and enable it to run on your computer. There are Linux alternatives to most software you can buy for Windows/Mac. Here is a short list:

- **Photo editing** (e.g., Adobe Photoshop): GIMP (sudo apt-get install gimp)
- **Fast web browsing** (e.g., Google Chrome): Chromium (sudo apt-get install chromium-browser)
- **PDF reader** (e.g., Adobe Acrobat Reader): Evince (sudo apt-get install evince)

So now you've done it! Or at least you've bothered to read to the end of this DIY. Either way, it means you're pretty awesome. And there are tons of awesome people like you out there in the Raspberry Pi community. There's a fanzine (*The MagPi*), an official forum (RaspberryPi.org), and in-person meetups (listed on RaspberryPi.org).

Even if you're not super interested in making your own computer, you can still apply the hacking philosophy to your everyday life. So many things are presented to us as black boxes that are the way they are, and we're not supposed to question why they are that way or to poke around and see if they might work better with a few adjustments. We're not invited to mess with the status quo. But as hackers, it's our responsibility to examine, tinker, and improve. That doesn't just go for computers; it goes for everything. ♦

Dream a Little Dream of Me

Stars shining bright above you, night breezes seem to whisper.
By María Inés

Thanks to Martyna and Sandra for modeling, and to Monika Łuczak for co-styling. All clothing vintage or thrifted.

GIVE UP GIVING UP

How to fight the self-saboteur in your head.
By Danielle

There's something you really want to do right now. Maybe you're thinking of performing on open-mic night at a comedy club. Or applying to your dream school. Or submitting your work to a magazine, journal, website, TV show, etc. Or trying a new sport or musical instrument. Or just asking someone out. It's something you've never done before, and it could get you one step closer to a dream of yours. But right this minute, you're already talking yourself out of it.

How do I know this? Because everybody does it. I myself do it all the time—I think of something that sounds like a good idea, and then find a way to sabotage it before I've even begun.

Why do we do this to ourselves? And why do *we*, especially—meaning girls and women—do this to ourselves? This is a sweeping generalization, and of course there are lots of exceptions and nuances, but rarely have I heard a male friend say, "Eh, they probably won't hire me anyway," or "I just don't think I'd be any good at it." Instead, they tend to try *everything*, and worry about the consequences later. (I think this is why so many of them ended up with broken arms from jumping their BMX bikes over janky ramps made of found wood and rusty nails.) This isn't to say that girls don't engage in risky behavior or make bad decisions, too—but since we were raised in a world that told us not to be too confident or assertive, we tend to second-guess ourselves more than boys, and that makes us say no to a lot of stuff just because we're scared of failing.

It really sucks, because over time, when you've said it over and over a million times, *no* becomes your default. You REALLY want to join the debate team, but you tell yourself you won't be any good at it and everyone will laugh at you. Or you want to learn how to play guitar, but your first thought is how

embarrassing it will be if you mess up a chord progression. Sure, if you talk yourself out of trying something, you are guaranteed not to fail at that thing—but failure is where all the learning occurs! That's the secret to getting good at almost anything: You stink at first, but you don't care—you keep doing it because you enjoy it (or you know you *will* enjoy it once you've gotten better at it). And then, after you've practiced doing it for a while, you get much, *much* better. Maybe you get *great*. You can't get there, though, if you don't give yourself room to fail at the outset.

There are, of course, plenty of times when it's a good idea to say no—you probably don't want to go to a club for the first time without friends, or try to drive stick shift without some practice in an empty parking lot. But when it comes to dyeing your hair or taking an improv class or learning to skate, why are you denying yourself a chance to really shine? And how do you learn to say yes?

You can, in fact, retrain your brain to focus on the positive sides of trying something— you know, like *This is a thing that I want, that might make me really happy*—instead of sabotaging yourself with negative thoughts. Self-sabotage involves a lot of negative self-talk ("What's the point, everyone will think I suck"); you need to counter that with a new kind of self-talk that's about how *great* you are ("It's gonna be so cool when I can shred on that guitar").

First, recognize how often you actually say no to things you secretly want to do. If it helps, write it down every time, or make a check in a notebook or something. Seriously, every time. A couple of years ago I noticed that I was talking myself out of doing a lot of creative things and I wasn't sure why, so I started carrying a tiny notebook around, and every single time I had a negative response to one of my own cool ideas, I drew a little line in it. After seven

days, there were 75 lines in the notebook! That's a lot of opportunities to become happier and more awesome squandered in a single week. (Granted, sometimes I was rejecting the same idea more than once— I don't think of 75 new cool things to do every week!—but that still seems like a lot of naysaying, right?) I never would have thought it was so frequent—it is so easy to underestimate how often you do this. That's why the first thing you have to do is try to keep track. Grab a pen and paper (or a smartphone) and start paying attention to your own brain for a bit. At the end of the day/week/month, look at how many times you've talked yourself out of doing something. Are you astonished? Now that you have a baseline, let's get to work.

Your brain is already really good at talking yourself out of stuff. What you need are powerful counterarguments. So, here are four of the more common self-sabotaging thoughts out there, and some strategies for silencing them:

"SOMEONE HAS ALREADY DONE THIS, AND THEY DID IT MUCH BETTER."

Yes, Steve Jobs was a genius. And you're probably not going to reinvent the personal computer tomorrow. But why should that stop you from trying? Jobs started with a garage and an idea. We still don't have flying cars or teleportation, and *someone* has to do it, so why not you? Your success is not directly related to anyone else's, and their success doesn't mean you have to stop trying. If either of those were the case, there would be only one book and one song in the world, because everyone else would have given up after that.

A great way to get over this type of thinking is to be a little patient with yourself. If you start messing around with computer parts now just to see what you

150

can make, in 10 years you might invent a cellphone that automatically recharges itself using solar power every time you're outside, or a robot that will walk the dog for you, and become a billionaire.

"PEOPLE WILL TELL ME I SUCK, OR LEAVE TERRIBLE COMMENTS."

Kathleen Hanna (of the bands Bikini Kill, Le Tigre, and the Julie Ruin) recently said in an interview in *BOMB* magazine:

Beyoncé isn't Beyoncé because she reads comments on the internet. Beyoncé is in Ibiza, wearing a stomach necklace, walking hand in hand with her hot boyfriend. She's going on the yacht and having a mimosa. She's not reading shitty comments about herself on the internet, and we shouldn't either. I just think, *Would Beyoncé be reading this?* No, she would just delete it, or somebody would delete it for her. What I really need to do is close the computer and then talk back to that voice and say, *Fuck you. I don't give a shit what you think. I'm Beyoncé. I'm going to Ibiza with Jay-Z now, fuck off.* Being criticized is part of the job, but seeking it out isn't. That's our piece to let go.

I mean, obviously *Be Beyoncé* is the best advice for everything in life, but I love everything Kathleen is saying here. It's not about just idolizing Beyoncé for her music/acting/videos/amazingness, it's about recognizing that being influenced by detractors is a *choice*. Time and energy are both finite resources—there's only so much to go around. You can spend them worrying about what other people think, or you can put them into your own projects, or into things that make you feel good.

Whether or not people criticize you is out of your control, anyway, so you have to decide that their commentary doesn't matter (really, it doesn't) and that it won't stop you from eventually ACHIEVING GREATNESS. Then, have so much fun while you're learning this new thing that the people criticizing you look like fools.

In the course of your entire life, you will have much more fun trying 100 new things than being great at one thing.

"I JUST WANT TO TRY SOMETHING NEW WITHOUT EVERYONE FINDING OUT OR HAVING EXPECTATIONS OF ME."

This is a legit worry, because sometimes people will want to project their own feelings onto your experience. Like, if your dad always wanted to learn how to skate, and now you're giving it a shot, he might be ULTRA interested in your progress in an annoying way—buying you a skateboard and loads of gear, following you around with a camera, talking about it at dinner—when you really just wanted to dip a toe in to see if you liked it.

If this is a concern for you, find a way to get started without much input, so you don't have outside pressure to stick with it. Whether or not you end up doing this new thing for the rest of your life is beside the point; it's much more important that you get into the *habit* of *trying stuff*. If you want to skate, can you borrow a skateboard from a friend and practice the next street over? Or, can you save some money to get your own stuff, and put it somewhere where no one will inquire about it for a while? What if you want to write, but you're afraid your ideas are terrible and you don't want any feedback on your early literary experiments? You can always keep a pen-and-ink journal, or hide your diary in a password-protected file on your computer—or, if you need your words to be somewhat public as motivation to write regularly, start an anonymous blog on a free site like Blogger or LiveJournal or WordPress, and disable comments.

"I'M AFRAID I'LL SUCCEED."

This one might seem weird—doesn't everyone *want* to succeed? Why would anyone be *afraid* of success? Well, I can tell you from a lot of personal experience that this is a real fear that can put you in a rut and hold you there forever.

Let's say you get really great at something, or you win a prize, or you try out for something big and get it. You'll probably start to get a lot of attention from other people, which can be uncomfortable enough for some of us on its own, but even worse, some of that attention is going to be of the hater variety. Some people might resent your success and try to make you feel bad about it. In these cases, you should always default to Beyoncé (see above).

But sometimes it's success in and of itself that we're scared of. When you've reached your goal in life, what do you next? Where is there to go from there? And what if you get there, right where you've always wanted to be, and you realize that you're still not happy? Or that you actually *hate* the Ivy League/acting/tennis/being a doctor/fashion/jazz music/etc.? Relax—success isn't some permanent mountaintop that you reach, then you're stuck there. Instead of concentrating on GETTING TO THE TOP, maybe define success as *whatever has the most potential to make you happy*—which will change many, many times throughout your life (sometimes throughout a single day). Keep chasing happiness, not success. That way you'll never feel like there's nowhere left to go.

Concentrating on happiness will also help you brush off other people's expectations. I have a friend who is easily the best photorealistic painter I've ever seen. Everyone expected her to go to art school for college—and she did, for a while, and she hated it. But she loves science! So she switched majors and now works in a biochemical lab. Everyone who sees her paintings in her apartment can't believe she doesn't paint for a living. Some people act like she's betraying her talent by not making it her life's work. But art school taught her that painting is fun for her only when she doesn't *have* to do it every day. You can let yourself be great at something without letting it take over your life forever, just like you can be good at something you grow to dislike, and then you can move on to something new.

And you don't have to be good at that new thing right away, or ever. Give yourself enough time and space to figure out what you like and whether or not *you* feel like sticking with it. Now is not the time to worry about whether you'll be a wild success. Get in the habit of positive self-talk and see where it can take you. That you're trying at all is enough. ♦

THE WORLD IS BOUND WITH SECRET KNOTS: *AN INTERVIEW WITH DAVID WILSON*

We talk to him about the Museum of Jurassic Technology, life's general impermanence, and being open to the possibility of wonder.

By Tavi

The Museum of Jurassic Technology looks like a humble little storefront on a street in Culver City, California. Upon entering, however, you find yourself in a maze of oddities—a row of microscopes on mosaics made of butterfly-wing scales, a hall of flower X-rays, tiny sculptures displayed literally in the eyes of needles (the sculptor timed his carvings by his heartbeat). At first it feels like being transported to another world, until you see what a loving representation it is of the wonders of our own. You might suspect some of the displays are made-up, or that footnotes, names, and the plaques and pamphlets sitting in the gift shop are fictionalized, until you come to love the ways in which the museum inspires that very act of questioning. Lawrence Weschler wrote in *Mr. Wilson's Cabinet of Wonder*, his 1995 book about this place, "It's that very shimmer, the capacity for such delicious confusion, Wilson sometimes seems to suggest, that may constitute the most blessedly wonderful thing about being human."

Wilson is David Hildebrand Wilson, who founded the museum in the late 1980s. Since then he's lived with his wife and daughter in an adjoining trailer and run the museum with the help of volunteers, visitor donations, and grants. I noticed while we were speaking that he would make these grandiose statements about life and humanity, but they were always prefaced with "I think." Or he would describe something, and find a better word for what he was trying to say two or three times, and list them all. You could hear his brain working. It brought back the sense of affection for uncertainty that I felt when I visited his museum in the summer, the same feeling I found when I read Weschler's book in the fall, and the same one I was overwhelmed with by the time we finished this interview. I might have burst into tears once we hung up? I DUNNO, YOU MAY JUST HAVE TO ~WONDER~. Read on, curious one.

TAVI Thank you so much for doing this.

DAVID WILSON Oh yeah, sure, I'm honored. Rookie looks great. How long have you been doing that?

Thank you so much. I started it September of 2011.

Can you tell what the viewership is?

I can, but I don't. I think if I look at the numbers it messes with my head.

It's funny—I'm the same way. If people write things about the museum I never read 'em. I'd rather not see it somehow.

I was reading an interview with Stephen Colbert yesterday, and he said reading about yourself is poison—even if it's positive attention, it just brings you outside of your head.

Oh yeah, it's easily as bad if it's positive as it is when it's negative. It's better to just avoid what you're doing and do it without a lot of external input. It can throw you off course.

How would you describe the museum to someone who's never heard of it?

I think typically what we say is that we're a small museum of natural history, history of science, history of art, and then everything else that comes along. We're inspired by older museums—200, 300 years ago, a museum wasn't a museum of a particular thing, it was a museum of everything. We don't think *all* museums should be that, but we think there's a place for that kind of museum, kind of an encyclopedic museum.

Would you say then that there's anything in particular that unifies everything you have on display?

There are definitely underlying, unifying principles to what we do, but sometimes they're kind of hard to discern, or hard to define. We have a motto, which you actually almost never see in the museum, but it's "Un translatio nature," which means "nature as metaphor." That doesn't really sum things up so much, but it actually is meaningful to us, because the kinds of things we like to put in the museum tend to be either natural phenomena or man-made—which, you know, there's no real distinction between what's man-made and what's natural, because humankind is pretty natural as far as I can tell. We find ourselves gravitating toward material and phenomena that have meaning in and of themselves, and that also suggest other levels of meaning—kind of radiating spheres of meaning.

It's interesting what you said about the line between man-made and the natural world being sort of blurry. To many people—and I always kind of thought this until I went to your museum—science and art are mutually exclusive. Some say it's science's job to tell humans that we're not important and art's job to declare that we are. How do you make them work together?

Essentially it goes back to a 17th century or even earlier designation of artificialia and naturalia—what is artificial and what's natural. It's kind of an act of hubris or pride, I think, to think things that are made by humankind are in some way out of the natural order. We're certainly, absolutely, profoundly part of the great glittering chain of being. I mean, look at

birds' nests—are they artificialia or are they naturalia? A bird makes this gorgeous nest, and that's considered a natural artifact—so why is that different for humans?

I read that you had this sort of epiphany in your late teens…

There was a moment when I was probably just turning 19—and it was through nothing I did, there just kind of came to me an opening of my mind and my understanding. It was inexplicable, but it gave a level of meaning to my understanding of life that I had never had previously. That experience lasted over a period of days. Towards the end of it, I became afraid that… I was just very concerned to not lose the understanding that came as part of that experience. And really, that moment has had a profound effect on how I [have] spent the rest of my life and spent the whole of my life's energy.

Do you feel like you've done justice to that realization?

I don't know that you can ever do justice, but I think I've spent the rest of my life kind of dancing around those understandings, because those understandings are really…I don't know how to describe it other than a sense of…meaning. That kind of understanding that things were exactly as they should be, and that there was infinite and intricate meaning in the order of things. It's really utterly incomprehensible. That doesn't really help. I don't know how else to describe it.

I think that in itself says enough, the fact that it is indescribable. What were you like as a teenager? What were the biggest influences for you at that time?

After that [epiphany], there was a certain change in my external demeanor. Prior to that, I had been somewhat introverted, but I still had a pretty active social life. But after that experience I became more introverted and spent a great deal more time reading and trying to delve into areas of human activity or natural phenomena that

reflected the kind of understanding that had come to me. I began to read Eastern philosophy—and this was not too easy to find at the time, in 1965; the culture has changed enormously since then. I also became interested in medieval times. I felt that… [*Tavi's dog won't stop barking*] Who is your dog?

I know, I've been quietly typing all-caps emails to my dad asking if he can let her in—

[*Laughs*] No, it's nice!

It's driving me crazy! I'm upstairs and she's right outside by my window, and I've been trying to quietly ask my dad—

You don't have to quietly do anything! You can go tell him if you want to!

I think I will if you don't mind; really quickly I'll go let the dog in!

Take your time!

[*A few minutes pass.*]

Problem solved. I'm sorry about that.

[*Laughs*] Do you live in Chicago?

I live in a suburb just outside, Oak Park.

So what do you do? Is this your full-time occupation, doing Rookie?

I mean, I'm 16 and I go to high school, but yeah, I mostly work on Rookie.

Is there an economic reality to it?

[*Laughs*] Unfortunately, yes!

There are so many different economies in the world. What we think of as money is just one of many. There are all these different kinds of rewards.

What have you found to be most rewarding about your work?

It's just, like, inexplicably rewarding on all fronts. I think ultimately the payment comes from watching people experience the museum. It's wonderful to go in and kind of discreetly be in the space with them. That's the primary reward.

Have there been any particularly memorable reactions?

An infinite number. I mean, yesterday I was up in the space-dog room [a room full of painted portraits of all the dogs who have ever been to outer space] and we just, as of this weekend, started to run in our theater a film that we made over the last couple of weeks. A few of us at the museum went to Central Asia, to Turkmenistan, to Pakistan, and very wonderful places quite far away, and shot a film, which we cut together far more quickly than normal. A middle-aged woman came out [of the theater] and said, "Sir, I just wanted to say that that film spoke to me in a way that I absolutely needed to hear right now." And you could tell it had an important effect, it communicated in some way something—and you could see this in her eyes—something that she really needed to hear. There was something in there that had true meaning for her, and I think that kind of thing is just exactly what you do all the work for.

How often do people recognize you, as you're trying to discreetly roam around? Did that change after the book?

The book didn't have that much of an effect. We actually didn't love the book. We love the writer, Ren Weschler—he's a wonderful human being and he's gotten to be a really good friend, and whenever he's in Los Angeles he stays in the adjoined trailer. He first wrote about the museum for a magazine article, in *Harper's*, and we thought, *This'll be gone in a month. This too shall pass.* And then a month or two later he phoned me and said, "Wonderful news—we've got a book deal!" And my thought was, *What do you mean, "we"?* [*Laughs*] There were certain things about his approach to our work that we felt were limiting, rather than expanding. But that was a long time ago, a decade ago or more. And it's been fine—it's just one in a great many events that have happened in our history. And not so many people actually read the book. We see about 25,000 people a year here, and I think five percent or three percent of them have ever heard of the book. So it didn't really change things so much.

I was also curious about the display of Ricky Jay's decaying dice. Of all the things you could get from a magician to show in a museum, why did you choose decaying dice?

I think that's a good example, in a way, of the kind of material that appeals to us. We had always wanted to have a gem and mineral hall, like, you know, they have at the Field Museum—that glorious gem and mineral hall—or the Museum of Natural History in New York. But we would probably never be able to collect enough in the way of gems and minerals to be truly significant. But then somehow this little hall [where all the dice are displayed], with the way that it's lit, looks just like a gem and mineral hall. We *love* that. So that's one level on which the dice are appealing to us. Another level is that there's a metaphorical overtone. Dice imply luck, so that exhibit is sometimes called "Rotten Luck," because, you know, decaying dice—there's kind of a play on words there. Many of those dice are loaded dice that con artists use to gain wealth unfairly, and there's something about that that appealed to us, too. And then there's the poetry of the decaying aspect of the dice, and decaying luck—because all things pass, and knowing that and holding that in mind (which is hard for

people of the age that you're mostly talking to, 'cause when you're at that age everything seems to be in front of you and possibilities seem limitless) is also really important for people. To understand that none of this is forever—which is maybe part of what happened to me when I was that age.

In a strange way I think that's a very comforting thought. Probably because just daily interactions give me so much embarrassment.

Yeah, and anxiety. To have that longer view, where you understand that all of this is impermanent, can be comforting. Liberating, actually. Anecdotes are great, so I'll tell you an anecdote. Just last night I was listening to the music of a person named Gurdjieff—do you know who he is?

No.

Gurdjieff was a philosopher at the turn of the century through the mid-20th century. Well, he was primarily a philosopher, but I recently learned that he also wrote music. Someone gave us a recording of some beautiful harmonium music that he wrote, and we've been listening to that. And that got me to go back and read about him—I had read about him before, but I wanted to refresh my memory. And—I wish I could find this quote and read it to you—he was saying essentially the same thing, that one of the most important things that he could offer was...wait, I found it. This is what he wants people to know: "Every one of those unfortunates during the process of existence should constantly sense and be cognizant of the inevitability of his own death as well as of the death of everyone upon whom his eyes or attention rests." So he's saying the same thing, which is the same as saying "memento mori"—you know, "remember death." There's really a lot to that. To hold death close to you at all times is *the* thing that can give meaning to life. How did we get started talking about this? [*Laughs*]

I don't know, but it's great. Oh, we were talking about the dice.

Exactly. And things going away.

You have this appreciation for these curious things, and that appreciation could've been expressed in many mediums that are more convenient. You could've been a writer or a photographer or just stuck to filmmaking. But instead it's expressed through this very inventive academic writing, and this questioning of what authority a museum has, and why—

Why a museum?

Yeah, or did it feel like you had no choice?

I don't know that I could say that it felt like I had no choice, but when that choice presented itself, it was an enormous relief. Because I'd always been looking for that, but it took *decades* to find it. I had begun in natural sciences in college, but then I went on and did filmmaking, and so I was torn between these two worlds—the world of natural science and the just amazing wonders, the kind of incomprehensible wonders, of all of that; and then [the world of] display and putting things into the world and being able to have an impact on people with what you put into the world. I knew I really loved that as well. So I really, really struggled with that [dichotomy] for decades, and I tried all kinds of things and could never really find anything that felt right. Until one day it dawned on me, like being run over by a freight train, that what I wanted to do was have a museum.

Do you ever feel like there is nothing left out there that could excite you, or that there is a shortage of things worth marveling at?

[*Laughs*] Completely the opposite. I have never even had that thought. That thought has never formulated in my mind. [*Laughs some more*]

That's very reassuring! I mean, I am a generally negative person, and I have to have a lot of energy to get my head to a place where I can keep an eye out for something that might be beauti-

ful or might spark my curiosity. I have no doubt that there are amazing things in the world, but often my pessimism makes me doubt that I am capable of appreciating them. This sense of wonder that you possess: Do you have to nurture it? Do you have to actively wrap your brain around it? How do you keep from feeling jaded?

[*Very long pause*] I'm up in the courtyard right now, and all the doves are out and looking at me, and it's great. They're not usually…they're all down low. We're not open today, and so I think during opening days they usually fly up high 'cause they get scared, but now they're all down towards the bottom, and it's just *great*. I *love* the doves. [*Pauses*] I think that everything in life comes down to, essentially, self and not self. In other words, understanding your existence or all of existence as atomized individuals versus seeing the whole— understanding your place, as an organism, in the whole great chain of being.

In my experience, singularity and isolation and jadedness are all parts of the same thing—they're all reflections of being limited by an understanding of yourself as separate and isolated from things around you. The more [you experience] a more permeable relation to other people and other things, the more naturally that sense of wonder comes. I think if you allow it, it can happen naturally over time.

In a lot of ways, the age of [your readers] is one of the hardest times in a person's life. I mean, they keep ramping up the difficulty in life as much as you can stand it, whoever has their hand on the dials. But [the period between the ages of] 14 and, depending on the person, 19 or 21 or something is excruciatingly difficult, primarily because of those issues—self, and having to establish a sense of self.

And feeling isolated in some way or another.

Oh, self and self-isolation are kind of synonymous. But I think you have to go through it. I don't think there's any way around it. And it's hard.

Well, that's a comforting thing. I just try to remember that everyone over the age of 20…I mean, it seems so impossible, but so many people have done it.

And most of those people have survived it.

I don't know if I'll leave this in, but I mean, for a while I was able to find my way around all of those general feelings, to keep myself busy, and then this fall, it just totally—

Went really hard.

Yeah. It was so strangely surprising. Like, I was always able to come home and read and watch movies and keep myself distracted, and suddenly it wasn't enough. Then kind of two things happened. One, I started listening to Fiona Apple.

[*Laughs*]

And then another was that I read the Weschler book, and I know you have ambivalence towards it, but—

Yeah, but I mean, don't let that affect you.

Just finding out the whole story of what inspired what you're doing, and the way that it all came together for you, and the sensibility that you bring to what you do, was extremely heartening, and…I don't know, if not for those two things, I don't know what would've happened. But thank you for what you're doing.

Oh yeah, sure. It's our job. But I think one of the best things you can do is just, as much as possible, to give yourself over to those activities that, in the long run, are aimed at really and truly a greater good. In more than just a knowable, physical, superficial way. But that's the most powerful way of doing it, to just *work*. Are you getting enough material to write anything?

Yes, thank you.

OK, and in case you're writing it and you need something else, just call again. ♦

DECEMBER 2012: FAITH

I haven't been writing on this site much lately. Recently I've felt so overwhelmed by the absolute horror that is EVER TALKING, EVER, that I've retreated in as many areas of life as possible. I wish I could say I've also resisted becoming a bad friend, but I have been so positive that everybody is absolutely disgusted by every stupid thing I have said or done in the past and that I am bound to say or do in the future that I have stopped talking to most of them. I also wish I could say I've avoided becoming a lazy student, but I keep getting distracted from the education part of school by noticing how creepy people can look when they're smiling, and how sad other people can look when they feel they're missing out.

This is a pretty good problem to have, because the thing I am afraid of (being alive), the vast majority of people manage day after day. Many of them are even happy. Many of them have more reason to be sad than I do. And when I consider that I am just one of billions of people on earth and how tiny we all are and what a brief moment in time this is and…HOLY SHIT THAT MEANS THIS IS THE ONLY TIME I GET HOW DO I MAKE THE BEST OF IT WITHOUT BEING A BAD PERSON? And how does it work that I think life is the worst, but I also don't want it to end? AND, why don't I have a more sophisticated analogy for this than how I felt when I finished the one and only season of E!'s *Pretty Wild*?

See? A really pretty good problem. But if a problem is big enough to keep someone from being a good person, it's worth examining.

In an attempt to talk to some people, I asked the Rookie staffers: "What do you do when you're so mortified by the daily embarrassment of living that you no longer want to interact with people?"

They had a lot of good advice ("Talk to a tree"—Jamia; "Hang out with a cat"—Kimberly). Lola sent me this quotation from Lester Bangs that felt so absolutely *right* that I copied it into my journal:

Just for the record, I would like it to be known by anybody who cares that I don't think life is a perpetual dive…I suspect almost every day that I'm living for nothing, I get depressed and I feel self-destructive and a lot of the time I don't like myself. What's more, the proximity of other humans often fills me with overwhelming anxiety, but I also feel that this precarious sentience is all we've got and, simplistic as it may seem, it's a person's duty to the potentials of his own soul to make the best of it. We're all stuck on this often miserable earth where life is essentially tragic, but there are glints of beauty and bedrock joy that come shining through from time to precious time to remind anybody who cares to see that there is something higher and larger than ourselves…I am talking about a sense of wonder about life itself and the feeling that there is some redemptive factor you must at least *search* for until you drop dead of natural causes.

I don't know what my religious deal is completely, but I have a lot of faith. I am sure that there is no shortage of goodness out there. I'm sure that potential and possibility and the fact that something can exist solely as an idea are enough for me. I'm also sure that soon enough, I'll retreat into extreme hermitry once more. By then hopefully the phrase "extreme hermitry" will have caught on and become the title of a reality show that airs on E! the same time *Pretty Wild* used to. And I will love that show's every embarrassment and make the most of it while it lasts. Just like I did with *Pretty Wild*. (And also life, if that wasn't clear.)

So, this month's theme is Faith. Happy holidays, and thank you, as always, for being here.

LOVE,
TAVI

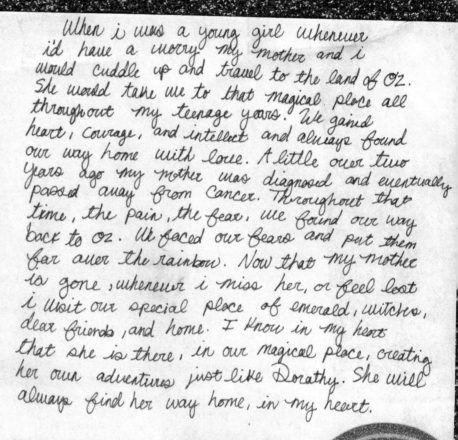

When i was a young girl whenever i'd have a worry my mother and i would cuddle up and travel to the land of OZ. She would take me to that magical place all throughout my teenage years. We gained heart, courage, and intellect and always found our way home with love. A little over two years ago my mother was diagnosed and eventually passed away from Cancer. Throughout that time, the pain, the fear, we found our way back to OZ. We faced our fears and put them far over the rainbow. Now that my mother is gone, whenever i miss her, or feel lost i visit our special place of emerald, witches, dear friends, and home. I know in my heart that she is there, in our magical place, creating her own adventures just like Dorathy. She will always find her way home, in my heart.

MISS YOU MOST OF ALL

A photo tribute to the ultimate comfort.
By Allyssa

Thanks to Sandy, Lauren, Nicole, Jessie, Jake, and Mike for modeling.

ON BEING A LATE BLOOMER

Success doesn't happen overnight.
By Emma S. Playlist lettering by Sonja. Tarot card photos by Eleanor, collage and illustration by Minna.

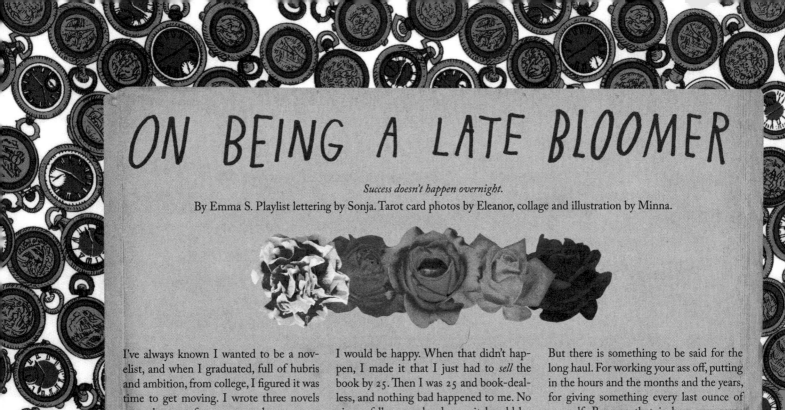

I've always known I wanted to be a novelist, and when I graduated, full of hubris and ambition, from college, I figured it was time to get moving. I wrote three novels over the next few years, each one more complicated and convoluted than the last. It perhaps should have been a red flag that my then–literary agent and I spent more time talking about who would star in the movie adaptation than we did about the book itself, but I was 22! What did I care? I was going to be an overnight success.

I was not an overnight success.

All three books were rejected. When I say they were rejected, I mean that my literary agents (I had two during this period) sent copies of my books to scores of editors, and every single one said no, over and over. This process lasted approximately four years. Four years is the time it takes to go all the way through high school! Some editors read all three books, rejecting me three times in a row. When I remember this period in my life, I picture those Whac-A-Mole games at carnivals, where a little furry badger pops up out of the board and you swing an oversize hammer at its head, and then it pops up out of a new hole and you whack it again, and again, and again. Every single hammer connected with my little badger head.

I kept popping back up, though. I was bruised and disappointed, but not defeated. What did those editors know? I was confident that I was a hard worker and a good writer, and that I had things to say. I set a deadline for myself—as long as I published a book by the time I was 25,

I would be happy. When that didn't happen, I made it that I just had to *sell* the book by 25. Then I was 25 and book-dealless, and nothing bad happened to me. No pianos fell on my head, no witchy old ladies cursed me, I didn't suddenly die in my sleep. Most important, nothing happened to my drive to write—there was no age limit on my imagination or creativity. This was a revelation.

The actress Susan Lucci became my guiding light. Lucci played Erica Kane on the soap opera *All My Children* for more than 40 years. I loved Erica Kane, the most powerful woman in all of Pine Valley, and so did the Daytime Emmy voters. For nearly two decades, Susan Lucci was nominated for best actress—but year after year, she lost. Susan Lucci lost that title *18 times* before finally winning in 1999. When she finally won, the entire crowd stood and clapped for several minutes. I wanted to be the Susan Lucci of novelists, so dogged in my pursuit of my goal that by the time I got there, everyone would be on their feet and clapping for me. Not necessarily because they loved my book (which would have been wonderful, of course), but because they knew how long I'd been trying and failing, how dedicated I was, how much I wanted it. Because they felt I'd earned it.

Now, of course there is something completely ludicrous about that idea—no one *deserves* a book deal or a Daytime Emmy; those kinds of things are based not on merit or character but on some equation of popularity and perceived earning potential.

But there is something to be said for the long haul. For working your ass off, putting in the hours and the months and the years, for giving something every last ounce of yourself. Because that is how you come to understand why you haven't been successful so far, and how you learn what you need to know to get there. And this kind of hard-earned success feels bigger than the overnight kind. If Susan Lucci had won the first Emmy she was nominated for, I'm sure it wouldn't have meant as much to her, and she wouldn't have gotten that standing O. And if I had sold a book back when I was 22, I would have taken it for granted—back then I thought that I "deserved" success just because I *wanted* it. I thought that the writing life was going to be easy, like living inside a bouncy castle, with no sharp edges anywhere.

By the time I finally sold my first novel at the ripe old age of 30, five years after my initial deadline, I'd done a lot more living—I'd gone to graduate school to study writing more earnestly, moved in with my boyfriend, married my boyfriend, had a bunch of jobs, made new friends, moved out of New York and then back—and when it happened, it made sense. When I got the call that the book had sold, I felt a tidal wave of joy, gratitude, and relief. I cried for days, more happy tears than I thought were possible. Because I didn't just feel "lucky"—though of course luck was involved. I felt proud of myself, because I knew everything that had gone into making this moment happen.

THE EMPRESS.

JUDGEMENT.

THE HIEROPHANT

THE DEVIL

THE HERMIT.

THE CHARIOT.

THE HIGH PRIESTESS

THE FOOL.

TEMPERANCE.

When that book came out, even though it had taken me years of work and rejection to get there, people acted like I had come out of nowhere, like an "overnight success." But look closer at any "overnight success" and you'll invariably find years of hard work. I recently watched *Part of Me*, the Katy Perry documentary, and was struck by how long it took for her to get to the moment when "I Kissed a Girl" became a hit—there were years of getting rejected by labels, getting dropped from labels, being told over and over that she would never make it, that no one wanted to hear the kind of music she made. Yeah, she was 24 when her first single hit, which is not "late" by anyone's calendar, but she'd been recording music since she was 17. Or look at Leonard Cohen—he didn't release his first album until the age of 32. Julia Child didn't get her famous television show until she was 51. Wallace Stevens didn't publish any poems until he was 38. A.C. Bhaktivedanta Swami Prabhupada founded the Hare Krishna movement when he was 70. Most of us will not be child stars or wunderkinds. Some of us will take a very long time to be successful at what we want to do, or to even know what we want to do. There is time for all of us to figure out what it is we want to do—and to change our minds over and over again, if necessary. No one is timing you.

There's a saying that I like, which has been attributed to both the Roman philosopher Seneca AND Oprah: "Luck is what happens when preparation meets opportunity." Yeah, it's cheesy, but it also happens to be true. So much of what goes on in your life is beyond your control. All you can do is work as hard as possible to get ready for those moments that might change everything. I don't believe in God, but I do believe in myself, and in karma, and in having patience, and in working my ass off. Being human is a complicated business, and when one issue in life (WHEN WILL I PUBLISH A NOVEL?!?) is resolved, others spring forward to take its place. It's important to pause long enough to feel truly grateful for whatever goodness has occurred—and then, yup, get back to work. ☙

HANGING OUT WITH JULIET CAPULET
BY ELEANOR

1. TALK SHOW HOST — RADIOHEAD
2. HAUNTIN' ME — KEEP SHELLY IN ATHENS
3. ANGEL — GRIMES
4. THE BEST PERSON I KNOW — CAT'S EYES
5. ONLY LOVE CAN BREAK YOUR HEART — ATLAS SOUND
6. REAL LOVE — BEACH HOUSE
7. BONFIRE — MEMORYHOUSE
8. OMINOUS CLOUD — BROADCAST
9. LOVE WILL TEAR US APART — JOY DIVISION
10. ROMEO HAD JULIETTE — LOU REED
11. BLOWN A WISH — MY BLOODY VALENTINE
12. PLAY DEAD — BJÖRK
13. FEATHER OF LEAD — LAMPSHADE

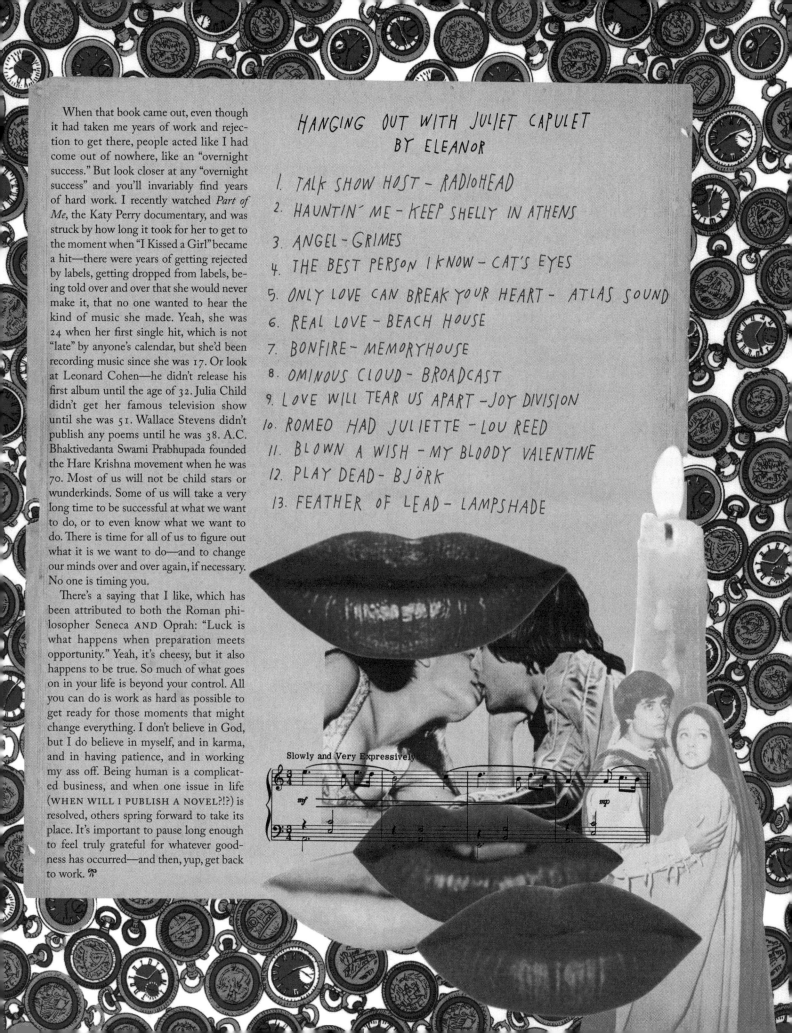

Slowly and Very Expressively

CITY OF ANGELS

They walk among us.
By Petra

Thanks to Sarah, Jacqueline, Brittney,
and Danielle for modeling.

I WANT TO BELIEVE

I have three main beliefs: science, feminism, and Allah. I still haven't reconciled them.

By Shanzeh Khurram

To say that I'm confused about religion would be an understatement. In just the past few years, I've gone from Muslim to agnostic to super-religious Muslim to now…when I don't really know what I am. Sometimes I feel like I should just forget about God and make a shrine to John Green and worship him instead.

I grew up in Pakistan, where almost everyone is a Muslim. My parents are Muslims, as are most of my friends, neighbors, teachers, and relatives. I went to a secular school in Karachi, but our teachers frequently gave religious lectures, and we'd start each day by reciting verses from the Qur'an. I was raised Muslim too, and for most of my life I never questioned the existence of God. I had been taught to believe, and I did—until I was around 14.

That was when I started having doubts about God. Where did he come from? Why did he create this world? All faiths say they are the one true religion, so who's right and who's wrong? These questions bothered me more and more with each passing day.

At the same time, I was getting really into science, which teaches me not to accept anything as true without solid proof. I like graphs and statistics and test results—things that are objective and quantifiable. I want detailed reports published in reputable scientific journals. I want full disclosure. I'm a fan of the scientific method.

And you know what is probably the most unprovable thing in the whole world? The existence of God/Allah/a higher power. Faith in God is necessarily blind faith, which cannot be quantified, and my science-loving brain does not like that at all. Believing in something with no proof makes me feel like an idiot, a fool. I would never believe in paranormal activity or hypnosis, so why should God be any different?

By my 15th birthday, I had become a total agnostic. But this didn't sit well with me, either. Agnosticism is at heart a belief in uncertainty, and I like being absolutely certain about what I believe. I found that when I didn't believe in God, I didn't believe in anything—I couldn't make sense of the suffering that I saw around me, and I just felt scared about life. This led to a full-blown existentialist crisis: I thought the world was absurd and meaningless and that nothing was real and that maybe it would be best if everyone just died and the world ended.

At 17, desperate to re-establish some meaning in my life, I enrolled in some orthodox Islamic classes. Fundamentalist Islam is nothing if not certain, and this kind of absolute faith calmed me, for a time. During this period, I refused to talk to guys and threw away all my CDs (OK, I just packed them into boxes—let's not get extreme!), because fundamentalists interpret the Qur'an as forbidding music as well as friendship between unrelated women and men (you're not even supposed to make eye contact with the "opposite" sex). I followed all the rules zealously, thinking the more of them I abided by, the closer I'd get to God.

After a month of super-strict religious adherence, I started to hate God. I thought he was harsh and sexist and that his rules were ridiculous and arbitrary. I was miserable without my music and without any fun in my life (I had decided that fun was sinful too, and that God would punish me for having it). In my desperation to find God, I had embarked on a rigid path that made me feel less connected to him, and to myself.

Most devout Muslims consider it a fard, or obligation, for all women to wear some kind of headscarf, and I did try, during this period, to wear a hijab. Before I go on, I think it's important to point out that the hijab is not the tool of oppression that most non-Muslims think it is. A lot of moderate Muslims wear the hijab too, by choice, and many fundamentalist Muslims are total feminists—in fact, for some Muslim feminists, wearing the veil is a feminist act because it prevents people from seeing them as just bodies and from judging them on appearance. By this point in my life I'd started identifying as a feminist, and I'd read so many stories by and about women who had found strength in the hijab that I thought it might do the same for me.

I dug out one of my regular old scarves and asked a friend to show me how to fashion it into a veil. The moment I finished tying it around my head, I burst into tears. I felt hidden, confined, restricted. I cried again when my father saw me in my new garb and started laughing. (My parents were, and still are, moderate Muslims, who are guided by a more liberal interpretation of the Qur'an and don't believe that wearing the hijab is necessary.) I cried all the way to school, where everyone gawked when I walked in—the self-proclaimed agnostic and outspoken feminist was now a hijabi? One of my friends even came up to me and told me to stop pretending.

The thing was, my friend was right. I *was* pretending. I had always hated it when Muslims said stuff like "a woman's modesty is her beauty"—it sounds to me like an attempt to control women, to keep us hidden and ashamed of our physical beings. And that's how I felt in my makeshift hijab—

not liberated but constrained. I stopped wearing it after just five days.

I know a lot of Westerners see Islam as a misogynistic faith, and it can be, just like Christianity or Judaism or Mormonism or really any other organized structure in our patriarchal society. And, just like almost any major religion, Islam is often used to reinforce traditional gender roles—by, for example, putting men in positions of authority over women, teaching that men and women are fundamentally different, and/or telling women to be good wives and mothers, subservient to their husbands/fathers/male family members, so that God will be pleased with them. I can't get with any organization that would limit a woman's choices so narrowly. Sometimes I wonder if religion is just a tool that those in power have used over the centuries to oppress and pacify the masses.

On the other hand, it was Islam that gave women the right to work, own property, and divorce all the way back in the seventh century, hundreds of years before the West granted women such freedoms. Some of the best scholars in the early days of Islam were women, like the prophet Muhammad's wife Aisha. The problem is that too many of today's Muslims dismiss the rights that were given to women from day one.

I've come to see the Qur'an as something like poetry—its meaning changes depending on how it's interpreted. Patriarchal readings of it will produce patriarchal results, and since I live in a patriarchal culture, those interpretations were mostly what I was exposed to growing up. But there are plenty of people—including the scholars Amina Wadud, Khaled Abou El Fadl, and Leila Ahmed—who interpret the book in a liberal, progressive, feminist way. Their readings make sense to me—a God who created women can't be sexist.

In the past few years I have had approximately 74,843,458,259 thoughts regarding Islam, God, feminism, and science. I've taken courses at orthodox Islamic learning centers and have read endless books of Islamic teachings. I've also researched most of the other big religions, but somehow I always return to Islam. That might be be-cause I was raised Muslim, but it's also the faith that feels best to me when I'm really being receptive to God. When I'm able to let go of my skepticism and believe in him, it is the most empowering, freeing experience ever. When I fast and pray in that state, I do so out of love for, not fear of, God, and prayer nourishes my soul in a way that I can't rationally explain. I feel a strange joy that is both ecstatic and tranquil, and my heart feels at rest.

Today I find myself wavering between a more moderate version of Islam and agnosticism—between God and science. Despite all my natural skepticism, I yearn for God. I don't want to be super-religious anymore, but I don't want to be an atheist either. I just want to connect to a greater purpose.

I have come to believe that Islam and science might actually be compatible. A lot of the early Muslims, like Averroes, Ibn Yunus, and Avicenna, were pioneers in the fields of science and medicine. The Qur'an also touches on such topics as embryonic growth and planetary orbits, which suggests to me that even though science can't prove God exists, it can be used to explain his creation. I look at everything he made with amazement and awe—everything from a blade of grass to the northern lights inspires a reverential sense of wonder in me and makes me feel connected to a higher power. Science and religion share this sense of awe and reverence in the face of the universe.

I'm also getting more comfortable with the idea of believing in something without seeing proof. After all, everything that science has demonstrated to be true was once totally unproven, but that didn't make it any less real. And there are a lot of things that science can't explain, like the placebo effect and why we yawn, but science and religion combined can help provide a better understanding of this universe. I can believe in science and religion at the same time.

I think it might even be possible to balance those beliefs while maintaining every bit of my feminism. I'm hoping this won't feel like a juggling act, but rather that those three threads can be woven together to make my connections to everything in the universe, and beyond it, that much stronger. When I attended lectures at or-thodox Islamic centers, I was surprised by how many of the women there were doctors, and one of my teachers, a woman who wore the niqab, cited scientific research when explaining parts of the Qur'an. These women are proof (ha) that I don't have to stop believing in anything I don't want to.

I haven't gotten where I want to be yet. I still have doubts about the existence of God. And I still struggle with some of the more misogynistic strains of Islam. But I'm getting closer. I am still trying to find my way back to God. I know that I will not find him through logic, but by following my heart. I believe that it will get me there.

LITERALLY THE BEST THING EVER: GOD

The most worshipful LTBTE ever.
Writing by Jamia, collage on this page by Beth.

My friend Meggan, a feminist theologian, once called me a "divining rod," by which she didn't mean that I can find water or other hidden treasures buried in the ground, but that I have an ability that seems just as uncanny—no matter where I am, whatever the situation, I can always find God.

When I was three years old, my mother taught me to sing spirituals and my father taught me to recite the Lord's Prayer, and those things taught me how to pray. I haven't missed a day of prayer since. I always start by thanking the most holy, the goddess, nature, the divine, and the big kahuna (who is so big they have countless names, including God, Allah, Shangdi, YHWH, Yahweh, Nana, Igbo, Elohim, Zhu, Hu, etc. etc. etc.) for the blessing of living another day.

God has always just made sense to me. The same way that some people feel sure that there is nothing beyond this physical world, that there's no such thing as a soul, and that all that awaits us after death is decomposition, I have no doubt that my soul has always known life beyond the body it currently inhabits, and that everything in our world is connected to and by something bigger, smarter, and stronger than we are. I've experienced this force when marveling at gleams of white light dancing on palmetto trees and hearing my grandma and aunties singing gospel music in church and in the kitchen. I've also felt it during dark times: deaths of loved ones, natural and unnatural disasters. I've bumped up against doubt many times and wondered how to make sense of how the merciful, compassionate, and loving God I believe in could allow bad things to happen— and I've come to accept my crises of faith as another pathway to learning about and connecting with that which is holy. I embrace that alienation as an essential part of my faith. Throughout all of it, God has walked with me, showing up to show me my blessings and to hold on to me during heartbreaks. My relationship with God makes me feel like I have an all-knowing, nonjudgmental, free therapist, teacher, and friend who listens to my soul 24/7 and never rejects me. This feeling has never wavered. My faith in religious institutions, however, has.

I grew up in a politically progressive household, but freedom of religion was not really an option for me growing up. I was expected to attend church every Sunday. I won extra points if I got up early for Sunday School. I was taught about "sins" (i.e., all the things that supposedly piss God off) and was told that being a "good girl" who honored her elders, never lied or cheated, and was kind to everyone was the surest path to heaven. One of my earliest memories is being dragged out of our Baptist church when I was very small for wailing from my pew after sitting still on a hard wooden seat in itchy tights and too-tight Mary Janes for three hours. My parents gave me a time-out and I never acted up in church again, but it wasn't long before I started to seriously question the confines, both physical and behavioral, that the church seemed to draw around worshipping God. It seemed to me, even as a kid, that God represented freedom rather than repression and restraint. I spent my childhood confused about why I was "bad" for not wanting to go to services even though I spent my private time reading the Bible, praying, and trying to live my life by the Golden Rule.

That confusion was the beginning of a long process of searching and questioning. I had always resisted the idea that I would only be saved if I conformed to other people's expectations of, and limitations on, me. I knew that my personal relationship with the highest power was more holy than anything I was being told in church. I started to look at the church's teachings with a more discerning eye, filtering what I was being told through my own strong sense of spirituality. I accepted the ideas that I believed in—like love, justice, service, and compassion—and rejected anything that smacked of injustice or bigotry, like homophobia and sexism. I liked talking to God about my most intimate yearnings and challenges without needing anyone else's validation that my approach was "right." With God, I could always be myself.

From the moment I let go of my blind loyalty to institutional rules and rituals, I became more comfortable with letting the divine spark within guide me in the right direction. It has never steered me wrong. My spiritual path feels like space exploration; the possibilities are as vast as the universe and as innumerable as the stars.

For a long time, though, I hid my spirituality. I was afraid that my secular liberal friends would think my beliefs were silly, and that my conservative Christian friends and family would worry that my open-mindedness would damn me to hell. I recall an atheist ex-boyfriend telling me that he was "surprised someone so smart could be so naïve." It annoyed him that I always believed that God was guiding me when he knew for sure that nothing exists but the cold reason of blood, bone, and dirt.

But then, a few years ago, I joined several interfaith women's circles as well as an intergenerational community that affirmed my right to my own distinct religious experience. Through my involvement with these groups I was able to reclaim my spiritual authority and give myself permission to carve out my own holy path without apology. (And by the way, no one—believer or nonbeliever—has rejected or condemned me.)

Today, my relationship with God feels unlimited. I talk to the Lord all day long. I take advantage of long subway trips and elevator rides to pray and meditate, to connect with the spirit, and to remind myself to be calm and compassionate in the midst of commuter chaos. Sometimes people look askance at me when they see me breathing deeply on the train with my eyes closed and my raised palms resting on my knees, but I just don't care.

It is my understanding that God is love, and that love motivates action. My commitment to activism has always been driven by the notion that living a life of service is one of the most sacred ways to give thanks. I learned this from my Baptist parents and grandparents, whose activism during the civil rights movement had roots in the African-American church, and from hearing stories about how slaves used spirituals as a means to communicate, educate, organize, and rebel in their quest for liberation.

I am now at a point where I feel comfortable acknowledging what led me to this point—a strong urge, a loud internal whisper, and a tingling shiver that I know well: my spiritual calling. After years of seeking, I've forged a new spiritual frontier: myself. Releasing myself from other people's expectations and allowing myself to receive God's blessings and wisdom in ways that feel honest, righteous, and real has been, in my life, literally the best thing ever. ✿

BEYOND BELIEF

A conversation about atheism, between atheists.
Writing by Jenny and Danielle, collage by Beth.

It can be kind of daunting to tell other people that you are an atheist. You get the question *"You mean you don't believe in anything?"* so many times that it starts to feel like a more polite way of saying "What's *wrong* with you?" A lot of people treat atheists like we're total bummers and/or intellectual snobs. When I was a teenager, my atheism felt like one more thing that made me weird and unlikeable. But nowadays, it is just one more thing that makes me me.

In the spirit of love and acceptance, I had an email conversation with my girl Danielle (who couldn't be more magical) on atheism—how we both got here and what it means and doesn't mean. —Jenny

JENNY So, fellow NONBELIEVER, how did you come to be an atheist?

DANIELLE It happened when I was a teenager, but it wasn't spurred by a specific event. My family was mildly Catholic (we were baptized, we celebrated Christmas), but religion was never pushed too heavily in my house. I think I had always questioned the role of religion in my life, and one day I just sort of realized, *Hey—I don't actually have to believe any of this.* I stopped going to church after my first communion, when I was seven or eight. What about you?

JENNY Well, my entire family is atheist—parents, grandparents, aunts and uncles, everyone. Religion was banned and religious texts were burned during the Cultural Revolution in China in the '60s and '70s, so there's an entire generation of Chinese, including both of my parents, who had no exposure to religion, or were brought up to believe that it was bad and bourgeois, etc.

I know a lot of Chinese people who are casually Buddhist, and I don't mean that in a pejorative way, but, for example, people in my family will honor certain Buddhist practices such as burning incense for our ancestors and visiting the deceased on Tomb Sweeping Day, but those practices have always felt more cultural than religious to me. It was never about faith in some kind of deity, it was more a way of organizing our day-to-day lives, of establishing rituals and building community.

I have this weird memory of these Jehovah's Witnesses coming to our house when I was in elementary school. I hid behind my father when he slammed the door in their faces. He used to say to me, "There is no God. God is money."

That scared the shit out of me because I was like, *Wait wait, my father has no soul. Money cannot be God!*

DANIELLE That is amazing.

JENNY But I've always felt in my gut that after we die, nothing happens. We become nothing and remember nothing; our lives just end. I mean, that was a horrifying thought to have as a child, but I had it, and I struggled with it, and I flirted with ideas of God and heaven and life after death and having a soul, but ultimately I knew in my heart that I did not believe any of that stuff.

When did you "come out" to your family and friends as an atheist, and how did they respond?

DANIELLE You know what? I never have! I never felt I had to, because my family doesn't place a lot of emphasis on religion.

Growing up, when we talked about religion, we talked about lots of different belief systems—including atheism [the view that there is no god or "higher power"] and agnosticism [the view that we can't really know if there is or isn't a "higher power"]. It was sort of a package deal—if you're going to mention religion, you can't talk about just one; it always came with talk about "options." I think this may be the first time I'm mentioning my atheism publicly.

JENNY That seems ideal to me!

DANIELLE And I don't start a lot of conversations about religion, so maybe that's why I don't feel that I've had to come out with my atheism too much? I think it only comes up when you are talking to someone who is intolerant in some way. As long as there is a base level of respect, I can talk to anyone about who or what they believe. If someone comes at me and is like, "I'm Buddhist," "I'm Wiccan," etc., I can be like, "Cool! Tell me about your life." I'm not hostile about being an atheist—but I also think that being an atheist is not an open invitation to try to convert me.

JENNY I know exactly what you mean. If someone is talking about their faith, my natural impulse is to listen and inquire, not to be like, "Yo, I am atheist. Gotta put that out on the table."

DANIELLE Do you struggle to talk about religion, or feel freaked out about it? I sometimes do. It seems to mean SO MUCH to people, and I'm always afraid of offending super-religious people by accident.

JENNY Oh yeah, I'm always afraid I'm going to offend someone who is religious. I think as you get older, at least for me, you start to self-select and meet people who are open and tolerant and able to accept views that contradict their own. But when I was a teen, I had encounters with people who were "threatened" by my atheism.

I remember once I was at this summer camp for philosophy nerds and me and a bunch of other high-schoolers were sitting around talking about religion and somehow it came out that I didn't believe in God. The other kids were like, "But surely you believe in *something*—you can't just believe there's *nothing*." I was sort of excited to articulate my thoughts on it because I had never done so before, so we ended up getting into a huge conversation about it, and one of the things that kept coming up was, like, "BUT YOU ARE SUCH A NICE, POLITE, THOUGHTFUL, SWEET PERSON," as if believing in God is the only thing giving us any reason to be loving and kind to one other. A couple of people asked me, "So if you don't believe in anything, what's stopping you from just stealing stuff and MURDERING people?" That question blew my mind—it assumed that religion and faith are the only way to regulate your behavior or formulate moral codes. Some of the really religious kids were bewildered when I told them, "The thing that stops me from stealing and killing is ME. *I* stop myself. I live up to my own expectations."

DANIELLE It is so weird that people think religion is the thing that keeps us from turning into savages—um, murder is still happening, even amongst people who believe in God!

I think this kind of thinking can lead people to sometimes use religion as an excuse for moral laziness. Like, "As long as I'm 'guided' by something, I don't actually have to put thought or effort into being a decent, engaged person." Catholicism, for instance, has the sacrament of penance and confession, where if you confess your sins to a priest and say 10 Hail Marys or whatever, you will be absolved of your sins. To me that seems both terrible (so you can just treat people like crap and then be given a clean slate?) and wonderful (redemption and change are nice!).

It's a shame that something as personal as religion is so often used to regulate others, too. I think that's what really turned me off from organized religion in general—most of the religious people I'd been exposed to wanted everyone to think like them, believe like them.

JENNY I can't get down with that either. I have a lot of respect for people who consider themselves extremely faithful and religious but are still like, "Let me do my thing and you can do yours."

DANIELLE Totally. Do you think it's difficult to be an atheist as a teenager?

JENNY It was mostly that I often felt left out at school. I remember reading books in English class and somehow everyone in my class got the religious references—I was the only person who needed all that stuff to be explained to me. And sometimes kids who weren't Christian would complain that their religions weren't given as much time and respect in class as Christianity—and I get what they were saying, but I thought the conversation should be not about how any one religion should get the same amount of air time as any other, but rather about respecting people of all faiths, including those of us who have *no* faith, equally.

And then when my teenage friends read Sartre and went through these "rebellious" periods of existentialism or nihilism or whatever, only to later return to some idea of faith, I felt like, *Dude, been there, done that my whole life, and still doing it 'cause it's not rebellion for me, and it's not a phase.*

DANIELLE I feel like atheism is often invalidated when you're a teenager because it's seen as just a way to rebel or to question what you know. But if you're figuring out your relationship to religion/spirituality, I think it's a good place to start from, to give yourself a blank slate and think things through from there on your own—which, especially at that point in your life, can be pretty revolutionary.

But it wasn't really weird for me to be an atheist as a teenager, because I didn't live

with people who were on my case about it; I can see how it would be more difficult if you are still forced to go to church every week, or you want to respect your family by sharing in their traditions.

JENNY I should add that when I was growing up, the impulse to "pray" for stuff was very much alive in me. The idea of being "good" and wanting goodness is so deeply tied to the idea of religion. So whenever I felt guilty about something or wished for good things in my life, I would end up "praying." When I was in middle school, a family friend was hit by a car and I was afraid he would die, so one afternoon I knelt by my bed like I had seen in the movies and I just kind of sat there for a while, not knowing what to say or whom to say it to. I just didn't know how to wish this man a miracle recovery outside the context of prayer.

DANIELLE We don't have a model, outside of faith, for valuing or demonstrating hope.

JENNY Does it scare you to think about what happens to us after we die?

DANIELLE I'm terrified of dying. But I don't think that's a bad thing—we're afraid because we don't know what happens after we die, but that lack of knowledge motivates me to be my best right now, in this experience of living. That sounds like something Oprah would say, but I guess what I mean is that I'm most afraid of dying when I feel like I'm not doing a good job of being alive. I definitely have introspective moments where I think, *If you died right now, would you die happy or fulfilled?* As an atheist, I don't have any comforting story to tell myself about a life after this physical life is over. Does it scare you to not believe in some idea of heaven?

JENNY YES, OH GOSH. (Is it weird that I wanted to type OMG but felt really self-conscious about using phrases like that in a flip way because here we are talking about how we believe there is no G?) I'm also terrified of dying.

DANIELLE (No, use the OMGs! They can just be *oh my gosh*es instead.) When I was a teenager, I used to lie down in my room and try to imagine what it would be like to be dead—not thinking, not hearing, not knowing anything. I think for a lot of people religion is a way to explain that nebulous place where we cease to exist.

JENNY I did the same thing! I would lie down in my room and try to evoke how it would feel to cease to exist.

DANIELLE I think we both needed to get out more.

JENNY When I was a kid, I started thinking about how I couldn't remember what it was like before I was born, how we have no memories of what it's like to not exist, and then I thought, *So this means that when we die, we will have no memories of what it was like to ever have existed.* That scared me, because I wanted to remember my mother and my father and my LIFE.

Then I thought maybe reincarnation would be a nice thing, but the thought of dying and being born all over again was terrifying too. *All* of it was terrifying. I wanted to believe in God, and I wanted the comfort of believing in heaven to keep me from obsessively thinking about death; but every time I tried to imagine heaven, or reincarnation, or life after death, the thought just felt completely empty. I felt no connection to the idea of an immortal soul—it didn't have the urgency of truth. The only thing that felt true was that when we die, we cease to exist—and that was terrifying. Some days I'd be watching cartoons and eating Twinkies and then suddenly it would hit me: *I'm gonna die. I won't know any of this one day or remember it ever happened.* I wanted so badly to believe otherwise, but it just didn't feel right.

DANIELLE I think for a lot of people religion is mainly about finding a community that shares your beliefs—getting together with family and neighbors over a common idea—which can be rad. I don't want to discount the positive side of religion, you know?

JENNY I sometimes envy the instant community that religion affords. And I'm very moved by the ways in which organized religion has contributed to so much beneficence in the world. I'm thinking about the very important and deep connection between the civil rights movement and Christianity in America, just to point out one of many examples. When I moved to San Francisco after college, I realized that most of the city's services for homeless folks were being run by churches, and I was like, "Dude, atheists, STEP UP YOUR GAME."

DANIELLE Sometimes being an atheist feels like there's extra room for apathy. Then again, maybe that's just who you are as a person—if you're apathetic, religion isn't going to fix that. But too often atheists are pitted against people who believe, and that's just damaging and shortsighted.

JENNY Yeah, it's not a good idea to pit atheists against people of religious faith like I just did right now. A love for compassion and a desire for more of it in the world does not have to come from religious faith, but it also very well can. I feel like not growing up religious has helped me recognize the things I think are good about religion, as well as the things I think are not so good.

DANIELLE It helps you stay a little objective.

JENNY Do you think it's arrogant of us to say we are atheists and not agnostic—that we don't leave room for the possibility of God or any god(s)?

DANIELLE I don't. When I was a teenager I used to work at a Catholic convent (long story), and I would constantly ask the sisters about their role in the community, or why they drove brand-new cars if they had taken a vow of poverty—things like that. The only answer I ever got was "Because!"—like I was a toddler asking why the sky is blue. But one day, one of the sisters said, "It is not wise to question religion as if you could possibly know the world at your age." And I was like, *Did you just dismiss my curiosity because I'm a teenager? How rude!* At that point in my life, I still thought that maybe one day I'd find the "right" religion—my atheism was more about not wanting to be Catholic than it was about knowing what I really believed or didn't believe. But that nun was so dismissive about what she saw as my arrogance that she didn't even recognize her own.

I'm not saying that it's OK to be arrogant as an atheist because others are arrogant about their religions—I'm saying that it's not arrogant to know what you do or don't believe, as long as you don't dismiss the beliefs of others as ignorance or naïveté. Being an atheist, for me, isn't about condemning religion or pointing out fault—I just want to go through the world without someone else's consciousness oppressing me.

Do you feel arrogant because you don't call yourself an agnostic?

JENNY I don't know. I guess for me it's like, how can it possibly be arrogant if my beliefs will never affect anyone other than me? If I don't try to convince anyone that I'm right and they're wrong? I will never shame someone for not believing what I believe. I will never support any legislation that restricts anyone's freedom to believe what they want, nor will I go to another country to try to convert the people who live there to my system of beliefs. I will never ask anyone to donate money to me so I can persuade other people to believe what I believe. I mean, I could go on and on. But it just seems the opposite of arrogant, because I am not denying anyone anything.

DANIELLE I want to print that on a pillow.

JENNY It can be powerful to ask yourself, OK, what if there is no higher power? What if there is absolutely no one, no deity who cares if I exist or don't exist? What if there is absolutely no reason or purpose for why I was put on this earth? Would I still want to be a more loving person and want the world to be full of more compassion, more kindness, more beauty? I'll answer for myself, and the answer is yes, yes, YES. ✿

BUILD YOUR OWN SHRINE

On the next spread you'll find a page for your own hero-worshipping purposes. Paste a photo of whomever you deem shrine-worthy and then show your love with the beautiful stickers our illustrators made just for you two. (Some suggestions: Beyoncé, the Beach Boys, pizza.)

Stickers by Allegra Lockstadt, Beth Hoeckel, Emma Dajska, Esme Blegvad, and Leanna Wright.

MAD LOVE

Rethinking the appeal of tortured romance.
By Jenny

The first time I thought I was in love coincided with the first time I had sex. The year before, I had written in my diary: *Ellen' let Mitchell touch her boobs, and now she thinks they're in love. Um, that's not love, that's called he likes touching your boobs.* But when it happened to me it was called love—real love that spun me on my feet.

I was 15 years old, and I swore I wasn't the type of girl who confused sex with intimacy. My need to be around him was as real and as urgent as my need to eat or sleep or shit, and yet I was hardly doing any of those things. I was just needing, needing, wanting, needing, needing, wanting, pining, needing, wanting, pining, crying, needing. We weren't officially boyfriend and girlfriend, but for three years we were somewhere excruciatingly in between. It was so physically painful that sometimes I could not get my body from the floor to my bed.

This did not seem strange at all to me. Love, the way I understood it, was *supposed* to be painful. Because if it wasn't, if it didn't make you breathless and fearful, if it didn't swallow you into the depths of its belly, spit you out, and leave you shivering and ecstatic, then it was something else. It was the kind of boring love that depressed me and was everywhere. It was the love of married people and their boring married lives. People like my parents weren't in love, I told myself. In high school, I was convinced that I'd seen my mother naked more times than my father had. When we went on vacations, my mother and I shared a bed and my father slept on a cot, and I often wondered if she preferred sleeping next to me. Their marriage looked more like a business partnership, whereas *love* was thinking there was someone in the world who completed you, and without that person we were all just half a being.

*All names have been changed.

These ideas didn't come from me. I had read Plato's *Symposium* the summer before junior year, and he said that human beings used to be completely round, but because we were too wicked, the gods cut us in half, and so we spend the entirety of our lives looking for our other half. Here was the most important figure in the whole of Western philosophy telling me that love makes you whole. Who was I to argue?

While I was in the early throes of my does-he-or-doesn't-he-love-me drama, I started to notice couples at school who made too much sense, like each person was super good-looking so of course they had to date. I felt sorry for them, because they would never know what it was like to love someone so much that it wrecked them. *That* was the kind of love that my favorite musicians sang about. That was the kind of love that was talked about in novels and movies and on TV, where people said things like "You're so beautiful, it hurts to look at you." Or: "I can't live without you." Or: "I would rather die than stay away from you."

So die. So don't live. So stop loving that person if it hurts, I was tempted to say. But I didn't really believe that. Instead, I thought: *I want someone to say that to me.*

The first time I fell in love with someone who loved me back, I couldn't stop smiling. I was 19. *I love him,* I thought every single second of my life. Instead of doing the reading for my classes, or even going to class at all, I was telling someone how much I loved him. "Is it bad that I don't care about anything?" I asked him. "I just care about this moment with you and the next moment with you and the next one and the next one."

When he went to study abroad in Japan, we talked on the phone every day for hours. The only thing that cheered me up was knowing that he was as miserable as I was. Except sometimes he wasn't. Some-

times he was happy, or at least engaged with the world and content to live his life in the present instead of looking back at the past, to a time when we spent an entire semester holed up in his dorm room. Those moments killed me. I didn't understand how he could feel anything but depressed without me.

"He should miss me so much that he literally wants to kill himself," I said to my friend. "Just kidding."

"You don't sound like you're kidding," my friend said.

Maybe I wasn't.

I remembered reading *Romeo and Juliet* in high school and thinking, *To be separated from your love is nothing short of death.* There's the part where Romeo sees Juliet for the first time, and she's so stunning that he falls in love with her right away. He says, "Did my heart love till now? Forswear it, sight! For I ne'er saw true beauty till this night." *Yes!* I thought. *That's how it's supposed to be!*

I once asked a college boyfriend about this girl he was obsessed with during his freshman year. She broke his heart, and he talked about her so much that she came to possess mythical importance in our relationship. He told me he had never loved anyone like he loved her.

"Never?" I asked.

"Oh," he said. "I mean, I'm sure I'll love you as much as I loved her one day."

"Thank you," I said. "I look forward to it." *I will strangle you in your sleep,* I thought.

After that, if a guy didn't declare that he was in love with me within a few weeks, or even better, a few days, I wasn't interested. *If you really loved me,* I thought each and every time I started dating someone new, *you would have known it the minute you laid eyes on me.*

But you know what? When I thought about it, Romeo and Juliet's relationship—if you can even call it that—was pretty disturbing. Within less than a week, they profess their undying love to each other and get hitched. Juliet delivers her famous "parting is such sweet sorrow" line, and the next time Romeo sees her she's unconscious from a potion that was designed to trick her family into thinking she's dead so that she won't have to go through with an arranged marriage to Paris. Romeo, with whom she has had about three conversations, was supposed to find her alive and whisk her away to a life totally cut off from her friends and family for all of eternity. GOOD PLAN.

As we know, it doesn't work. Romeo thinks Juliet is dead and kills himself, and when she wakes up, she kills herself too. They literally die for love. But is the tragedy of Romeo and Juliet that a family feud prevented two star-crossed lovers from being together? Or is it that they never gave themselves a chance to see if they were even compatible before going to drastic lengths to be a couple? Because literally hours before Romeo meets Juliet, he's hopelessly in love with her cousin Rosaline. When Benvolio advises him to get over her, Romeo is indignant:

He that is strucken blind cannot forget
The precious treasure of his eyesight lost.
Show me a mistress that is passing fair,
What doth her beauty serve but as a note
Where I may read who pass'd that passing fair?
Farewell. Thou canst not teach me to forget.

I mean, the guy is convinced that no other woman can compare to Rosaline and that he will never forget her, and then he goes to a party and TOTALLY FORGETS HER.

Juliet is a 14-year-old virgin when she decides to commit to Romeo for the rest of her life. When I was a 14-year-old virgin, I thought I was head over heels in love with someone who used emotional blackmail to get chicks. I have also fallen in love with, at various times, someone who turned out to be an ardent Rush Limbaugh supporter, several someones with really gross Asian fetishes, someone who regularly passed out on other people's lawns from drinking too much, and, maybe worst of all, someone who had married his long-term girlfriend

a month before telling me that he wanted to run off with me. Each of these people was the love of my life. Or rather, the love of that particular point in my life. These boys were at their dreamiest and most perfect before I knew much about them, when they were capable of playing a role in whatever fantasy I needed them to be part of.

When I was 23, a poet in my MFA program followed me into the girls' bathroom and told me he would follow me anywhere. We fell in love so fast I could not even tell you how exactly it happened. From the moment we met, we spent every single night together. Our love was showy and fraught. He signed all of his letters "Your Owen" and I signed all of mine "Your Jenny." We streaked outside in the rain. Our friends were convinced we lived in a permanent state of undress. We'd go weeks without seeing any other humans. When one of us felt even the slightest hint of sadness, the other one did, too. Early in our relationship I suggested that we spend a night apart. Just as I was about to leave, he suddenly became so woozy and feverish that he couldn't stand up. We ended up going back to my apartment, where I made him soup and held him in my arms until morning.

"I'm madly in love with him," I told every single person I knew. We depended on each other for everything—forgetting that once upon a time we both lived entire lives without each other, and those lives weren't necessarily miserable. But I was obsessed with someone who was obsessed with me, and we were both obsessed with being in love. It was wonderful, it was unsustainable, and eventually it destroyed us both.

Why do we have to be *madly* in love? Why does love have to drive us mad? Why can't it drive us to health? A healthy relationship gives each person in it room to have interests and desires outside of the relationship. When your happiness depends entirely on one person, you are not in a healthy, loving relationship.

When I was younger, I focused so much on falling in love that I completely failed to consider what it would mean to *stay* in love. And I still don't know what it means exactly, but I do know that I don't

want to spend every day of my life reeling from it. I know that I want my story to go on long past the first thrilling kiss. After Romeo and Juliet have sex for the first time, Juliet wishes to keep him as a pet, a plaything who always remains by her side. He's totally into it, but she reconsiders and confesses, "Yet I should kill thee with much cherishing."

In the end, "much cherishing" is what ends Romeo and Juliet's lives, and it's what ended Owen and me. We broke up after three years together. The thrill of how quickly we fell in love was all but replaced by the chokehold we had on each other. I had to accept something painful: Just because you fall for someone, and just because that initial fall is stupendously, indescribably wonderful, doesn't mean that this person is right for you in the long run.

Last month, I went with my parents to the dentist to get a cavity filled. My mother ducked out to get some groceries while my father and I were in the waiting room. I noticed that he had his phone clipped to his belt.

"That looks so dumb," I said.

"Well, I don't miss your mother's calls this way." And he didn't. My mom called five times, always to ask some trivial question, like whether she should get shiitake or king oyster mushrooms. And each time, my father picked up. As we were walking to the car, I noticed that my father still walks on the side of the road closest to the cars. "In case a car gets too close, it'll spare you and your mother," he always said.

I used to think that was unnecessary and annoying. But now I know that it's an act of love. That all of it is an act of love.

As thrilling as it is, love can't always be desperately intense and all-consuming. I think there's another kind of love that is possible, one that doesn't kill us. Maybe instead of wanting to disappear into love, we might decide to emerge more fully because of it. Maybe true love encourages us to embrace the ugly, boring parts of each other with as much tenderness as we would the plainly beautiful parts. For years, I was dying for love, but now, finally, I think I'd prefer to love someone so much that it *doesn't* hurt at all. ◈

WITH YOU AND WITHOUT YOU

A photographic remembrance.
By María Fernanda

My dad died recently, and everything has been complicated and hard for me to fully understand. I needed to make something to help me process the situation a little better. This series of photographs was inspired by Día de los Muertos (Day of the Dead), a very important Mexican holiday that takes place on the first two days of November. It is customary to visit the graves of our departed loved ones and make altars and decorate them with flowers, candles, and sugar skulls. It's a way of celebrating life by celebrating death, bringing us closer to our memories and to one another, and forcing us to abandon our fear of death and to embrace the little time we have on earth. I grieve for my dad, and even though he's not around anymore, I know he is with me every time I think of him.

Thanks to Zaid Díaz for styling, Kenia Filippini for modeling, and María Rangel Isas for modeling, styling, and art directing. Special thanks also to Miaus and Manolin.

JANUARY 2013: MYTHOLOGY

Happy New Year, Rookies!

The new year is like a birthday in that it seems like a much bigger deal than it is. Like, the difference between 2012 and 2013 sounds huge, but is today *that* different from yesterday? Did my 13th birthday mean I *didn't* pee my pants the very same night I supposedly became a young adult? According to my now-defunct Snoopy pajamas, OBVIOUSLY NOT. Still, change of any kind brings hope and makes you feel like this will be the year you finally become Oprah. You probably won't, but the thought that it might be conceivable is motivating.

This month's theme is Mythology: lies, exaggerations, legends, the works. Hannah really wanted us to do an ice queen/1920s-flapper month, so somehow it all kind of made sense together. Our Mythology heroes are Björk and Josephine Baker. And a bunch of Greek gods, Narnia characters, and ladies of the Harlem Renaissance.

Last January I did an acrostic poem for the month's theme, so I guess I'll try again this time, just to close this out:

M is for My, it's the new year already!
Y is for Yowza, it's 2013!
T is for This poem is not as strong as last year's.
H is for Hi guess 2013 is not going to be that great after all? ("Hi" as in when you go into the word "I" with a breath of exhaustion, because you are sad, because you are realizing that 2013 is not going to be that great after all.)
O is for Oprah, who I will never be.
L is for Like I should just give up now and not even go back to school in a week when break is over.
O is for Oh my god, break is over in a week.
G is for Guhhhhh.
Y is for You know, maybe 2013 won't actually be so bad [and the rest of a monologue a cartoon character would recite about optimism].

Yeah, no, we'll all be fine.

LOVE,
TAVI

I KNOW WHAT I DON'T KNOW

I could fill a library with the books I've told people I've read.
By Joe. Playlist lettering by Lisa Maione.

Just the other night, I finished reading *The Great Gatsby*. I was about a decade too late by public school standards, and I wish I hadn't waited so long, because it's as awesome as everybody said it was. But more than that, I wish I hadn't wasted so much time in high school and beyond pretending I had already read it, feeling ashamed as I bobbed and weaved through conversations, trying to hide the holes in my knowledge.

Technically, I never lied—I just did a lot of listening when F. Scott Fitzgerald came up, and pretended I knew what made someone "a Daisy" or "a Nick." Last summer I was on a boat trip, and I nodded along with everyone else when someone made a crack about "the light at the end of the dock." I caught the reference, but not the context. When it came time to come up with an opinion on the Baz Luhrmann adaptation, I watched the trailer with the same excitement as my friends, but I didn't bother explaining that my enthusiasm was due to a lingering Leonardo DiCaprio fandom and an unceasing obsession with *Romeo + Juliet*. Similar fakery accompanied several other conversations concerning White Men You Mustn't Miss, including James Joyce and Vladimir Nabokov.

This secret shame, like most, is actually quite common. How many times have you heard—or muttered yourself—something like "Oh, yeah, I've read parts of it..." or "I saw it so long ago that I barely remember what happens"? In truth, you may never have cracked the cover or read anything beyond a Wikipedia entry, but somehow that's harder to say. These white lies are often arbitrary, backed by our own hierarchy of personal tastes and how we think they might serve or betray the way we wish to be seen. For instance, because of my anti-

fantasy bias, I'll proudly tell you I couldn't get past the first chapter/scene of *The Lord of the Rings*, but no one in my life knows that entire chunks of the Rolling Stones' discography are foreign to me—including some of what I'm told is the good stuff, like *Some Girls* and *Tattoo You*. And I like the Rolling Stones!

No one has time to really take in all of culture, but that's only part of my excuse. Also at work are the comfort of settling with stuff I already know—what's unfamiliar can be scary!—and just plain laziness. I've seen all six seasons of *The Hills* more than once (thank you/hate you, Netflix) and will often put on an episode I know by heart (in which Lauren calls one of her friends "shady... evil and conniving") rather than dive into a John Cassavetes film—I hear *Husbands* is good?—that I haven't watched, but feel I should, for whatever reason.

Embarrassment about such gaps in the media libraries of our minds depends on the outside world being able to take a look at those libraries, which is weird, right? In the age of the Facebook profile, being seen as savvy and smart means knowing, and usually flaunting, certain cultural touchstones. Books, movies, TV shows, bands, artists—they can all signify different personality traits or ideologies that we want others to know we have, whether it's alternative edginess or introspective sensitivity. The novels we carry around (Sylvia Plath for the tortured), the band tees we choose to wear (Kate Bush for the kind of out-there), and the screenshots we post to our blogs (*Clueless*, always *Clueless*) broadcast these interests in the hope that some of the feelings they elicit in others will reflect back on us.

As a teenager, I wanted to be the kind of kid who liked Hunter S. Thompson,

with all the badassness that implied, so I devoured a bunch of his magazine articles, bought a few of his books, and mourned his death with a homemade patch on my JanSport. I rented *Fear and Loathing in Las Vegas* for me and my friends to watch on a Friday night and understood about as much of it as a sober 16-year-old could, but I didn't finish the book until years later, because it was dense and I had homework.

While we're at it, here's a by-no-means-complete list of Books I Pretended to Read in High School:

- *The Bluest Eye* by Toni Morrison
- *Catch-22* by Joseph Heller
- *A People's History of the United States* by Howard Zinn
- *Slaughterhouse-Five* by Kurt Vonnegut
- *A Farewell to Arms* by Ernest Hemingway
- *Heart of Darkness* by Joseph Conrad
- the final act of just about every William Shakespeare play

What can I tell you? This stuff isn't as fun when it's assigned. I've since caught up on some, and I hear the rest are great.

I was more concerned with punk music back then anyway, but I couldn't actually sing you a song by the Misfits or Crass either. It's not that I was a total poser—the Clash, the Ramones, and Operation Ivy were branded onto my soul—but I was trying to keep up with an unrealistically completist standard. The list of amazing things in all mediums and genres has built up for centuries and never stops coming, like a Tumblr dashboard scrolling to infinity, filled with everything you absolutely need to experience *right now* or forever feel left out. Keeping up with new stuff—*Community*! Jennifer Egan! Dirty Projectors!—while also being well-versed in the old and influential—*Twin Peaks*! Tom Wolfe! Nina Simone!—is not just overwhelming, it's impossible.

I had imagined college to be the period in one's life for catching up, when you're literally paying for the privilege of getting to spend your time reading "important books," pausing only to see cool bands or watch obscure art films. For four years, my chief responsibility would be to devour culturally significant words and images. When those years passed in three and a half blinks and I felt no closer to cultural completion, it became obvious the game (which I had created in my head) was rigged against me. (I still get anxious under towering bookstore shelves, an endless reading list looming over me.)

Well, enough. I'm done pretending. Never again will I read/watch/listen to anything out of peer pressure (though I guess I'll watch *Downton Abbey* if everyone keeps telling me how great it is). Books and shows and movies and music should be a source of pleasure, thought, and enlightenment, not social anxiety. Cultural knowledge is not a contest; you don't get an award for Most Lines From *The Larry Sanders Show* Memorized, or Correct Pronunciation of Every French Philosopher's Name. Trying to keep up with everything is exhausting, and pretending that you've kept up with everything is worse. Openly admitting what you don't know is not only a huge relief, it also makes it possible to learn from those around you, people who have their own voids that are bound to be different from yours. I remember nervously confessing to a friend that I had only a cursory knowledge of the writer Philip Roth—and he didn't laugh at me. He gave me some recommendations.

As soon as you give up trying to win some nonexistent prize, there's the freedom to really marinate in the good parts of discovering new things, or returning to old favorites without guilt. Listen to one album for the entire summer, reread your favorite passages in a play over and over again, or watch a whole season of *Law & Order* even when you already know the verdicts. I used to spend more time downloading music than listening to it, amassing a comprehensive collection I'd never get to. These days, I only keep about five albums on my iPod at any given time—infinite choice freaks me out!

When I actually read it, not to brag about it but just for fun, *The Great Gatsby* was really enjoyable. Now I *really* understand what it means to be a Jay, or a Tom, or a Daisy, or a Nick—but more than that, I'll forever attach the experience of reading that book to a specific moment in my life: a wet winter day in Brooklyn, awaiting a delayed flight to the South. It will be just as memorable as a humid English classroom. And I still have a lot to look forward to. ☆

SHOEGAZE SNOWSTORM
BY MEAGAN FREDETTE

1. BROTHER – CHAPTERHOUSE
2. HEART IS STRANGE – SCHOOL OF SEVEN BELLS
3. STAR SAIL – THE VERVE　4. HITHERTO – COCTEAU TWINS
5. BLUE CREAM SKY – EXPERIMENTAL AIRCRAFT
6. PULSE – I BREAK HORSES
7. IN YOUR HEART – A PLACE TO BURY STRANGERS
8. NOTHING MUCH TO LOSE – MY BLOODY VALENTINE
9. STARRSHA – RINGO DEATHSTARR　10. THE GARDEN – TAMARYN
11. WILD – BEACH HOUSE　12. NEVER-NEVER – LUSH
13. 40 DAYS – SLOWDIVE　14. DREAMS BURN DOWN – RIDE

SIRENS' SONG

Mermaid vibez all day long.
By María Fernanda

Thanks to Ana, Citlalli, Natalia, and María José for modeling.
Clothes and styling by María Rangel Isas. Styling assistants:
Abril Ventura, Zaid Díaz, and Betty De Anda. Thanks
also to Chuyin, Manolin, and Miaus for their help.
Rings from Du Aquarelle.

TRUTH OR SCARE

Separating fact from fiction when it comes to sex and other stuff.

By Lola

A couple of weeks ago, my editors asked me if I would put my skills as a nurse practitioner/sex-haver to use by debunking some of the most prevailing myths out there about sex and our bodies and other stuff that seems to generally cause confusion. I went to the Rookie clubhouse (a mythical place that should exist) and asked my fellow staffers to tell me what they'd been told over the years, which led to a pretty amusing discussion wherein all sorts of urban legends were trotted out: One girl heard that masturbating too much causes the vagina to dry out (nope); another's mom told her that douching with Coca-Cola after sex would kill sperm (no, and also: sticky). Misinformation and rumors spread for all sorts of reasons, ranging from the innocuous (imaginations, y'all) to the seriously effed (authority figures who want to discourage sexual exploration by any means necessary), and I couldn't possibly tackle everything in one article, but I tried to identify some running themes and set the record straight, because the truth matters.

Here are some common lies, in various Important Categories:

VAGINAS

THEY ARE DIRTY AND THEY SMELL BAD.

That wet spot in your drawers throughout the day is your vagina cleaning house. Vaginal fluid helps maintain a relatively acidic pH situation in your vag, preventing bacteria from causing infection. How much discharge is "normal" varies from vagina to vagina, so you should familiarize yourself with what's typical for you—that way, you can pick up on any sudden changes in color or volume or smell, which could indicate an infection. A healthy vagina is not odorless, and it's not supposed to smell like roses either, so you don't need to use any specialty products like douches to "clean" it—just water is good, and just on the outside. If you prefer to use soap, use an unscented one that's less likely to cause irritation—again, only on the outside! The inside is self-cleaning. Amazing, right? Your vagina has got it covered.

THEY STRETCH LIKE A SWEATER AFTER A LOT OF USES.

No! The vag is not like a sweater. You don't have to worry about its stretching with wear. It's a muscle, and like other muscles in your body, it can flex without losing its shape. Frequent penetration, whether we're talking large penises or hands or vibrators

LIFE SKILLS 201

Let nothing stand in your way.

By Krista

Last year we tackled such essential life skills as haggling, apologizing, and landing a punch. Since then, we have grown. We've changed. We've mastered those basic life skills, and now we are older, wiser, and ready to tackle new challenges. That's right, folks, it's time for round two: intermediate life skills. That's *intermedias vita peritias* in Latin. (We're so smart now.)

1. GIVING/ACCEPTING A COMPLIMENT

Compliments are great. They give us a lift, brighten our day, make us feel accepted and appreciated. The whole world loves them, and lots of people use them as a shortcut to get to know someone, which is usually a sound strategy. Say it's hard to make conversation with a girl you just met? Compliment her shoes/book choice/nail art/ability to belch loud enough to be heard in a crowded auditorium—anything that you *honestly* like about her upon first impression. She gets some recognition, you come across as friendly, and everybody wins!

Except it's not always so easy. Maybe someone compliments a dress of yours that you HATE and only wore because you haven't done laundry in a month. Maybe the attention makes you nervous or uncomfortable. Maybe you feel like no one ever flatters you, so when a girl with amazing style tells you she likes your sweater, you are *deeply suspicious* that she's making fun of you. None of this matters, because unlike many areas in life involving social etiquette, compliment giving and receiving do not exist in a gray area. There's a right and a wrong way to handle them.

If you're getting a compliment, no matter what it is, the best possible answer is: "Thank you." The end. Even if you don't believe the compliment, be graceful and gracious and just say those two words. If you say, "Oh, this? I've had it for years, I kind of hate it," you're basically telling your flatterer that they have crappy taste. If you say, "Really? I kind of feel like my singing voice sounds like a high-pitched squirrel's," it seems like you're fishing for a second compliment.

If you're giving a compliment, mean it. It won't come off very sincerely if you half-heartedly praise someone when you just can't think of anything else to say, or if you actually hate something and are just so startled by it that you offer a, "Wow, are those…oh, rubber cowboy boots? *Interesting*." (Mothers are awesome at this.) Girls can smell a fake compliment from miles away, so let's be true to one another.

2. STOPPING AN OVERFLOWING TOILET

You're at a friend's house, and you need to poop, so you do. You flush, and then you

or anything else one might use for pleasure, does not change this fact, and nothing short of having a baby will noticeably alter muscle tone. Even then, this is not the case for every person, and the change is not usually dramatic or irrevocable—like any muscle, the vagina can be exercised by contracting and relaxing it (aka Kegel exercises).

PERIODS AND TAMPONS

A PERIOD IS A GEYSER OF FRESH, RED BLOOD.

One Rookie said that she used to think her period would involve "beautiful red blood seeping sweetly out of [her] vag, and not sometimes incredibly dark to the point of looking poo-colored," and another believed that once you started menstruating, the blood would "just keep gushing." No. Here's the deal: Most people get their period for about a week every month, or technically every 21 to 40 days for three to seven days in a row. But it usually takes three to five years after your first period for your cycle to become regular, and even then it can be unpredictable if you're not taking hormonal birth control. There's also huge variation in the consistency of menstrual blood—your flow can change from light spots to clumps that resemble loogies, which usually form during the heavier part of your cycle. The blood can vary in color from bright red to almost black, and usually gets darker toward the end of your cycle, when it's not being dispelled as quickly, so it's not as fresh when it finally comes out. Despite apparently widespread fears of menstruation being like some sort of flash flood, you only lose about four to 12 teaspoons of blood during each round.

There are exceptions. If you truly are gushing blood to the point where you're changing your pad/tampon every hour because it's soaked, or you're experiencing a lot of pain, this could be the result of several issues—endometriosis, hormonal imbalances, cervical polyps—and treatments vary. Go see a doctor, who can help you relieve the pain and make sure that everything is OK.

TAMPONS WILL "TAKE YOUR VIRGINITY"...

First of all, only you can decide what constitutes "losing your virginity" (if you even want to define sexual experiences with that paradigm). But even if you go strictly by the "broken hymen = not a virgin" formula, this myth doesn't really hold water: Not every person born with a vagina has a corona (the technical name for the "hymen"), and if they do, it's rare to have one that fully covers the vaginal entry. Coronas are different—most are ring-shaped, with openings that are large enough to accommodate a tampon without breaking. Actually, it's rare for a corona to "break" at all; it tends to stretch or experience minor ruptures from various activities, sexual and otherwise.

...OR KILL YOU...

Toxic shock syndrome is a severe bacterial infection that isn't caused by tampons notice…it's not going down. Ohhhh no, it's not going down, ohmygod the water is rising, OHMYGOD IT'S GONNA OVERFLOW!!! THERE'LL BE TURDS EVERYWHERE AND AHH THE HUMILIATION.

OK, steady! Breathe! I will not let this happen to you. Here's what you do: If the level of water in the toilet bowl is higher than usual but no longer rising—like the toilet just won't flush, but there's still "stuff" in it—find the toilet plunger, which should be next to the toilet, put the plunger over the hole in the bowl, and push it up and down a few times. This will make a sick suction noise. Usually the toilet will clear in just a few seconds, and then flush normally. (Yes, this means the toilet plunger will touch your poop and pee. That is its lot in life. Rinse it off in the clean toilet water, and put the plunger back where you found it.)

If the water is already at an alarmingly high level and rising rapidly and with no sign of stopping, DUDE. Take the lid off the back of the toilet RIGHT NOW (it's heavy, look out!) and set it down anywhere. Then reach into the cold toilet water (ick, I know, but it's clean, I swear), and lift up the float. The float is the thing inside the toilet that looks like a black balloon. The second you lift this up, the water will stop running. Keep holding the float up, and bend down to where the pipes connect the back of the toilet to the floor. See that little valve? Turn it to the right to shut it off. Now the water has stopped running; the toilet cannot overflow, so let go of the float. Find the plunger and give the toilet a good plunging. The water level in the bowl should start going down. When it's down to a level that looks safe, turn the water back on, and you should be good to go. Crisis averted. And aren't you handy?

3. GETTING AWAY FROM A STRANGER WHO IS SCARING YOU

Chances are, at some point, you will be in the immediate vicinity of someone who is either deliberately behaving in an alarming way—like a guy on a crowded train who is touching you in a manner that doesn't seem accidental—or behaving in a frightening way because they are mentally ill.

Let's say you're on a bus and some guy is ranting, yelling, or otherwise acting outside the range of accepted social behaviors and making everyone uncomfortable. He is making you nervous, but not targeting you personally. This is the kind of situation where most people will sit tight and try to ignore what's happening, and if you feel safe in the crowd and the person is not being violent, you could choose to do the same.

But that doesn't always happen. Situations change quickly. Let's say the guy decides to get in *your* face and start yelling, or sidles up next to you and starts making sexually harassing remarks that no one else can hear, or touches you, or calls you a bitch because you won't talk to him—the list of what a person can do in public to make you seriously uncomfortable, furious, embarrassed, and scared is long. This is not a situation where you sit tight and ignore the person. Y'all, if a person is scaring you, or even staring weirdly at you in a way you don't like, GET UP AND MOVE.

themselves, but has been associated with tampon usage in less than half of cases, because tampons can rub against the walls of your vagina, allowing certain dastardly bacteria to enter your bloodstream. One Rookie wondered if TSS was related to bad hygiene, but it isn't—even if you accidentally leave a tampon in for a week, you will probably not develop TSS (fewer than one in 100,000 menstruating women per year do). You're probably more likely to meet someone in a band called Toxic Shock Syndrome than you are someone who's actually suffered from it, but it *is* a medical emergency, so in the unlikely event that you develop any of the symptoms—a high fever, red rash, vomiting or diarrhea, or low blood pressure (whose symptoms might include dizziness or fainting)—take out your tampon and head to the nearest ER. If you're really apprehensive about TSS, you might consider switching to low-absorbency tampons, which are thought to reduce the risks by creating less friction, or you could try the Diva Cup, a reusable receptacle for your menstrual blood.

...OR ELSE DISAPPEAR, NEVER TO BE HEARD FROM AGAIN.

At the deep end of your vagina is your cervix, the doughnut-shaped entrance to your uterus. If you've never had a baby, the doughnut hole is about three millimeters wide. I ransacked my apartment to find something that was comparable in size, but nothing was small enough. (Maybe a really tiny bead?) Point is, tampons can't get into your uterus, let alone float around the rest of your abdomen. It is possible to forget that you put a tampon in, or for it to get lodged in an area of your vagina that you can't seem to reach, because your cervix changes position throughout the menstrual cycle. If this happens, wash your hands, sit on a toilet, and bear down like you're pooping, then do a sweep of the inside of your vagina with two fingers. If you still can't reach it, trust me, you won't be the first person to visit a doctor or healthcare provider for a lost tampon.

SEXUALLY TRANSMITTED INFECTIONS

STIS ARE FOREVER.

Only two STIs cause lifelong infections that can't be cured (but can be treated): herpes and HIV. Herpes outbreaks can be painful, although they tend to decrease in intensity and frequency over time. HIV is a serious chronic illness that can develop into AIDS, which doesn't have to be fatal, but can be. Most of the others—including chlamydia, gonorrhea, and syphilis—are treated with antibiotics.

HPV, or human papilloma virus, is its own case, which pleases HPV, because it's on this "I'm special and mysterious" head trip. Although it's technically not curable, 90 percent of HPV cases are cleared by the body's immune system within two years. You can treat the symptoms of HPV—genital warts and/or precancerous cells—

If you're taking public transportation, move to another part of the bus or to another train car, or get off at the next stop (as long as there are people around and the person isn't following you). If you're in a store or a place of business, tell an employee, leave the place (only if there's somewhere safe for you to enter close by), or, if you feel really scared, call the cops. Don't worry about being rude—this person has forfeited all rights to polite interaction. If you feel physically threatened, don't hesitate to loudly announce it to the people around you, which sometimes embarrasses a harasser into leaving, and alerts everyone else that they need to watch this guy. It's sad that we live in a world where we have to think about stuff like this—I mean, why should you have to move at all? Ugh. But no matter how unfair or infuriating it is, you can't necessarily count on other people to help you, so it's best to have a plan of action.

4. KNOWING WHAT TO SPRING FOR

There are things in life you can buy at the dollar store or find abandoned in alleys and take home. Then there are things you might think about spending a li'l money on, because quality actually matters. Everyone's list is different, but here are some loose guidelines.

Things you should never take for free:

• Fabric furniture of any type that is sitting outside. No matter how sweet that couch is, it could have bedbugs, it may have been rained on, it might be a lapdog's favorite pissin' spot. This goes quadruple for free mattresses!
• Secondhand nonstick pots and pans. Hand-me-down pans usually have scratched bottoms at the very least, and once it's been scratched, that coating can start to flake off into your food when you cook. Studies suggest that nonstick coating does not do good things to our bodies. (Besides, the pan will become less nonstick over time.)
• A kitten or puppy or bunny from a box. Unless you're ready to be that bebeh animal's mummy for the next 6 to 14 years.

Things you can buy cheap or thrift:

Almost everything! This includes hard furniture, room décor, glassware, clothing, and bags. If you've never been in a Dollar Tree, your life is about to change.

Things that you might consider investing in:

• Tampons. Cheap tampons—like off-brand ones, or the weird kind you get from the machine—hurt. You deserve the best menstrual support.
• Your skincare regimen. Does your face soap cost $15? Is it keeping your face zit-free? All right then. I'm not saying you can't explore other options, but if it's the only thing that works, it's worth it.
• Q-tips. Knock-off Q-tips suck. I don't know why.
• Toilet paper. All of those opposed to chafing, say "aye."
• A winter coat and boots. These are the articles that you will use to shield your fragile epidermis from possibly subzero

by having them removed by your doctor. We're still learning a lot about HPV, and the guidelines for testing and treatment are constantly shifting, but your takeaway on this subject is this: GET VACCINAT-ED AGAINST HPV. The vaccine is called Gardasil and is recommended for people of any gender between the ages of 9 and 26. It's currently available in at least a quarter of the world's countries. It doesn't protect against every kind of HPV, but it covers the most prevalent strains. (If you're a minor, you will likely need your parents' permission to get this vaccine, but thankfully more parents are learning how important it is.)

YOU'LL KNOW IF YOU OR SOME-ONE YOU'RE WITH HAS AN STI.

STIs are tricky little bastards: The most common ones, including chlamydia and HPV, most often have no symptoms at all. Other STIs can masquerade as other infections—trichomoniasis causes vaginal itching, discomfort, and discharge, just like a yeast infection or bacterial vaginosis. Early HIV infections sometimes look like a flu, and then the symptoms can disappear for years. Herpes is visible only during an outbreak, which can be so mild that you don't notice it, but it is always transmittable. (While we're on the topic: A herpes outbreak usually looks like cuts or sores, not a single raised bump, so relax about that ingrown hair.)

Since you can't know if someone else is STI-free just by looking, the only way to be sure is to get tested, and ask for your partner's results (and this goes for everyone, no matter what kind of sex you're having or whom you're having it with). Besides total abstinence, the only things that will significantly reduce your chances of getting an STI are condoms for blow jobs, anal sex, and vaginal sex, and dental dams for oral sex on girls.

Pap smears do not test for STIs. They test for one thing only: changes in your cells caused by high-risk (cancer-causing) strains of HPV. They don't test for the low-risk strains of HPV, which still cause warts, or any other STIs. There is no one test for everything, and a lot of healthcare providers won't automatically test for STIs, mainly because many of them won't even bring up sexual behavior during a routine exam. Help them out. If you want to be tested, ask your provider at the beginning of the visit.

PREGNANCY AND BIRTH CONTROL

JUMPING JACKS, HOT TUBS, AND/OR DOUCHING CAN PREVENT PREGNANCY.

OK, deep breath. Here are some of the things that can't get you pregnant: feelings, toilet seats, sperm that's been hiding from the sex you had two weeks ago (sperm can live for up to five days inside your body, but not on, like, your bed sheets). Conversely, the following things will not prevent pregnancy: having it be the first time you've had sex, having sex during your period, exercising, douching afterwards, doing it in a body of water. Short of abstinence, birth

temperatures. Winter is not fun when your jacket doesn't really do much and your boots have poor traction.
• Sheets. The higher the thread count, the nicer they feel. It seems like such a silly thing to splurge for, but you spend *a third of your life* in bed.
• Meat. If you eat meat, it can be worth it for you, animals, karma, and the planet to buy meat that was raised responsibly in a free-range or no-cage environment without antibiotics (and this tends to be more expensive).

Of course, it's OK to splurge on anything, if it's your money and you've budgeted for it. Just don't confuse "affording" something with putting it all on a credit card.

5. FARTING AND GETTING AWAY WITH IT

Maybe you're the kind of person who doesn't think twice about farting—it's natural, right? If you have to fart, you fart, and that's the end of it.

But maybe you're not there yet. Maybe you just got a new girlfriend or boyfriend and they are not aware that someone as adorable as you farts like a Holstein cow. Maybe you're alone in a public bathroom with your nemesis. Maybe you are always on the lookout for new and innovative ways to fart without anyone knowing it was you.

It just so happens I have two tips for you: (1) If you need to fart, try to get some distance from other people. Then discreetly hold your butt cheeks apart (hands on the outside of your clothes) and slowly, gennnntly, let it out. Go easy. The fart will be silent. Potent maybe, but silent. Practice with this one until you feel confident. (2) If you are around other people, you can do what my sister and I call "crop-dusting." Move away from your original position and/or friends who will know it was you—act like you're wandering aimlessly to check your phone or look at something, whatever—and then fart as you walk by groups of strangers, finally returning to your friends free of telltale stank.

6. CURING HICCUPS FOR REAL

Hiccups are annoying, though not quite as annoying as smartass friends offering useless hiccup cures. (Drink water from a glass upside down! Pinch the skin between your thumb and forefinger! Hold your breath!) I get them all the time—usually riiiight when I settle into a chair at the library, or I decide to flirt with a barista. So here is the Best Hiccup Cure I Have Ever Encountered: Get a glass of water. Take a HUGE sip. Hold the water in your mouth, and try to swallow it in eight or so separate swallows. The hiccups will nearly always desert you. #truestory

7. REMOVING BLOOD STAINS FROM SHEETS AND UNDERWEAR

Let's say you wake up in the middle of the night with a warm feeling "down there." Yep, you bled through your tampon/Diva Cup/pad, your favorite underpants, *and* your jammies, onto the sheets. Awesome.

But, really, no biggie. Get up, take off the clothes that are bloody, even if the stains are already mostly dry, and dump control is the only thing that prevents pregnancy. We don't have room here to get deeply into your options, but a quick overview: The most effective methods of birth control are the IUD and the implant, because they reduce the possibility of human error (you have to remember to take the pill every day and apply the patch every week, whereas the implant can last for three years and an IUD for five or more). Only condoms protect against both STIs and pregnancy, and using both condoms and another method of birth control (like the pill) is the surest way, if you're having penis + vagina sex, to be safe in all regards.

PULLING OUT IS AN EFFECTIVE METHOD OF BIRTH CONTROL.

Hot topic! This is a myth with a little bit of truthiness. Some studies estimate the failure rate of withdrawal to be 18 percent, which is only slightly higher than that of condoms. But! For teenagers, the failure rate for pulling out is closer to 40 percent in the first two years of use, so while you can argue that it's better than nothing, it's not *that* much better. The biggest follow-up question here tends to be whether pre-come can get you pregnant. Various studies have found either no or low sperm counts in pre-come, which means the consensus is that it *probably* can't, but there is no guarantee. And pulling out does not prevent you from getting or giving an STI.

IF YOU HAVEN'T GOTTEN ACCIDENTALLY PREGNANT BY THE TIME YOU'RE IN YOUR 20s, YOU ARE PROBABLY INFERTILE.

This is a persistent myth, and a couple of Rookies reported having friends in their 30s who still believe it. Listen, just because it hasn't happened yet doesn't mean it can't happen, even if you've had unprotected sex on a number of occasions. If you have an intact uterus and working ovaries, you are probably fertile for three or four days of your cycle, around the time of ovulation (when your ovaries release an egg), and even though this usually happens midway through the cycle, it's hard to predict. And because sperm can live in your body for up to five days, it's even harder to estimate your window of non-impregnability. It's possible that not ever getting pregnant was just dumb luck, and there's no reason to assume that you don't have to take precautions or fear that you won't ever have children. Someone is considered infertile only after they've been actively trying to get pregnant for a year, because it can take totally fertile people that long even when they're trying their very best. Getting a period every month is a pretty good sign that you are capable of getting pregnant.

ABORTIONS ARE DANGEROUS.

Abortion is a safe procedure when done in a medical setting by trained professionals. To put that in perspective, studies indicate that the mortality rate for a first-trimester abortion (the first 14 weeks of pregnancy) is 14 times lower than that for childbirth. When performed in the first trimester, an

'em in the bathroom sink. Pull the sheets off the bed and put them in the bathtub. Stop up the drain in both the sink and the tub and run COLD water over everything, focusing extra water power on the stains. When everything has soaked, you've got lots of options:

- Put club soda or fizzy water on the stains until they fizz, then blot off the stains with a washcloth or paper towel.
- Use a laundry stain stick.
- Use dishwashing soap and blot.

Then you can wash everything as usual in the laundry. Blood usually comes right out (unless you're Lady Macbeth).

8. FAKING SICK

Let us not talk about why you might need to fake sick. The point is that the day may come when you do, and you'll need to do a convincing job or you will shame me.

Many sick-shamming amateurs try to fake sick a lot, or on the day of whatever it is they don't want to go to or do. This is obvious and childish, and requires little effort on an authority figure's part to see right though. Therefore, the first key to faking sick is this: Don't do it very often, or you'll have no credibility.

The second—and most important—key to faking sick: Start early. You need to plan. If it's Thursday you want off, start coughing a little at the dinner table on Tuesday night. Don't draw attention to yourself. If a parent asks you if you're OK, say you're fine.

Come Wednesday morning, it's time to increase the coughing. It's also time to look not-so-good, because the grooming routine is the third key to faking sick. Don't wear *any* blush. If you usually wear eyeliner or eye shadow, don't, but do the rest of your makeup as usual. You'll look "off," but no one will be able to pinpoint exactly why. If you have both glasses and contacts, it's a glasses day. If you don't wear makeup, consider either applying too much moisturizer (for a sweaty sheen) or none at all (for a dried-out, dull look). Whatever makes your hair look not-greasy, don't use that, and don't brush your hair too much either. At this point, if asked if you're OK by anyone, still say, "I'm fine," but do it in a weaker voice.

Come home markedly worse than you left. Run around the house or hold your head between your legs to get red cheeks before going inside, then draaaaag yourself through the front door (assuming a witness is home). Cough around adults. If asked to dinner, say you're not hungry, and eat reeaalll slow. Don't participate much. At this point, if someone asks you if you're OK, say, "Yeah, I dunno. I'm not feeling too good." People living with you will begin to remember that you've been kind of off for a couple days now. Maybe cough your way to the bathroom in the middle of the night, especially if the bathroom is located next to parent doors.

Thursday morning: showtime! This is where you pull out all the stops. Obviously, yes, keep coughing, and find an adult and say, "I don't feel so well," or maybe even, "I think I'm gonna throw up." Head for the toilet. Do the nauseous hangout. Put your face over the bowl. If you don't fake sick

abortion is an outpatient procedure, which means you can go home the same day, and it takes about 15 minutes; in the second trimester, it is also an outpatient procedure, but it takes longer and requires more time for preparation. (If you're looking for more information about these procedures, check out PlannedParenthood.org.) Having an abortion does not affect your ability to get pregnant, stay pregnant, or give birth in the future. None of your future partners will be able to tell that you were ever pregnant.

There are so many more myths out there, and I wish I could tackle them all. (I did not mention, for example, that oral sex does not refer to making out or having phone sex, as some Rookies once thought.) But seriously, if you have questions about anything, please email us at youaskedit@rookiemag.com and we will try our best to find answers for you. ✱

very often, this will usually do the trick. Plus, smelling toilet water might induce some plausible retching. For extra drama, you can always weakly protest a guardian's decision to keep you home: "But I was supposed to hang out at [insert name of friend your mom doesn't like]'s today!"

I always thought I was a brilliant sick-faker, but it turns out there is an even better one. It's my friend Jen, whose mom is a registered nurse and was completely certain Jen was trying to trick her every single time she said she felt sick. Jen was forced to come up with advanced faking techniques such as the false high temperature, which she explains as follows: "Once your mom puts the thermometer in your mouth, and she's sitting there watching you so you can't run it under hot water or hold it up to a light bulb, make sure your mouth is completely closed, and then rapidly rub your tongue along the thermometer, as fast as you can. The friction creates a quick 'fever,' and it just looks like you're swallowing spit."

One parting word of advice: Don't try this on days when you can't make up the test. ✧

HANGING OUT WITH THE WHITE WITCH

BY HAZEL

1. DESTROY EVERYTHING YOU TOUCH – LADYTRON

2. OBLIVION – GRIMES 3. FOREST FAMILIES – THE KNIFE

4. HUNTER – PORTISHEAD 5. ONLY SNOW – THE BLONDE HUDSON WEEKEND

6. WHITE – BLOUSE 7. STOLEN CHILDREN – PARENTHETICAL GIRLS

8. COLD AS ICE – ATLAS SOUND 9. IN THE COLD I'M STANDING – M83

10. COOL AS A FIRE – CHAIRLIFT

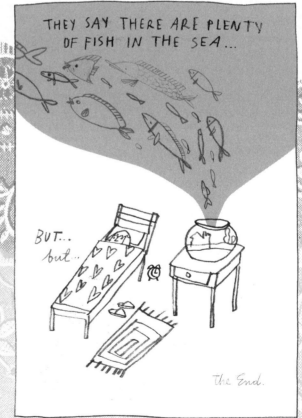

THE INVENTION OF SEX

It's all up to you.

Writing by Cindy. Playlist lettering by María Inés.

You know that thing when two of your friends get together and they're madly in love and they're having sex for the first time, or it feels for them like they're having sex for the first time, and they're all over each other and it's PDA overload and you and the rest of your circle are going, "God, it's like they think they invented sex"?

Well, actually, they did. And so can you.

You may think that there's a "right" way to have sex—judging from some of the questions we get for Ask a Grown and Just Wondering, you do, and you're worried that everyone but you knows what that is—and I can't say I blame you. If you get most of your ideas about sex from the media, popular culture, and porn, you've been taught that there are a handful of scripts that your getting down is supposed to follow—because, hey, this is how *everyone* does it.

Well, hell no. There is no such thing as "doing it right," because there is no "right" way to do something that is, after all, a private and recreational activity. Were you nervous the first time you ate ice cream that you might do it wrong?

My point is that there are no formulas. There is no recipe. Really great sex is a new invention every time you have it. You make it all up as you go along.

Every sex partner you will ever have is different. Every body has different sensitive spots (not just the obvious ones). It's fun finding them on your own—using your fingers, your lips, your tongue, your hair. Everyone reacts to pleasure differently—with different sounds, words, movements, facial expressions. Everyone has different moods, and different ways they feel like having sex during those moods (not to mention different reasons for *not* wanting to have sex on any given day).

Don't try to follow anyone else's narrative. Create your own. All you need is a sense of curiosity and wonder—and a basic understanding of the fundamental workings of your own and your partners' bodies, which is why sex education is so important. (And no, porn doesn't count here. Porn is entertainment, not education. If you use it as a source for real information, you will end up with a skewed idea of what sex is, how people's bodies actually work, and what is actually pleasurable to people you're touching. Not to mention that you'll know nothing about protecting yourself from infections, diseases, and unwanted pregnancy.) Once you have a good grasp of the basics, you can improvise: What would happen if you did...*this*? Or tried...*that*? Every great discovery comes from experimentation—putting different things together and seeing what happens. Adding and subtracting ingredients, and gauging how they react to one another. Sex is no different.

Here are some ways to experiment with your sex life, to make it your very own.

REINVENT YOUR BODIES.

It's amazing how sexy a random body part that you've never even thought about can be when you're stroking and admiring it on a loved one. And you may discover new erotic potential in previously unconsidered parts of your own body when someone else focuses on them. It could be an anklebone, a fingertip, an elbow...

There's a great movie by the French director Eric Rohmer called *Claire's Knee*, where the protagonist becomes fixated on that part of the title character's body. In Michael Ondaatje's novel *The English Patient*, Count Almásy is doing what we all do when we're crushed out—obsessing about her to a friend—and he says, "What is the name of that hollow at the base of a woman's neck? At the front. *Here*. What is it, does it have an official name?"

Your body is a wonderland. So is your partner's. Explore, discover, feel your way around—literally. Make new maps of each other's bodies. Find all the hidden treasures.

CREATE A NEW LANGUAGE.

Because we so rarely get to talk frankly about sex in public—especially us girls and women, and especially in the more sexually repressed parts of the world—the language of sex is pushed to the margins, to things like porn and dumb song lyrics and dumber books about how to "pick up women." So it's up to you to make up your own language, which is a really fun burden to carry.

You and your sex partner get to invent a vocabulary with which to express desire, appreciation, ecstasy, and love. In fact, let's start with an exercise for all of you reading this: I have been trying for years to come up with a word for giving head to a woman that's as good as *blow job*. *Cunnilingus*, *pussy-eating*, and *muff-diving* are just too technical and/or gross and/or unwieldy to catch on. We need a term that's as succinct and catchy as *blow job*—because the easier and more fun it is to talk about something, the more people will talk about it, and the more normal it will be to expect it from your partners.

(A tip for those of you just starting out on your sex life and feeling a little shy: Every request you make will be much better received when preceded by "You turn me on so much, and you'll turn me on *even more* if you…" This is where inventing your own language is useful—give whatever it is you want your partner to do some fabulous-sounding term. And when they say, "What's that?" you say, "Let me show you…")

MAKE UP GAMES.

What do you really love doing with your partner? Are there things you never thought you'd do, but now you really want to try them with her/him? Your dynamic is going to be different with every person you're with, and different with a single person from one romp to another—and your desires, like everything else about you, will shift and change constantly over the course of your life. Sex is a playground, and changing it up is a big part of the fun. I had this friend a while back who would talk to me about her love life, but *never* mentioned anything about sex. So I was startled and amused when one day, after meeting a new man (whom she'd go on to marry), she said to me out of the blue, in a tone of dreamy wonderment, "Isn't sex wonderful? It's like Six Flags, in bed." Well, she's English, so she said Alton Towers, which is the UK equivalent of Six Flags, but you get the gist. She was finding out, maybe for the first time, that with the right partner, sex really is the best amusement park there is, and you and your partner get to invent all the rides.

REINVENT EACH OTHER.

You may have many sexual partners in your life. You may have one. (You also may have none, if you choose, but you have probably already figured out that this article is not for you and stopped reading long ago.) But no matter the number (and a big one is no better or worse than a single-digit one), the ones you'll treasure most are the ones who taught you things about yourself that you'd never really known before. There's the partner who gets you to understand why people sometimes describe sex as "mindblowing"—I mean, my wish for all of you is that every time you have sex, including the first, is like this, but in the real world that isn't necessarily the case. There's the partner who makes you realize that you like something you had little to no inkling about—like role-playing, dominating someone or being dominated, or something that's unique to you. The one who flips all your gender expectations around. The one where you thought you were straight, but it turns out you're not, or not always. The one where you thought you were gay, but turns out you're not, or not always.

☆ ★ ☆

And by the way—sometimes inventions go wrong. Maybe things combust and there's an explosion in the lab that breaks things. Maybe those sizzling elements touch each other and fizzle out in a damp squib. That's OK. You learn from mistakes. It's what experimenting is all about. And when things don't turn out so great, the best possible thing you can do is laugh about them. When you start having sex and you're nervous and a bit insecure, it's easy to freak out and lose your sense of humor. Don't. Laughing about something together, admitting that that particular position was nowhere near as fun as everyone else seems to think, and coming clean about feeling awkward relaxes both of you and takes the pressure off. So, maybe your last experiment was a bust. The wonderful thing is, there are so many more you can come up with! Never stop discovering. ☆

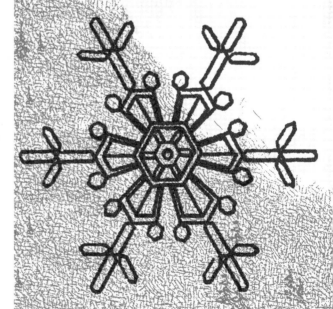

CRYSTALLINE
BY ELEANOR

1. AMPHIBIAN - BJÖRK
2. EN GALLOP - JOANNA NEWSOM
3. SHADOUT MAPES - GRIMES
4. THE FOG - KATE BUSH
5. THE WOLF THAT LIVES IN LINDSEY - JONI MITCHELL
6. MASTER'S HANDS - CHARLOTTE GAINSBOURG
7. JOURNEY IN SATCHIDANANDA - ALICE COLTRANE
8. BIRDLAND - PATTI SMITH
9. EVENING OF LIGHT - NICO
10. SMOKEY TABOO - COCOROSIE
11. SOLUSH - KRÍA BREKKAN
12. ALICE - COCTEAU TWINS
13. ASOZAN - ODIOO
14. TRY TO MAKE YOURSELF A WORK OF ART - JULIA HOLTER
15. WHAT ELSE IS THERE? - RÖYKSOPP

COSMIC DANCER

A little appreciation for the universe. By Clara Pathé and Chrissie.

Set design by Clara Pathé and Chrissie. Makeup by Lenaig Delisle. Styling by Elvia Carreon. Models: Natasha, Marissa, Andrea, and Christin of Coriolis Dance Collective, as well as Aaron and Hy. Thanks to Hy, Madison, Molly, and Fred for their assistance, and to Lucky Vintage in Seattle for lending us clothes.

MY KIND OF GUY

I had no idea that being a man would make it so hard to be myself.

By Tyler

When I was three years old, I told my dad I was a boy. He assumed it was a typical toddler linguistic mistake, but I knew better. I knew I was a boy, and every night before I went to sleep I prayed that I'd wake up with a "boy's body," by which I guess I meant a penis, which I didn't have. I was born with a vagina, so my father understandably thought I was a girl, as did everyone else but me.

In middle school, that time when everyone's priorities shifted to looking hot, being cool, and above all fitting in, I tried my best to emulate the girls in my class. I copied their makeup, miniskirts, short shorts, and high heels. I bought a subscription to *Cosmo*, thinking it would teach me how to act like, feel like, and be a girl.

By high school, I had stopped trying to fit in. I hid under a hoodie and sweatpants every day and never took off my headphones, lest someone actually try to talk to me. I didn't know it then, but I was depressed—clinically so—and in total denial of the truth I had so clearly understood and proclaimed at the age of three.

Finally, when I got to college, all those years of repressing that truth, of trying to be someone I wasn't, took their toll. My depression became so severe that I had to reduce my class hours from full-time to part-time, and there were many days when I couldn't even drag myself out of bed to walk the 200 feet to the dining hall, so I just wouldn't eat. Even the parts of my life that used to be fun—singing, hanging out with my friends—became a struggle. I knew I had to do something before depression swallowed me whole, but what?

That summer, the one between my freshman and sophomore years of college, I got a job as a camp counselor. I was assigned to co-lead, with a male counselor, a group of 12-to-14-year-olds, most of whom were boys. Hanging out with those boys reminded me how I felt when I was

a kid. I related with them way more than I did with the female campers. The boys liked me, but they didn't see me as one of them—I was the "girl counselor." And I was surprised by how much that hurt. It stung the way it does when someone insists that you're…anything that you know for a fact that you're not.

As camp wore on, it became harder and harder to tolerate being the "girl counselor." I developed intense anxiety and was constantly on edge—when I was told I couldn't take off my shirt when we went on a field trip to the beach, I became furious.

That was the alarm bell that finally woke me up from years of self-denial. Obviously I had some strong, significant, but deeply buried feelings about my gender and identity, feelings I could no longer ignore. I started looking up stuff about gender online and examining my own emotions and memories pretty much constantly. I knew I didn't feel like a girl, but that still left me a lot of options. Was I androgynous? Genderqueer? Figuring out (or I guess remembering) that I was a guy took a long time, but when I got there, I just *knew* it was right. It's hard to explain the feeling—how do cisgender people "know" what gender they are? You just know. And once I knew, I wanted to change my life, to stop pretending to be something other than what I truly am. I knew the only way I was going to stop feeling miserable 24 hours a day was by transitioning.

Transitioning means changing the way you live and the way you present yourself to the world to more accurately represent the gender you identify yourself as. There are lots of different ways to do this. Some people take hormones as adults, or hormone blockers for children who want to delay puberty until they've decided what gender they want to live as. Others choose to have what's known as sex reassignment surgery, in which one's genitals, breasts,

and/or internal reproductive organs are changed or removed. Some people opt for a combination of surgery and hormones. Some choose neither and are content transitioning in other ways: using a different name, going by a different pronoun, dressing differently, and/or behaving differently in public, e.g., using a different bathroom, going out for the boys' vs. the girls' soccer team, etc. How a person decides to transition, and what they are transitioning from and to, are as deeply personal as their reasons for wanting to do it in the first place—and all of them are equally valid.

Physically transitioning via hormones and/or surgery is a long, often difficult process. In the U.S., most doctors won't give you hormones or perform genital surgery until you've jumped the significant hurdle known as the Real-Life Experience. The RLE is a specified amount of time (in the U.S. it's usually between three months and a year; in some places, like the UK, it can be longer) during which you live as the gender you are transitioning to "full time," everywhere you go, including in your own house. It usually entails coming out to everyone in your life, name and pronoun changes, and a makeover designed to help you "pass" as the gender you identify as. (I was lucky with this last part—throughout my RLE I usually passed for a 12-year-old boy, even though I was a 20-year-old person who was born with a vagina.)

In some ways the RLE is well intentioned: It's supposed to give a transitioning person and the people in their life time to adjust to their new gender identity, and to make sure they're not "rushing" into a major operation. But it also functions as a test to see if a person is "*really*" transgender, and that never made sense to me. What does being "really" transgender even mean? And as for the concern that someone might "rush" into this—I've never known a trans* person who had not already spent years agonizing over their identity and researching their options before their first medical consultation. Why not have people prove that they *really* want a nose job by making them wear a prosthetic nose for a year?

You have to show your doctor proof that you've completed your RLE, which comes in the form of a letter from a therapist that you've been seeing regularly throughout. Any licensed therapist can give you your RLE completion letter, but not all are familiar with the protocol, so you usually have to find someone who specializes in gender issues, otherwise known as a "gender therapist." Some gender therapists are content just discussing the experience with you; others assign you homework and require recommendation letters from employers, teachers, and/or other doctors.

I think therapy in general is a great idea for any trans* person, because being gender-nonconforming in a transphobic, homophobic society can be very isolating, and it's helpful to have a safe space where you can sort out your feelings and ask questions. But having to prove the validity of my identity to a therapist was decidedly unhelpful.

There was only one gender therapist in my area (I found him online), so that's who I saw. During my first appointment, he asked the usual questions: *How long have you known you are a boy? Do you feel trapped in the wrong body? Do you hate the body you have now? Have you always?* All of these questions rely on the trans* person's acceptance of traditional gender roles, and expect them to conform to the stereotypical trans* narrative (knowing from childhood, experimenting with gender from childhood to present day, hating one's body and feeling "trapped" inside it). Your diagnosis as "really" trans* depends on your falling in line; different experiences are not accounted for. But it's not uncommon for someone to realize they're trans* as a young adult, having had a perfectly happy childhood in which they felt their gender matched their assigned-at-birth sex. Why do we have to hate our bodies or feel that they're "wrong" in order to be allowed to transition? Am I not "really" trans* because I loved my body, but preferred one that would better reflect my identity?

As I was pretending to absorb the therapist's lecture on what "being a man is all about" ("being the breadwinner, taking care of a woman"), he paused to point to my feet and said, "You can't wear purple shoes anymore." I was wearing my favorite Vans. I didn't have the guts to correct him ("They're *maroon*"), nor to add that I had left my purple ones at home, the ones that matched my purple phone case and backpack. I didn't speak up about his heterosexism or his misogyny either, because I just wanted to get through this process as quickly as possible and get my hormones. If that meant not wearing my favorite shoes for a year, fine.

During your RLE you're supposed to learn the behaviors and social expectations attached to the gender role that you're taking on. This didn't sit well with me either—why would you be encouraged to conform to the gender-based expectations of a sexist culture? But my three best guy friends were thrilled. They couldn't wait to initiate me into the world of "manhood": roughhousing, going out for beers and all using the same bathroom (and half-jokingly telling me to "man up" when I couldn't finish my beer); and deeper stuff like talking to me about what it meant to them to be a man, a son, a brother. I observed male body language and speech patterns: Men are socialized to take up more space than women; when walking, men lead with their shoulders instead of their hips. (I also tried to change the way I talked, but I couldn't eliminate the vocal inflections I had learned from 20 years of female socialization. To this day I am still all "Hi! How *are* you?! So excited to see you!" when I see someone, even [especially] someone I'm not actually excited to see.)

Suddenly I had to run everything I did, said, and even thought through a new filter: Was I crossing my legs in the right way? Did my walk resemble that of a runway model or of a football player? Did I *really* need to rant about how the best songs on *Bionic* were all written by Sia because Sia is an amazing genius? I felt that I had to disown anything "feminine" I had ever liked or done so that everyone around

me would see my transition as valid. It felt like my gender identity was starting to eclipse my personal identity.

During this time I was reading a lot of blogs and watching vlogs by trans* guys who were documenting their transitions online, and so many of them seemed to place a lot of value on being "man enough," which meant rejecting anything "feminine." They scrutinized one another's behavior closely, calling out anything that didn't conform to their idea of manhood. I'd see posts like "You want to dye your hair pink? OBVIOUSLY YOU ARE JUST A TRANS-TRENDER. NO REAL MAN WANTS TO DYE HIS HAIR PINK. STOP GIVING TRANS GUYS A BAD NAME." This made me so sad. A lot of trans* guys seem to feel that embracing their new physical "masculinity" means a wholesale rejection of anything "female," aka misogyny. I don't understand how someone who knows what it's like to be treated as female and to be discriminated against (via sexism, heterosexism, and/or homophobia) can subject others to the same discrimination. Aren't we, as trans* people, trying to show society that gender is a spectrum, and many of us don't fit where we have been assigned?

I finally finished gender therapy in June 2011. I got my proof-of-RLE letter, and I was prescribed testosterone. I had spent a total of eight months agonizing over every last bit of my personality, speech, body, and appearance just to get a piece of paper to drop off at the pharmacy. As soon as I got my prescription, a weight was lifted from my shoulders. I no longer had to prove myself to anyone or conform to anyone's stereotype of what a "real man" is. I could paint my nails without fear of being scolded by peers or told by a therapist that I was "obviously confused" or "simply a girl with tomboyish tendencies"—I was just a dude who felt like wearing nail polish, and if anyone disapproved I could show them my middle finger (its nail a pretty sea-foam green). I felt free to define myself however felt right to me. Gender isn't about measuring up to someone else's expectations—it's just a way to be the person you already are. ✧

my mom. wasn't she beautiful?

FEBRUARY 2013: *Passion*

Happy February, Rookies!

This month's theme is Passion, and the best way to introduce it might be to ask that you go download and listen to "Blame it on my wild heart" by Stevie Nicks.

Where is the reason?
Don't blame it on me,
Blame it on my wild heart

This sentiment has become a personal mantra of some sort. This past fall, I started diagramming every lyric Stevie Nicks has ever written, and found that her songs are often about these adventurous, puzzling women, probably all wearing cloaks, most likely also holding doves, always challenging those around them, always asking a series of questions, and always having a ton of feelings. Kinda like all of us at Rookie this month.

Look, I am as disgusted as you right now. Even writing this feels kind of silly—the word PASSION is way overused and corny, and who am I to say I'm some special emotional snowflake? But the alternative is to write something ironic and removed, and I hate that—I'm obviously already making an effort with this, why pretend that I don't care?

The process known as "growing up" is riddled with Pandora's boxes. The negative of every circumstance becomes more and more visible, and you have to accept it if you want the positive, too—be it in a friendship, an opportunity, or listening to an album that might do something to your breathing for a moment instead of keeping you up and busy. I used to accept the negative by believing it would all one day pay off as material for my EGOT-winning body of work based on the horrors of my life and personality, making it all worth it. I used to scheme, basically. But bad experiences are no longer a means to an end for me. Since I became especially enamored by Stevie a year ago, they have become enough for me all on their own—certainly acceptable, and even invigorating. As difficult as it is to convince myself of this when such experiences are actually taking place, I really do think I prefer a life of emotional range to one that's consistently happy. It's not that I believe you need the bad to appreciate the good—as Dave Foley says, pie does not taste better because somebody somewhere has AIDS—but I do believe that there's a difference between happiness and fulfillment, and I think the latter is more for me.

My goofiest-sounding secret is that I also believe in magic. Sometimes I call it God and sometimes I call it light, and I believe in it because every now and then I read a really good book or hear a really good song or have a really good conversation with a friend that seems to have some kind of shine to it. The list I keep of these moments in the back of my journal is composed less of times when I was laughing or smiling and more of times when I felt like I could feel the colors in my eyes deepening from the display before me. Times in which I felt I was witnessing an all-encompassing representation of life driven by an understanding that, coincidence or not, our existence is a peculiar thing, and perhaps the greatest way to honor it is to just be human. To be happy AND sad, and everything else. And yeah, living is a pain, and I say I hate everyone and everything, and I don't exude much enthusiasm when sandwiched between fluorescent lighting and vinyl flooring for seven hours straight, and I will probably mumble a bunch about how much I wish I could sleep forever the next time I have to wake up at 6 AM. But make no mistake about it: I really do like living. I really, truly do.

I hope you like this month.

LOVE, TAVI

Rhiannon

SMASHED

Falling in and out of love with your first favorite band.
Writing by Pixie, illustration by Kendra.

Can't live for tomorrow... Tomorrow's much too long

I wanna turn you on

I. FIRST TIME THAT I EVER SAW YOU

The summer of 1993, I would have followed my cousins Tracy and John anywhere. They were siblings, 13 and 14 years old, and I was 12; and though that's not a big gap in terms of actual chronological time, the dividing line between *teenager* and every age that comes before it is clear, strong, and immovable. To me my cousins seemed *impossibly* cool—worldlier and more mature than I could ever hope to be. They dressed cool, they listened to music by bands no one else had even heard of, and they seemed to discover trends ages before they trickled down to me and my friends.

That summer, our whole extended family went on vacation together to Cape Cod. Tracy and John had an effortless way of navigating the beachfront stores, finding perfect accessories for their ever-evolving identities, while I straggled behind, trying to look like I belonged with them, in their world. It is to my cousins' credit that they never tried to ditch me; with my giant glasses and my abundance of orthodontia, I certainly wasn't helping their cred, though they made me feel cool by association.

They were going through a grunge/alt phase that summer, so they introduced me to bands like Mudhoney and Sonic Youth, and to songs by bands like Nirvana and Pearl Jam besides the ones they played on the radio. But they could also speak knowledgeably about hip-hop, dance music, jam bands, punk, pop—pretty much everything—and when they did so, I paid attention, trying to soak up as much information as I could. I wanted to know everything they knew, to like everything they liked (well, maybe except for the jam bands—sorry, dudes).

Before that trip, I just listened to whatever my older sister listened to—mostly Top 40. Under Tracy and John's tutelage I basically exchanged one set of secondhand tastes for another—one that was definitely more sophisticated, but no more *mine*.

Then one day my cousins decided to walk into one of those ramshackle old beachfront record stores—the kind that smell like sand and patchouli and decaying wood and greatness—and while they combed hungrily through the racks, I found myself transfixed by a poster on the wall with a picture of two mischievous-looking little girls sharing what looked like a popsicle. The poster advertised a record that had just been released about a month before (and is now—gulp—20 years old). I didn't know anything about it, or the band, but I remember thinking that their name—the Smashing Pumpkins—was kind of scary, since it describes a violent act, but also kind of funny, as it evoked an image of, like, the Monopoly Man looking at a pumpkin and declaring it "smashing." The funny/scary juxtaposition spoke to me, because I had just entered a phase where I dealt with my anxiety by trying to find the absurdity in everything I feared.

I noted the name of the album—*Siamese Dream*—but I didn't buy it that day, because I knew my mom wouldn't react well to the song title "Silverfuck." But I kept thinking about that photo of the two girls. Soon after that I heard the first single from that album, "Cherub Rock," on the radio, and was immediately captivated by the loud, trippy guitars and the anthemic chorus. I asked John what he thought of the Smashing Pumpkins and he said they were "pretty good," but he didn't seem super into them, which I liked, because this was something that could belong to *me*, not to my parents, not to my sisters, not to my cousins. This was something that was mine to love, sight and sound.

II. FREAK OUT / AND GIVE IN

Having covered the first two stages of falling in love—curiosity, then a crush—I moved on to step three: obsessive adoration. This kicked in when I saw the video for "Today" on MTV. It features the lead

Pumpkin, Billy Corgan, as a bummed-out ice cream man who ditches his regular route to drive into the desert, where makeout sessions and paint fights ensue.

It was the first time I'd seen the band outside of promo shots in magazines, and whatever magic their visuals + their sound created when they came together, it worked on me. I felt instantly, deeply connected to them, like they'd been waiting for me, painting that ice cream truck, hanging around in that desert, until I caught up.

The song had a singsong melody accompanied by fairly dark lyrics ("Can't live for tomorrow / Tomorrow's much too long / I'll burn my eyes out / Before I get out"), which hit my sweet spot of silly and sinister. The music was quiet and loud, happy and angry—an optimist's howl attempting to break through a dark and scary chaos. As the guitars swelled I felt a rush of triumph, like I was overcoming something.

"I wanna turn you onnnnnn," Billy growled. *Mission accomplished*, thought 12-year-old me. The Smashing Pumpkins became my first musical passion, and like all obsessive loves, it burned too hot to last.

Over the next few years, I begged my mother to take me to the mall so I could buy every Pumpkins album I could find (luckily she never noticed the swear on *Siamese Dream*)—and when I couldn't find a bootleg or an import at the regular record stores, I implored her to take me to the specialty ones. My room was plastered with Pumpkins posters, my drawers filled with band T-shirts. I drew the SP symbol on basically everything I owned. By the time I got to high school, when the band released their biggest album ever, *Mellon Collie & the Infinite Sadness*, I was spending most of my study-hall time writing Billy's lyrics in my notebooks, and I never went anywhere without at least four Pumpkins CDs to listen to. I cut my hair short and convinced my mother to let me get plat-

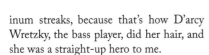

inum streaks, because that's how D'arcy Wretzky, the bass player, did her hair, and she was a straight-up hero to me.

I fell in love with the Smashing Pumpkins because I felt like Billy Corgan was the only person on earth who understood what I was going through, because he wrote about sadness and confusion and love and darkness and anger and did so in a perfect storm of sarcasm and angst, that 1-2 combination of "fuck off" and "please love me" that felt very familiar to teenage me (and, I imagine, many other people). It was music that I could cry to, rage out to, get excited by, and find solace in. But falling in love with your first favorite band is all-consuming: You're not just falling for a sound, but also for an image, an idea, the people behind the entire endeavor, and the atmosphere they create. My love for the Pumpkins even spilled over into my actual love life: My high school boyfriend was just as obsessed with them as I was, and the band was something we bonded over and, later, something I turned to for help dealing with a very angsty breakup.

III. GREAT LOVES WILL ONE DAY HAVE TO PART

The last time I saw Billy Corgan in person, it was the year 2000 and I was being rescued from a pit filled with aggressive bros who seemed determined to kill everyone. I was 19, and the band was roughly eight months away from breaking up. I remember being lifted by a security guard and making brief eye contact with Billy, dream of dreams, and giving him a "Sorry I almost died down there, I wanted to stay!" face, to which he raised his eyebrows in a "What are you going to do?" kind of way. He looked bored to me, but maybe I was just projecting—four years earlier I would gladly have broken several ribs and possibly a leg to watch the band play "Starla."

Driving home from the show that night, I didn't feel my usual post-concert euphoria. I wasn't drowning in pure bliss—there was a drop of something new in the mix, or maybe some ingredient had been removed, but I felt a little off. I felt a little less. It was that feeling where you still love someone but you're no longer in love with them. Of course, I wasn't the same person I'd been when I saw that poster seven years earlier. The band had changed a lot too. When Billy finally announced the band's breakup, I was somewhat relieved. I had spent my adolescence slavishly devoted to them, and they had spent their young adulthood catering to obsessive fanatics like me, and maybe it was time for all of us to take a break from one another.

IV. YESTERDAY THE SKY WAS YOU

It's hard to explain what exactly happened to our love. Maybe I outgrew the songs, or the memories I'd attached to them, or maybe I wanted to feel the same way I felt when I first heard them, which was impossible, because I wasn't 12 anymore, and instead of listening to the songs and imagining what my teenage life would be like, I'd actually gone out and lived it. Some of it was as beautiful and hopeful as the songs promised, some as heartbreaking, and some of it was disappointing, as I hit my 20s in a tailspin of depression and didn't know how to keep alive the spirit of optimism-within-darkness that the band had often given me.

Falling out of love with your favorite band is a strange kind of heartbreak. It's hard to accept that some loves are temporary, and that something that once defined your identity and helped you feel safe and understood can't do that for you anymore.

It's also hard to admit that someone you once thought could do no wrong, can. The band's breakup was so bitter that it made me hear the music differently—what had been comforting now sounded heavier, nastier. And some of the records Billy Corgan put out in the years that followed just weren't for me, which forced me to face the fact that he had his own visions and goals and that "perpetually re-creating within Pixie Casey the feeling she had when she was 12" was probably not among them. On Twitter, you often see groups of fans directly scolding their idols for changing in any way. I get it; I hate change, too. But you can't stop people and things and the world and your life. What you can do is learn to let go.

V. I'LL HEAR YOUR SONG / IF YOU WANT ME TO

I'm grateful for everything the Smashing Pumpkins did for me. They helped me through some truly dark days, encouraged me to write poems (terrible ones, but those can be just as important), and gave me access to a secret world that I had discovered all on my own. They were my first obsessive love, before I'd ever fallen in love with a person. And in a way they prepared me for that scarier kind of love: The deep connection I felt to the band and their music was good practice for eventually allowing myself to connect with another human being.

To this day I have a soft spot for anyone who tells me that the Pumpkins were their favorite band in high school—I feel like we would have been friends, or made out, or at least spent hours talking about Billy Corgan's lyrics and/or silver pants. But I also know that at some point one of us will make fun of how obsessed we were, and the other one will laugh it off, and we'll lock it up and distance ourselves from how *intense* we used to be, and how *emotional*, and how *embarrassing*. Why are we so eager to disown our younger selves? Maybe we're trying to avoid getting lost in nostalgia, trapped in our own memories. Maybe we're ashamed of how angsty we used to be. Or maybe we just remember how much it hurt to go through those times.

Last June, I was having a crap day, and, on a whim, I downloaded *Oceania*, the new album by a new version of the Smashing Pumpkins in which every member besides Billy has been replaced. I wasn't sure what to expect, but as I listened to the opening notes of the first song, "Quasar," I suddenly felt 12 years old again, bouncing my head around and dancing in my computer chair. It was the first time in a long time that listening to a Pumpkins record was *fun*. It was nice to know that even though I'm not that obsessive kid anymore, I haven't abandoned her completely. That, like my cousins did that summer on Cape Cod, and the Pumpkins did for my entire teenagehood, I could accept her. She needed that, and she still does. ❦

B.C. + P.C. 4EVER!

Love at First Sight

What is it? Is it real? A semi-scientific inquiry.
Writing by Jane Marie. Playlist by Pixie, art by Minna.

Here's what it feels like when it happens: First my earlobes get kind of hot and then my hearing goes all *wahWAHwahWAh*. Next, I feel warm in my cheeks and my stomach sort of drops like going over a hill and my fingers tingle and my heart starts to race. Only then does my brain engage, but all it says is "Go get that person and put their body inside our body and keep it there until the day one or both of you die, which will hopefully be at the exact same time 70 years from this moment." Love at first sight: It is what dreams, rom-coms, and the best, totally realistic and achievable R&B love songs are made of! But "love at first sight" can also produce some of the most comical, epically disastrous breakups possible. I should know. It's something of a habit of mine.

My last one was about five years ago. I was freshly divorced (from a totally other love-at-first-sight situation) and had just moved to New York to work on a TV show. One of my jobs was to find and license the music on the show, only it wasn't like the music on *Glee* or anything, it was mostly instrumentals. So I spent a lot of time getting in touch with musicians to get

permission to use their music. We wanted to use a song by this one musician—or group? I had no idea. So I Googled them, found their Myspace, and got hit with a ton of love bricks. Looking back, the picture wasn't even good—his eyes were squinted, his lip curled into a snarl. But at the time I didn't interpret that as "grumpy and angry," but rather as "icy and alone," which led to the thought, *This man needs some warming up!* I knew exactly nothing about him, except that he was a solo artist, not a group; I was 29 years old and already divorced once. I don't believe in fate, or destiny, order, God, or a "plan." But I literally thought, when I saw his picture, *This person was MADE FOR ME.*

I read his bio and learned that he lived in another country, which was no obstacle to our perfect union, as far as I was concerned. Within a few days we'd exchanged two emails and I was telling friends over dinner that I'd "finally found my person." He could've been a mass murderer for all I knew, or had a girlfriend, which he did, which I DID know about, and here I was thinking the "stars had finally aligned" or something? Oh, and this was maybe the 10th time in

my life I'd had this rare, magical experience so far. The first was in sixth grade, with a boy who never spoke to me but gave me his ID bracelet *through a friend* and let me wear it for a week before having that friend ask for it back. And the last time, when I was almost 30, it felt *exactly* the same, so you can see how much I learned from each of the eight interceding experiences. Nothing! But I blame nature—and not going to therapy soon enough.

There are biological and psychological causes for this overwhelming "love at first sight" feeling, and none of them involves some grand scheme where the universe creates two people who are perfect for each other and then waits 17 years to orchestrate entire school systems' sports programs to ensure that they meet at an intramural volleyball tournament. The reality is that love at first sight is all in your head. You are actually making the whole thing up! Let's look at the science.

There was a study done in Dublin recently that suggested that if you're attracted to someone based on looks alone, you'll probably still like them after talking to them for five minutes. Scientists

cootie catcher

fortune teller by ginette lapalme ♥

HOW TO FOLD

REINFORCE CREASES

BOTTOM TOP TOP CLOSED

HOW TO USE

1. ASK A YES OR NO QUESTION
2. CHOOSE SHAPE. SPELL IT OUT
3. CHOOSE FLAP. COUNT LETTERS
4. REPEAT STEP 3 5. CHOOSE FINAL FLAP. OPEN AND READ YOUR ANSWER

* cootie catcher is never wrong *

there set up a speed-dating event and showed the participants pictures of everyone they were about to meet. If someone was attracted to another person based on their picture, it turned out, there was very little that the object of this attraction could say during such a short meeting to negate the attracted person's initial desire. After their five-minute "dates," the volunteers stuck with their appearance-alone choices 63 percent of the time. Which isn't a *huge* majority, but my point is, this is what is happening when you fall in "love at first sight": Your brain is going, "Oooh, that person is fine. And they are wearing a T-shirt of a band that I like! C'MON, LET'S QUIT SCHOOL/WORK, PACK UP OUR STUFF, AND MOVE AS SOON AS POSSIBLE TO ANOTHER COUNTRY TO BE WITH SOMEONE WE HAVE NEVER EVEN TALKED TO!" It doesn't work like that, brains. You have to actually get to *know* people. Ugh, brains are so stupid!

You want to know what's worse? The next thing that happens is that your brain reacts to this total stranger like they're a drug you're addicted to. Dr. Helen Fisher, a biological anthropologist at Rutgers University, looked at MRIs of people in new relationships who described themselves as "madly in love," and noticed that the reward and craving center in our brain—the ventral tegmental area, which happens to be the same place that jumps into action when someone uses cocaine—goes kind of nuts when we think about the person we're in love with, and releases a ton of dopamine, aka the "pleasure chemical." Over time, the more dopamine your brain gets, the more you want. So if someone, upon first glance, causes that part of your brain to fire, you might be on your way to becoming basically *addicted* to being around them. For all you know, they could have a totally incompatible sexual orientation at best, or hate rap music at worst, and here you are already under their spell.

Think about the strongest crush you've ever had: At the beginning of the crush, you can't stop thinking about this person. Your only goal is to be near them as much as possible, and when you are, you've never been happier. This is awesome and can remain awesome if you get really lucky, but if you happen to fall in love with a jerk because you didn't take the time to get to know them before you put all your eggs in their basket, it can be the most ridiculous situation in the world. Now think of when you've been your most heartbroken: You long even more desperately for that person and recall only the most romantic, positive parts of your time together. You feel more attached to them than when you got to be with them several times a week. How is this possible after they clearly stated that they don't like you anymore and want you to go away? Because your brain craves the dopamine that they trigger, and addiction is stronger than reason. (Tangent: Let's all practice not crushing on people who don't like us.)

There are countless other biological variables involved in falling in love, including hormones and genes, but what about the psychological factors? I know people hate to get Freudian in these conversations, but reduced to their simplest possible rendering, Sigmund Freud's theories on what we find initially attractive in other people sound pretty right-on to me. Back in the late 1800s, he posited that our first "romantic" feelings are directed at the people who raised us when we were babies. This doesn't mean kids have literal amorous feelings toward their parents, but that since as an infant you depend wholly on your caretakers for your happiness and comfort (or discomfort), they're the first people you look at with all-consuming adoration, and this love you have for them builds the architecture in your brain that will later house your crushy feelings. When you're older and scanning the world for appropriate crush objects, you'll try, whether you know it or not, to find people who can comfortably live there too—strangers with qualities that you find familiar because they remind you of how your parents treated you, or how they treated each other, or both. This works for both good and ill: If you had amazing parents or guardians who respected each other and treated you with love, care, and compassion, not only will you expect the same from a partner, you will naturally be more attracted to people who treat you that way. But some of us didn't have the greatest parents—maybe they were cold or they fought all the time or were abusive—*those* are the familiar qualities that our traitorous brains will be looking for, and we will fall for people who have them without being able to explain why except to say that we *understand* these jerkfaces and feel comfortable with them and not with some weirdo nice person. AUGH! It's totally unfair.

If you've ever had an instantaneous crush on someone that turned into a tumultuous and ultimately unsuccessful relationship, think about that person now. Focus on what attracted you to them in the first place. If it was the same exact thing that made going out with them not that much fun, I'd be surprised if that quality didn't remind you of someone from your past. (You might have to really focus to remember anything unpleasant about them—and again, you can blame science: Studies have suggested that our brains kind of protect us from reliving the pain of negative experiences by conveniently focusing on the good stuff and blurring out the bad.)

I should say here that even though love at first sight has never worked out for me, it's not a disaster for everyone. Some people get lucky and run into someone at a party who is wonderful, trustworthy, and loyal and who makes their dopamine go nuts, and then they develop a perfect mix of pleasurable chemicals and optimism about the person that can sustain a relationship over the long haul. In fact, in such lucky cases, "love at first sight" actually gives your relationship an advantage: According to a 2004 study from Ohio State University, if you get that positive feeling from someone during your first encounter and you do end up dating, it's more likely that you'll still feel that way about them nine weeks later. It's a totally irrational and premature trust based on a fantasy, sure, but that illusion allows you to communicate with your crush more freely, and thus become closer to them. It's kind of a self-fulfilling prophecy: You can picture yourself with this person forever, so you treat them in a way that would foster long-term closeness, and sometimes you hit the jackpot and you end up falling actually, truly in love with a great person. But it all starts out the same way, with a drug: dopamine.

If that describes your relationship, congratulations! But let's say you're like me, and "love at first sight" is a warning sign that you are about to go down a painful, time-consuming dead-end path. What do you do instead of trying to bend the universe to allow you to spend every waking moment with that person you saw *once* at a party a few weeks ago?

What worked for me was kind of a four-pronged approach to developing saner relationships:

1. Determine the kind of relationship and partner you want, setting aside the thought of any particular person. Make a list, even! Would you like someone to call you twice a day, or is once a week enough? Someone who wants to spend their life in academia, or someone who hopes to one day manage the store they've been working at since freshman year? A person who is very close to their immediate family or more of a loner? An emotionally expressive person or one who plays it close to the vest? There are no right answers, only right answers *for you*, so be completely honest with yourself. For example, I know that I need kind of a *lot* of attention from my love object. I need them to remind me often that they care about me, because it's easy for me to forget. On my list, which I actually did put in my phone along with a few tips from my therapist, I wrote:

• Absolutely available: no spouses or significant others
• Loves his mother
• No substance abuse
• Buys me flowers when we won't see each other for a while
• Texts or calls often and promptly

I used to try to be the "cool girl" who totally rolls with the punches and is unfazed when her love interest doesn't call or text for a few days. I was confident in other areas of my life, and too embarrassed to admit that I wasn't always that way in relationships—that I needed a little extra handholding in the beginning to feel secure. It didn't help that I had a pattern of choosing partners who fed my insecurities and acted like it was a drag to reply to my phone calls or show in any way that they were thinking of me. But then I learned a miraculous thing in therapy that I'm going to pass on to you: It is never weak to ask for what you need. Furthermore, it turns out that my old axiom, "If you have to ask for it, it doesn't count," is dead wrong. In fact, it can mean even *more* if you ask someone for something and they give it to you just because they *know you want it*, even if it goes against their habits or instincts. Once I started looking for someone who wouldn't mind sending me a sweet text once a day, occasionally buying me flowers, and calling me their girlfriend, it turned out not to be embarrassing at all.

2. Slow down in the beginning; take some time to get to know the person before you go all in. Say you're trying to quit smoking, but you're craving a cigarette really bad. You know that smoking one will immediately make you feel better, but you also know that long term it'll kill you, so you have to overcome the desire for instant gratification with logic, reasoning, and a genuine desire to change. It's the same way with the drug called love at first sight. Tell your dopamine receptor to calm down—you'll get it some more drugs in a minute, but right now you're trying to be reasonable. Work hard against indulging your addiction to this new "perfect" stranger so that you can determine if they have the qualities you're looking for in a partner (refer to your list), and so you can spot any red flags.

3. Have faith that if you want it, you can find romantic love and attraction with someone who doesn't immediately drive you wild. This is the hardest one. If you find yourself generally drawn to people who are good for you, skip this paragraph. But if you, like me, always get it wrong, maybe you need to step outside your comfort zone and date against your "type." This will mean that you might not get that big dose of dopamine upon first glance, but trust me—it can come later. I'm not talking about dating someone you don't even *want* to like, but if you find someone who meets your list of requirements, and you like hanging out with them, think about giving them a chance. This isn't the same as stringing someone along, telling them that you care for them more than you do—that's unfair, and it can be really hurtful. I'm just saying spend time with the person. Go on dates, be friends, flirt, and see what happens. A lot of us have had the experience of falling in love with someone we used to think of as "just a friend"—it's totally possible, but you'll never know if you just write off anyone who doesn't make your brain chemicals go crazy right off the bat. Which leads me to:

4. You don't have to take every crush seriously. Sometimes crushes are just a fun way to learn how to draw new initials graffiti-style—they do not all have to lead somewhere. It's even fun to have five crushes at once, one for each of your different alter egos. "Love at first sight" is a feeling, not a commandment. Wallow in it, fantasize, blush when you talk to her/him/them, and enjoy it, but take it easy if you can. More often than not the person will end up doing something unattractive enough to cure you of your crush before anything exciting happens anyway!

But what if you've never been in love at first sight? Does that mean there's something wrong with you? No! You deserve a gold star, because you, my dear, are a well-adjusted, reasonable person unfazed by wayward chemicals and un-dealt-with childhood traumas. You will most likely have a much easier time finding true love than the rest of us. Or you might not even be interested in romantic love at all, which would be such a relief, and I am jealous of the time you are spending trekking through Nepal, or writing a book, or becoming president, or doing really complicated origami.

So, after I had crossed an international border to be with him, and lived with him for a while, things with my last LAFS (ha!) started to go downhill, and then degenerated even more, until we finally had this exchange (*over the phone*):

Him: I don't love you.
Me: What? [*aaand crying*]
Him: Eh, it happens. People stop loving people all the time. You need to accept that.

And that was that. That breakup hurt so bad that I finally stopped trusting my own heart (more precisely, my own eyes) when it came to guys. For whatever reason, there is a bug in my system where if I meet someone who makes me feel all swoony right away, I can pretty much guarantee that they're not going to make me happy in the long run.

I was single for a few years after that. Anytime I found myself attracted to someone, I ran fast in the other direction. Meanwhile, I started going on dates here and there with people who didn't zing me off my feet, just to see what I'd been missing. Turns out I'd been missing a lot! And being treated with respect and kindness made up for not getting the dopamine rush I chased for so many years.

Then one day I ran into a friend after a comedy show, and after we'd exchanged some niceties, he asked if I was dating anyone. I told him no, and he said, "Great. You should go out with my friend Julian." He showed me a picture on his phone of a sweet-faced guy holding a bouquet of flowers—the kind of picture that, if I'd seen it a few years earlier, I'd have been like, *He's a nice-looking young man. Yawn.* He had none of the brooding, none of the just-under-the-surface anger, that I am naturally such a sucker for. But now I was like, *Oh, wow, that's…different. He looks…sweet? Sure, I'll give it a try.*

On our first date, my earlobes didn't get hot, my stomach didn't do flips, my heart rate was steady. No magical fairy dust fell over my eyes when I laid them on him—but now, a few years later, I'm DROWNING in it. Love at first sight has nothing on the feeling I get from the fresh flowers my husband sends every time he has to leave town, along with a note that says "BRB." ☺

the smiths

THIS CHARMING MAN: AN INTERVIEW WITH MORRISSEY

"My life as a teenager was so relentlessly foul."
Interview by Amy Rose, illustration by Kendra.

I don't think I really need to introduce you guys to Morrissey, but just in case: He's been an icon for, oh, more than three decades now. He began his career in the early '80s as the frontman (and heart) of the Smiths before going solo in 1987, and he is notorious not only for his music, but also for his political activism, especially when it comes to animal rights (he recently cancelled a performance on *Jimmy Kimmel Live* because the cast of A&E's *Duck Dynasty* was also scheduled to appear).

Moz has been hugely important to so many of us over the years because his songs are relentlessly passionate, and he celebrates his individuality rather than being marginalized by it. No matter how dark his lyrics get, he never loses sight of the beauty and humanity in other people and himself. His music has saved my life many times, so it's hard to express just how much I love him, and how absolutely blown away with joy and gratitude I was when he graciously agreed to answer some questions via email for Rookie.

AMY ROSE You started writing music when you were in your teens, and you published books about James Dean and the New York Dolls in your early 20s. What was your creative process like as a young person, and how has it changed?

MORRISSEY Those weren't books, just juvenile essays, and thoughtless rubbish at that. I had no creative process, just pain, which I mistakenly assumed might be creative process. Well, it wasn't…

The way you address alienation in your music really resonates with your fans. Do you think a certain degree of loneliness enriches our lives? Is it OK, or even good, to feel alone?

Everyone is, in fact, alone. Being contractually tied to another person—in marriage, for example—accentuates the loneliness, because you have effectively allowed the state to determine your obligations to someone, as if you can't trust and manage your own feelings by yourself. Anyway, I see humans as essentially solitary creatures, and this is not changed by surrounding ourselves with others, because they too are solitary. Life is a very serious business for the simple reason that nobody dies laughing.

What were your greatest aspirations as a young person, and would you say you've achieved them?

My greatest aspiration was to make it through the coming week. As a teenager I found life to be inevitably disgusting, and I could see no humanity in the human race. When my time in music began, I found all my goals were reachable. For the first time ever in my life, I spoke and people listened. I had never known such a thing previously. My life as a teenager was so relentlessly foul that I still can't believe I actually survived it. Perhaps I didn't…

What political causes mattered most to you back then, and are they still important to you now?

War, I thought, was the most negative aspect of male heterosexuality. If more men were homosexual, there would be no wars, because homosexual men would never kill other men, whereas heterosexual men love killing other men. They even get medals for it. Women don't go to war to kill other women. Wars and armies and nuclear weapons are essentially heterosexual hobbies.

But the most political gesture you can make is to refuse to eat animals. It was so when I was a teenager, and is still the case now.

What music or movies or artists do you recommend to your teenage fans today that they might not know about?

The arts have diminished, because we are now living through a time when we are encouraged not to think. No one making music wants to waste time struggling with art. A group like the Sex Pistols would

never again be allowed to slip through, and there is no such thing in 2013 as a popular artist who sets their own terms for success. Whether it be Beyoncé or Justin Bieber, we see singers who have absolutely nothing to offer anyone as they walk offstage clutching three Grammys in each hand.

Many of your lyrics deal with self-preservation in a world that can sometimes be less than gentle. You strike a balance between acknowledging personal hardship and pain and fiercely appreciating beauty. What helps you to see the loving and good parts of life during tough times?

If I feel it, then others surely must. That's the only thought that sustains me.

At the end of each of your shows, people rush the stage and try to hug you or hold your hand. You're always very gracious about it in a way that many artists aren't, but how do you feel about it?

In recent years I saw McDonna live, and no audience member reached up toward her to try to touch her. I see this so often with artists who we're told are global stars. It is a big lie. Or else, you might possibly be a big star, but you are not loved. My audience has an urgent need to touch, to shake hands, to move out of their seats, to defy so-called security, to make physical contact. They don't simply sit and observe, but feel the urge to act. It's a great compliment for me, and one that most Grammy winners could probably never imagine.

One of our readers said that she realized you two were soulmates when she noticed she was wearing the same color nail polish as you at one of your shows. I'm sure our readers want to know: Where do you find good cruelty-free products?

It isn't difficult these days, because lots of companies have abandoned animal testing, mainly because they know people no longer want animal-tested products—for moral reasons, but also because of the logical realization that a test on an animal doesn't have any bearing on how human skin will react to the same ingredient. [Some of the major companies] have started to turn their backs on animal torture, and that's very encouraging. And some companies—Clarins, for example—say they do not test on animals, but they won't print this information on their products. But if there were any real concerns for public safety, then cigarettes, which kill most of their customers, would never be sold.

How would you describe the experience of writing your forthcoming memoir, and what do you hope readers will take from it?

I think autobiography is mostly self-worship, or personal mythology. In my case, self-disgust is the spur, which doesn't mean it isn't poetic or elevated or even funny.

What would you like to achieve, as a person and an artist, in the years to come?

I have no vision of the future. I never have. There is nothing to consider other than today. I'm saving tranquility for when I'm dead.

If you could tell your teenage self one thing, what would it be?

I am still my teenage self. If you think that we all step through a door marked Adult, or that we sign a Grown-Up Document, you're quite wrong. We remain as we always were, and that, alas, is one of life's many nasty tricks. ◊

Everybody knows this is NOWHERE

Photos by Petra, collage and illustration by Minna

As long as we can
sail away

was thinkin' about   what a friend had said,
was hopin' it was...   a lie...

Teenage Love

FOR LOVERS ONLY

I thought I knew, but now I know that rose trees never grow in New York City...

Literally the Best Thing Ever: Stevie + Christine

Their relationship survived Fleetwood Mac, and that's effing amazing.
Writing by Jessica, illustration by Brooke Nechvatel.
Playlist by Pixie, art by Minna.

In 1977, Fleetwood Mac released *Rumours*, a magical, haunting, complicated album detailing the breakups of the two couples in the quintet, and it quickly became the best-selling record of that era. The band had begun in the '60s as a dude-ish blues-rock outfit, but in the early '70s two women were added to the lineup: the British keyboardist/singer Christine McVie and a California-by-way-of-Arizona singer called Stevie Nicks.

In the band photo on the album's back cover the two look like the same stripe of hip and witchy gals, but in their music they were opposites. Christine's songs were breezy, romantic, direct—all smiley faces and hearts. Stevie's songs were plodding, mysterious, and bittersweet—she sang about drugs, the man she'd loved (Mac guitarist Lindsey Buckingham), and her best girlfriends (she wrote the demo "Think About It" to support Christine during her divorce from Mac bassist John McVie). The two wrote an equal number of songs on this album, but the only number one hit ("Dreams") was Stevie's. Onstage, Christine sat behind the piano, while Stevie, who couldn't play any instruments and so was given a tambourine, took center stage, twirling in her diaphanous gowns and enchanting the audience. She was the spectacle. Christine was the background.

In any true girl best-friendship, I think it's natural to feel like one of you is the Christine, the competent one in the shadows, while the other is the Stevie, the dazzling rock star with natural charm. If you're the Christine, your friendship is like a passport to another life, and you feel extra-lucky that you get to know the private, life-size version of your sparkly friend. I know, because in seventh grade, *I* was the Christine, and my best friend, Jennifer,* was Stevie.

Jennifer was a master flirt who didn't seem to come with the default mortal fear of boys that the rest of us did. She barely cared what anyone thought of her, period. And of course, since she didn't care whether the boys paid attention to her, that's all they wanted to do. They'd even meet up with her at the mall, which all the other girls in our junior high marveled at (the boys never wanted to go to the mall).

I was not a girl that boys wanted to get to know, but being Jennifer's sidekick meant fielding endless questions about her from them, and there was a funny power to that. I was the one she hung with on the epic boring days, the one who knew who she really had a crush on. Friendships can be wholly different on the inside, and privately, Jennifer and I were equal. How other people saw us had no bearing on our closeness.

Christine had been in Fleetwood Mac for about five years before Stevie joined. When the band's drummer, Mick Fleetwood, proposed adding the songwriting duo Lindsey and Stevie to the lineup, he arranged for Christine to meet them. Recounting that meeting in the Fleetwood Mac bio *The First*

---

*This name has been changed.

30 Years, Christine said, "The last thing I was thinking about at that point was another girl in the band. I had been so used to being the only girl!" But Stevie and Christine hit it off from the beginning. "I liked her instantly," said Christine. "She was a bright, very direct, tough little thing. I liked her not because she was like me—quite the contrary. We're complete opposites…The one thing we had in common was a good sense of humor." If the two women hadn't become friends, the band wouldn't have become what it did.

The first Mac record that the pair made together was 1975's self-titled album, and listening to Christine's congenial "Over My Head" vs. Stevie's brooding "Rhiannon," you can sense the difference in their personalities. Then came *Rumours*. During the making of it, both Stevie and Christine broke up with their dudes, who were obviously still in the band—and in the recording studio, and in their faces all day every day while they were working in Sausalito, California. The ladies rented a condo overlooking the San Francisco Bay and retreated there while the rest of the band stayed up all night partying in the studio accommodations/rock & roll frat house. Christine and Stevie talked through their heartbreaks and hopes for the future, encouraged each other, and hid in each other's rooms when their exes showed up drunk and yelling in the driveway, according to Ken Callait, who produced *Rumours* and co-wrote a book about it.

The band toured sporadically during the recording, and while "Over My Head" had given Fleetwood Mac their first hit in America, "Rhiannon" made it so girls started showing up to the shows in flowing lace dresses and silk hats and screamed when Stevie came on stage. When *Rumours* came out, it made the whole band hugely famous, but Stevie became an icon; the press dubbed her the "Queen of Rock." Christine got no such honorific—she wasn't the co-Queen, or the Queen of Piano Rock, or even, like, the Princess.

You'd think that sort of thing would cleave even the most solid of friendships, especially given that the women were also creative collaborators making art that was all tangled up in self-expression and ego. From the outside, you might assume that there was some competition between them, and that Stevie was winning it, because Christine seems subdued and plain and, well, Stevie is Stevie. She wore a top hat. But you never hear anything about jealousy or resentment between them, and if there were even a drop of it, don't you think you would? People love to discover this type of tension, as if there can never be two of anything when it comes to women. It's possible that Christine saw in Stevie what I saw in Jennifer: a rare person naturally suited to the spotlight. And maybe Stevie saw in Christine a genuine talent who didn't crave or need fame.

The band reunited for a tour in 1997, but a year later, Christine, who had developed profound anxiety about air travel and performing, quit the band for good. Now Stevie was "the only girl" in the band, but she wouldn't accept the mantle without Christine's blessing (which was freely and gladly given). To this day, Stevie laments her friend's departure. A month ago, she told the *Guardian*, "I'd beg, borrow, and scrape together five million and give it to her in cash if she would come back. That's how much I miss her." ☻

sisters of the moon

BEST FRIENDS

Happy Galentine's DAY

1. Let's Get Together – Hayley Mills
2. Run the World (Girls) – Beyoncé
3. Girls Just Wanna Have Fun – Cyndi Lauper
4. 22 – Taylor Swift 5. Wannabe – Spice Girls
6. Umbrella – Rihanna feat. Jay-Z
7. Where My Girls At – 702
8. Amigas Cheetahs – The Cheetah Girls
9. Can't Hold Us Down – Christina Aguilera ft. Lil Kim
10. Stronger – Britney Spears
11. Independent Women Pt. 1 – Destiny's Child
12. This One's For The Girls – Martina McBride
13. Dancing Queen – ABBA

Songbird

GOLD DUST WOMAN

MARCH 2013: *MYSTERY*

Hi, Rookies!

Welcome to March's theme, Mystery. On our minds this time around: David Lynch, Alfred Hitchcock, and all the eeriness of the regular ol' suburbs. I think the appearance of normalcy almost always ensures a bit of darkness underneath, so this month we'll be looking at the kinds of mysteries that have been right in front of you all along. In case you just get SO SWEPT UP in the theme that you start walking around in a trench coat and spying on your neighbors, here's a playlist I made of some menacing music to act as your soundtrack.

In Every Dream Home a Heartache

1. I'm Glad I Never… - Lee Hazlewood
2. Satan's Theme - The Rondels
3. Girl Afraid - The Smiths
4. TV Set - The Cramps
5. Halloween All Year - The Orwells
6. He Hit Me (And It Felt Like a Kiss) - The Crystals
7. Basement Scene - Deerhunter
8. Undertaker - CocoRosie
9. Because - Elliott Smith
10. Bad Things - Cults
11. Bad Seeds - Beat Happening
12. Poison Ivy - The Rolling Stones
13. What's the Ugliest Part of Your Body? - The Mothers of Invention
14. Runaway - Del Shannon
15. Blue Velvet - Bobby Vinton

Thank you, as always, for being here, and may you power through this end-of-winter slump with all the episodes of *Scandal* and midnight snacks in the world.

LOVE,
TAVI

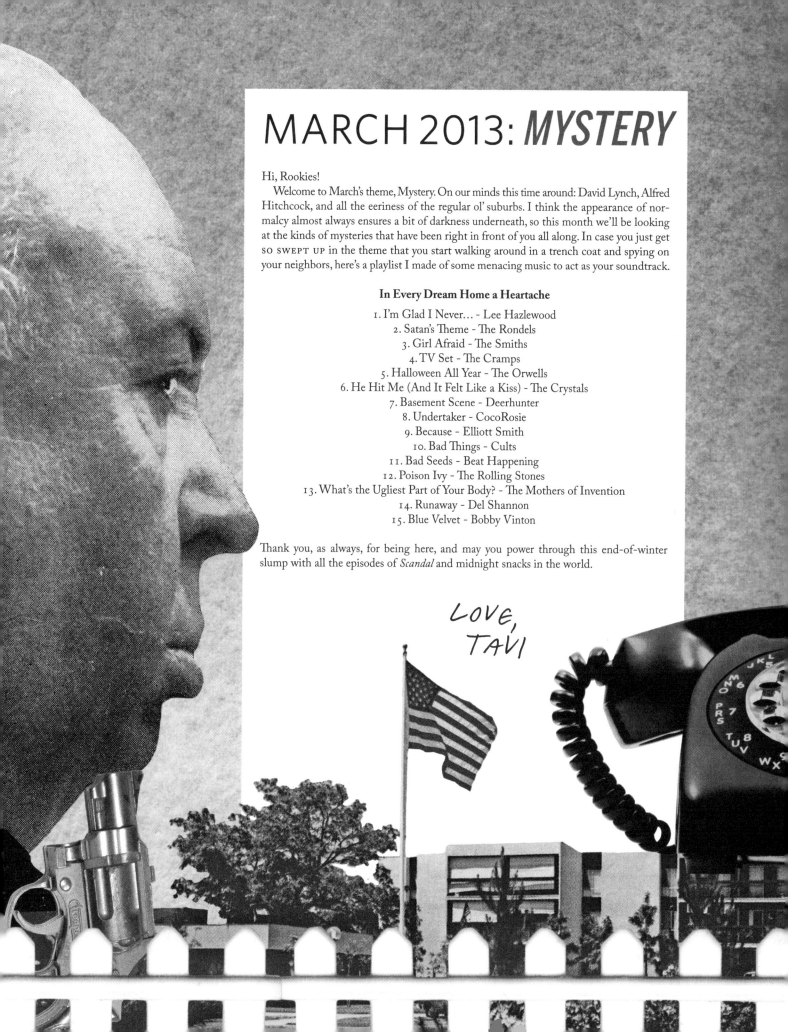

THE GREAT WIDE OPEN

When your whole world is flat, empty, and directionless, the options for fun are pretty limited.
Writing by Julianne, collage by Beth. Playlist lettering by Tavi.

The first thing you realize when you open your eyes in Cheyenne, Wyoming, is that it is flat. In all directions. It is panoramically, 360-degrees flat. Houses dot the landscape, and the sky is pierced with the occasional yellow arches or the red Pizza Hut font or the party sombrero on the Taco John's sign. But it's still so flat that you feel like you're looking out at the ends of the earth. The horizon merges with the plains the same way the sky bleeds into the ocean, and so the feeling is that of being on an island, in complete isolation. Landlocked. If you never left Cheyenne, you could grow up feeling like nowhere else existed.

I grew up there. Like many small towns, it was a fine place to spend a childhood. Most everyone I knew had a backyard to play in, and there was minimal crime and decent public schools. I spent many of my days at my grandma's house, playing in her garden with any number of my more than 50 first and second cousins, and when the sun would set she would call us inside, where warm tortillas and chili verde waited on the table. When I was little, everyone in town seemed to have a smile on their face and a good word to say about their neighbors.

But then I hit adolescence and opened my eyes—figuratively, this time—to the fact that I was living in a remote place in the least populated state in America, and there was a huge world beyond its borders. I became incredibly restless and depressed. I longed to live in a more sophisticated city like Oakland, California, where my mom had taken me to visit my aunt, or my true dream destination, New York City, which I idealized after watching *Party Girl*. I started to feel like there was nothing intellectually stimulating for me in Cheyenne. I didn't want

to be there, but more important, Cheyenne didn't want me there either. It was one of those small towns that try to pretend teenagers don't exist. Unless you were involved in organized sports, which I wasn't, there was very little for young people to do. No rec center, no "cool teen hang-out spot" (if those aren't mythical everywhere). Beyond the mall and the movie theater, and infrequent trips to Denver to see bands play, the whole scene was deadsville. Young local bands put on shows at the VFW occasionally, but those were few and far between—though my friends and I looked forward to them more than we did our birthdays.

We had to make our own fun. Of course, when your whole world is flat, empty, and directionless, the options for "making your own fun" are limited. Like many of our peers, we experimented with alcohol, weed, and sex—stealing away illicit moments made our lives slightly more interesting, and it made us feel connected to other teens across the country in cities much more glamorous than ours. But mostly, we drove around aimlessly. And sometimes we went to the silos.

If Cheyenne's defining quality is its flatness, its secondary feature is that deep in the country, its tumbleweed-smattered plains—yes, there are actual tumbleweeds there—are peppered with abandoned military silos. We knew about a few of them, the ones where high school kids had gone to hang out for years. They are huge concrete structures with two walls that form an L shape—remnants of the Cold War under the purview of the nearby F.E. Warren Air Force Base. Inside are gargantuan steel girders, two round strips of bolted metal that are aimed heavenward and emptied of their bounty: missiles designed to deliver nuclear

weapons. (The Warren AFB "can neither confirm nor deny" that such missiles were ever housed there.) The statues on one side of the entry to the base were exact-size replicas of Peacekeeper missiles, the favored weaponry of the Reagan administration, and this was just 10 miles from the house I grew up in. In the '80s, my sadistic older cousin used to tell me that if the Soviets ever decided to attack they'd hit Cheyenne first, just to make me cry.

But in my teen years, in the '90s, long after most of the weapons had been reportedly carted away, I was not scared, but curious. The silos were our version of an urban myth, passed down from a previous generation of high schoolers: *Did you know you can party where the bombs were?* If one of us managed to finagle car keys from our parents for the night, we'd drive out into the horizon, past the city streetlights into the pitch black, seeking those silos in the dark, armed only with vague directions we'd obtained from older sisters and brothers and, occasionally, someone in the car who'd been there before. It felt like we were trying to get off the island.

My high school friends and I bonded over Sonic Youth, feminism, and our mutual desire to leave Wyoming as soon as possible. We'd dream about what it would be like anywhere else while scribbling poetry and chain-smoking over bottomless cups of coffee in shit diner chains. Going to the silos, we wanted to see if the inky

darkness would somehow transport us to another place. But we were also seeking out our own narrative, trying to figure out how being from this odd, sparse part of the country cvonnected us to the rest of the world. We'd drive north past the paved thoroughfares and the strip malls, then east out onto Four Mile Road, and make a left after two miles, where the streets became gravel. Then we'd slow down to a few miles per hour with the high-beams on, past the ranches, where horses and cows grazed on the dry grass like they had for centuries, until we reached the closest silo—the one we visited most often.

We'd walk up the short hill from our cars to a flat concrete platform (I can't remember if there was a sign warning us not to trespass). Once there, we wouldn't do much. We'd sit around and gossip about who was pregnant, who was doing a fanzine, and who had scored weed from their parents. We'd maybe spray-paint the concrete walls with hearts or our names—Marie, Steven, Julianne—immortalizing ourselves alongside 10 years of seniors before us. Sometimes a kid would have a six-pack of Coors and we would split it among eight people. Out there, surrounded by cows and grass and buffalo—yes, buffalo— the only indication that humans had ever found Cheyenne was the silo itself. The silos didn't have roofs, so you could climb onto the lowest part of the girder, just a few feet up, and look at the stars, imagining what had been here before. If the moon was waning we'd be enveloped in darkness and we'd tell stories about

the Cheyenne and Arapaho tribes, who once hunted bison on these very plains. We'd imagine the homesteaders who had made their way into the American West in the 1850s, building one-room houses and setting up ranches, some of which still existed. There was always some sort of ghost story, usually tied to a young pioneer woman who'd gotten lost in the harsh blur of winter and whose spirit wandered the lands to this day, crying out for her family. We'd scare ourselves with that story, told in the pitch black, the only light coming from the tip of a cigarette or joint.

I think we also felt sad. We related to that girl, lost in the dark, wishing only to find her place. There at night, we couldn't see past our own hands, and a girl in a blizzard would have seen less. It felt like an apt metaphor, all of us blind and feeling our way, inch by inch. This whole country holds strange secrets and lost souls, and out there it was like we could feel all of them. The history of this land had led to *us* here inside this silo, where it was so quiet and dark that we could hear the ghosts moving endlessly around us.

There was an incident or two, like the time my older, drunken boyfriend fell into a hole in the concrete and we had to help him out using a blanket as a rope. (I broke up with him shortly thereafter; his physical resemblance to Kurt Cobain no longer made up for his Cobain-like proclivities.) Then there was the

time I backed my car up at the wrong angle and slammed into the Firestone twins' flashy red Fiat, and we all agreed to lie and say it happened in a friend's driveway so our parents wouldn't find out where we'd been. But my memories of those nights are mostly quiet. If we stared into the galaxy long enough, we could lose ourselves, merge with the land and the sky. We'd stay until midnight, when we had to return to make our curfew.

Eventually, my best friend and I moved to New York City, where the streets are radioactive in the way I always wished for. The plains claimed most of my classmates. Many are still in Cheyenne, with kids and houses and husbands. Some of them died—drugs or suicide—and I imagine them with the silo spirits, wandering the ranches on the outskirts of town, looking for a home that will accept them.

We did normal teenage things back then—renting *Sleepaway Camp* or *Sid & Nancy*, eating pizza, pretending to do homework—but the silo trips defined me in a way I only understand now. I processed vastness there. I saw something beautiful but also not quite right. ◆

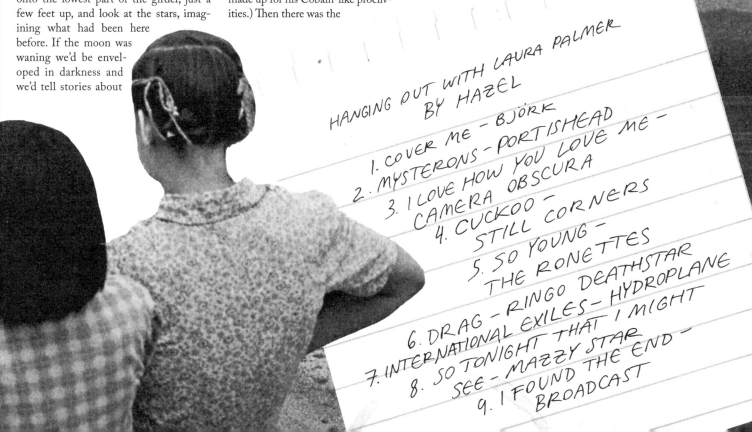

HANGING OUT WITH LAURA PALMER
BY HAZEL

1. COVER ME - BJÖRK
2. MYSTERONS - PORTISHEAD
3. I LOVE HOW YOU LOVE ME - CAMERA OBSCURA
4. CUCKOO - STILL CORNERS
5. SO YOUNG - THE RONETTES
6. DRAG - RINGO DEATHSTAR
7. INTERNATIONAL EXILES - HYDROPLANE
8. SO TONIGHT THAT I MIGHT SEE - MAZZY STAR
9. I FOUND THE END - BROADCAST

Actual Size

How I fell in total love with my own body.
By Gabi

Like most fat adults, I have wasted years of my life feeling shitty about my weight and trying, through diets, to reach an arbitrary number on a scale, each time feeling worse about myself than when I started. It took a long time, but I figured out how (and why) to stop doing that. Here's how it happened.

I somehow managed to make it through the majority of my childhood with pretty healthy self-esteem. Once in a while my grade-school classmates made mean comments about my chubby body, and it hurt my feelings, but overall I thought I was pretty rad.

That changed in seventh grade, when I transferred schools because I wanted to be challenged academically. I was an overweight biracial girl who went from being one of the smartest and most popular kids at my public school in Detroit to feeling like the complete opposite at a prestigious, overwhelmingly white private school in the suburbs. I didn't have the same skin color, body type, education, or social status as my new classmates, and I began to question how I could have ever believed I was smart or attractive. Though I was eventually able to get good grades and regain confidence in my intelligence, my feelings about my looks were not so resilient.

This was my first real encounter with the Fantasy of Being Thin, which is the idea (that so many people buy into) that life will magically improve once you reach your "goal weight." The fantasy intensified when I entered high school. Unlike my middle school, my high school was coed, and I developed crushes on lots of guys. I was constantly daydreaming about how wonderful my life would be once I was skinny—how all the boys I liked would love me, how all the girls I hated would be jealous of me, and how blissfully happy I would be. While I recall

long stretches of time during those four years when I wasn't obsessing about my body, somewhere along the way I managed to try the Atkins Diet, the Master Cleanse, and countless other weight-loss regimes. I'd inevitably give up after a few days or weeks and then berate myself for yet another failed attempt at thinness. I graduated high school weighing noticeably more than I had when I'd entered.

My first significant weight loss came the summer after graduation. This is every fat teenager's dream, right? To shed your former identity and enter college as someone new? My mom, who had encouraged my past dieting, was more than happy to help. She'd heard about a local clinic that had a summer weight-loss program for teens. We attended the informational meeting together, where we were told about success rates and reasonable expectations. My mind was made up—I was going to do this.

After getting the green light from a doctor, I started going to weekly classes where we learned about "healthy eating" and exercise. In retrospect, I think this program was absolutely horrid: Instead of teaching us about balanced eating and nutrition, they gave us prepackaged meals and weight-loss shakes, and taught us to count calories. We were actually encouraged to drink diet soda because it had no calories! (There's nothing wrong with choosing to drink diet soda, but I find it misleading to suggest that it's good for you.) Alas, it *is* possible to lose weight on such a program, and I did. Watching the numbers drop made me feel high. I started running three times a week, for hours at a time. I meticulously tracked every single calorie that entered my mouth. When the program ended two months later, I'd lost even more weight than I'd anticipated.

I was convinced I'd keep dropping the pounds in college, but things didn't go quite as planned. Like most people's freshman years, mine was filled with lots of Easy Mac, cheap beer, and midnight pizza runs. I stopped losing weight and started gaining. Then, that summer, right before school started again, I got sick. I could barely get out of bed for a week. While at the doctor's office, I picked up a pamphlet on HIV and scanned the list of symptoms of the disease's onset. I realized I had every single one. I freaked out, absolutely convinced I was HIV positive as the result of one or two unprotected sexual encounters. At the time, you had to wait three months after possible exposure to be sure the test results were accurate, and so began 12 weeks of torture. To make matters worse, right around this time, the guy I was madly in love with broke up with me.

I didn't talk to anyone about what I was going through. Instead, I fell into a deep depression and alternated between crying hysterically and feeling numb. I barely made it to any classes. My hair started to fall out in chunks from stress. I contemplated suicide. And, yes, I lost weight. I was absolutely terrified and miserable and thought I was dying, and meanwhile people were telling me how great I looked. I was closer to my goal weight than ever, but happiness couldn't have seemed further away.

By the next semester, I'd gotten over the heartbreak, my health had improved, and my tests had come back negative. This was all obviously a huge relief, but my body image issues picked up right where the other stuff left off. Any excitement from the weight loss was soon overshadowed by feelings of not being thin *enough*: I was back to my ninth-grade size, but I was still the heaviest in my group of friends, and I couldn't fit into the largest pants at most designer stores.

It was at this point that fate intervened, in the form of LiveJournal. I'd discovered the social network/blogging platform in high school, and had been casually using it as a sort of personal diary. Then a college buddy introduced me to the LJ communities—groups filled with folks who shared common interests: fashion, celebrities, TV shows, cooking, you name it. I joined a few and slowly started interacting with people, eventually making friends and forming deeper relationships. Because we didn't know one another in real life, everyone seemed comfortable sharing their secrets and insecurities, without fear of judgment.

One group, Fatshionista, called itself "a place to discuss the intersections of fat politics and fat fashion." I'll be honest—I had never heard of "fat politics," nor did I have any interest in it. I joined simply because I loved fashion and the idea of sharing style tips with a community of other fat girls. I checked the site daily, scrolling through endless posts in which large women shared photos of their outfits. At first I found myself judging their bodies and their clothing choices: I'd look at women in baggy T-shirts and matronly dresses and wonder, *Why would she want the whole world to see her looking like* that?

But over time, something funny happened: Without any conscious effort, I started to see those women's bodies differently. I no longer saw them as gross or unattractive. As I became more active in the community, I found myself browsing the more political posts, the ones criticizing our culture's obsession with dieting and thinness. It got me thinking, and I decided to take a small step: I'd take a break from reading tabloids and mainstream lady mags that compared bodies or doled out advice for slimming down, and instead focus on positive portrayals of bodies that looked more like mine. Over time, fat bodies began to look not only normal, but beautiful, to me. And eventually, slowly, I fell in love with my own.

My next step was to make a conscious decision to stop having conversations about

other women's looks, on the internet and in real life. I stopped participating in negative body-talk with friends—I tried to be supportive of their concerns about weight, but I refused to engage with the topic. It's amazing how when you exercise positivity and compassion toward others, it magically turns inward—this one effort made an unimaginable difference in how kind I am to myself.

All the weight I had lost in the previous few years, I gained back—hardly a surprise, since I'd lost most of it by undereating and getting sick. This time, though, I didn't beat myself up about it. I let go of my need to constantly monitor my caloric intake. I allowed myself to *enjoy food* again. I graduated from college at my heaviest weight, and I was more in love with my body than ever. I started a blog that encouraged other women to have fun with fashion regardless of their size, and that has since become my career! I now get emails from girls who say that scrolling through my photos has kept them from feeling ugly or worthless.

When people ask me how they can stop hating their bodies, I always suggest that they limit their mainstream-media intake and replace it with body-positive media.

LiveJournal is pretty much dead now, but the fat-positive movement is going strong on Tumblr (check out activists like Jessica Luxery and Margitte Kristjansson); there are tons of plus-size fashion blogs (Franceta Johnson and Nicolette Mason are two of my faves); and the former Fatshionista moderators, Lesley Kinzel and Marianne Kirby, now write regularly about body politics for xoJane. *These* are the things I choose to look at daily, and I can now appreciate other women's bodies—of all sizes—without judgment or jealousy. I read mainstream magazines again and I watch TV with a critical eye, which allows me to avoid internalizing the endless body-shaming messages that used to make me feel inferior.

As I get older, I find that I'm more interested in educating myself about how certain foods can help bodies fight sickness and disease. This past year I've made a concerted effort to eat more whole foods and less processed stuff—and it's actually been *fun*. Now I'm able to choose healthy options because they make me feel great, not because I think it will lead to weight loss, and I can't tell you how freeing that has been. I may drop 50 pounds as a result of the changes I'm making, or I may not lose an ounce. Either way, I'm fine. ♦

LAST CALL

My father is going to drink himself to death, and I just have to live with it.

By Esme

My father is an alcoholic. And for almost 20 years, as far as I was concerned, that was no problem. It was just another thing about him: He loved the Beatles and racing cars and drinking constantly. He drank pastis on vacation in France, vodka whenever he had money, and golden cans of lager at all other times.

After my brother was born, it was decided that my mother would go back to work while my dad stayed home with us, mainly because he had forgone any kind of a career over the previous decade in order to play guitar in bands with his brother. He would spend his days cooking tomato sauce, cleaning the house, and downing cheap wine from cartons that he had stored on high shelves, out of our reach. I always understood that Stoffer—which is what everyone calls him, and which he likes to be called, so I will do so here—was an alcoholic, but the word meant very little to me. His drinking was completely out in the open; he was honest about it to the extent that he'd sip from what he called "a traveler" (basically a mini bottle) every morning on the walk to school. "Ahhh," he'd say to us, jokingly, "breakfast of champions!" It didn't bother me, because it didn't seem to infringe on our relationship. He was always there to pick us up from school and correct our homework and play catch in the park with a cigarette behind his ear and an open container by his side.

It dawned on me years later that his drinking had been a huge factor in my parents' divorce, which happened when I was six, but even that had barely changed anything: My parents moved to apartments on the same street in West London, so the four of us were often together. Stoffer still came over to walk us to school every day, far beyond the point of necessity. Once I was older, he'd hold my uniform blazer under his arm while I had a quick cigarette before

class. Then he'd kiss me on both cheeks and say, "Do the right thing today, OK?" He never appeared drunk—to this day, I've seen him tipsy maybe three or four times.

Then, a few years ago, everything changed. I was 19, returning home from a summer abroad to find him standing at the gate looking pin-thin and noticeably shrunken. He told me he had a doctor's appointment booked for that very afternoon. That appointment turned into a referral to a specialist, who promptly sent us straight to the hospital. We found out that Stoffer had cirrhosis, a liver disease that causes scarring of the organ tissue and can be fatal if not treated. He was only 57, but he looked more like 75. His rickety limbs were covered in lesions where his skin had become dry and irritated. The doctor said that if Stoffer quit drinking immediately, he had a chance of recovering; if not, he would suffer complete liver failure or any of a number of equally serious complications within two or three years. I immediately burst into tears. Stoffer, on the other hand, was entirely unperturbed. "Thank you, doctor," he said, standing up. "But I'm a rock & roll musician, I've been drinking and smoking since I was 10, and I'm just about having a ball." It was the answer I would've expected from him, but I freaked out. I felt like my eyes had snapped open to an evil I couldn't believe I'd never noticed before.

When I was 15, my mother coaxed my brother and me into spending an afternoon at Alateen, an offshoot of Al-Anon, which is a support network for people whose lives have been affected by someone with a drinking problem. My mum wanted to make sure we hadn't developed any deep-seated issues as a result of Stoffer's alcoholism. The meeting was interesting, and the people were nice, but I was sure it wasn't for us—then I noticed my brother sobbing as we left. I asked him what was wrong, whether he'd wanted to talk more about Stoffer. "No," he said, wiping his

eyes. "It just upsets me, listening to those stories. I feel bad for those kids—it must be awful. Dad isn't like that at all."

At the time, I felt almost proud that this was true. But after I found out what he'd done to his liver, and after I'd heard him proclaim that he had no intention of changing his behavior, things started to look different. I reconsidered things from my childhood that I had previously glossed over. Stoffer made it clear to us when we were little that childcare bored him "to tears," and while he was essentially a loving and devoted father, he was also irritable and moody. Despite his laxity on things like watching TV and brushing our teeth, he would spank us when we misbehaved, and he would occasionally lose his temper over what seemed like trivial matters. I started modeling when I was 12, and I remember once talking about a photo shoot that my friend had just done. Stoffer didn't approve of my modeling—he thought it was "banal"—but he suddenly got nasty and laid into me for not booking as many jobs as my friend had: "You'd better raise your game, Esmerelda, or you're going to go nowhere." (He doesn't remember this.) I chalked that up to Stoffer being a jerk rather than a drunk, but now I wondered if his drinking had altered his perception of reality, as well as my own.

More frustrating was his attitude: He'd been given another chance and the time for action was now, but he seemed to have no interest in taking any. I boiled with anger. I was angry at my father's parents for having allowed him to get away with a lifetime of drinking; I was angry at my mother for having married him in the first place; I was angry at myself for not having noticed his illness sooner. But mostly I was angry at him. He and I were close. When I hit my teens, I suddenly shied away from my mother, especially when it came to discussing personal stuff—I felt like we no longer understood each other. She always seemed disappointed in my grades or my hair or the short skirts I wore to school. In the meantime, Stoffer and I developed a genuine rapport that I didn't have with anybody else. My brother, my father, and I became a sort of gang, and Stoffer transitioned from parental figure to something like an older brother. We'd sit around his house, listening to Jimi Hendrix records, and I talked to him about things I never discussed with my mother: boys, sex, periods, drugs, dreams, nightmares. My friends adored him, and whenever they came over he would hang out with us, smoking pot and giving my girlfriends advice on how to handle their latest crushes. "The lying little bastard!" he'd interject during the telling of a boyfriend scandal. Or: "He should be so lucky!"

I couldn't imagine a future where I'd break up with a guy, or go on a job interview, or get married without consulting Stoffer first. But his response to his illness made it plain: He was choosing alcohol over us. He goofed around with the nurses at doctor's appointments. He seemed incapable of or uninterested in doing the most basic things for himself, like eating proper meals or bathing twice a day to heal his raw skin. We were supposed to stick together and look out for each other—I would never let him down like this.

I decided it was my responsibility to bring Stoffer to his senses and save his life. I started to harangue him about his drinking. I cried to him on the phone. I tried to appeal to his softer side, weeping about all the grandchildren he'd never get to meet. I tried to scare him by listing the unpleasant physical ramifications of his illness, like renal failure and stomach infections. I even tried to bribe him with numbers for weed dealers, thinking pot could be a replacement for the booze. Nothing worked. He'd act irritated by my concern and hang up on me or storm out of the room, or he'd try to reassure me by flippantly saying, "I'm not going anywhere, I have the constitution of an ox," which only told me that he was so blinded by his need for alcohol that he had ceased to accept reality. It was completely exhausting. I also felt very alone. I tried to recruit my mother and brother on my crusade to Save Stoffer, but they both told me quite plainly that they were OK letting him make

his own decisions about how to live his life—what little he had left of it. They were willing to help take him to doctor's appointments and fill prescriptions, but I was the one nagging him to eat and rubbing lotion on back sores that he couldn't reach.

I worried about him constantly—every time he didn't pick up the phone or was late to meet me, I was sure he'd suddenly keeled over in the middle of the street, breakfast of champions still in hand. Anxiety permeated my entire life: I skipped classes to take him to hospital appointments. I'd spontaneously start crying during conversations with friends. I called Stoffer obsessively several times a night just to make sure he was OK. I agonized about going on trips and vacations in case I never saw him again. It was as if I'd been saddled with a huge baby, one who was dependent on me, but too heavy to lift and impossible to care for.

After months of beating my head against a brick wall, I realized something would have to change. My mum repeatedly reminded me that alcoholism is a disease (I've since learned that Stoffer's great-grandfather was a bad drunk), and that Stoffer was so blinkered by it that the idea of an alternative lifestyle was completely unfathomable to him. Worse, it was completely unappealing. "Never you mind all of that," he'd tell me as I sobbed. "I'm having the time of my life." I had no choice but to accept the reality: He had decided to keep drinking until it killed him, and I was acting as though he had already died. If I didn't come to terms with what he was doing to himself, I would waste whatever time he had left, and I didn't want to live with that regret. My change of heart was neither sudden nor gradual nor even really conscious: I just understood one day that Stoffer's alcoholism transcended his role as a father or a friend, and if I wanted to keep him on as either of those things, I would have to move forward.

I started to treat the alcoholism as a curse that had taken hold of my dad decades before I was even a twinkle in his eye, and this made me understand two crucial points: First, it was beyond anyone else's control, and more important, it had absolutely noth-

ing to do with me. In a way, it helped me see Stoffer as his own person. We often think of our parents as existing for us, to please and help and take care of us. But Stoffer had his own needs and his own agenda and it was his right to do what he wanted. Growing up, I almost deified my dad, and when he got sick I spent a lot of time hating him for being a selfish bastard. Now I've come to see him as just a human.

People still don't really get it. Family members continue to deride my father for his selfishness, or laud me for my "strength" in dealing with "a shit-kicking drunk," as Stoffer cheerfully calls himself. I don't think of it as strength. Any strength I might have had was used up trying to solve a problem that wasn't mine to solve. I just did what I had to. I'm not making excuses for him when I try to explain that he can't help being the way he is. In a perfect world, my dad wouldn't do anything I'd have to defend. But addiction is its own animal, and imagining Stoffer as helpless against it was the first step in forgiving him.

It's been almost two years since Stoffer got sick, and he still drinks as much as he ever did. I try to ignore it. I pretend that it isn't an issue. I've grown accustomed to his frail appearance, though I catch myself checking for signs of further deterioration. He's mostly given up on going to the doctor—there isn't anything they can tell him that he hasn't already heard and ignored—but if he ever does need to be accompanied to an appointment, he goes with my brother or my mum. When he talks about his illness, I urge him to "do the right thing," just like he used to tell me when we said goodbye at my school gates.

Sometimes when we're sitting around, laughing and joking and trading stories, it makes me sad to think about how badly I'm going to miss him, whether that's in three months or three years. But most of all, I feel lucky to have been able to sit around and laugh and tell stories with him at all. ◆

Use Your Words

If psychic powers are the cost of admission to knowing you, you'll be awfully lonely.
Writing by Emily G. Playlist lettering by Tavi.

I was having a bad day the other day. It was raining, I kept dropping (and breaking) things, I got a parking ticket—pretty standard bad-day stuff. I called my "main hang," Kumail, for comfort, and here's how the conversation went:

Me: Hey honey, how are you?
Him: Oh, pretty good. While waiting for this meeting I talked to this guy for like an hour about cosmetic dentistry. It turns out that it's hilarious, and also slightly sinister.
Me: OK.
Him: [*Something else about cosmetic dentistry*]
Me: [*Imitating his voice*] "And how are you doing today, Emily?"
Him: Yeah, how's your day going?
Me: Oh, OK. I got a parking ticket.
Him: Oh, that sucks. What do you want to do tonight?
Me: JUST GLOSS OVER MY MISERY, WHY DON'T YOU?!
Him: …What?

Has this, or anything like this, ever happened to you? Do you ever find yourself waiting impatiently for someone in your life to respond to your signals that you *need…something*? Do you find yourself disappointed when it isn't offered to you without your asking for it, and more upset than you were to begin with? I don't just mean in romantic relationships—this kind of thing happens all the time with friends, parents, siblings, and anyone else you feel close to.

I was a practicing mental-health therapist from 2003 to 2010, and in that time, I saw lots and lots of clients of just about every kind, with all manner of mental and emotional problems. But there was one particular pattern of behavior, one that plagued many if not most of my clients as well as myself (please refer to the above example), a pattern I came to see as one of the most maladaptive things you can do to any kind of relationship—something that might reduce your anxiety in the moment, but which over the long (or usually just slightly less short) run makes things much, much worse. And that pattern was: expecting other people to be psychic. This is when you have in mind an outcome that you'd prefer and an idea of how you'd like your loved ones to behave, and then you get upset when those expectations aren't met—but you've skipped the crucial step of *informing people* of those expectations. It can sound like this:

"He should know that I don't like onions on my sandwich by now."

"It's our anniversary! Where are my flowers?"

"Can't she tell that I'm upset right now?"

"How could he make fun of my parents? Doesn't he realize I'm really sensitive about that?"

"Is she gonna ask me about the big test that I was worried about? She'd better, or I'm gonna be pissed."

In each of these situations, the speaker is asking someone to have mind-reading powers. They're essentially requiring, as a baseline minimum for dealing with them, the ability to magically KNOW what they need without their having to resort to what is really our very best and most efficient means of communication, as a species: words.

I guess in my fantasy version of my phone call with Kumail, he would have fig-ured out how bummed I was just from the sound of my voice, and responded by (a) asking me about my day without prompting, (b) telling me everything would be OK, and (c) suggesting we go get pho together. Because that's what I wanted. So why didn't I ask for it?

Perhaps because it's still hard for me, even as a grown, feminist woman, to seem "demanding." Maybe because I am usually so easygoing that I feel somehow defective when I require attention. It certainly isn't because Kumail wouldn't have been willing or able to do anything I asked of him—he just didn't know what I wanted. Because I didn't tell him. Thus damning myself to an evening with no pho, no comfort, and an even worse feeling in my gut. It was a self-fulfilling prophecy.

Now, I can hear some of you saying, "But doesn't it take the magic out of things if you have to tell someone how to treat you? Shouldn't they just *know*?" And that's a nice thought, especially for those of us who tend to do a lot of heavy lifting in our relationships (whether it's necessary or not), but nope—no one can be expected to *just know* every thought and feeling in your head! And if psychic powers are the cost of admission to knowing you, you're going to be awfully lonely.

If you, like me, have a hard time seeming "high maintenance," remember that the person you're in a relationship with is there because they care about you and want to be around you. Having days when you need more attention than usual is fine. Expecting that someone else will know when those days are is not. Even if you are soulmates/best friends/parent and child, that does not mean that you can anticipate the other person's every single want and need. And if you take the plunge and actually ask for what you want, how much warmer and fuzzier is it to have someone listen to you and then do what you request, just because it makes you happy? Sure, someone can eventually learn that if you say, "I've had a bad day," they should immediately offer you a hug, but that takes time, and it's never 100 percent. Communicating with someone is way preferable to presenting them with a test they cannot pass, a mystery that can't be unraveled, and thus making sure that they constantly fail to meet your expectations.

But Emily, WHYYYYY would anyone make sure that they were constantly disappointed by other people? I know, it sounds crazy! But the real truth is that a lot of us force our partners or friends to let us down over and over so that we can blame *them* for the lack of perfect harmony in our relationship, because we're scared to admit the truth, which is that right now…we'd rather be alone. Expecting psychic behavior can function as an impenetrable suit of armor that protects you from the nitty-gritty of relationships. Maybe you're not really ready to be that close to someone else. Maybe you're still feeling hurt over your last relationship/BFF-ship. Maybe a lot of shitty things happened to you when you were a kid that make it really hard for you, now, to trust anyone, so you find sneaky ways to push everyone away. These are all totally reasonable ways to feel (though I do think you gotta work on that trust thing—I'm not saying *everyone* needs some kind of emotional intimacy with other human beings in their lives, but I am saying that I have never heard of someone who didn't, and I was a practicing therapist for seven years). But it's not fair to punish other people for their lack of X-Men-level powers.

Now I can hear the rest of you saying, "This sounds like it'd be really squirmy and difficult to do," and guess what? You're right. It can be hard. The best relationships are filled with squirmy difficulty from time to time. Not only do you have to actually know your own emotions and what you want, you also have to be willing to be a little bit vulnerable and let the other person in on what's happening inside you. Admitting that certain kinds of jokes upset you,

or that you need comfort, can make you feel naked and exposed. But if it's someone you're close to, showing vulnerability can only serve to make you closer. If your sincere requests end up being fodder for jokes, or dismissed, maybe this person isn't someone you should have a close relationship with. Good thing you found out now!

But how do you do it? How do you break this "unreasonable expectation → inevitable disappointment" pattern that's created when you expect people to read your mind? Even though I strive for transparency and fairness in all my relationships, I still have to work on it too, as you've seen. Here's what "working on it" looks like for me:

1. SEE WHAT'S HAPPENING FROM THE OUTSIDE.

During interactions that feel too full of emotion for me, I imagine that I am watching what's happening between my husband/mom/friend and me on television. (What a boring reality show this would be.) This is a great technique any time you find yourself reading between the lines of an actual conversation too much. If someone were watching your interaction on television, would they be like, "Oh smack, he's totally ignoring her!" or would they be like, "Here are two people discussing what they want to eat"? If the viewers at home can't tell how you're feeling from your words and body language, maybe your crush/dad/BFF can't either. Bringing this level of objectivity to your interactions, now what do you do? Glad you asked:

2. NOW GO INSIDE: FIGURE OUT WHAT YOU'RE FEELING AND WHY.

When you feel disappointed by what a loved one said or did or didn't say/do, what is going on inside you, where no one else can see? Do you expect that on your birthday, the whole day should be devoted to celebrating? Other people may not know that. Did you get a haircut, and then get irritated when no one mentioned it? You may love your haircut and want your friend to gush about it; you may hate it and think that your friend's silence means she hates it

too; or you may feel neutral about it and are waiting for your friend's judgment to help you figure out how you feel about it. Any of these things could be true, but from the outside, you just look like a girl sitting there quietly with a fresh new haircut. If you can articulate *why* you're disappointed, you might be able to spot the point where you were expecting telepathy from other people, and then go back and communicate what you need. And no fair saying "I'm just mad!" Anger always comes from somewhere, and it's often just a mask for fear or sadness. What are you actually feeling? Be honest with yourself. You might have to keep digging for a while, asking yourself harder and harder questions until an answer comes up that rings true.

3. FIGURE OUT WHAT YOU WANT, HOW THE OTHER PERSON CAN HELP, AND WHETHER IT'S A REASONABLE REQUEST.

Now that you know how you're feeling, you can start to focus on what you want. How can the other person help you feel better? What would make you feel cared for? What would give you the little morale boost you need? Examples of perfectly reasonable desires and requests: extra attention, a latte, to be left alone, for someone to clean up after themselves, to be not teased. These, on the other hand, are examples of unreasonable requests:

"Stop being stupid." "Just understand me." "Take care of everything." Reasonable requests are specific and (somewhat) easily done; unreasonable ones force the other person to translate what something like "understanding you" means. If you don't know concretely what you want, neither will the other person.

4. COMMUNICATE YOUR REQUEST.

This is where all that fun vulnerability we discussed earlier comes into play. Take a deep breath, look the other person in the eye, and use this setup: "I am feeling ____, and would like you to ____. Do you think that'll work?" Always keep things in terms of what you are feeling and what you are requesting (not ordering) from the other person, rather than how they "messed up" and how much it hurt you. The key here is "I statements." Instead of saying, "You are really bad about knowing when I've had a bad day," say, "I've had a bad day and would love it if you could give me a neck massage." It just frames things more positively. Now, if the situation involves extra onions on your sandwich, you might feel like *expressing how you're feeling* is a bit much—in that case you can skip straight to the request. The most important thing is that you communicate your desires clearly, rather than using sneaky backdoor methods to get what you want. Sneaky backdoor methods, by the way, include things like crying when you're not that upset in order to be comforted, picking a fight with someone about something random when you're irritated that they're not reading your mind, and guilting someone into doing things for you.

None of this is going to come easily for you right away, especially if this is a pattern you established a long time ago and have been perfecting for years. But if there are things you want in this life—and I hope there are—you are going to have to make your desire for those things known, no matter how risky that feels. The alternative is that you never get what you want, and you simmer with resentment about it for the rest of your time on earth. There is no third possibility wherein everything you've ever dreamed of just magically falls into your lap, however much I wish there were.

People are terrifying, and relationships are hard, but people are also the best, and relationships make us human and everything else more bearable. The millions of ways we interact with all of the people in our lives will always (I hope!) be a forest we're all stumbling through together. But it's nice to have a couple of signposts to guide us along the way. ⟡

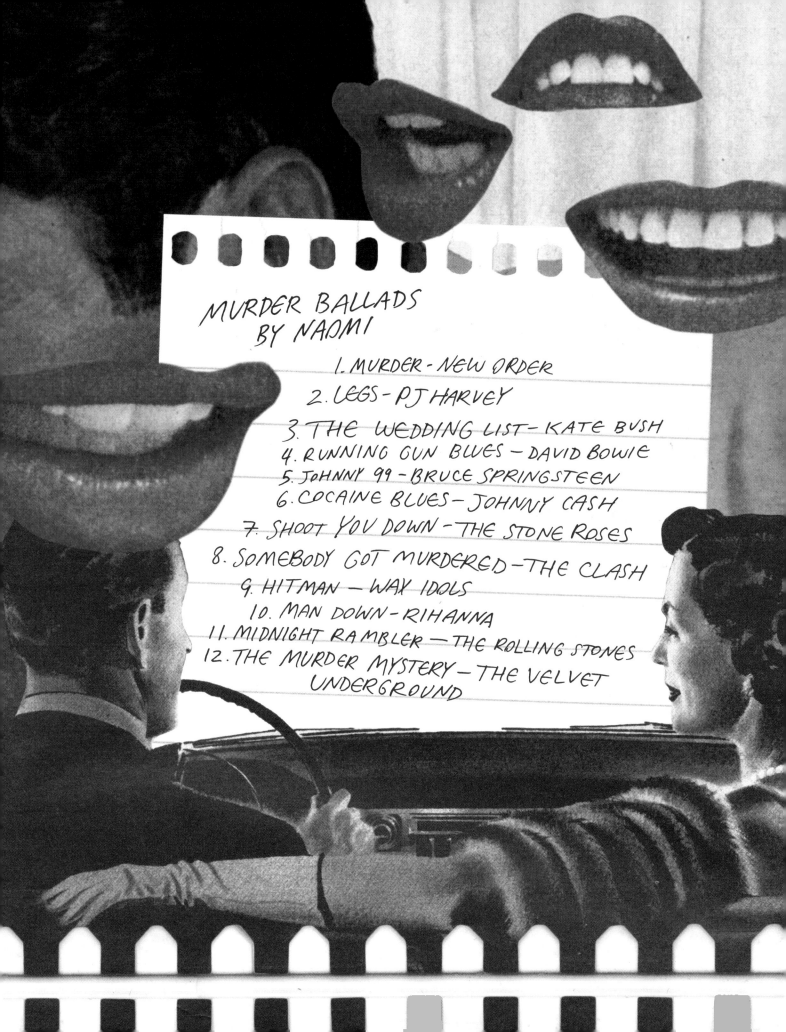

MURDER BALLADS
BY NAOMI

1. MURDER - NEW ORDER
2. LEGS - PJ HARVEY
3. THE WEDDING LIST - KATE BUSH
4. RUNNING GUN BLUES - DAVID BOWIE
5. JOHNNY 99 - BRUCE SPRINGSTEEN
6. COCAINE BLUES - JOHNNY CASH
7. SHOOT YOU DOWN - THE STONE ROSES
8. SOMEBODY GOT MURDERED - THE CLASH
9. HITMAN - WAX IDOLS
10. MAN DOWN - RIHANNA
11. MIDNIGHT RAMBLER - THE ROLLING STONES
12. THE MURDER MYSTERY - THE VELVET
    UNDERGROUND

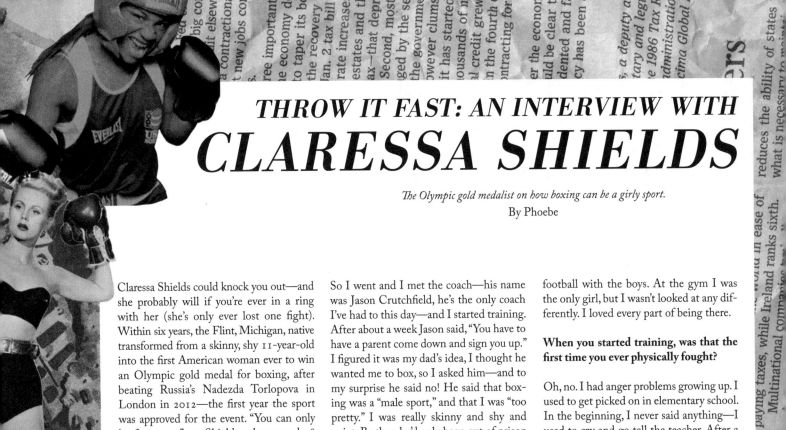

THROW IT FAST: AN INTERVIEW WITH
CLARESSA SHIELDS

The Olympic gold medalist on how boxing can be a girly sport.
By Phoebe

Claressa Shields could knock you out—and she probably will if you're ever in a ring with her (she's only ever lost one fight). Within six years, the Flint, Michigan, native transformed from a skinny, shy 11-year-old into the first American woman ever to win an Olympic gold medal for boxing, after beating Russia's Nadezda Torlopova in London in 2012—the first year the sport was approved for the event. "You can only be first once," say Shields, who turned 18 just a few days ago. "I feel like I did a good job." Here, she tells us how we can follow her ass-kicking example.

ROOKIE What led you to start boxing?

CLARESSA SHIELDS Well, I'm really sentimental. If I keep getting signs about something, I usually go with it. When I was nine, my dad had just gotten out of prison. He'd been in jail for seven years. One day we were just riding around, and he mentioned that he had wasted so much of his life, and he wished he would have stuck to what he was passionate about. I said, "What was that?" And he said, "Boxing." Right after that, he mentioned that Laila Ali took after her father, [the boxer] Muhammad [Ali]. I was like, *OK then*. I figured if I could box and I was really good at it, he'd be really proud.

Then one day I was walking to the store and I bumped into my friend Eddie outside Berston Field House, which is this little rec center, and I was like, "What are you doing down here?" and he's like, "I'm boxing." That was the final sign. Everything said *You gotta do this.*

Did that make your dad happy?

So I went and I met the coach—his name was Jason Crutchfield, he's the only coach I've had to this day—and I started training. After about a week Jason said, "You have to have a parent come down and sign you up." I figured it was my dad's idea, I thought he wanted me to box, so I asked him—and to my surprise he said no! He said that boxing was a "male sport," and that I was "too pretty." I was really skinny and shy and quiet. By then he'd only been out of prison for two years, but he thought he knew me, right? He thought I was so fragile. He's like, "Not my baby girl." So I didn't talk to him for two days. On the third day he picked me up from school. I still wouldn't talk to him. He drove me to his house, and when we went inside, it was like an intervention. His wife, my stepbrothers, and my stepsisters were all sitting at a table waiting on me. And they all voted on whether I should box or not, and my dad just went with the majority—and everyone said, "Let her try it." Thank god they voted in my favor! I found out later that my dad thought I was going to quit. He thought I would get beat up and learn my lesson, and wouldn't want to do it anymore.

But you kept going to the gym?

Other than my grandma's house, that was the first place I ever felt accepted. I could be what I wanted to be and who I wanted to be and how I wanted to be. It wasn't a crime to sweat. It wasn't a crime to run around. It wasn't a crime to hit something hard. Growing up, you know, people are always telling you that you have to be a girl, you have to keep your hair done. They tell you to wear the right clothes and not play football with the boys. At the gym I was the only girl, but I wasn't looked at any differently. I loved every part of being there.

When you started training, was that the first time you ever physically fought?

Oh, no. I had anger problems growing up. I used to get picked on in elementary school. In the beginning, I never said anything—I used to cry and go tell the teacher. After a while, you just snap. I got into my first fight in third grade, and all I knew was that a girl had made me mad. I didn't think, *I'm about to beat her up.* I thought, *I'm about to make her leave me alone.* I just had a thing that if somebody disrespected me and they didn't stop when I said stop, I had to put them in line—boys and girls. In fifth grade the teacher wrote on my report card, "Extremely dangerous." But sometimes they hit me first. I had to do a whole lot of standing up for myself.

Everyone says that violence doesn't solve anything, but do you think it actually helped in these situations?

Well, once I started boxing in the sixth grade, it became a fact of life that I could defend myself if I was messed with. If somebody tried to fight me, I didn't have to run. But like I said, boxing really opened me up to who I wanted to be. It helped me control my anger. It gave me the discipline to not just go out and fight whenever somebody disrespected me. It gave me the confidence to talk, and I started to talk out problems. But I do think it's important for women to learn self-defense. It's good for every woman to have the security to know:

I can protect myself. Boxing just helped me in every way. I don't know where I'd be without it. It even helped me find God.

How is that?

By the time I was 12, I'd fought and won three fights. I knocked the other girl out each time. My fourth fight was a lot harder. My grades had dropped in school, so my aunt told me I had to quit the gym until my grades came back up, and I was out for a month and a week. As soon as I came back, my coach was like, "I got you a fight." So the day of the fight rolls around and the girl looks over at me and says to her parents, "I'm going to stop her." I just turned red. We got in there, and that girl fought me back. I got the best of her—in the last 10 minutes, she was crying—but after I won, I realized, OK, I'm going to need God to help me in school, and to help me fight girls like that.

Do you ever feel bad about the fact that winning involves hurting someone else?

No. If you think that, you're in the wrong sport. I always think about it like this: Yes, boxing is an aggressive sport. It's a sport where you've got to hit people. But either they're going to hurt you first or you're going to hurt them. Which one you want? So I decide: I'm going to get her before she gets me. All friendship is forgotten until the match is over.

What's the worst injury you've sustained?

I don't get hit that much! I recently pulled a muscle in my back. I've had a black eye and a busted lip. I don't worry about it. Again, I'd be in the wrong sport if I did.

When did you decide you wanted to go to the Olympics?

I don't know how it happened. When I was 13, my coach called me and said that boxing was going to be a sport at the Olympics, and that I was going and I was going to win. I thought he was drinking. He said, "You're the best." I didn't believe it then.

What sorts of sacrifices have you had to make to be good enough to get to the Olympics? Do you feel like you're missing out on a lot of teenage experiences?

Oh, of course. I've had to cancel on many birthday parties and movie nights. I even ruled out dating for a long time. You want to be focused and you don't want to mess up. Even when I wasn't fighting anytime soon, I had to make sacrifices. Not hanging out with my friends was big. I had to cut off some family members because of their actions. There's just a certain lifestyle that I've got to lead. I can't be around people who are drinking or smoking. Yeah, I can go to a party, but a lot of parties in Flint—there'd be trouble, and my coach didn't want me around that, and I didn't want to be around that. And just hanging out with my friends or with boys—you don't know, stuff happens. But I felt like if I focused on boxing, I knew what would happen.

I find the Olympics somewhat stressful to watch, because the athletes have devoted so much time—in some cases, their whole lives—to this one event, and what if they have a bad day? How do you deal with that pressure? Were you anxious going into the ring in London?

No. It's the moment that you've been waiting for. I mean, yeah, *I've been waiting for this and if I mess up it's over*—that's a horrible thought. But one thing I've learned in boxing is: Get your emotions in check. Boxing isn't so much about the physical part—it's about the mind. The mind controls the body. Going into a fight, I eliminate everything. And when I say everything, I mean *everything*. I mean people who are not going to want to see me fight harder. I mean situations—whatever they may be. When I get in the ring, I think, *I worked hard for this, and I have something to fight for.* You don't train hard and get yelled at by your coach and cut off your boyfriends just to make it to the Olympics and lose.

How did life change for you after that?

It changed tremendously. I mean, people recognize me. I see them do a double take, like, *Is that her?* People want autographs and pictures. It's hard to go to the mall. I got a sponsorship, and I have an agent who's working on getting me some endorsements.

I read that you were surprised that you didn't get more endorsement offers after your win. You didn't receive nearly as much attention as Gabby Douglas, for instance. Do you think that's because gymnastics is considered a more glamorous sport?

I don't know, maybe. But gymnastics has always been one of the top sports in the Olympics, and women's boxing is new to it. And people have this image of what a woman is and what a girl is. When you look at gymnastics, you think it's a pretty girl doing flips. It's actually a lot harder than that—I can't do a flip like Gabby Douglas—and they have to train just as hard as anybody else. But I think it's mostly about how long it's been around and what people like to see. To a lot of people, a girl isn't someone who will get in a ring and hit other girls—or get hit. Once we get over that, I think women's boxing will have more support. Maybe it will be looked at as a "girly" sport.

Do you have any advice for teenage girls who want to box?

Try it. Boxing's not for everybody, but don't be afraid of what people will say about you.

Do you have any tips for throwing a good punch?

Throw it fast. I can't really give an exact answer, because that's a secret. ♦

WILL BE BOYS

A report from both sides of the male gaze.
By Tyler

I'm sure you've heard the expression "boys will be boys." People use it when a seven-year-old boy pushes his female classmate off the playground slide. (That means he has a crush on you!) When a 12-year-old boy snaps the bra strap of the girl next to him at the lunch table. (He's just joking around!) When a 16-year-old boy walks by, swivels his head, and loudly exclaims, "Damn, I'd tap that ass!" (It's a compliment! It's just hormones—he can't control himself!) As a trans* guy, I don't buy any of these excuses. I think he *can* control himself—it's just easier to blame biology than to unpack years of privilege and learned behavior.

Before I knew I was transgender, I presented as female for 19 years, and I was on the receiving end of all the behaviors I just described. In middle school, some of my guy friends would lay their hands on the seat of my chair so that when I sat down they could grab my ass. It made me angry, but I didn't think I was allowed to be. *Aren't I supposed to be flattered by the attention?* I wondered. Whenever my girl friends and I got upset or offended by a bra snap or a butt grab, the boys would say it was "no big deal," and I think a part of us believed them. To tell a teacher would have been social suicide—these guys were part of our group, and we knew better than to get them in trouble. At the same time, I was molding myself to be a girly-girl, someone boys wanted, because I thought that's what I was supposed to do. Even if I didn't enjoy that kind of attention, I felt like if I had no worth to boys, I had no worth at all. I gauged what to wear by my male classmates' reactions. If their jaws dropped at my short-shorts, I was doing something right. If they made fun of a particular shade of lip gloss, I never wore it again.

Sophomore year, I was struggling with depression. I started dressing in hoodies and sweatpants to make myself less visible and more comfortable. Still, there was no escaping the leers of the boys at school. My male friends frequently offered unsolicited opinions on how I could be sexier. "You should wear tighter clothes," they would say, and I'm not sure I could count the number of times it was casually suggested that I get breast implants. The few of them who wanted to be more than friends sometimes let a hug linger for too long, or worse, tried to kiss me when I'd made it 100 percent clear that I didn't feel the same way. Part of me felt like I couldn't say no, like it was my job as a girl to go along with it, and so sometimes I did. I'd learned—from movies, from classmates, from family members—that testosterone makes boys perpetually horny, that they "need" to act on their impulses, so in my mind, they, like the occasional stranger at the mall who would take advantage of a crowd to grope me before quickly walking away, couldn't help what they were doing.

I had no idea how much I put up with or brushed off as normal until I started to transition to a male-presenting person when I was 20. Suddenly, I was "one of the guys." People tend to assume that transitioning is about me becoming something else, but in a lot of ways my experience is more related to how other people treat me—what they assume about me based on physical characteristics. For instance, I've always been really small. I'm the person friends lift in the air when they hug me, the one who always gets stuck in the middle seat on car trips, who crawls into tight spaces to retrieve missing items, who wins limbo contests. I've never been the

go-to person for any type of strength-related task. But early on in my transition, an older woman pulled me aside at the supermarket and asked me to help her carry three cases of water bottles to her cart. *Wow, strangers expect things of me as a man*, I remember thinking.

People—colleagues, friends of friends—started asking me to do things like grab a beer and watch football, and I, ever the good listener, became privy to attitudes that made me even more furious about all the harassment I had silently endured before my transition. A while ago I was out with some co-workers, one of whom I'll call Carl. Carl started telling this story about the previous night's exploits: The girl he was sitting next to stole his beer and took a sip from it (possibly accidentally), so he grabbed her face, turned it towards him, and kissed her. Then he said, "You owed me!" I guess she didn't react too badly, because it was clear Carl was pretty proud of himself for this slick move. He went on to complain about how all the girls at the current bar looked "like dykes." I didn't say anything, because it was a work function and I really wasn't sure how to respond. Another night, a friend of a friend pulled me aside at a party and started telling me about a recent hookup. He described the girl he was with as a "prude bitch" because she didn't want to have sex with him. When I told him that the girl didn't owe him anything, he said, "I thought you were a man," and walked away.

The way the world saw and treated me changed so rapidly, but the way I saw the world hadn't changed at all. On one hand, I had this newfound male privilege—I noticed that people tended to respect my personal space more, and nobody suggested

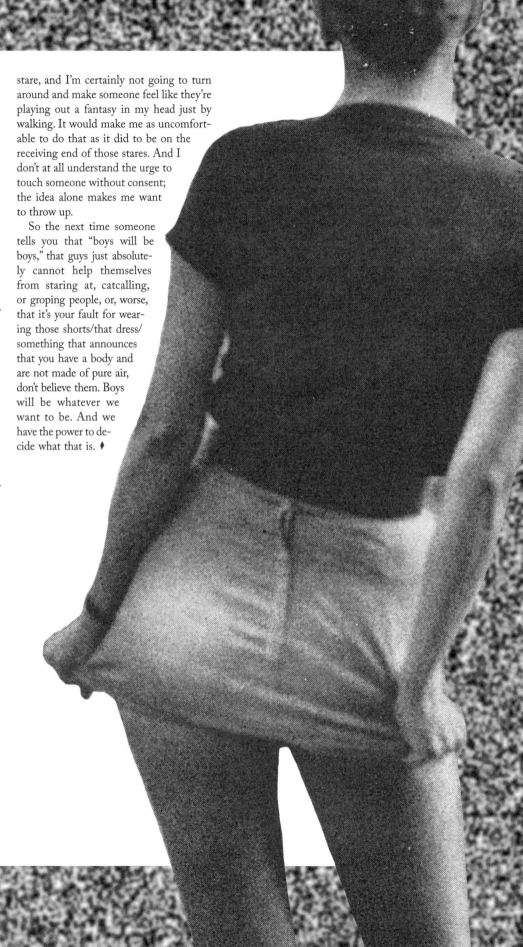

I sit on their lap to make room—but on the other, it was assumed that I shouldn't be scared walking alone at night. Whenever my guy friends got too drunk, they'd stumble across campus by themselves at 2 AM. I was now expected to do the same, even though I'd been raised to think that was dangerous, and still do.

I've heard from a lot of trans* guys who worry that starting hormone therapy will turn them into incredibly aggressive and horny people who can't control their anger or their sex drives. I can't answer for everybody, obviously, but I can say unequivocally that taking hormones didn't change who I am inside—it just changed my body to better match that person. The first year of hormone replacement therapy, which for me meant weekly or biweekly injections of testosterone, is often equivalent to what adolescent cis males go through over a period of two to five years during puberty. While it's really exciting to experience the "right" puberty, it's filled with just as much awkwardness as the first time around, only everyone else grew out of their awkward phase years ago. As a 20-year-old summer camp counselor, I had worse acne than my 14-year-old campers. I was growing out of my shoes overnight, waking up aggressively scratching my stomach due to rapid hair growth, and squeaking whenever I tried to sing a Mariah Carey song.

When I compare my first puberty with my second one, I can say that testosterone definitely amped up my sex drive. I found that I was aroused more easily—by images of hot celebrities or porn or just watching my girlfriend contemplate what to write in a text message. If I randomly thought about something that turned me on, I had trouble willing myself to turn it off and think about something else. But this idea that men *cannot help* gluing their eyes to your ass as you walk down the street? I'm sorry, but that's bullshit. The dosage of testosterone I was getting during certain early stages of my transition put my levels on the high end for males of any kind; and yet somehow I didn't, and don't, have to *leer* at people. Yes, I see attractive people on the street and I notice them, but I'm able to control myself. I'm not going to stop or

stare, and I'm certainly not going to turn around and make someone feel like they're playing out a fantasy in my head just by walking. It would make me as uncomfortable to do that as it did to be on the receiving end of those stares. And I don't at all understand the urge to touch someone without consent; the idea alone makes me want to throw up.

So the next time someone tells you that "boys will be boys," that guys just absolutely cannot help themselves from staring at, catcalling, or groping people, or, worse, that it's your fault for wearing those shorts/that dress/something that announces that you have a body and are not made of pure air, don't believe them. Boys will be whatever we want to be. And we have the power to decide what that is. ♦

JUST THE TWO OF US

An early Mother's Day card from the only child of a single mom.

By Dylan

It wasn't my mom's vision of what she wanted for my childhood, watching big chunks of my family life break off and melt into nothing. But these things happen. Over the course of three years, starting when I was 12, my parents separated, rejoined, lost money, and finally divorced.

My dad moved out. I never wanted to live at his house so I didn't. I saw him once a week for dinner, but my mom was the one who raised me through high school and into college. She and I stayed in our old house, which she was now solely responsible for maintaining. She was also suddenly 100 percent in charge of feeding, clothing, and watching over me, her only child. This was all happening as I was becoming an official teenager—a defining moment in almost any mother-daughter relationship, but the departure of our family's third member meant no one could act as a buffer and a foil to offset any intensity between Janet and me.

It's been noted that by the time they split up, my parents' relationship was long past its expiration date: They were trying to make it work for my sake, because that's what "good parents" in a "good family" do. My mother still expresses regret that she wasn't able to provide me with the family she'd pictured for all of us nor the feeling of stability that she imagines would have come with it. To her, family meant a "warm house" in a "nice neighborhood" with a mom and a dad. What we ended up with instead is a two-person team: a single mother and her only child.

♦ ♦ ♦

"I had a tough time letting go of the dream of home, safety, and family," my mom said when I talked to her about all this stuff again for this article. "For so long, I walled myself off from the harsh realities. Then, as a cockeyed optimist, I held out the hope for redemption. I thought it would be better for you if I held the family together. It was unspeakably tough to face facts, move forward, and take care of us."

When I hear her talk like this now, it hits me how hard it must have been for her to simultaneously mourn her failed marriage and her vision of the "perfect family," get her shit together to take care of the two of us, and deal with my anxiety as all these tumultuous changes were happening in my life. The dissolution of my parents' marriage was one thing, but I accepted it and moved on quickly. My dad was always more of a hardass, so there were ways in which their divorce made the house a lighter place for me to live. What truly unsettled me was the financial insecurity that followed, when we had to sell our dream home after owning it for only nine months, not to mention cut back and re-evaluate every dollar we spent as a family. Things that used to be givens, like annual trips to my visit my cousins and my private school tuition, were now uncertain extravagances. As my mom was dealing with splitting from her husband, losing her job, and the house she could no longer afford gathering dust on the market, I broke down in angst frequently, always at home, always at her.

"*Wahhhh,*" I'd fake-sob. "You don't even understand, today was *sooo* hard and I have *sooo* much homework, I can't even touch a pan right now."

"I pay for this house," she'd reply. "Do you like living in this house for free?"

"*Wahhhhhhh…*"

I would glare at her over another one of her gourmet dinners, blaming our nightly meal for my high school weight gain (when really it was all the beer I had begun to drink on the weekends). Every Sunday night, inevitably stuck on an essay due first period the next morning, I would take her to task for sending me to a prestigious all-girls high school—because, even though the education was fantastic and I knew it, it was, like, totally *ruining my liiife and it's your fault!!!* When she sent me opportunities to do paid graphic design work for her and her friends, which both funded my funtimes and built my portfolio, I bitched endlessly about the workload. Basically, I was insufferable. And yet she suffered me.

My mom: "Dylan, I think you're being too hard on yourself here. You've always been a great kid, with a good work ethic and remarkable authenticity. I love that about you. When it came to giving you guidance, it was actually easier with your father out of the picture. Everything became so clear. My voice was true. I knew what to do. I could see your confidence and faith in yourself building." All right, Janet's pretty spectacular. To stick up for, and to stick *by*, the mess that I was is an act of extreme trust and love that I still feel unworthy of.

Eventually, though, I got the new picture. My dad's sudden absence meant a lot of things, obviously, but one of them was losing around a third of our household workforce. "It was down to the two of us," my mother said. "We both needed each other, and I needed you to pitch in. Anyway, it was the right thing for you at your age, even in an intact family." I mean, she has a good point. And I'm thankful that I was forced to finally take responsibility for the stake I had in the physical and emotional state of our household. If I didn't put in my share of cleaning the floors, earning my own spending money, and walking the dog (who was technically *mine*, after all), who else would? And if I was feeling like a brat (approximately 73 percent of the time between the ages of 12 and 18), acting on that feeling would drag 100 percent of the house down, because there was no one else at home for either of us to interact with (besides Sammy, who was actually a really good buffer when he needed to be).

◊ ◆ ◊

My friend Aki's parents divorced around the same time as mine, and when we lived together we had a lot of late-night talks over bowls of cereal (hashtag college) about what it was like growing up with a single mother. I asked her for another one of those sessions, without the cereal this time, for this piece.

"Why were we so shitty, anyway?" I asked her.

"After my parents' divorce, as I was on the brink of becoming a teenager, I began to see my mom as an individual being, rather than the holy, unblemished, and infallible mother that I wanted her to be. I wasn't ready for that," Aki said. "My mom used to say that I was punishing her for being a person. I used to scream back some asinine teenage remark, but by the time I hit my late teens, I began to realize that that was exactly what I was doing. I was punishing her for living her own life out of anger over the lack of control I had over mine."

Our new life had lessons for my mom, too. "What I learned about relationships didn't save a marriage that was doomed by a chasm in values and loss of trust," she said. "But I became a better person. I understood for the first time how to express my needs while honoring others. I asked you to consider my feelings and contribute. Seeing you now, I'm kinda happy about that."

Just like with Aki and her mother, I had a hard time adjusting to this new version of my mom, this woman who trusted me and treated me like an emotional equal. A mom who expected me to consider her feelings as well as my own. But I had to start seeing her as a person, not just as Mom, so that I could eventually feel like an adult with her. I was called on to act like a grownup before I really was one, but it helped me mature in a way that I'm proud of now.

◊ ◆ ◊

On each of my birthdays, my mother reminds me of a theory that she holds dear: that before each person is born, the future-baby spirits choose who their parents will be. I've always been baffled by her fondness for this notion, since her own mother was depressed, unstable, and unsupportive. Why would anyone consciously choose such a mean mom?

"Well, needless to say, when I first heard that little adage, I nearly retched," she told me. "How messed up was I to pick *my* mom? I have lots of regrets. I just try and leave them in the rearview mirror. But one

decision I'm endlessly happy about: to be a mom. I was overwhelmed about being pregnant, then *it was you*. And I knew." If I had picked her, she said, she was going to be worthy of that choice. "When I stepped outside myself and watched myself with you, I marveled. I knew I was doing pretty good. I didn't know I had it in me! Mother's Day is my favorite day of the year now."

Whether I chose Janet Tupper way back when I was a speck of cosmic dust, or if it was just the luck of the draw, I couldn't have hoped for anyone better to have on my team. Just me and her, figuring it all out together: That's what family looks like to me. And it feels like this is what we were supposed to be all along. ◆

THE GREAT UNKNOWN

How to deal with doubt.
By Danielle

I've made a lot of questionable decisions in my life, and I've had to live with a fair amount of doubt about them as a result. I can't even imagine what life must be like for people who are not constantly filled with uncertainty or anxiety about the choices they've made or are about to make. *How is that possible?* I wonder. *How do they go through the day without wondering whether they should have gotten the coat in black instead of turquoise, or if they should have signed up for that French class instead of taking another study period?* And I know I'm not alone. We get a lot of Just Wondering questions about this very topic: *Is it normal to not have any idea what I want to do in life? How do I develop interests and passions? What if I do this and it messes up my entire LIFE?* Doubting Rookie readers: I hear you!

Of course, other people—like friends and especially family—love to give us their unsolicited opinions on these matters, often pressuring us to do one thing or another. When I dropped out of college after a year and moved across the country, my family completely freaked out: What was I planning to do for money? Where was I even going to live? I had no idea. It was an adventure, I told them. I would be fine! And I was—eventually—but there were just as many scary, am-I-going-to-be-able-to-afford-food parts as there were awesome fun parts, and I found myself wondering if I made the right decision *a lot.*

But doubt can be a good thing. It means you're thinking seriously about what you want, and thinking about it is one of the first steps toward figuring it out. Also, it's totally normal to try and avoid regret. Sometimes you need to consider how things might shake out in order to decide whether or not you can live with every possible outcome. Here are some things to keep in mind if you're agonizing over your list of pros and cons, worrying about worst-case scenarios, or just generally confused about what to do.

THERE IS NO SUCH THING AS THE RIGHT DECISION.

When you're trying to make up your mind, one thing that can totally paralyze you is this idea that there is a foolproof choice—a clear-cut path to happiness—and that if you choose wrong you'll end up miserable, and possibly living in your car and eating beans out of a can. In reality, every decision you make can (and probably will) have some positive *and* negative consequences: You picked a great college, but your awful roommate made your first year hell. You took the job you always wanted, but you are getting paid a lot less than you asked for. The objectively *right* decision is a myth. You can only consider what's best for you *right now.* And decisions are what you make of them. Did you quit the school soccer team because you wanted more free time and now you're bored? See if there's a local league, or use the time to try something totally new, like volunteering or taking acting classes.

YOU DO NOT NEED PERMISSION TO LIVE THE LIFE YOU WANT TO LIVE.

A lot of you probably want to make your parents happy, and that's great, because they surely want to do the same for you. Unfortunately, it's not always possible to please everyone. I don't want to be a downer here, but it's your life, and your parents aren't going to be around forever—I know, I'm sorry, but sometimes you need to think about that and ask yourself if you want to become a 50-year-old doctor who wonders what her life could have been like if she had pursued marine biology or mixed-media art.

We hear from readers all the time who are worried about what to do after graduating from high school or college. Most of the time, your parents encourage you to take a pragmatic route because they want you to have some security, and they also want to know how much longer they have to pay your phone bill, put gas in your car, and give you money to go to the movies (your parents are so nice, go hug them).

A lot of our decisions come down to risk versus reward: Stay in school and get on the career track as soon as possible, or take two years off to be educated by the School of Life. Either option can end up working out or leaving you feeling like you made a huge mistake, and that's scary enough as it is—the last thing you need is someone else's vision of what's right for you complicating the matter even more.

IT'S NEVER TOO LATE TO CHANGE (YOUR MIND OR ANYTHING ELSE).

Remember this! This is what we doubters always have to fall back on! Uncertainty often stems from the belief that you can do something that so catastrophically messes up your life that you will never recover from it. Even if things do take a turn for the worse, life is full of second acts! People reinvent themselves all the time. Remember when Martha Stewart WENT TO JAIL for insider trading?! Yeah, I barely do either, because now she's back and stronger than ever. Regret doesn't have to be a major factor if you don't wallow in it, and a bad decision only feels permanent if you let it. Chalk up your mistakes to life lessons, and transfer schools, move cities, change majors, start over.

JUST BECAUSE THINGS DON'T WORK OUT THE WAY YOU THOUGHT DOESN'T MEAN YOU'VE MADE A MISTAKE.

If you feel like you want to do something that other people tell you is useless, keep in mind that what is useless to them might be highly valuable to YOU. And if your screenplay or your band doesn't "pay off" right away, that doesn't mean it wasn't worth a try, or that it isn't fun (a big payoff), or that it isn't worth it to keep on trying. The worst that can happen is that you eventually decide to do something else, and at least then you are free to do so without wondering what might've been.

YOU MIGHT NOT EVER REALLY KNOW WHAT YOU WANT TO DO, AND THAT IS PERFECTLY FINE.

Sometimes not knowing what to do is a matter of not knowing what you *want* to do. But you know what? It's OK. You don't have to have a passion for any one thing, or be working on a spectacular project every minute of the day. Plenty of people go through their whole lives not knowing what they want to do, or they figure it out much later. (Alan Rickman got his first movie role at the age of 46.) On the flipside, I knew for a fact that I wanted to be a fashion designer in middle school, and I followed that dream all the way to college despite the fact that many people thought it was impractical, because I loved it! Then I went to school to study fashion—and it turned out I didn't actually love it. I just wanted to make clothes for myself. And now I'm a writer, and everything worked out OK. You learn as you go along, and even people who appear to have it all figured out often don't. You're still young, your interests can change, and you may never be the type of person whose passion dovetails with a career, which is why we have hobbies.

THERE ARE PEOPLE YOU CAN TALK TO ABOUT ALL OF THIS.

Doubt can lead to anxiety, and anxiety can cause you to suffer from paralyzing indecision—it's a vicious cycle. If thinking about this stuff makes you physically sick or want to hide in your bed forever, it's prob-ably time to bring in a pro. I have sought out therapists and doctors a lot in life, most recently when some major life decisions were keeping me awake at night. My doctor said that it's totally normal, but she wanted to do a physical anyway, and the tests showed several non-serious things that might have been contributing to my emotional state. Your brain is part of your body (duh), so if you feel like something is off, don't hesitate to see someone.

It doesn't necessarily have to be a doctor—it's also nice to just talk to friends or anyone you trust about your feelings. Maybe your school has a guidance or career counselor. Or, if what you're freaking out about is What You Will Do When You Grow Up, find someone who's doing what you're considering doing and ask them how they decided on their career and what challenges they face. It's easy to worry yourself into a corner and feel trapped by indecision, so don't keep all of your concerns to yourself.

Doubt is inevitable, but it doesn't have to dictate your life. I've had major doubts about decisions that turned out to be great, and have been gung-ho about plans that turned out to be terrible. But the worst-case scenario is rarely as terrible as you think it will be, and anyway, my "bad" decisions showed me that I have the strength to adapt and be spontaneous, so it was worth it.

Remember that as much as you think and plan and scheme, your life will probably not work out exactly how you want it to (or think you want it to) right now. And if you need a little push to help you with a hard choice, think of it this way: *Not* making a decision is a decision in itself. It's a decision to keep things exactly the same, just out of fear of the unknown. And that would be the only real mistake you could make. ♦

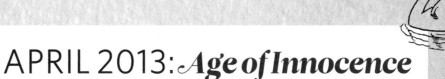

APRIL 2013: *Age of Innocence*

Well hi! We have a few items going up in the Rookie shop in the coming weeks that I am so stoked to tell you about:

ROOKIE AXE™

Here at Rookie, we firmly believe that women can do whatever they want, and that includes smelling like a 12-year-old boy. We've collaborated with Axe to bring you a scent that will make you feel especially…*strong* and stuff the next time you buy shoes, give birth, or march for voting rights. Feminism!

REBEL BOY: A MEN'S RIGHTS ZINE

I get that some things are really hard for women, but does anyone ever think about the *men*? One of my favoritest authors, Tucker Max, wrote and printed this manifesto on men's rights in the style of the classic Riot Grrrl zines of the '90s. In it you'll learn all about issues men face every day, like women not laughing at their jokes and being mad about rape and stuff. Features contributions from Rookie heroes Daniel Tosh and Seth MacFarlane.

VINTAGE MAXIPADS

We've always been strong advocates of wearing vintage clothing. Stuff from the thrift store is usually the cutest and the cheapest. Why stop at clothes, though? We've scavenged our favorite secondhand shops for adorable vintage maxipads, and now we're making them available to you. We found every color from brown-beige to pale beige, and we promise they'll boost your self-love.

OK, April Fool's. For real, this month's theme is Age of Innocence. Here's what I said about it in an email to the staff:

What does it mean to lose your innocence? Is it your first kiss, the first time you have sex, the first catcall, first time you drink/smoke? Is it sudden or gradual?

We're not talking about a whimsical, infantile idea of innocence. Anaheed said innocence is safety. I'd say it's stuff like safety and comfort and unjadedness and openness. Ironically, I was much more cynical at 11 than I am at 16. With the loss of innocence can also come maturity. All of it is kind of bittersweet.

I often feel that life is a series of events that require you to choose between blissful ignorance and the scary process of seeking truth. Sometimes it's too late to do the former without lying to yourself. And sometimes it's OK to lie to yourself. I think a bit of delusional narcissism is necessary for most creative endeavors, and certainly for sharing them. It's probably delusional for anyone to think anyone else should care what they have to say, but if you don't believe that, you'll never make anything, and if you really love creating things, that simply won't do. How do you get there, as a creative person? How do you brainwash yourself?

How do you stay in touch with your innocence as you grow up? How can you return to a state of wonder? I've been doing it on my walk to school by matching up the music on my iPod with my outfit and the weather and the buildings I pass. I'm just like a five-year-old about it, and it's perfect. I'm more enthusiastic about and in awe of silly things as a teenager than I was as a child. When you're little, your standards for the things that excite you aren't low, but they are simple. And while that's a beautiful thing, I think it's even better when you have a broader spectrum of emotions to connect to something over. When you're drawn to something not only because it's happy and immediately gratifying, but also because it's complex and often dark or sad. That's why an album doesn't sound special the first time you listen to it, but really hits home once you've been through some stuff.

I hope you like it. As always, let us know if we miss anything, or create it and send it along.

love, tavi

The Royal Party

The girls with the most cake.
By Olivia

Thanks to Ashlee, Julianne, Alina, and Marisol for modeling,
and Cooper Campbell for his assistance.

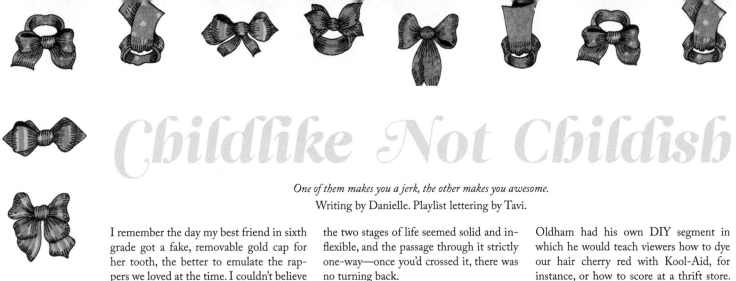

Childlike Not Childish

One of them makes you a jerk, the other makes you awesome.
Writing by Danielle. Playlist lettering by Tavi.

I remember the day my best friend in sixth grade got a fake, removable gold cap for her tooth, the better to emulate the rappers we loved at the time. I couldn't believe her parents would buy it for her *and* let her wear it—it seemed so cool, so *grown up*. Plus, I knew she had to go into the city to get it, which added to its aura of sophisticated danger. I, meanwhile, was still watching cartoons on TV, and crocheting and knitting clothes for my dolls.

Soon I noticed that my friend was starting to hang out with different people, and that she wasn't coming over as often after school to play kickball in my backyard. I now know that trying on new friends is just a natural part of growing up, but at the time I felt abandoned. Now that she was ready to be older, my friend was leaving me behind in Babyland. I felt like I was deficient in some way: abnormal, immature, *childish*.

By ninth grade most of the girls in my class had cast aside their Barbies and sticker books in favor of high heels and lots of makeup, which made me nervous. I wasn't ready for that kind of self-sexualization—I would rather stay home and paint or watch *E.T.* for the hundredth time than go to a dance or hang out in the park to look at the cute boys I would see the next day in school anyway. There were a lot of things I looked forward to about being a teenager and then an adult—e.g., staying out as late as I wanted, eating ice cream any time of day or night—but I wasn't ready to give up all the things I loved about being a kid.

And I was convinced I would have to give them up. You know how people say you should enjoy what you have now while you're alive because "you can't take it with you" to the grave? That's how I felt about the transition from childhood to adulthood: You had to leave your childish things behind. The dividing line between the two stages of life seemed solid and inflexible, and the passage through it strictly one-way—once you'd crossed it, there was no turning back.

In my family, crossing that threshold meant taking on a whole list of new responsibilities. While as a kid I earned my mall money by sharing after-dinner dishwashing duties with my brother, once I became a teenager I'd have to do laundry for the entire family all by myself. I'd have to pay for more of my own stuff, too, which meant I'd have to get a job, and that wouldn't really leave me any time for knitting or doodling or yet another *E.T.* screening. (Repeated viewings of that movie couldn't have helped my fear of adulthood, now that I think back on it: The grown-ups in it are uniformly horrible, and the children get to ride around on flying bicycles.)

Here's another thing: Growing up, I never saw any of the adults in my life having *fun*. They all seemed super serious all the time, and super *tired*—I assumed it was from working all day at jobs they didn't seem to like very much and then coming home to houses and apartments that needed to be maintained, which would have been more than enough, but I didn't even factor in the time they spent raising and tending to me and carting me around to all of my million after-school activities. But no matter what the reasons, the image they gave me of grown-up life was dire, stressed out, exhausted, and bleak. I was terrified of growing up and becoming like them and losing all of the simple joys of youth; but I was also afraid of being left behind and missing out on all of the pleasures and freedoms that the adult world had in store. And I got stuck there, with this impossible choice.

Then came "Todd Time." Back in the early '90s, on the first iteration of MTV's *House of Style*, the fashion designer Todd Oldham had his own DIY segment in which he would teach viewers how to dye our hair cherry red with Kool-Aid, for instance, or how to score at a thrift store. On the episode I happened upon, he was reupholstering a chair from the flea market using some cheery fabric, a glue gun, and some safety pins. This blew my mind. I loved the flea market! I loved making new stuff out of old stuff! And this guy—this Grown Man—was doing this for a living? It was so cool to see an adult with a job they didn't hate—a job that in fact involved doing the very things that *I* loved—and he was obviously having fun while he did it. Believe it or not, this was the first hint I got that adulthood didn't mark the end of fun forever.

After that revelation, I started paying closer attention to the adults around me, and I noticed that they didn't all look like the responsibilities of life and work had put them through the ringer. Some of them, like my eighth grade art teacher (who was basically Joni Mitchell), had jobs that they seemed to enjoy. It began to dawn on me that there was more than one way to be an adult, and that not all of them involved giving up your childhood hobbies. It turned out that there wasn't actually a hard line between childhood and adulthood: You can hold on to the parts of being a child that nourish and comfort you, that make you feel like yourself and help you become the person you want to be.

Suddenly adulthood didn't seem so scary anymore. I got a job, bought a car, went away to college, dropped out, dropped back in, and eventually became an Official Old, with a job and a spouse and a house and everything. But I never stopped doing the things I liked, and many of those "childish" hobbies turned into skills that have been invaluable in my adult life: I still do all that crafty stuff, and all that time spent

noodling around by myself while the other kids were sweating it out at school dances taught me how to be happy being alone, which so many people don't know how to do and which has been incredibly useful to me. I now see all of my grade-school interests and proclivities, which were so often dismissed as "childish" by my classmates, as my way of staying connected to the part of me that can still feel wonder, and that's willing to be entertained by simple things that make me happy—the *childlike* part of me.

Here's the difference between *childish* and *childlike*: Childish behavior in anyone who isn't an actual child is obnoxious. It's ramming your cart into random objects at Target for no reason; it's throwing a temper tantrum when you don't get your way; it's refusing to apologize when you've made a mistake. Being childlike, on the other hand, is immersing yourself in something just because you love doing it. It's being open to liking things that aren't "cool," without pretense or explanation, because they make you happy. It's the ability to be

curious and interested without worrying what anyone else might think. It's pretty badass, when you think about it.

So many of you send us variations of the question "How do I figure out what I'm passionate about?" Well, you should know that you're already doing some of the greatest things! A lot of the stuff you like now could end up being a source of lifelong joy for you, and it's important to keep things in your life just because they make you happy—not everything has to contribute to a career decision or larger life plan. High school is stressful enough as it is, you know? In fact, being childlike is *especially* important when you're a teenager—a period when you're changing constantly, and sometimes confusingly, and are meanwhile being barraged by messages about what is *acceptable* and what is *cool* and how you *should* act/look/be— because it will keep you connected to some truth about yourself. It allows you to ignore everyone else's input so you can figure out what you want for yourself. And it's easy enough to do: Just tap into what it felt

like to be a little kid with a free afternoon. Five-year-olds don't worry that it's "juvenile" or "uncool" to play in the sprinklers in their underwear or stare out the window for a while making weird sounds with their mouths or spend an entire hour just *coloring*. This is why no five-year-old ever says they need help figuring out what they're passionate about.

So what if it makes you happy to play with Legos long past the recommended ages on the box, or have sleepovers until you graduate from high school (or beyond)? Or maybe you just really love making tiny movies, or getting together with your friends to be goofy. Don't feel like you have to give that stuff up, hunker down, and *get serious* about your *future*. You're not just doing something you love; you're also learning how to give yourself permission to revel in life a little bit. If you make a habit of this, it can lead to your becoming the kind of person who knows what she wants, too, and who pursues it without apology or compromise—and there is truly no better kind of adult to be. ⋈

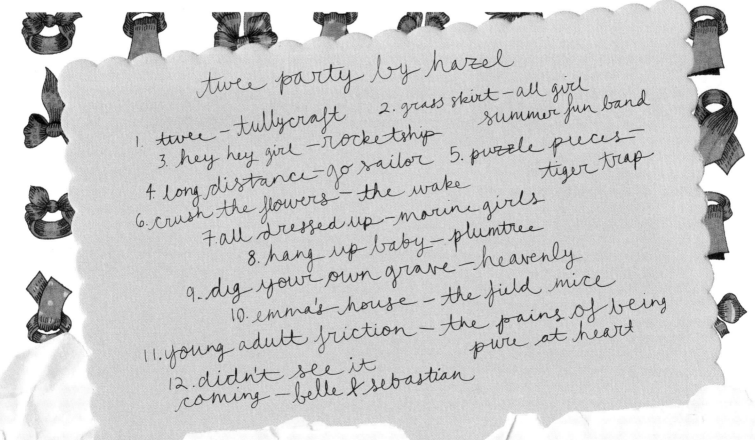

twee party by hazel

1. twee – tullycraft　　2. grass skirt – all girl summer fun band
3. hey hey girl – rocketship
4. long distance – go sailor　5. puzzle pieces – tiger trap
6. crush the flowers – the wake
7. all dressed up – marine girls
8. hang up baby – plumtree
9. dig your own grave – heavenly
10. emma's house – the field mice
11. young adult friction – the pains of being pure at heart
12. didn't see it coming – belle & sebastian

The Complete Guide to Kissing

Smooch unto others as you would have them smooch unto you.
Writing by Krista, illustration by Ruby A.

Well, it's happened. You've found someone you like. Someone you have a crush on. This is HUGE. OK, this happens all the time—but this time it's different: *This* time, this person you've been secretly obsessing over for*ever* and who is so cute and sweet and nice and funny and smells good and is UGH SO PERFECT...this person LIKES YOU TOO. You like *each other,* and it's *amazing,* like a needle-in-a-haystack, no-one-has-ever-felt-this-way-before, I-can't-believe-we-found-each-other sort of thing.

You start hanging out more. You maybe go on a few dates. And then you want to kiss him or her.

This idea of kissing them starts to occupy your thoughts. You're thinking about it all the time, and every time your beautiful perfect adorable crush talks, you can't bring yourself to take your eyes off their mouth. You are staring creepily at their lips *a lot.*

Then one day your crush comes over and you're playing video games on the couch (well, *they're* playing video games; you're watching the light from the screen reflecting off their face out of the corner of your eye) and...you snuggle a little closer.

Crush takes eyes off video game and sets them on you. You and crush lock eyes. And suddenly you both *know:* This is *it.* Your First Kiss is about to happen. You lean in and suddenly you're in their face space, inhaling their warm breath, and then you gently, gently touch your lips to theirs like a butterfly who can't decide whether to stick around or fly away and then it's like a dam breaks and you've both wanted this SO MUCH and your crush grabs you and suddenly you're *really* kissing and it's so easy and so fun and so *perfect* and the music swells and as you lace your fingers through your crush's you can feel in your heart that this is so, so right, and that was your first kiss—and it was better than you ever could have hoped.

That's how every first kiss with someone new would happen if life were perfect. But we all know how life really is, and while the first time you kiss someone is often absolutely lovely and wonderful and great, it can also be awkward, funny, terrible, gross, and occasionally—let's face it—really, truly awful.

You don't have to look far to find stories about kissing, images of people kissing, whole entire songs about kissing...but what about the actual MECHANICS at play? What if you don't care about the context or narrative surrounding the kiss but want solely to learn *OMG what to do with your mouth* when you finally start kissing people? Like, is there a "right" way to kiss? Major, fatal mistakes to avoid? *What if you're a bad kisser and you don't even knowwwwww???* This kind of information is a lot harder to obtain. UNTIL NOW.

I'm about to break down for you, step by step, the four basic types of kiss. (When you've advanced beyond these, you won't need my help.) But first let me reassure you: Kissing is not hard, you do not need to stress about it, and you are most likely going to be an excellent kisser (maybe you already are). Kissing is just getting to know someone in a new way (like a handshake, but with your lips!), and all the good manners and putting-each-other-first type things we already do on the regular with our friends can easily be translated to kissing. If you're a thoughtful, considerate person already, you'll probably be a thoughtful, considerate kisser, without even trying very hard. The Golden Rule applies here: Kiss unto others as you would have them kiss unto you. (Don't worry if you aren't sure how exactly you would have someone kiss unto you—we'll cover that here.)

One final caveat: Don't feel like you have to follow anything I'm saying here. The truth is that *any* way of kissing is just fine, so long as you and your collaborator in this endeavor are enjoying yourselves. It really all boils down to your style. What follow are just some basics to get you started and help you on your own trip down Lip-to-Lip Lane. (Yes I just said that.)

KISS TYPE 1: THE FIRST KISS WITH ANYONE, EVER

Ooooh, this is so exciting. *First kiss!* Yeah!

But before we get down to logistics, your first step should be asking yourself, "Do I

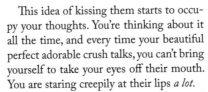

really *want* to kiss this person, or do I just feel like I *should*?"

If you've never kissed someone, please do not listen to people you hang around with who act like it is *everything*. Judging by the number of emails sent to our various advice outlets each month by kiss virgins worried about either catching up with everyone else or *not* catching up with everyone else, you're in good, abundant company. No matter how old you are, you are not the only person your age who hasn't had their first kiss. There's nothing wrong with starting your kissing career before any of your friends, and there's nothing wrong with graduating from high school or college without having touched your lips to another human's. This isn't a race, and it's not like if you don't have your first kiss *now* the window of opportunity will slam shut forever. You have all the time in the world. And don't worry that people will ostracize you in college or that no one will want to have sexytimes with you when they find out that you're not super experienced: College is full of virgins, including some kiss virgins, and being a curious, engaged partner is way more important than how many people you've done stuff with.

Also: If someone wants to kiss you but you don't want to kiss them…don't. It's OK. It doesn't matter if they gave you a ride home or paid for the movie or took you to prom or saved you and your entire extended family, plus assorted pets, from a burning building: You don't owe *anyone* close personal access to your lips. Plus, you'll be kissing people for the rest of your life, so why not wait until you really want to?

When your first kiss does happen, here's something else to keep in mind: It might go really great or really badly or totally boringly or kind of weirdly or any of countless different ways, but no matter what happens, remember that **your first kiss does not determine your kissing future.** It's a kiss you'll remember, almost certainly, but it's still **just one kiss.**

OK. ON TO THE NITTY-GRITTY.

I think the hardest part about first kisses is not the kissing itself, but knowing how to initiate it.

HOW DO YOU KNOW WHEN YOU ARE ABOUT TO KISS OR BE KISSED?

Sometimes it's obvious and the kiss happens in a really predictable setting. Your first kiss might be a dare, or part of a game. You might be going out with someone—let's say it's a girl—and she tells people at school that she's going to kiss you. (This is a rare gift, because now you have time to properly freak out about it with your friends.) When you're young, first kisses often happen at or after school dances, or at the end of the night when you're going home from a place you went to together, either just the two of you or with a group.

Thankfully, if you're both into each other, it's usually pretty easy to tell when a kiss is about to happen. One of you might be looking intently at the other's face for longer than normal. You might feel shy or nervous or like you want to laugh. A pretty good rule of thumb is: If someone's face is really close to your face, and they're looking at you intensely, or you guys are laughing about something but your faces are WAY CLOSER THAN IS NORMAL FOR FRIENDS and you feel a kind of charge in the air—then it might be kissin' time. If you feel like it, lean in a little closer, and do…

KISS TYPE 1(A): THE INTRO KISS

This is the first kiss you ever have with a new person. It's simultaneously a greeting and announcement ("Hi! I like you!"), and a way for you to get a sense of how the other person kisses, to see if it's compatible with the way you like to kiss.

Here's how you do it:

1. Lean in.

2. Check to make sure that your crush is also leaning in toward *you*. (You don't want to be moving your face, eyes closed and lips puckered, toward someone who is playing *Bejeweled* on their phone, totally unaware of the plane that's coming in for a landing…on their face.)

3. Optional: Close your eyes. (When in doubt, I say close 'em: It's traditional, and it

solves the problem of how weird it would be to see another person that close up.)

4. Tilt your head to the right or left—if your partner is starting to tilt in one direction, you go the opposite way. This is so your noses don't collide before your lips do. If you can't tell which way the other person's gonna tilt, your best bet is to go right. I'd say most people go right like 95 percent of the time. (And if you make a miscalculation, just laugh it off and keep going.)

5. *Gently* touch your lips to your date's lips. No big SMACKS (you're not kissing your grandmother or your dog); no wide-open mouth (you're not trying to devour them). Just your lips, about as open as they are when you're just breathing through your mouth.

6. At this point, you can apply a little pressure. Your lips are doing that kissing thing you do when you kiss your pets and relatives, but like 80 percent softer, and your lips are lingering on theirs about 500 percent longer. Hopefully by now your date will have started kissing you back, just as gently. And hoooraaaaay, you're kissing!

If the idea of kissing someone's mouth is still a bit scary, and/or you're really shy, you can always try…

"KISS TYPE 1(B): CHEEK KISS/ SMILE COMBO

1. You're sitting next to your crush. You really want to kiss him/her but really don't know how to start.

2. Quickly, like a sparrow, you dart in, kiss the side of their cheek, and then, when they look at you, you grin adorably at them while biting your lip. (This works really well for same-gender first kisses when you're not sure if the other person is interested in girls, because if they react like "Um, what are you doing??" you can act like ha ha ha NOTHING, you're just really friendly and love hanging out with them!)

An Intro Kiss is *not* about making out. It's a gateway kiss–the kiss that lets you know whether someone (a) likes you the way you like them and (b) feels right to kiss.

Kissing is actually pretty hard to describe, you guys. Is this nice, soft intro kiss good? Do you like it? Is everyone happy? Great! If you want, you can stop here. Orrrrr you can advance to…

KISS TYPE 2: FRENCH KISSING

I know this feels like a major jump, but french kissing just means using your tongue, and you can definitely use your tongue without SERIOUSLY MAKING OUT. If your tongues touch, you're frenching. The end.

So you're Intro Kissing, lips only, and it's nice, and you're liking it, and you want to go further. Try opening your mouth juuuuust a little bit more. (Your date will probably open her or his mouth more too, either because they've done this before and know what's up or because they're following your lead and are enjoying this as much as you are.)

With your mouth open, gently (*gently* is the key word here, folks) touch your date's tongue with your tongue, then tongue-retreat back to your own mouth. Don't like SHOVE YOUR TONGUE IN THEIR MOUTH without any warning, or stick it really far back in their mouth. There's nothing necessarily wrong with that per se, but for the first-time french kiss with someone? Give them a minute before you go licking their molars. Your partner will probably understand quickly what's happening, and will hopefully touch *your* tongue with *their* tongue. *Soft*. Gentle.

Your tongue is pretty relaxed during all this, but never totally idle—keep it moving in a calm, languid way, like licking an ice cream cone. Don't give your partner a totally flaccid, listless tongue, but don't stiffen up either, for either of these two extremes is equally gross to receive.

Once you've started frenching, you can always go back to kissing sans tongue. Retract your tongue and do some more Intro-style kissing. Vary open-mouthed tongue kissing with closed-mouth kissing. (If you keep your mouths open the entire time, things can get pretty sloppy fast.) Keep kissing with your lips, and add just a *touch* of tongue here and there. It's much

better that way, and you can move into MAKING OUT later.

KISS TYPE 3: MAKING OUT

Making out is when you've been kissing for a while and there are open mouths and frenching and the tongues are…not being quite so polite. Making out is when your arms are around each other and the tongues are really going at it and you're kissing for longer than, say, 30 seconds. A makeout session is basically you and your partner trying to get as close as possible without actually consuming each other. Hands roam all over the place; you will probably get turned on. This is the most intense form of kissing, and it can last for a very, very long time.

But no discussion of kissing would be complete without mentioning the basic anti-kiss: a kiss that's the opposite of all the ones we've talked about so far. And that is:

KISS TYPE 4: THE NON-SEXUAL PECK

The peck is what your mom gives you on the top of your head, or the way you kiss your dad, grandpa, grandma, or other relation on the cheek. The peck is affectionate but completely nonsexual, and that is why in movies, when the hero wants to kiss a girl goodnight and she very obviously turns her face so he can kiss her cheek, we all know NOTHING is going to happen between them. If someone is aiming for your mouth and you turn your head dramatically and on purpose, that is, in our society, a clear-cut "You're nice but no thanks, I'm not romantically interested" signal. A peck can hurt someone's feelings, but sometimes you don't feel romantic about someone, and it can't be helped.

So now we know the basics. Great! We're kissing! (Not with each other.) It's fun! Hopefully! But sometimes it isn't. Things don't always go smoothly, not even for very experienced kissers. So now it's time for:

KISS TROUBLESHOOTING

Bad breath: So you want to kiss someone, and they want to kiss you, and you lean in, and they lean in, and…oh wow. WOW. This person has HORRIBLE breath. I mean the

kind that is so terrible that you can almost *see* it hanging in the air. What do you do?

Welllll…how much do you want to kiss this person? Is this a first kiss with someone you've had a crush on for ages? Is this your boyfriend of three months? What's the situation here? It's obvs up to you, but I would say that if you really, really want to kiss this person, and you've never kissed them before, you might want to go for it. Just this once! Of course, this is only if you like them enough to deal with this unfortunate situation in the hopes that next time will be a bit…mintier. A gross, but hopefully worthy, sacrifice.

But if you know this person a little bit better than that, you can totally say, "Hey, do you want some gum?" This can be embarrassing for the poor girl/guy, though, so try this trick: If you suspect kissing might happen at any point when you're out with someone, you cannot go wrong by putting gum or mints in your pocket and offering your date one while chomping on one yourself, before kissing ever has a chance to happen. Act like you just always eat mints, and it's super-natural to offer one to her/him.

And of course if it just doesn't seem worth it, at the moment you become alerted to the situation, when your lips are close to theirs, you are well within your rights to retreat and say vaguely, "You know what, this just doesn't feel right." (And if you're on the other end of this, please don't be ashamed. Bad breath is easily treatable and not a reflection on your character. If you brush and floss regularly, didn't just eat a bunch of onions and garlic, and you don't smoke, ask your dentist and/or your regular doctor to help you figure out what's going on. Nip the problem in the bud—isn't it worth it if it means MORE KISSING?)

Slobbering: You're kissing, you're frenching, and…your date thinks it's their mission in life to swab your entire mouth with their tongue. To them, a sexy kiss is the wettest, sloppiest one possible. They are licking your lips, the inside of your mouth, they may even (yes) *lick your face*. WHAT THE HELL IS GOING ON THIS IS TERRIBLE SOMEONE HELP.

Slobbering is dreadful and often inflicted by someone who really really really wants to

kiss but has very little experience doing so. They're trying to make the kiss really sexy, and for some reason they think this is the best way to do so. They are wrong. They must be stopped immediately. Here's how:

1. Pull away from the slobberer.

2. Assuming you like this slobberer, smile.

3. Say, "I like kissing you really softly, like this."

4. Then demonstrate what feels nice to *you*. Kiss your partner very gently, throwing in a little bit of tongue, but WAY LESS than they were using with you.

5. Pull away. Smile. (You are so friendly and encouraging and not at all humiliating!)

6. Then lean in to give them another chance. Your partner (if they are not stupid) should immediately try to emulate what you just did. If the new kiss shows *marked* improvement, congratulations! There's hope. If, however, the new kiss is just as bad as—or *worse* than—the original slobbery kiss…I'm so sorry, hunnybun, but this person might not be ready for the hotness of your kisses. (Unless, of course, sloppy kisses are your jam. Who knows? Everyone likes different things.)

Oddly aggressive kissing: You're kissing, you're frenching, and…your date has totally taken over. They're kissing you really aggressively, maybe grabbing the back of your head *hard, shoving* their tongue in your mouth and pushing it around. Their teeth *actually touched your teeth*, and you didn't like it. Meanwhile, you are clearly not matching their level of forcefulness and…gusto. This person is totally disregarding your body language, which is communicating that you are not really into this kind of kissing at all.

One thing you can do here, if you're really uncomfortable, is put a total stop to the proceedings, go home, and watch *Downton Abbey*. You can try again some other time if you feel like it, but maybe you won't, and that's just fine.

But if you want to keep kissing them, but not in the way where you feel like you're being mauled by a bear, try these steps:

1. Stop kissing your partner immediately, and pull away from her/him.

2. Give them a surprised/confused look, and then slowly and carefully begin kissing them again. You can put a hand right under their collarbone as a signal that you want them to stay on their side of this kiss rather than tackle you. Your hand is resting there, not actually pushing them away. (If you're continually physically pushing someone away and they keep ignoring it, this is worse than a bad kiss. It's coercion, it's force, and the only positive thing about it is that it lets you know right away that this is not a person you want to be involved with.)

3. If this beast still isn't getting your message, stop again, explain to them how you *want* to be kissed, and demonstrate this preference on their mouth. This is their last chance: If this doesn't fix the problem, take your leave. Go find someone else to kiss. Kissing is supposed to be fun, you guys!

Now, like I said, maybe none of this advice applies to you. Maybe you have your own idiosyncratic kissing technique; that's awesome, since knowing what you like in terms of kissing will help you figure out what you like sexually for the rest of your life. Maybe you're the girl who LOVES the feeling of a slack wet tongue resting in your mouth like a dead squid. Again, congratulations; you have a jump-start on knowing yourself.

My point is that there's no "right" way to kiss. There's only what you like, and what your kissing partner likes, and whether and how you two match up. Wait until you're really and truly ready, and then embark on a lifetime of practice (the fun kind). ✾

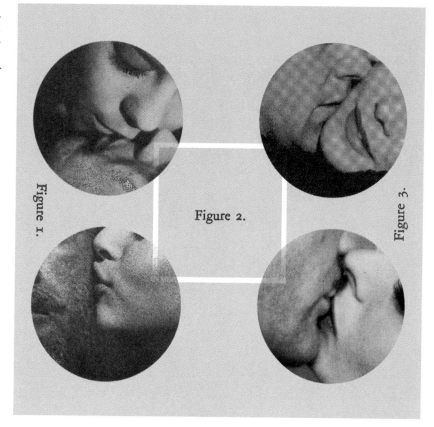

Figure 1.

Figure 2.

Figure 3.

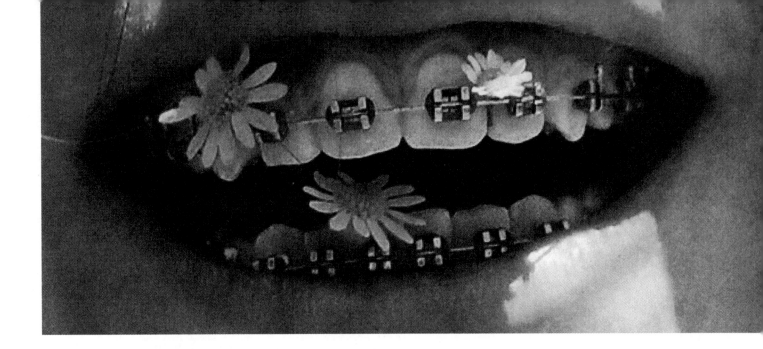

gentle on my mind

Let's make some old memories.
By Erica

Thanks to Beth and Eira for modeling, and to Recollection Vintage for the clothes.

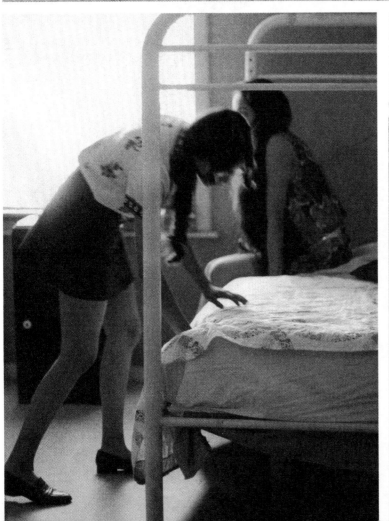

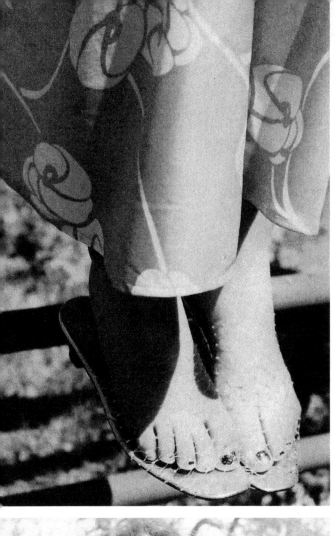

Stay Curious: An Interview With Molly Ringwald

"I felt like the most ill-equipped teenager out there."
Interview by Maude Apatow, illustration by Allegra.

A few months ago I got a really nice tweet from Molly Ringwald. I was excited, because I admire her and have kind of always wanted to be like her. I asked if I could interview her and she said yes, so I avoided her for a month. Sometimes when I really admire someone I'm afraid to talk to them because I don't want to embarrass myself. My dad told me I was being crazy and kind of rude, so I emailed her and set a time for us to talk.

Molly Ringwald starred in some of my favorite films, including *Sixteen Candles*, *The Breakfast Club*, and *Pretty in Pink*, all directed by John Hughes. She's also done a lot of theater, and right now she's on *The Secret Life of the American Teenager* on ABC Family. Not content to limit herself to an amazing three-decade-long acting career, she's also written two books (*Getting the Pretty Back* and *When It Happens to You*), and she recently released her first jazz album, *Except Sometimes*, which includes a great rendition of "Don't You Forget About Me" from *The Breakfast Club*.

I met Molly at R+D Kitchen in Santa Monica, and I immediately ordered a water because when I am nervous I drink water so it looks like I am doing something. She is so nice and cool, though, that she instantly put me at ease. She is actually so much more than *cool* but I can't think of a more apt word to describe her. After the interview she told me she didn't have a ride home, so my dad and I drove her. I forgot why she needed a ride but I am so glad she did, because I got to spend another 15 minutes with her. Now I know where she lives, but I won't tell you. Actually I already forgot. Here is my interview with Molly Ringwald.

MOLLY RINGWALD So, have you done a lot of these?

MAUDE APATOW Not really. I get so nervous, I feel like I'm acting so crazy.

Don't worry about it.

Thanks. So…your jazz album just came out. Was it fun to make that?

Yes! My dad's a jazz musician, so I grew up singing jazz—I did that before I did anything else. It was like coming back to my roots.

Weren't you in *Annie*? Was that your first acting job?

That was actually what kicked me into acting more than singing. Somebody heard me sing and suggested I try out for *Annie*, which was doing its first West Coast production. I was 10 years old and listening to the soundtrack all the time. So I flew to L.A. to audition.

What was the audition process like?

It was one of those huge cattle calls. It was exciting, but I was really shy when I was a kid—I'm still kind of shy. The only time that I wasn't shy was when I was onstage. I was so nervous to be around all these other girls [who were auditioning]. We started out with all these [girls], and then it kept getting narrowed down and I kept making the cut every time. Toward the end [of the process] I think I would have been devas-

tated if I hadn't gotten the part. That's why I think acting is so hard on kids.

What do you think about letting kids act?

I have three kids, and I won't let them act for exactly that reason. I feel like there's a time when kids should just be able to be *kids*. And, you know, acting is really a business. But of course my eldest daughter is nine and that's all she wants to do. Sometimes I think I'm kind of pushing her to be an actor by denying her the right to do it. [*Laughs*]

When you started acting, were you put in situations where you were the only kid around?

Yeah, I was always the youngest person around. For years.

How did that feel?

I loved it. It was hard for me at the time to relate to people my own age. That was sort of ironic: I became sort of like the "every teen," representative of all teen America, but I felt like the most ill-equipped teenager out there. There were a couple of years when I was terrified to be around kids. Kids are mean!

That's how I feel—I've been around so many adults that it's scarier being around kids.

How old are you?

I'm 15.

Right, so you're sort of getting out of the really mean stage. I think like 13, 14 for girls is the worst. I was terrified of them. When I was acting during that time, it inspired so much envy and jealousy and teasing, you know? I had a tough time in school. But later I got so confident from what I was doing outside of school that I didn't really care what they thought.

Do you have siblings?

I do. I have my sister, who's three and a half years older than me, and my brother is a year and a half older than me.

Do you ever fight with them?

Oh, definitely. My sister mostly.

Sister—yeah.

You know, I think sisters just do that. We were a very close family, but looking back on it I think [dealing with my success] was hard for [my siblings]. My sister was basically like Claire in *The Breakfast Club.* I kind of based [that character] on her—not *her* specifically, but just in that she was a really popular girl in school. She was very well liked. And I never felt that way—she was my closest connection to popularity. So to go from being the most popular girl in school to having a sister who is like the most popular girl in the *country*— she didn't know how to handle it. And my brother just felt kind of invisible, you know? It's hard. It messes with the balance of the family.

Right. Let's talk about your books. What do you get out of writing that you don't get out of acting?

Coming from a long career of having to do what other people tell me to do, it's nice to have control over what you're making. I think [writing is] the most pure expression that there is. No one else really does anything to your work. They edit you, but they're all *suggested* edits, so I don't have to take them if I don't want to. If you're acting in somebody else's movie, even though you can contribute and you can ad-lib and have opinions, ultimately you're not the creator.

My mom wanted me to tell you that she has loved you since she was a kid.

I love her, she's very funny. Did you always get along with her?

Yeah.

Always? Have you never gone through a period where you didn't like her?

I mean, I go through like small periods, but I have a really good relationship with my parents. My mom's like my best friend. I feel like I have more in common with her than [with] any of my friends.

Do you ever feel the need to individuate or to be different?

I've gone through stages where I tried to rebel, but it was kind of stupid because my parents are so nice that I have nothing to rebel against.

That's nice. I feel like my daughter has been rebelling since the day she was born.

My sister's like that. What is the most important advice you ever got from your parents?

The most important advice I got from them was to do something other than act. They were always impressing upon me how important it was to develop other skills and talents, and I think that's served me well throughout my life. So I try to impress that upon my kids, you know, whatever they're interested in, to not just put everything into one thing, but to stay curious.
    Also, uh, not that much TV. For the first four years of Mathilda's life we lived in New York, and our apartment was so small that there was no place for a

TV, and she didn't have any interest anyway. And then a couple of years ago we moved [to L.A.] and got a TV and all of a sudden all she cared about was television. So we put rules on television, the computer—any device. That is really hard, but I think it's been good for her.

We have no TV on weeknights.

When I told Mathilda there was going to be no more television during the week she lay down on the coffee table and sobbed for like half an hour.

[*Laughs*] My sister does the same exact thing!

It was like she lost her best friend! But after that she started to do stuff during the week again. She started to draw and paint again, and now she's into doing stop-motion animation. She's doing claymation videos.

Oh, that's cool! Are you nervous for when your kids are teenagers?

I am, but I try not to be. I look at somebody like you, and I think you're a really good example that shows me that it's possible she's going to be OK. I just try to look at [teenagers] that are good examples and hope I can steer my kids in that direction. Shailene Woodley, who played my daughter on *Secret Life*, she's another one. She's grown up now—I think she just turned 21—but she's an amazing example of someone who had a great relationship with her mom and a very strong sense of herself [as a teenager]. But ultimately as a parent you're just a custodian. Your kids are yours, but they're not really *yours*. You have to kind of guide them in the right direction, but they're going to make their own choices and their own mistakes, just like I have.

But I will admit that sometimes, in the middle of the night, I'll have anxiety attacks thinking about my kids, like, *What if she tattoos her face?!* That would break my heart. Have you seen kids at your school do that—tattoos on the face?

I've seen the lips, which I don't get—you pull your lip down and there's a tattoo.

Oh, that's awful. I don't get that. What kind of books do you like to read?

I'm reading a lot of books right now. We just read *The Catcher in the Rye* at school. I loved it.

I love *The Catcher in the Rye*!

[The rest of] my class didn't seem to like it that much. My teacher seems bored with it.

I read *The Catcher in the Rye* when I was doing the John Hughes movies, and when I look back on it today, I had no idea that I was making, in a way, a *Catcher in the Rye* in this set of movies that would continue to exist for generations. I mean, that book came out in 1951, and people are still reading it.

I feel like I can relate to it now!

I felt like it was *me*! Have you read [J.D. Salinger's] *Nine Stories*?

No, but I just got it. It's sitting next to my bed.

It's so good.

I just read *Room* by Emma Donoghue. Have you heard of that?

I haven't, no. What is that?

It's from the perspective of a five-year-old boy whose mom got kidnapped when she was 19 and locked in a shed, and he was born in the shed, and that's all he knows. I liked it. When I was telling my mom about it, she didn't want to hear about it.

Yeah, there's certain things that when you have kids, you can't…like, I never particularly liked violence in movies, but now if there's violence perpetrated on children, I can't watch it. It makes me physically sick.

See, I really love that stuff. And then I just get obsessed with it and it makes me upset.

Do you like to write fiction?

Kind of. I've been writing. I wrote a lot when I was younger—like two years ago—but I haven't been writing at all lately because of school and technology. I wrote an article last summer about how my addiction to Twitter, Instagram, and Facebook has affected how much I write.

Yeah, I remember that.

It's awful. The second I finish my homework, I go on my phone for an hour and then I go to sleep. And I don't make any time to write or do any of the things that I want to.

See, I feel the exact opposite in that I was tweeting for a while, and then I kind of took a break, and I've been trying to get back into it. And I can't quite do it. People can be really vicious on Twitter. It's hard

not to take it personally. I mean, I can read one nice thing after another, and then one person will say something—

And you only remember the one bad one!

Yeah. It reminds me of being younger and being attracted to the one guy in the room who wasn't looking at me. Eventually you grow out of those behaviors, but Twitter brings me right back to that. Why should I care about what this loser—who probably has, whatever, 12 followers anyway—thinks, you know?

I read them all. I'm on Twitter all day long. I've gotten a little better because I feel like it's messing up my brain for real and I can't focus on anything else. It's so bad. A couple of years ago Harry Styles tweeted me to wish me a happy birthday, and some One Direction fans attacked me. I got around 2,000 tweets and I'd say 60 percent of them were awful. I can't even believe that people do stuff like that.

What advice do your parents give you about that? Just get off [the internet], and don't look at comments?

They say you just have to choose not to focus on that.

It's so hard, though. We won't let our daughter post her face on YouTube, but she got around that by making these little claymation things and posting those. So I said to [my husband], "We have to disable the comments." I just don't want people to say mean things [to her]. That's why I don't want my kids to be involved in show business until they graduate college.

Do you feel like [show business] messed you up as a kid? You seem to have gotten through it really well.

I was incredibly lucky and had a tremendous amount of success at a young age, so during those years it was fine, you know, because I was successful. But then going into my 20s, when I had to grow up, it was really hard. When you're in your 20s you're actually not that much more grown up than you are when you're in your teens, but everyone expects you to be in this different place. And once you've become really famous or successful, there's always a backlash. It's part of human nature: We want to build people up and then tear them down. If I were considering an acting career now, with the way technology is, I don't know if I would have made the same decision. I don't know if I could have dealt with it.

Because of things like Twitter and people being mean?

And TMZ and all that. The kids who are really famous now have to deal with so much more invasion of privacy, and if you don't have a strong family background—if you don't have parents that are intelligent and good and not into exploiting their kids—you don't have a chance. But even though I have truly great parents, I don't think I could deal with that. I think I was really lucky that I got through it all. You know, statistically, if you look at most of the kids that are acting, most of them don't grow into healthy, well-formed human beings. I have very mixed feelings about it all. Whenever Mathilda says to me, "Why can't I do it?" and I give her all my reasons, she says, "Well, *you* did it. Do you think you're more special than me? Do you think that you're smarter than me?" You know, no, no, I don't—it's just that I was lucky. I think it's more unsafe now. You're required to give so much more of yourself than you were back then. When I started, you were able to have a private life and a public life. Now you're expected to be on display all of the time, and if you're not, they get angry.

What were you like as a teenager?

I thought I knew everything when I was a teenager. I was very opinionated and I really thought that what I knew was the answer to everything—and that my parents knew nothing. I was probably unbearable in a lot of ways.

I guess that's how we all feel.

I felt like my parents didn't understand. I loved them, and I still do, but I never considered my mom, like, my best friend. There were things that I could never talk to her about—like sex. I probably err on the opposite side of things—I want to talk about everything with Mathilda, so sometimes I rush things a little bit. When she was in preschool she was interested in how babies are made, and we had this book, *Where Willy Went*, about a little sperm in a race to try to get to the egg. So she already knew about the sperm meeting the egg, but she didn't know how [the sperm] got there in the first place. She asked me about it and I said, "You really want to know?" And she said, "Yeah." And I just blurted it all out. It took about seven minutes. I told her the whole thing. She was like wide-eyed and I said, "Was that what you were expecting?" She said no. I said, "Has anyone talked about this at school?" And she said no. So I said, "Well, was it a surprise?" She said no. And then she said, "I mean yes." I said, "Well, that's it." And then I had to tell all of the other parents [at her school], "Hey, by the way, if you hear [your kids say] anything about the penis getting bigger and blah blah blah, uh, this is where it came from." My husband was just shaking his head. It was really embarrassing. [*Laughs*]

Do you think she was ready to hear it, though?

She was not ready at *all*. I totally jumped the gun. Because six months later she said, "Mom, do you want to know how babies are made?" I was like, "Yeah, sure," thinking to myself, *I told you this whole thing.* And she said, "Kissing."

[*Laughs*] Tavi wanted me to ask if there's anything that you would like to tell her teenage readers. Words of advice.

I sort of make it a policy not to give advice, because I think everyone has to figure it out on their own. The only thing I will say—which is not original, because

Dan Savage did a whole campaign on it—is that it gets better. I think it's important for teenagers to remember that life is always changing. However you feel right at this moment, you're not going to feel that way in an hour or tomorrow. It's ephemeral. And I think it always gets better.

How did you and Tavi meet?

I write for HelloGiggles, and the founder, Sophia Rossi, introduced us. This is the first thing I've ever written for [Rookie], so I'm excited.

Did I tell you that I interviewed the comedian Demetri Martin last week?

I love him.

He's great. He has a book coming out, and I took him to the Museum of Modern Art in New York and we walked through an abstract-art exhibit because his book is an art book. I didn't record the interview on my phone because I didn't want to take up the space on it, so I used somebody else's recording device, and it kept turning on and off.

That's my worst nightmare.

When I got home I wanted to make sure that certain things I said weren't recorded, so I had to listen to this whole conversation. I was like, *Oh my god, why am I talking so much?* I was interviewing this guy and I didn't stop talking. And I kept saying, "Oh, that's great." I'm like, *How many times are you going to say that?* Or *How many times am I going to say the word* like? Demetri kept saying all these very intellectual thoughts [about the art], and all my thoughts were like, *Why isn't this in my house?* Like, *I just want this in my living room.* You know, total consumer. But yeah, you should pick up his book.

Thanks for doing this, Maude.

Thank you so much! Now I'm scared it didn't record! 🎀

No More Nice Girls

Hijacking the backhanded "compliments" that have been bumming me out.

By Sady

When I was 18, I was released from the confines of homeschool into the wide, exciting world of college. I quickly discovered I was woefully unprepared—not for the academic part, which I knew would be rigorous, but for dealing with all those *people*. At that point I had never dated anyone. I had never had a beer. I had neither kissed nor been kissed. I had not, for the prior couple of years, *spoken* to anyone unless it was absolutely necessary. I'm not blaming home education for my dismal lack of socialization—I know that the normal homeschool experience includes a lot of interaction with the outside world. But such was not the case for me. I had used homeschool as an excuse not to interact with anyone outside of my immediate family. I entered college with a nervous desire to make friends, but zero understanding of how that process actually worked.

When you are severely socially stunted, other people can sense it. Not that I made it very hard—I provided lots of clues. There was the wild, deer-in-headlights look on my face when I found myself in a room with more than three other people, the fact that I didn't get 98 percent of people's pop culture references, and my habit of, after someone told a joke, asking for clarification. At one point someone said they wanted to "take me out," and I said, "You mean like with a gun?" You know, fun, sexy, cool stuff like that.

But despite all of this frankly off-putting behavior, dudes seemed to *love* me. Let me be more precise: The *worst* dudes loved me. Everywhere I turned, there was a 28-year-old pot dealer who lived on his brother's couch, or a senior who made it his business to nail as many freshmen as possible, or, once, during my summer internship, an older man who taught my friend math at community college. They were popping up like awful incubi every 30 seconds, ready to yank the glasses off my face so they could remark on how "pretty" I was underneath them, or to

gently brush my horrified face with their creepy pot hands, or to just lean in and purr, "You're great. You're so *innocent*."

First of all: EW. Second: I was not "innocent." I was a shut-in. Being attracted to me was like wanting to date E.T. And yet somehow, the precise lack of social skills that made me…challenging, let's say, to hang out with also apparently made me downright irresistible to a certain type of guy: the kind that is easily intimidated by women who can do scary, threatening things like make eye contact and converse with others out loud. One look at me and these guys surmised that this E.T.-like creature (so childlike in her ignorance of our earthly ways!) would be more open to their fumbling, grabby modes of seduction than a reasonably experienced and assertive young woman might be. Other girls would surely tell them to get lost. Me, you probably could have trapped by putting a line of Reese's Pieces on the floor.

Now, there's nothing wrong with being innocent. With innocence comes the kind of trust that keeps you open to the world around you. Once you've been scuffed up a bit by life it's hard not to close parts of yourself off as protection; to remain playful and curious is difficult and brave. *Innocent* can be a genuinely appreciative, respectful compliment that means someone likes your fresh perspective and your lack of cynicism.

But it's amazing how, in a patriarchy, anything—even a genuinely noble virtue—can be used to belittle women. Because when those guys in college leered at me and told me I was "so *innocent*," they didn't mean it as a compliment (I didn't ask them, but you know it when you hear it). My inexperience made me vulnerable, and that can be a siren's song for anyone (not just guys) who needs to feel stronger than the person they are pursuing. They seemed to sense that they could get away with all sorts of BS with me because I wouldn't know that I could (and *should*) call them out on any of it. For example: TOUCHING

MY FACE. WITHOUT MY CONSENT. I must stress: This happened MORE THAN ONCE. More than a decade later, I am NOT DONE being creeped out by this.

There are other words like this: *sweet*, for example, and *pretty*. Neither of those is a bad thing to be, but somewhere along the line someone decided that these were *girly* qualities, and if they were associated with girls, they must somehow signify inferiority and weakness. Add to this mix the contradictory yet simultaneous fear of women and girls that comes with sexism and you get a culture that fetishizes helplessness in women (because if we think we're supposed to be weak and helpless, maybe we won't figure out that we're not). So "sweet, pretty, and innocent" isn't just a description, it's become an order. That's what girls are *supposed to be like*.

The image of girlhood that we're taught and sold is pink, it's happy, and it's non-threatening. It involves canopy beds and no discernible desires excepting the endless one to please and appease others (especially men), and perhaps to occasionally roll around in a field of flowers, giggling. Now: If someone were to offer me a pink canopy bed I would take it, no questions asked. But actual girlhood (as any girl knows) isn't really like that. There are sharp angles, corners, and shadows, and erasing those from the picture creates an unrealistic ideal that no real person can ever live up to—plus, it leaves out a lot of the interesting stuff.

So here's what I propose. Let's counter the verbal hocus-pocus that turned these strengths into weaknesses with some word-fu of our own. Let's add some of those shadows back in, and make those virtues powerful again. Here are some other ways to think of those words—feel free to replace *sweet*, *pretty*, and *innocent* with these alternatives in your head whenever you hear them, or just know that when someone says you seem "so innocent," they mean you're learning stuff and that means you're awesome. Here we go:

SWEET → COMPASSIONATE

Like innocence, sweetness can be an admirable quality. When Jane Austen describes someone as having a "sweet disposition," you like that girl—you get the sense that she's generally open to life, that she has a generous spirit that isn't likely to sour under adversity. But then you have the diluted-by-patriarchy meaning, which is "nice all the time to everyone ever and everyone likes her the most because she's never been angry or sad or stressed out or had even a mild headache." From babyhood, girls are praised for being "sweet" and "pretty," while boys are more likely to be called "big" or "smart." And so girls become women who haven't learned how to do a lot of stuff that's pretty important in life, because that stuff isn't "sweet." It's not "sweet," for instance, to tell somebody to back off, or to demand better treatment. It's not "sweet" to tell a misinformed blowhard who's dominating the conversation that he's wrong. It's not "sweet" to tell somebody you're not interested in dating them, or to cut a toxic person out of your life. Later on, it won't be "sweet" when you ask for a raise at work. It's not "sweet" to campaign for political office, protest an injustice, or report a sexual assault.

To give sweetness back some of its former glory, think of it as a form of compassion. Compassion is a real, deeply felt understanding of the fact that everyone in this world experiences pain, and that pain always sucks, for everybody. It's an honest desire to help other people get through their pain, to lessen it or prevent it when and how you can.

You can be kind to others without being polite to everyone all the time; and you can be outspoken, demanding, and downright disagreeable without being a bad person or a "mean girl" (another epithet that's flung around to oppress girls—do you ever hear anyone being called a "mean boy"?).

Another wonderful thing about compassion is that it's not damaged as you get more scuffed up by life—in fact it tends to grow over time. Every hard day you've ever had, every hurt or trauma you've experienced, is actually a strange kind of blessing—it's a door into the suffering experienced by others, a chance for you to realize, even when you're overwhelmed by your own pain, that *this is what it's like for other people, too.* Pain is terrible, and you shouldn't seek it out. But when it happens—and it always happens, to everyone—it can help to realize that through it you are learning about a part of the human experience that you will one day be uniquely qualified to help other people live through.

PRETTY → CONFIDENT

Oh, "pretty." Where would I be without you? I would be living a far more centered and less insecure life without the memories of that one year in college when I pretty much ate only tuna salad sandwiches without mayonnaise, and also I would pick the bread off, and people would kindly tell me that I "looked tired" almost every day, probably because I was somehow surviving on two to three handfuls a day of celery and cold tuna. That is where I'd be without the concept of "pretty."

Pretty things are pleasant to look at, and it's hard to see how that could be turned into a bad thing, but leave it to a male-dominated culture to define *pretty* as "a female human that we have deemed fuckable," i.e., a person with genetically assigned perfectly symmetrical features and a body that is thin but curvy and that doesn't need to use a wheelchair to get around, and who is graceful and young and preferably blond, doe-eyed, and white. If you have ever been in love, though, you know that at the height of it the object of your affections was the most beautiful sight in the world to you, right? So you have to acknowledge that there is a culturally understood definition of what's pretty, and then there's what all of us weird, complicated human beings actually find pretty, and those two sets are far from identical. Attraction is subject to powerful, mysterious forces way beyond the scope of the dominant beauty ideal. It's a good idea to tune in to those forces, the ones that tell you what you want and what makes you happy, and turn the volume way down on (a) what everyone else thinks you should want, and (b) what you imagine other people think of you. And while you're at it, try to think less about how you look, and more about how you feel. (This is not always easy, I know, especially if you are a teenage girl on planet earth.)

To do all this, you need confidence, which, like compassion, is something you gain by living. The more you get to know the specific person you are, the more qualified you'll be to realize both what you want and what makes you worth wanting.

INNOCENT → LEARNING

Innocence is often used to mean "seems young and vulnerable in a manner that would allow me to get away with wacky bullcrap." The people who are attracted to that are, not surprisingly, the kind of people who are really super into getting away with wacky bullcrap, which is why telling girls to aspire to that version of "innocent" is basically like saying "the zoo is much more fun when you actually climb *into* the tiger exhibit."

But *young? Vulnerable?* Those things are wonderful. They mean you're open to experience. You're not set in your ways. You have the confidence to change your mind. You're not less than anyone else just because you haven't been around as long as they have. Your mind is alive to and engaged in the world in a way that's hard to hold on to later in life. You're *learning.*

The idea that girls are supposed to stay "pure" is a trap designed to keep you from getting out there and exploring the world—because, you're told, it will only rough you up, sully you, make you less. But learning is not a trap. It means that you're standing in front of failure and embarrassment and disappointment—and joy, and surprise, and all the other good things that come with experience—and you're ready for them. That you're not afraid to explore. It means you're ready to grow up, even when that process scares you. I can't think of anything braver or more powerful than that. 🌱

The Good Witches

Photos inspired by a Swedish Easter tradition.
By Eleanor and Beth Siveyer

For these photos, Eleanor, Beth Siveyer, and Arvida Byström were inspired by the Swedish tradition of Easter witches: Young girls put on their mothers' silk scarves, recycled sheets, or old dresses and exchange feathers, flowers, and handmade cards bearing the slogan "Glad Påsk!" (Happy Easter!) for candy.

Photos by Eleanor. Art direction by Beth Siveyer. Styling by Nao Koyabu. Thanks to Arvida, Hanna, and Maria for modeling, and to Christina Corway at S: Management for hair and makeup. Thanks also to Beyond Retro, J&B the shop, and Paper Dress Vintage for providing clothes.

black girl lessons

A tragically inevitable rite of passage.
Writing by Jamia, illustration by Allegra.

The first time it happened to me, it cut my insides up so bad that my stomach still churns every time I think about it. I was in first grade. My family had just moved, so I was the new kid in school. I was also one of a small handful of African-Americans among a sea of white students, which made me even more conspicuous. But it didn't bother me much: I made friends, got good grades, and had fun. One day at school I heard a couple of kids talking about an upcoming birthday party for one of our classmates, Mandy.* They said that she had invited the whole class, but it was the first I'd heard about it, so I figured she must have forgotten to put my name on the list because I was new. (I was so naïve that no other possibility occurred to me.) I made a

This name has been changed.

mental note to alert her of this oversight the next time we crossed paths.

I ran into Mandy later that day on the playground, when we were both in line for the tire swing. I still remember the rainbow-colored striped shirt she was wearing, slightly discolored and stained from the sandbox, and her Velcro KangaROOS. I asked if she'd forgotten to tell her mom to send me a party invite, and she just stood there and looked at the ground for a long time. Then she narrowed her blue eyes, tossed her dirty-blonde curls, and said, "Mom just doesn't like blacks. She just doesn't like them in her home, because she says you guys are bad."

I had an instant physical reaction to her words—they grasped at my throat, making it hard to breathe and impossible to speak. I felt confused, hurt, humiliated, outraged. Even though I've experienced many other painful incidents since then, my heart has memorized the intricacies of that initial ache; many years later, trying to describe to an inquisitive white friend what it feels like when I witness or directly experience prejudice, I found myself going right back to that playground. "I feel hurt, and then angry, and then sad to the point where it is hard to breathe," I told my friend. "And then a gust of energy rises from my toes, twists my tummy, squeezes my heart with its imaginary fists, and then pushes up through my throat with a burning sensation that surrounds my face." In those moments I am stricken with a paradox: total paralysis and asphyxiation coupled with a frenetic vigor that could lift me off the

floor, propel me like a cannonball into the offending target, and destroy everything in its path with the force of a gale. But most times, I told her, holding in everything I'm feeling is what stings the most.

I was reminded of my encounter with Mandy again this year, in February, on the night of the Academy Awards. I was in California, grinding away at a work event, not watching the broadcast. At some point in the evening I took a second to glance at my Twitter feed, and I saw the tweet that you've no doubt heard about by now—the one where The Onion, in an attempt to be funny, called the nine-year-old Best Actress nominee Quvenzhané Wallis "a cunt."

I reread the tweet to make sure my eyes weren't playing tricks on me. I blinked with disbelief—they wouldn't really write that about a *child*, would they? But sadly, that was just a vestige of the same naïveté that had convinced me that Mandy had simply forgotten my party invitation.

As I felt my innards contort in that familiar and disconcerting way, I realized that I was foolish to have been surprised for even a second. Quvenzhané Wallis, after all, is not Elle Fanning or Chloë Grace Moretz or any other well-known (and white) ingénue. And, contrary to the protests of several internet commenters who argued in the days that followed the incident that Quvenzhané's race was irrelevant, I believe it matters. Like many others who understand the long history of black women's bodies being objectified, undervalued, oversexualized, and exploited, I doubt that a similar joke would be lobbed so cavalierly at a white girl.

Quvenzhané's experience was infuriating but, to anyone who'd gone through it themselves, immediately recognizable as a tragically inevitable rite of passage: our first encounter with racism. Up until that moment most of us naïvely assume that the world is basically fair. And then someone says something that reveals what other people think of us, and we start to understand what it means to be a black girl in a racist, sexist world.

I received my moment of enlightenment courtesy of Mandy that day on the playground, and its lesson was reinforced countless times in the years that followed. When I was not much older than Quvenzhané is now, men routinely called me a "cunt" and the N-word when I ignored their obscene comments on the street. I once, also as a child, literally fought off a delivery man who tried to accost me in my home and said disgusting things about my "exotic" heritage and "wanton sexuality."

So it did not surprise me, but it broke my heart, to watch another little girl—one who happens to be brimming with talent and apparent joy—go through this rite of passage. Jamilah Lemieux put it just right in *Ebony* magazine: "I wish that Quvenzhané could enjoy her newfound fame without these hard-earned black girl lessons, but they would have caught her on the block, in the classroom, on the internet at some point even if she hadn't garnered an Oscar nod."

Now this offensive tweet from a publication with close to five million followers is part of Quvenzhané's story, and she'll probably be reminded of it for years to come. This was a coming-of-age moment, a first lesson in the hateful indoctrination most black women are subjected to over and over in our lifetimes. It seems that even in 2013, no one can escape this ugly education.

Not 17-year-old Gabby Douglas, who, following a gymnastics performance that earned her an Olympic gold medal, endured negative reviews of her hair, and who faced backlash after speaking out about racially motivated harassment at her gym in Virginia.

Not Malia Obama, whom commenters on conservative blogs targeted with racial slurs a few years ago, when she was 11, for simply wearing a T-shirt with a peace sign.

Not 14-year-old Amandla Stenberg, who played Rue in *The Hunger Games* and sparked the ire of racists on Twitter for looking exactly the way her character was described in Suzanne Collins's book: dark-eyed and dark-skinned. It was devastating to see tweets from people who said they were less sad about Rue's death because of her skin tone, and others who decided that they were less "pumped" about the book because she was black. The irony of the situation is that Jennifer Lawrence played Katniss, a character whom the author described as having dark hair, gray eyes, and olive skin. The same people who were angered by what they erroneously considered to be Rue's inaccurate physical representation weren't at all bothered that Katniss was being played by a fair-skinned natural blonde.

And, of course, not me. After that moment with Mandy, any time people treated me unfairly I had to wonder if it was because of my actions or the color of my skin. Racism has a way of permeating even the most mundane exchanges: I go shopping and am followed around the whole time by salesclerks who repeatedly inform me of the cost of the clothes in their store. I get accepted into an honor society at school and one of my classmates hypothesizes that I got in via affirmative action, not my academic performance. And on and on. While I've always maintained my own sense of inherent worth and dignity, it has been exhausting.

But, you know, I always have an optimistic heart. And it's always holding out for people to grow, change, and treat one another better. It can be really discouraging to see how far we still have to go and how much work still needs to be done before we can create a world where we're all judged not on how we look but on how we are, but I'm stronger every day because I'm still here, I'm surviving, and I'm using my voice. When I need to blow off steam, I vent with friends and family who understand and trust my perspective. I nourish myself by speaking up when someone makes a racist (or sexist or homophobic or otherwise bigoted) joke or comment, even when I'm scared to make the situation uncomfortable. And I try to tell my story as much as I can, because it's important for me to let other black girls—and those who love us—know that they're not alone. ✿

This girl's name has been changed.

The Importance of Angsty Art

Sometimes it's good to be bad.
Writing by Jenny, illustration by Leanna.

When I was four years old, I started recording stories for my parents, who were living in a place I knew little about except that it was on the "other side" of the world and called New York City and bodies had to travel through clouds to get there. My extended family of grandparents and aunts and uncles sat down with me every week or so to record my stories on tapes that they would stuff into envelopes padded with old newspapers and mail to my parents.

"You're a born storyteller," my family told me.

"I know," I said, solemn, serious, blithely confident.

My parents saved these tapes and gave them to me when I was in high school. *This is the beginning*, I thought to myself when they handed me the box labeled with my Chinese name, Zhang Jia Ning. *This is where it all started. This is when I decided— no*, knew *I would be a writer, when I knew I couldn't be anything other than a writer.*

When I went home for winter break my first year of college, I made myself listen to one of these tapes and had a small, solipsistic cry-fest. It opened with my auntie's voice, strong and trembling, telling my parents how much we all missed them and how much we hoped they were not struggling too much in New York. She started to tell my parents about the things that were happening in Shanghai, how we were all doing well and looking forward to the warm promises of spring.

"I want to talk," I said, interrupting my aunt in the middle of her story about my uncle's new business venture. "I'm going to

tell a story, a story, a story…" I repeated this until I had silenced everyone else. I spoke aimlessly about a cow, a swallow, some whales, flowers that fall from the sky, and a beach with no fish, water, or sand.

"Do you like it?" I asked in the middle, and again when it was over. "Mama, Papa. I am thinking of you. I'm getting better at telling stories. My teacher praised me. I miss you so much. I think about you every day. Why aren't you here with me?" There was more, but I couldn't finish listening to it.

I was 17 and, for the first time ever, experiencing some pretty serious writer's block. It was weird, because the year before, when I was still in high school, I felt like I had so much to say. Like, SO MUCH. I filled up several spiral-bound notebooks that year with poetry and little short stories and fragments that were somewhere between straight-up prose and barely disguised diary-style bitching and moaning. I wrote all the time: on the eight-minute bus ride to school, on the eight-minute bus ride home from school, during my classes, during my free periods, during my lunch periods. I wrote instead of figuring out how to socialize with my peers. I wrote instead of figuring out how to talk to my parents. I wrote instead of listening to my baby brother after I had promised him that we could "play all day." I carried a notebook, or sometimes several notebooks, with me everywhere I went. Everything was a potential poem or story: the way my English teacher picked at the mole next to her nose; the way my father would suddenly start singing the chorus of "Sad Movies"

in the middle of dinner after I complained about having a "sad, miserable life"; the time I saw a child outside of St. Mark's Bookshop slap his mother on the mouth and how she responded, "You do that again and I'm going to push you in front of a moving bus the next time you cross the street"; the time I went downstairs to get an orange and found my mother sitting, her face tear-streaked, in the dining room, and she said, "I miss my family"; the way I responded with a single "oh" and then ran up the stairs without getting the orange. I truly felt I had been put on this earth to write all of this down, that my writing was, in a way, *a gift*, and that one day it would be recognized as such!

Though my brain had been storing praise and swelling with greedy self-congratulation for some time, my senior year of high school was when I definitively crossed over to being insufferably cocky. I actually had thoughts like *I am such a good writer that it's kind of embarrassing for everyone else in the class.* When my teacher handed back our writing assignments, I'd think, *Yes, I know, I know, in all your 10 years of teaching you have never read anything as stunningly beautiful as what I turned in last week. Join the club.* A few things had led to this point: a fairly steady stream of compliments from my teachers, the couple of nights when I summoned the ovaries to perform some of my poetry out loud at a few open mics that ended in standing ovations, and a month-long screaming match with my mother over my declaration that there was no way in hell that I would study medicine or law when I got to Stanford, because I was going to be a writer.

"Starve me if you want," I told her. "But you can't force me to not write."

"I can and I will," she said.

"I never thought you would stoop to child abuse."

"Why don't we talk about it later," my grandmother would often plead.

"No point," I said. "I'm never changing my mind."

My notebooks from that year were particularly whiny and hit some screechingly high notes of torture.

This was why I had to be committed to my writing. Writing *had* to feel like life or death, because if it wasn't the most important thing in the world to me, why was I staking my relationship with my mom on it?

"I'm fighting for my life," I wrote in my diary. "That's what she doesn't get. Writing is my life. If I can't write, I can't live."

🎀 ❀ 🎀

And then something happened that pushed me over the edge—I got myself an education. At Stanford, I pretty much announced myself as an English major the day I got there. I raced to fulfill my prerequisites so that I could sign up for a poetry seminar *and* a fiction seminar in the same quarter. I remember staying up all night to write a 20-page short story for my fiction workshop and then staying up a second consecutive night to finish a poem for my poetry workshop. In the week that followed, I was giddy and buzzing with anticipation of how much mothafucking praise was about to be heaped on me by my teachers and classmates. *Someone is probably going to say, "This is literally the best thing I've ever read in my life,"* I thought to myself the night before class.

And someone did say that, but more people said that the pacing in my story didn't make sense and that I had failed to characterize the protagonist and that I relied on mystery and withholding to mask the fact that my story lacked depth or any real meaning. My teacher more or less insinuated that my prose was drunk on its own lyricism and completely neglected to tell an actual narrative. One of the workshop critique letters I received from a fellow student said something like "Sorry, I actually had to put your story down at one point, because I was so frustrated and annoyed by it."

My poetry was apparently even worse. The teacher was notorious for being brutal during workshop, and there was a rumor floating around that a student had once fled the room in tears. *That shit's not happening to me*, I told myself. *If anyone is gonna be in tears, it's going to be the other students…FROM BEING SO MOVED BY MY POETRY.*

I don't think I need to say who went home after class in tears. I don't think I need to spell out who, upon getting back to her dorm room, immediately looked up the word *puerile*, hoping, hoping, hoping it meant "genius" or at least "pretty good," but knowing, knowing, knowing it did not.

My literature classes didn't help. My professors stressed the importance of approaching a text with detachment, with a critical gaze rather than an emotional one. There wasn't a place in academia for gushing or ranting. There wasn't room to simply say, "I loved this and I don't know why." One had to use academic jargon. One had to be methodical and thorough. It was like listening to a song and wanting so badly to get up and dance, but instead of dancing, you have to sit there and think about why those sounds made you want to dance and consider the exact mechanics behind the formula of a danceable song. And I didn't want to do that. I just wanted to dance. I just wanted to read. I just wanted to write. I didn't want to deconstruct lines of poetry or do a close reading of Faulkner's usage of semicolons.

The more English classes I took, the less pleasurable it became to read and write. I started to dread it. I started to take fewer risks. I started to become concerned with matters of taste. I started giving a shit what other people thought. It was like becoming a teenager all over again, a time when the more I understood about the world, the more fearful and timid I became. It was like when I wore a white crotchet sweater in sixth grade without a bra and my friends were all like, DAMN, I CAN SEE YOUR NIPPLES, and my awareness of my own body suddenly soared and I went from jumping around the playground without a worry to agonizing over getting dressed in the morning, because once I knew that the way we dress invites scrutiny, I could not forget it. The same with my writing—I couldn't forget what I was learning, and the more I learned, the less free I felt.

🎀 🎀 🎀

My hero, the poet/seer/activist Ariana Reines, once said in an interview:

I want to say something about bad writing. I'm proud of my bad writing. Everyone is so intelligent lately, and stylish. Fucking great. I am proud of Philip Guston's bad painting, I am proud of Baudelaire's mamma's boy goo goo misery. Sometimes the lurid or shitty means having a heart, which is something you have to try to have. Excellence nowadays is too general and available to be worth prizing: I am interested in people who have to find strange and horrible ways to just get from point A to point B.

For two weeks, I could not write this essay because I was afraid my essay on bad writing would be…badly written.

🎀 ❀ 🎀

I couldn't listen to those tapes of me telling stories for my parents because the amount of joy evidenced by the way I kept going on and on and on, and my total obliviousness to how boring my stories were, seemed so…*desirable*. The tale of the cow and the whales wasn't *good* in terms of plot or character development, and it was never going to win me a spot in the Kid Genius Hall of Fame, but telling those stories made me *feel* good. It made me feel less small and less frightened in a world that didn't always remember me or notice me or take care of me. Making up those stories and recording them made me feel like I could deal with my parents' absence. In a way, they helped me survive.

Why are we so quick to ridicule our angsty teenage feelings? Why do we feel a need to make fun of our "bad" poetry? Why is it embarrassing to be earnest, to take our feelings so, so seriously, to insist on our pain and to compare it to the stars, to the seas, to volcanic eruptions and cosmic voids that we can never completely comprehend? What is wrong with that?

I read good writing all the time, and it's not even good. Most of the time when I read articles and essays in widely respected news outlets and magazines, the experience of perusing that heavily polished, finely wrought, carefully constructed prose is one of mind-numbing boredom, or maybe an *eh*. When I pick up one of the novels that the *New York Times Book Review* says we should all be reading, I often think, *This is perfectly adequate, but is there more? There has to be more.* My hesitation to name names here is partially due to professional manners, but it's also further proof of the tyranny of the good—I do not want to be excommunicated from the literary world for questioning what I'm expected to revere.

But…what if the glut of great writing out there isn't even that good? Maybe good writing has yet to live up to the shining promise of the bad writing that we save in our journals, that we lock in diaries hidden under the bed, that we seal in letters and keep in boxes instead of sharing it with the world in a more calculated attempt at art? That is the writing we do when we are so seized by terror or love or misery that we actually allow ourselves to write down what we must, must, must say, moments when we allow our raw and formless thoughts to survive and take up space.

When my first book of poetry came out, I posted a few videos of myself reading the poems on YouTube. I know maintaining faith in humanity is pretty much contingent on never ever looking at YouTube comments, but I went against good judgment and looked. One of the comments

I don't mean to just romanticize our early longings to create art as some kind of purer state or a more ideal mode of creation. It's not about merely feeling nostalgic for a time when I was so unselfconscious. It's about remembering what it was that I loved so much about writing in the first place. I started writing not because I wanted to one day be a Very Important Figure in the Western canon, but because I loved it, all of it—telling stories, playing with language, making up words, inventing new forms of address. And that love, as tacky and cringe-y as it may be, is always in danger of being shamed out of existence, and we must not let that happen.

I can't remember the last time I sat down to write a story without thinking, *Oh god, is this any good?* It's been well over a decade since I could lose myself in writing fiction for hours and hours without being seized with paralyzing fear—fear of sucking, of being a shitty writer, of being derivative, of writing something that could be described at best as "minor." I can't remember the last time I read a novel and didn't immediately have some kind of instinctive critical reaction to how the characters were developed, or how language was being employed or underemployed or something. It's like watching a scary movie and thinking about how the severed limb looks too clearly like a prosthetic instead of feeling genuine fright at the sight of a severed limb. I want to scream, not analyze. I want to feel something without giving in to the impulse to articulate it, to deconstruct it, to bestow upon it intellectual teeth and arms and legs.

was, "Was this written by a fifth grade boy with psychological issues? This isn't a fucking poem, it's a bunch of garbage."

A few months ago, a poem I wrote about the Empress tarot card was published on the literary webzine HTMLGIANT. I zipped right past the positive comments and zeroed in on the sole negative one: "At first I misread the bio. I thought it said that the poem was written by a teenage girl. Which would make more sense."

I know both of those comments were supposed to be mad-clever ZINGERS aimed at my self-esteem, meant to shame me and put me in my place, but instead, I was happy to be compared to a fifth-grade boy and a teenage girl. In fifth grade I wasn't worried about whether my stories were well crafted. When I was a teenage girl I wasn't fretting over whether my emotions had the potential to disrupt tradition. I wasn't stressing about whether my writing would one day change the entire landscape of Arts and Letters in America. I was writing because it felt good.

I thought about the notebooks I filled in high school, the ones that I'm still too scared to revisit—not because I think my bad writing will make me cringe, but because I'm afraid my bad writing will make me yearn to write like that again. I'm not talking about writing poems that compare my loneliness to a black hole or my love to a prairie devastated by fire; I mean writing with tremendous heart and without concern for taste or craft or the entire wretched literary canon that has come before me, the literary canon that is still mostly populated by boring, uninspiring white dudes whose writing will never change my life. If I let myself reread those old notebooks, I might want to return to a time when I was driven only by big, terrifying, excessive emotions that resist intellectualization (and monetization and professionalization). I'm not ready for that. For now, at least, I will not be embarrassed. I will not reject my bad writing. I will be glad that I once placed terrible meaning in clichéd descriptions of love and bad metaphors for loneliness. I will be grateful for my briny, bubbly, tumultuous adolescent feelings and enthusiasm. I will finally finish listening to those old tapes. ❧

What I Wish I Knew About
My Period

Pointers for those who menstruate or are about to.
Writing by Elizabeth, illustration by Emma D.

It was Labor Day weekend, the last free days of summer before school started. I woke up in my best friend's bed and felt weird. I got up to pee and saw that there was a darkish stain on her sheets where I had been lying. I felt sick to my stomach, because I knew the worst thing ever had happened: I had gotten my period. I was 10.

I had always been the youngest in my class, but 10 years on the planet is not a long time to prepare for the reality that your body can now *make babies*, and in exchange for this superpower you will be tortured for three to five days per month with any or all of the following: painful body-twisting cramps, zits, headaches, mood swings, and, not to put too fine a point on it, BLOOD coming out of your VAGINA.

Needless to say, I'm older now, and I have been dealing with my period for what seems like forEVER. So I thought I'd share some of what I've experienced and learned with any early—or late, or medium—bloomers out there.

(Quick note before we start: This article is for anyone who gets their period, regardless of gender.)

1. GETTING MY PERIOD WASN'T LIKE IT WAS FOR MARGARET IN *ARE YOU THERE GOD? IT'S ME, MARGARET*, AND I GUESS THAT WAS OK.

When I read that Judy Blume book in elementary school, it was my primary source of menstruation information. Have you read it? It's all about this girl Margaret and how badly she wants to get her period. Margaret and her BFFs (slash frenemies)

Gretchen, Nancy, and Janie looked forward to their periods so intensely that they PRAYED FOR THEM and lied about getting them before they had. I was so confused by this—puberty scared the *hell* out of me. And the scariest thing about it was the idea of getting my period—it just sounded like a very uncomfortable physical situation that comes with a lot of responsibility.

Aside from waking up and feeling dread, I can't recall anything about the Day I Became a Woman. I assume I told my friend's mom what was going on and then went home and told my mom? But I don't know. I do remember wanting to cry, or maybe I did cry, and feeling embarrassed and convinced that everyone at school on Monday would just *know* what had happened.

I've since read that fewer than 10 percent of girls get their periods before they turn 11. But since I was the youngest kid in my grade, most of my peers were almost 12, and so it's very possible that I wasn't the only girl in Mr. Manfredi's sixth grade class who had to wear giant maxipads (ugh) under her acid-wash jeans. I wish I had known that then, because I felt really alone. (Once I had to go to a sleepover while I had my period and I was so mortified that someone would see a pad in the garbage can that I snuck out to the garage when no one was looking and put it in the trash can out there.) It would have been nice if someone had told me that there's nothing shameful about getting your period—and also that it's OK not to be really psyched about it. But no one talked to me like that, because I didn't have any hippies in my life.

I also had no one to turn to for answers to my myriad questions, such as:

How much blood is actually coming out of me?

It can feel like gallons, especially when it gets on the sheets or, ugh, on your clothes. (It happens.) It turns out that it's actually less than six tablespoons a month. And it's bloody, but it's not all blood: It's mixed with fluid from your cervix and your vagina, and clumps of tissue from your uterus (these look like blood clots and are often called that, but they're not).

Why are cramps so terrible, and what exactly is happening?

Basically, puberty is your body telling you, HEY NOW, I'M PREPPED UP FOR A BABY! even if at this point in your life *you* are not ready for that. During your menstrual cycle, an egg is released into your uterus (aka "the womb"), which starts building up its walls to make it a safe place to grow a baby. But if no sperm comes over and fertilizes that egg, your U is like, "Oh, OK, I guess we don't need all this extra padding," so it contracts, or tightens up, to get rid of it—aka you get your period. If your uterus contracts too hard, it can hurt. Sometimes it hurts a lot. How much it hurts is different for everyone. A bad

cramp can feel like someone is squeezing your abdomen and twisting it in their fist just for fun. I consider this the worst part about being magical enough to create life. I guess it's a small price, but *jeez*. (With this, as with all physical stuff, if it hurts a lot lot LOT, see a doctor ASAP.)

How exactly does a tampon work? Is it gonna get swallowed up inside of me or fall out?

A tampon is a little cotton plug with a string. It sits inside a little tube, with a littler tube inside that acts like a plunger to push the tampon into your vagina. (They also come tubeless, but I would wait till you are really comfs with using them before you switch to no-applicator tamps.) Here is a quick tutorial for beginners:

1. Wash your hands.

2. Assuming you're inserting your tampon in the bathroom, it helps if you stand with one foot on the tub or toilet (it changes the angle of your vagina so it's easier to slide the tampon in).

3. The applicator tube has little ridges on the side to make it easier to grip. Hold the applicator with your middle finger and thumb right at those ridges.

4. Position the applicator so that the tip is touching the opening to your vagina. (A Quick Note on Your Anatomy: Your vagina is the passageway that leads to your internal reproductive organs—your cervix, uterus, et cetera. It's not any of the stuff you can see from the outside, like your labia and clitoris. The external organs make up the vulva, which no one ever talks about even though that's what they're usually referring to when they say *vagina*.)

5. Slide the applicator into your vagina until your thumb and middle finger are touching your vulva. Then use your index finger to (gently) push the smaller tube all the way into the larger tube. This should be a fairly smooth operation. If it hurts going in, stop, pull the tampon and applicator out, put a pad in place, and make a doctor's appointment.

Once you've pushed the whole thing in, gently pull the applicator out. The tampon should now be in your vagina, with the string hanging there where you can see it. If you give the string a li'l tug you'll see that the tampon is pretty solidly in there. If it comes out easily, take it out and grab a NEW ONE and try again. It won't get swallowed up inside you—your vagina stops at your cervix, and the tampon can't get past it.

To remove a tampon, I recommend sitting down on the toilet, grabbing the string, and pulling downward. Do this BEFORE you pee, or you will just have to pull on a peed-on string. (If you can't find the string, reach into your vag with your thumb and index finger, grab the end of the tampon, and pull.)

If you're not into the idea of tampons, there are lots of alternatives, including disposable or cloth pads, sponges, and the Diva Cup.

2. YOUR FRIENDS ARE THERE TO HELP, BUT TAKE THINGS AT YOUR OWN PACE.

My mom came of age in the '60s in a strict household, and I am willing to bet that she has never used a tamp in her life. So no li'l cotton bullets in our bathrooms, anywhere. And where did that leave me, a young girl in contemporary society who was terrified of (a) talking to her mother about her period and (b) getting blood all over everything everywhere? Basically in a diaper. As in, extra-long Kotex Super maxipads, which were what my mom had around. They were like nine feet long and as thick as the September issue. Just terrible. But I didn't know anything else…until two years later, when I went to sleepaway camp.

When you live in a small cabin with a bunch of other girls for seven weeks, you end up sharing *everything*. It's very freeing and liberating and also kind of gross (in a good way). Most of my camp friends went to private high schools in Manhattan and were therefore *verrrrry* sophisticated (I was a public-school kid from Jersey). When Julie and Melissa learned that the reason I was skipping group swim was that I had my period (You know what's worse than a giant Kotex? A giant WATERLOGGED

Kotex), they were aghast. They marched me into the bathroom, sent me into a stall with one of Julie's Tampax, and stood outside the door. TIME TO LEARN.

"OK, take your shorts and underwear off," one of them ordered. "Now face the toilet, and put your foot up on the lid."

"Wait, what? Why?!"

"I don't know, it makes it easier. Just do it."

"OK."

"Put it inside you, but only as far as where your fingers are holding it."

"OK."

"Now push the end in."

"I—I can't."

"What do you mean, you can't? Push HARD!"

"I CAN'T! OWWWWWW! WHAT? THIS HURTS! IS THIS WHAT IS SUPPOSED TO HAPPEN? THIS HURTSSSSS."

I tried again a couple more times that summer, but I could never push that damn thing into my vagina. My theory is that my corona, the anatomical part formerly known as the hymen, was the kind that totally blocks the entryway to the vagina, because when I had intercourse for the first time when I was 16 it hurt like a bitch and I bled a lot—and afterward tampons were no problem.

3. WAYS TO DEAL, WHAT TO USE, AND WHY SEX ON YOUR PERIOD IS MORE THAN OK.

Dealing with uncomfy stuff when you have to be in public most of the day:
If men got their periods, the first day of each cycle would be a paid vacation day—I believe this with my whole heart. The first real day of my period is agony. My contact lenses are uncomfortable, my head throbs, I feel bloated, that annoying zit I spoke of earlier finally shows up, and my cramps make me wanna lie fetal on the floor of my office.

I use a period-tracking smartphone app to remind me when I'm about to get my monthly (writing this essay has led me to realize that I wanna use all the corny old-school euphemisms for "period" WAY MORE OFTEN in my life). I've been tak-

ing two Aleves the night before to get ahead of the extreme uterine thrashing I am about to deal with, then I just keep 'em coming every eight hours throughout. I've discovered that naproxen (the active ingredient in Aleve) works better for my cramps than ibuprofen (the stuff in Advil), but you might be different—take whatever works best for you.

Also, during my period, I try to put my coffee addiction on hold for a day or two and drink caffeine-free tea instead. Caffeine makes my cramps worse, and I find tea soothing (and green tea helps with my bloatiness).

Things you can do in the privacy of your own home:
I asked for a hot water bottle for Christmas a few years ago, and it is the best gift I ever got. Fill it with almost-boiling water and then lay it down on your lower belly. Stretch out and breathe deep. It feels awesome. It's time to bring back the hot water bottle, you guys—it will be your best friend!

Until you get one, though, if you have bad cramps you can try lying down in the tub and running a hot shower, positioning the showerhead so the water is hitting your abdomen. This sounds weird to type out here as a recommendation for some reason, but it really works, I swear!

This next suggestion is even weirder, and just as anecdotal as everything else I'm telling you in this article, but here goes: As an adult I noticed that my cramps were worse when I had a tampon in. I mentioned this to a few ladies whose opinions I trust, and they suggested I switch to unbleached tampons. I did, and I swear, my cramps are significantly less intense now. Could this be for real?! I have no idea, and I don't think anyone's ever done any tests regarding this wild theory. But since it takes all kinds of chemical-y stuff to bleach cotton, it seems like a good idea to go with the unbleached anyway. The fewer chemicals I am sticking into my vagina the better, right?

I know that there are a lot of you out there who will tell me that there is an even better way to keep chemicals out of my vagina, and that is to use the aforementioned Diva Cup or a sea sponge, but I just haven't

been able to go there. I can't see myself having to empty and reinsert a small cup during an afternoon bathroom break in the 10-stall public ladies' room in my office. But if these options seem favorable to you, I recommend looking into them.

Orgasms are super helpful:
You know how I told you that cramps are your uterus contracting to push out unneeded stuff? Well, a contraction is a muscle tensing up. And you know what helps relieve muscular tension? Orgasms. Orgasms are just a pretty good way to be NOT TENSE all around. Actually, maybe the *best* way. Again, this isn't scientific fact, but I can vouch.

Obviously, the easiest way to have an orgasm anytime you want/need is to masturbate. (It might take you a while to learn how to give yourself an orgasm, but put in those hours: It's worth it.) I'm not sure if you realize this, but there's also another way to have an orgasm, and that is by having sex with another person. NOW I KNOW that a lot of people are not so eager to have sex during their ladies' time. Maybe you feel physically tired (legit) or not your sexiest (all in your head). But sex on your period is the same as sex at any other time of the month—or possibly better, because you have extra lubrication. It's not all that messy, either—just lay a towel down on the bed/rug/chaise/table/wherever you get down to business, and go for it. Period sex is **no big thing**.

🦋 🦋 🦋

OK then! These are all the things I wish someone had told me before I got my first period, and in the couple of years that followed. Most of all, I wish I had found someone to talk to! I had so many questions and fears about the whole business, and I think I would have been so much less self-conscious, and so much HAPPIER, if I had only had access to some friendly advice. So, talk to your friends! Talk to your cool older cousin or aunt or sister or your best friend's cool mom or your OWN cool mom. And read *Are You There God? It's Me, Margaret*, because it's a really good book. ❈

First Date

The promise of a perfect day.
By María Fernanda

Styling by María Rangel Isas. Thanks to Sofía and Fer for modeling. Special thanks to Gibran.

the year i learned everything

A short story about being scared and doing it anyway.
By Roxane

1.

It is summer in a dead-end town. There's not much good to say about that. I have been spending a lot of time at the community center pool. The lifeguards at the pool are all ugly so it's kind of a waste of time. I always hope I'll see a cute boy there and I like how the hot pavement feels when I walk barefoot. One of the lifeguards, his name is Jason Miller. He's in college and still has terrible acne. I feel sorry for him. Acne is supposed to go away when you're in college. You're supposed to grow into your looks. He seems pretty lonely. Even though he wears sunglasses all the time, he stares at me. I always set my towel right next to his lifeguard stand and make sure to wear my skimpiest bikini. I feel like I'm doing a good deed. Sometimes, after he jumps in the water to help a kid who can't swim or whatever, he climbs back into his seat and water from his body drips on me. He tastes like chlorine and sunscreen. I keep waiting for him to ask me out. He knows I'm going to be a senior this year; I told him. I think he's afraid of girls. My brother says men who are afraid of girls are gay, but Jason Miller isn't gay. When I roll onto my back and see him staring at me, I also see a rise in his swim trunks. Last week I saw him at the Skate & Bowl with some of his friends. He's the best-looking of the bunch so you can imagine how ugly his friends are. They were all bowling and really getting into it like total fucking losers. I mean honestly, it's *bowling*. My dad bowls. Bowling is the only thing that makes him happy but he's old so he has an excuse. These guys are like 19 or 20 and bowling makes them happy.

There's no hope. Anyway, Jason Miller was sitting off to the side drinking a beer. He must have a fake ID. He looked lonelier than he does at the pool. I sat next to him and started drinking his beer. He didn't say anything so I stared at him and slowly drank every drop of that beer and he stared right back and when I finished I set the glass down. He said, "You're welcome," so I said, "Thank you." Then my friends came looking for me. I squeezed his thigh, surprised by the muscle, and he turned bright red. I slid my hand higher to see how red he could get. I would have stayed longer. I wanted to stay longer. I would have squeezed other parts of him but I had to go. I want Jason Miller real bad.

2.

My perfect summer of lying out at the pool was too good to be true. My dad made me get a job, said I had to *earn my damn keep*. I decided to get the worst job I could think of to punish him, something that would make him embarrassed when word got out. You know how it is in this town. I forgot what my mom said about my dad, how he has no shame. Now I am stuck waiting tables and washing dishes at a crappy chain restaurant. They don't even really cook the food there. It comes frozen and they reheat it like a frozen dinner. Sometimes when people try to get real fancy with their orders, I want to tell them look, you're being served microwaved food, you should have just stayed home. I'm the only girl who works in the kitchen. The line cooks spend most of their time staring at me even though I wear a T-shirt and jeans every day. I like to be comfortable and let's face it: I run so much I look good in most anything. By the middle of my shift, I may as well be competing in a wet T-shirt contest, only there's nothing sexy about it because I'm all sweaty and I stink like fried onions and potato skins and fish sticks. I hate working. I hate standing on my feet all day. I hate seeing what's left on people's plates when they're done eating. People are gross. You wouldn't believe what comes my way. Sometimes I wear gloves so I don't have to touch anyone's DNA but then it's harder to hold on to the dishes and when I break dishes, my boss, Fat Willie, he gets really fucking mad and threatens to fire me but he won't because he likes staring at my ass and every other part of me. Most of the guys I work with don't speak English and they have greasy hair and porn-star mustaches. They make me wish I had paid more attention in Mrs. Morales's Spanish class because I know they're talking about me. I hear things like *la gringa* and *culo* and *concha* and I can just tell they're saying some nasty shit. I'd tell them I'm nasty too but I don't want them to get any ideas. There are enough boys around here who have ideas about me.

3.

The only time I get to see Jason Miller now is after work. I miss seeing his pale skinny body sitting in the lifeguard's chair. I miss him staring at me while little kids sort of drown, their lips slick with spit and pool water. The way he looks at me turns me all the way on. No one has ever looked at me like that. He came in a couple weeks ago.

I was sitting at the bar, on break, drinking a soda, trying to flirt with the bartender so he'd serve me a real drink. That bartender must have been gay because my tits looked perfect in my tank top and I was doing dirty things with a straw. He barely acknowledged me. He's an asshole. Jason Miller walked up to me and put a hand on my shoulder, totally freaked me out until I turned around and saw his ugly face, which isn't ugly at all, just messed up with acne. He said, "You work here now," but he wasn't asking a question. He said it more like something finally made sense. He looked kind of happy about it and asked me if I wanted a ride home after my shift. I said yes even though my brother was coming to get me. By the time I got off work, I was in the worst mood, hot and sticky, my T-shirt stained with I don't know what, and there was Jason Miller standing in the parking lot next to his car looking at me like I wasn't hideous and that kind of made me angry. For the first few minutes I didn't even say anything. We sat in the parking lot and he kept tapping his fingers against the steering wheel so I grabbed his wrist and said, "Stop doing that." He blushed real hard, said, "Sorry," and then he said, "Should I take you home now?" I said, "I don't know, should you?" He suggested we go to the pool and I shrugged. When we got there it was real dark and it felt like we were breaking the law or something so of course I was really into it. He had a 12-pack of Natty Light and a beach towel and thank god there was a moon that night or we would have killed ourselves in that pool. Jason Miller handed me a beer and started undressing. I thought that meant we were going to fuck so I slammed the beer real quick, which made me sick as hell. My head was spinning and the beer sloshed around my stomach with the chicken fingers I ate earlier. I didn't want to puke in front of a boy I actually liked so I tried to hold it together. I'm a party girl. I know how to rally. Jason Miller, he stood at the edge of the deep end in baggy plaid boxers. He smiled, wiggled his toes, threw his arms in the air, jumped and did a perfect dive into the water. He barely made any sound. It was like on TV. He swam toward me, and his arms in the water made such a pretty sound. He said I should come in. That boy raised himself out of the water and kissed my knee and held his lips there for a long time. When he pulled away, he said, "The water's fine, just like you." He smiled and I felt so hot and heavy and for a second, I didn't know what to do. It was confusing. Normally with guys, I know what to say and how to move things along but with Jason Miller I drown. I thought about how nice it would feel to swim in the pool naked, to feel clean, to let water touch me everywhere the way I wanted a tall, skinny boy with bad acne to touch me everywhere. I told him to close his eyes and he did and that made me feel even funnier. This boy makes me crazy like he knows me even though I never tell him much about myself. I got undressed, and for a minute I stood there, completely naked at the community pool. I thought about how mad my dad would be. That man has strange ideas about who can and can't see me naked. The ground was still warm and there was hardly any breeze. I felt like I was about to have the best night of my life so I took a deep breath and did exactly what Jason Miller did. I threw my hands into the air. I jumped.

4.

When I dove in the pool I stayed under water for a really long time, staring at Jason Miller's skinny legs kicking out and pulling back together as he treaded water. I think he started to worry because he joined me beneath the surface and held his hands open like he was asking, "What's up?" I grinned and swam toward him and I don't know what came over me but I kissed him. It was soft and watery and how good it felt surprised us both because we kept staring at each other. The chlorine hurt my eyes. I didn't care. I didn't look away. I ran out of air and my chest was going to cave in so I pulled away. As I floated to the surface, he held my hand and floated with me. We were in a different world, where it was possible for a girl like me to like a boy like him and for a boy like him to like a girl like me. I was sad when we broke the surface. My chest was pounding so I took a deep breath and another deep breath and another deep breath. Jason Miller closed the distance between us and wrapped his arms around me. We floated together toward the edge of the pool but we never seemed to reach it. We didn't talk but I wanted to say something to Jason Miller, something important we would both remember.

5.

Billy Tomasetti came by work. I've messed around with him before. He has sweaty hands and works in a pizza parlor. He always smells like sauce and hot cheese. When you work in a restaurant, you always smell like something that once was good. When it clings to you that smell somehow goes bad. Billy never says anything nice but I don't say anything nice to him either. He found me out back by the Dumpsters. I was smoking and sitting and wanting to be alone before I walked home. He had a brown paper bag in his hand, a bottle of warm malt liquor. When I saw him walking toward me, I wanted to throw up. I threw my cigarette into the Dumpster and told Billy I had to get back to work but he laughed. He said he knew my shift was over. He came up real close, his chest pressed against mine. He told me to open my mouth and I don't know why, but I did. He started pouring malt liquor into my mouth and soon my face felt numb. Billy killed the rest of the bottle in like 30 seconds. It was crazy. I've never seen anyone slam back that much beer at once. Billy asked me if I wanted to go fool around and I told him the truth and said, "No." He laughed some more but it wasn't a real laugh. It was like he pretended I was saying something really funny. Billy grabbed my boobs and squeezed hard. I tried to slap his hands away and he shoved me into the wall. I felt numb from the malt liquor so I didn't mind. I mean, I minded but there was nothing I could do about it so I let it go. "Don't be such a tease," Billy said. I told him I wasn't being a tease. I told him I wasn't in the mood. He slid his hand down my pants. I don't know what he was looking for but he didn't find it. Finally, when I didn't respond, he said, "Fine, just blow me." I shook my head and all I could think about was Jason Miller and how he would never talk to me ugly or touch me ugly. Doing anything with Billy felt like lying to Jason Miller and I don't want to ever lie to Jason Miller. Billy wasn't interested in what I didn't want to do. He pushed me down to my knees and I got so mad because the ground was greasy and gross and I didn't want to blow him but I also knew the easiest way to get rid of him was to get it over with. It was miserable at first but then I left myself, pretended it wasn't me on my knees. When it was over, I spit onto Billy's shoe and he laughed again and said, "I thought you always swallowed." I told him it was the last time. He shrugged. I'm pretty sure that's the last I'm going to see of him. I puked into the Dumpster and went back inside to finish refilling the salt and pepper.

6.

Jason Miller only kissed me that night at the pool. He held me close in the warm water. His fingers pressed against my spine and found the small of my back and locked there. I liked how his bare, damp chest felt. After we kissed, I closed my eyes and pressed my cheek against his shoulder, the bone of it. He didn't try anything more even though I wanted him to. I would have let him do anything he wanted. That's how I am with boys. I don't even think. I pretend I'm not there and let them touch me and taste me and take me. Sometimes I like it. Since I went to the pool with Jason Miller, I haven't wanted to let another boy touch me. I don't want to forget what his hands felt like on my skin. I know myself though. I'll probably do something I don't want to do. After a while, it got cold and we were both shriveled up something awful. My whole body ached as I pulled myself out of the water. I was so sleepy. We dressed quickly and Jason Miller took me home. After he dropped me off, after he kissed me on the cheek and said he would see me around, I sat on my front porch for a good long while. I sat there, my hair still wet, smelling like chlorine, and I got mad because he was supposed to want me. I called him and before he could say anything, I shouted, "Why didn't you

fuck me?" and he said, "Because when we have sex I want to touch you in some place clean and soft and warm and safe, not the public pool where, honestly, you don't want to know all what happens in that water." I didn't know what to say. I sat there stupidly, holding the phone to my ear. He listened to me breathe.

7.

I work with a guy named Manny who also goes by his given name, Manuel, or Manuelo or Manuelito, depending on who he's talking to. He's one of the line cooks and his arms are lined with tiny burn scars from all the grease splatter. Sometimes when I look at his arms I want to connect the dots with a Sharpie. Manuelo is a small man, shorter than me, but I'm pretty sure he has a killer body. When he hugs me his chest is rock hard and hot. He likes to play soccer, and when he's on break he hangs out back, bouncing a soccer ball off his feet, kicking it against a wall, sometimes faking like he's trying to score on an invisible goalie. Manuelo has three children; two are still in Mexico. Sometimes we sit on the loading dock eating fries and pickles, or Mexican food he brings from home, the real stuff, not that shit from Chevy's. He shows me pictures of the kids he had to leave behind and tells me in days and months how long it will be until he sees his babies, *sus bebés, sus queridos, otra vez.* He always holds the pictures carefully, cradled in the palm of his hand. I get jealous of his kids even though they live in a really small house, far away from their father. My dad would never show anyone a picture of me and he doesn't know how to hold things carefully.

8.

We were lying on the hood of Jason Miller's car at the overlook on the edge of town when I turned and pressed my hand against his face. He flinched and tried to push my hand away but I wouldn't let him. I felt bad for once thinking he was ugly. There is nothing ugly about that boy. He's the most perfect-looking person I know because you can tell he is good. I like his face. In seven weeks he's going back to

school. I will still be here and people will think they still know me. Boys will think they can do whatever they want to me, that I will let them. I will know they are all wrong. I'm not sure if Jason Miller is my boyfriend but when I'm alone at night I pretend he is. I say *Jason Miller is my boyfriend* over and over like that will make it true. I asked Jason Miller if he was going to forget me when he went back to school with all the beautiful girls he must meet every day. He said he wouldn't. I'm not stupid like most girls who believe any old thing a boy tells them. I believed him even though I shouldn't.

9.

Jason Miller brought me to the apartment he shares with three other guys. The place was a pit, well, the shared areas, but his room was really nice. I could tell he cleaned up because I was coming over. The place smelled like Lemon Pledge. I appreciated that. We watched reruns of *Law & Order* and the detectives kept saying the word *Miranda* until it started to sound funny and we laughed every time. I yawned after a few hours and Jason Miller asked if I was ready to go home. I shook my head. I said, "I'm spending the night." He asked about my parents and I told him they don't give a damn where I sleep. He nodded and went to his dresser and grinned as he threw me a T-shirt. When I started to pull my dress over my head, he turned away. "You don't want to look at me?" I asked. "Not without your permission," Jason Miller said. I told him he could look and he turned around real slow and watched me undress. The shirt he gave me was from the school he goes to and it smelled like him and also chlorine. I took my time. He started breathing funny and well, you know. It's not hard to tell when a guy likes your body. Jason Miller stripped down to his boxers and crawled into his bed with me. It was narrow but we fit together nicely. I was so sure we were going to finally have sex and for once I really wanted it. He turned the lights out. We lay facing each other. I could barely see him because there wasn't much of a moon. His breath smelled nice. Finally, I leaned into him and kissed him.

He made my lips tingle and it wasn't just because his lips were chapped. I said, "You can have whatever you want, Jason Miller." He kissed my cheek and my neck and my collarbone. He slid his hands along my ribcage, down to my thigh. "Anything I want?" he asked. I nodded and rolled onto my back. I don't know why but I felt a little sick to my stomach and I kind of wanted to cry so I covered my eyes with my arm. Jason Miller pulled his hand away and said, "What's wrong?" I shook my head and swallowed what I really wanted to say. He pulled my arm away from my face and I started crying really hard. "I only want to hold you," he said. He asked if that was OK. I whispered, "Yes."

10.

The morning after I spent the night at Jason Miller's crappy apartment he woke me with coffee exactly how I like it. I didn't even hear him leave to get it. I was so tired and I slept so hard because I knew it was safe to sleep hard next to a boy like Jason Miller. I don't think I've ever slept so good my whole life. I sat up and crossed my legs and he stared at them the whole time. I'm never going to complain about running again. It totally pays off. I pulled the T-shirt further up my thighs and set my coffee on the end table before pulling his hand between my thighs. "Last night's offer still stands," I said. Jason Miller looked at me strangely and I thought maybe he didn't like me anymore because we hadn't fucked yet. "Why do you always do that?" he asked. I had no idea what he was talking about. "Do what?" I said. He slid his hand up my body and held my face and it kind of freaked me out because he was so gentle. "You don't have to make everything about sex." My face suddenly felt really warm and I was nauseous again. I got out of bed and pulled my pants on, accidentally spilling my coffee, and I knew I was about to start crying again and I didn't want to do that. I said, "You're an asshole. I was trying to do you a fucking favor, you freak." He called after me but I ignored him. I ran out of his apartment holding my shoes and I walked the three miles home barefoot. All I heard was a loud ringing.

11.

I haven't spoken to Jason Miller in three days. I'm pretty sure he's done with me but I've also seen him sitting in his car out in front of my house. I don't know what the hell his deal is. He's called my phone a few times but I don't answer. I'm sure he's just calling to say something mean. I probably deserve that. You should have seen his face when I called him a freak. That was a low thing for me to say. Still, I don't want to hear anything mean from him. I am going to pretend he's as nice as I needed him to be, wanted him to be.

12.

Something really gross and annoying happened after work today. When our shift ended, Manny offered to give me a ride home but instead of taking me home, we sat in the mall parking lot and he kept drinking from a bottle of cheap tequila. Manny offered me some but I didn't want any. I haven't had a drink since that encounter with that perv Billy Tomasetti. The radio was on a Spanish station so I only understood every other word or so. When a song came on that Manny liked, he slapped his hand against the dashboard and sang along. He got totally wasted and I started stressing out that he would kill us when he drove me home. He talked a lot about his family, how much he missed his wife, said she was fat but beautiful, *una gorda guapa*. I felt real sad for him again but I also wanted to go home and take a shower and go to bed. He's been weird at work lately, always looking at me like a man instead of like a friend, grabbing my ass when I'm walking to the line to get a new order. I kind of expected him to be better. That was my mistake. The air in his truck was too hot and thick and I didn't know what I could possibly say to make him feel better about being so far from the people he loves but at the same time I wanted to tell him it could be worse, that he could be living with people who didn't love him at all or who loved him wrong. When I told him I wanted to go home, it's like he instantly sobered up. He looked at me real angry. I know that look so I reached for the door handle but I couldn't find it and my hands were shak-

ing and it was so dark. He slid across the seat and started feeling me up and licking my neck. His breath smelled and it was the worst. I told him I was the same age as his oldest kid but I don't think he could hear me. I kept fumbling for the door handle and when I finally found it, I started jetting across the parking lot but he ran after me and tackled me to the ground. He is way faster than he looks.

13.

The parking lot was completely empty but I still screamed. I remembered how strong he felt when we hugged and knew I was done for. I looked up at the stars but it was mostly cloudy so I couldn't see much of anything but the lamppost nearby. I tried real hard to leave myself but I couldn't and that made me panic. I didn't want to be in my body for what he was going to do to me. My knees and hands were all scraped up and killing me but I stopped moving even though this sharp, nervous pain was ripping through my chest. Manny licked my neck again and then my face and his hands were everywhere. I knew there would be bruises. I still couldn't leave my body so I screamed again because what Manny was doing was so messed up. I used all the Spanish curse words I know, which are a lot because all the guys at work do is curse—*pinche* this and *chinga* that. I finally lay real still thinking if he thought I was dead he might stop. He was on top of me and looked at me, his eyes half-lidded, but I turned to the side. He didn't deserve to look into my eyes and I don't know why but suddenly he stopped and muttered, "Dios," and got off me. That was one of the best feelings ever, that he decided to leave me alone. I stood, started to walk away as fast as I could. He grabbed my arm and said he didn't rape me. It was ridiculous for him to split hairs like that. He said he would drive me home but he didn't say he was sorry. That's what he should have said. "Don't fucking touch me," I told him and I said, "Chinga tu madre," because I know that's serious business. I pulled my arm out of his hand and kept walking. I didn't run because I read somewhere that when confronted by a rabid dog you should walk, not run, so as not to let them smell your fear.

14.

I was too tired to walk home and I was sore and fed up with everything. I went to the bus stop in front of J.C. Penney's and called Jason Miller. It felt like forever before he answered but he eventually did. I tried to explain I needed him but I couldn't think right or say any words right and I could still see Manny sitting in his truck at the far end of the parking lot. I told Jason Miller I needed a ride really bad. Instead of hanging up, he asked me where I was and was super calm about it. He told me to hang tight and then my battery died so I sat there and hoped Jason Miller would actually come. Ten minutes later, Jason Miller's car raced across the parking lot toward me like he was running from the devil. It was kind of awesome. He pulled up where the bus normally stops and didn't even turn off his car. He just got right out and came into the shelter and when he looked at me he knew something totally fucked up had happened. He tried to come close but I slid all the way down to the end of the bench. I kept shaking and couldn't say anything. I saw Manny slowly pull away and finally felt like I could breathe again. Jason Miller noticed me staring at Manny's truck as it disappeared. He sat on the opposite end of the bench and said, "Look at me," but I couldn't. "OK," Jason Miller said. "It's going to be OK." It got colder and I was so sore and tired. "Do you have a bathtub?" I finally asked, turning to look at him. He nodded and we stood and as I walked by him, Jason Miller handed me his hoodie. When I put it on and wrapped myself in the warmth from his body, I felt a little better.

15.

We didn't talk during the drive. I had nothing to say. One of his roommates was home when we got to his place and that asshole whistled as we walked through the living room and said, "Way to level up." "Fuck off," Jason Miller shouted and that made me feel good, that he wouldn't let anyone treat me wrong when he was around. I sat on the edge of his bed while he ran me a bath and then he gave me some privacy. I tried to take the hoodie

and my shirt off by myself but I pulled a muscle or something wrestling with drunk Manny. I sat on the toilet and called for Jason Miller. "I need help," I said, "but I don't want you to freak out if my body looks fucked up under my clothes." He clenched his jaw and agreed and then he pulled my arms over my head and was so gentle taking my shirt off. It hardly hurt at all. I stood and he helped me with my jeans and underwear too and he hissed when he looked at me because my knees were scraped and my elbows were scraped and there were bruises everywhere and he started to say something but I shook my head. I said, "Don't," because it would hurt too much. Jason Miller helped me into the tub and it felt so good to be surrounded by hot water. I said, "You can stay." I said, "Don't go." He sat on the toilet. He said, "You are so beautiful," and then he said, "Tell me what happened." I was so tired of always keeping terrible things to myself that I told him about Manny and Billy Tomasetti and the stupid losers I've slept with and this horrible thing I've never told anyone about and the whole time, Jason Miller listened close and careful. When I was done I said, "I get why you don't want to fuck me," and he said, "I want you real bad. I'm just waiting until you're ready."

16.

He wanted to meet my parents. The night before I invited him over, I told him that wasn't necessary, that my parents held no illusions about my virtue and dignity. He stopped smiling. He said, "But I do." I felt hot and heavy again like I did that night at the pool. I got angry, told him not to treat me so nice, walked away, walked away so fast it was hard to breathe. He ran after me, his feet pounding the warm pavement. He grabbed my shoulder and tried to turn me around but I fought him and started crying and got even angrier because I cry ugly. He let me fight him and throw my fists into his chest and he held me so tight it was like he was trying to pull me into his body. When he showed up at my house, I peeked through the window next to the front door. He was shifting from foot to foot and looked so young and scared. I didn't want

anything in my house to hurt him. I turned and leaned against the door and exhaled. I can't even explain how I felt. Maybe I felt everything, all at once. Jason Miller rang the doorbell again and my father yelled, "Someone get the fucking door." When I opened the door, Jason Miller smiled. He looked at me hard, and lifted my chin up with one finger. "What's wrong?" he asked. I shook my head and leaned into him and whispered, "These people don't deserve your respect." He squeezed my hand and thrust a bouquet of pink daisies into my face. "These are for you," he said. They smelled sweet and clean and I loved them. Jason Miller wrapped his arm around my shoulders and we went into the den where my parents were watching television and drinking box wine, putting on a real classy display. Jason Miller extended his hand toward my father but I shook my head. My dad looked up and grunted, nodded toward the empty loveseat, where Jason Miller and I sat, our knees touching. My dad looked at my boyfriend, well, I guess he's my boyfriend, we still haven't talked about it, and he said, "You're about what I'd expect, not much to look at." Jason Miller turned so red, all up his neck and through his ears. I stared down at my feet but I held Jason Miller's hand real tight. I know it had to hurt but he didn't wince or pull away. He held my hand too, just as tight, tighter even.

17.

After he met my parents, I didn't think Jason Miller would ever call again. My mother was checked out the whole time, like she always is, staring at the TV, never blinking. My brother was out with his friends. We ordered a pizza, my mother couldn't even be bothered to cook, and ate from paper plates like animals. Jason Miller told my father he was majoring in mechanical engineering, said he had good prospects, like it was 40 years ago, like he was speaking to a man who cared about the future prospects of the boy his daughter was seeing, like my father was a man who deserved to know anything about me. When it got to be too much, when my skin felt cut up and raw, I said, "Let's go to my room," and Jason Miller blushed again. He blushes more than any boy or girl I've ever known. As we left the room, Jason Miller said, "I'm going to be a good man to your daughter." My father waved his arm, then let it hang limply at his side. Good men make him uncomfortable. Men who are interested in his daughter make him uncomfortable. My father is the jealous type. Jason Miller and I sat on the edge of my bed. I couldn't look him in his face, didn't want him to see my eyes because then he would see the truth of me. I was bleeding even though there was no blood and Jason Miller didn't try anything, didn't feel me up, didn't push me onto my back and try to choke me with his body. He sat with me until the bleeding stopped. He kissed my neck and we stretched out on my bed and I covered his legs with mine and I fell asleep listening to his breathing. In the morning he was still there and I looked at him and saw the man he's going to be and maybe even the woman I could be with him. I tucked two fingers into his belt loop and understood he was a boy I wouldn't have to hold on to too tight.

18.

I had to know what our deal was so I finally asked Jason Miller if he was my boyfriend. We see each other every day now and talk all the time and we totally make out but we never go all the way which is mostly fine by me. I love making out with him but it confuses me that he doesn't fuck me and that's why I'm never sure if we're actually dating or not. I think bringing up the boyfriend-girlfriend thing is the only time he's ever gotten really mad at me. "How could you ask me that?" he said. "You are unbelievable." He was real indignant which I found adorable. He said, "Of course I'm your boyfriend," and then he got really nervous and asked, "I am your boyfriend, right?" We were at a really nice restaurant, sitting in a booth, the kind with real leather seats. We were both dressed up and everything. I covered his hand with mine, dragging my fingers back and forth across his bony knuckles. "You are my boyfriend," I said. "I was just making sure." He asked me if I was going

to work the next day but it was my day off and that seemed to make him pretty happy. He said, "Good." When I asked why, he wouldn't say but I got excited, thought maybe we'd do something really cool. He showed up at my house late in the afternoon and said we were going on an adventure. I wore a sundress he likes and straightened my hair so it hung down my back. The look in his eyes when I got in the car—I know I looked good. We drove into the city and he took me to a baseball game. I've never been to a big-time sporting event before. He used his fake ID to buy us beers and we ate eight hot dogs between us. He explained about baseball and what was happening and only a little of that was boring. He bought me souvenirs including one of those big foam hands, which I have always, always wanted. After the game, I don't know how, but we went to this really tall building, all glass and steel. It was so beautiful. The guard let us in and we took an elevator to the roof. There was this whole scene set up with white Christmas lights and a blanket and food and I didn't understand at first, thought we had interrupted someone else's date so I started tugging on his sleeve but he said, "Baby, this is for us," and I said, "I hope you always call me baby." That word sounded so pretty when he said it to me.

19.

When I went back to work, the first person I saw in the kitchen was Manny. I went to the sink to start on the prep dishes and when I turned back to look at him again he started walking toward me. I was scared all of a sudden and tried to back away from him but there wasn't anywhere for me to go. I reached into the nasty sink water, feeling for something sharp, and I felt a little better when I found a knife handle. I held it there under the water. Manny looked at the ground and mumbled something I couldn't make out. I shook my head and he said, a little louder, "I'm sorry for what I did to you the other night. It wasn't right. I hope you can forgive me." He rolled his *r*s. I tried to figure out what to say. I didn't want to forgive him. I'm tired of forgiving people who don't deserve it and who

aren't really sorry for the things they have done. I let go of the knife and heard it land softly at the bottom of the sink. I wiped my hands on my apron. I said, "I thought you were my friend," and then I took my apron off and I walked out of that kitchen. I didn't want to work there anymore with that sad man who thought it would be OK to fuck me in a deserted parking lot when I said no and screamed and begged him to stop. It was still light outside and I started running and I didn't stop until I got to Jason Miller's apartment. I pounded on the door and when he opened it, he looked so worried. "What's wrong?" he asked. I stood on the tips of my toes and kissed his face. I kissed his hands and I wrapped my arms around him and said, "Thank you," and I said, "I'm going to say it first even if it freaks you out. I love you." He said, "I've been saying *I love you* in my head since I first saw you stretched out under the lifeguard chair."

20.

Jason Miller went back to school and we still haven't fucked and it stresses me out. I want to know I will see him again and that he still likes me. On our last night together I shared my concerns and he said everything was going to be fine. He started tickling me and kissed me and I swear our lips and tongues were practically glued together for hours. If I never did anything but kiss Jason Miller for as long as I know him, I'd be fine. He's a great kisser. He doesn't slobber all over me and his lips have gotten soft now that I make him use Chapstick. He brushes and flosses so his breath is nice and he doesn't choke me with his tongue. When we kiss he feels me up but it's not gross. He touches me like he cares about what happens to my body. It makes me want him more. I like wanting him. The wanting leaves me feeling kind of edgy but in a good way. Since school started, we talk all the time and he sends me silly texts and emails and I started applying to colleges because it seemed like a good idea to have a plan. I run a lot and ignore most people at school because I've always hated them anyway and I know one way or another I'm getting out of here. It's weird but boys have totally left me alone. They can see I belong to someone who matters now.

21.

Every month I take the train to see Jason Miller at school. He introduces me as his girlfriend and his friends are nerdy like him but really nice. I've fallen asleep next to him more times than I can count and he's never forced me to do anything. Sometimes I worry one day he'll change and become more like the other boys. When I tell him such things he takes me seriously and says he understands why I might worry. He doesn't make me feel stupid or silly. The weekend after Thanksgiving I gave him a blow job under a blanket in his tiny dorm-room bed. I did it because I wanted to taste him and make him feel good and make me feel good. He didn't force my head down. He just kept stroking my hair and saying "oh god" over and over. When he was about to come he tried to push me away but I held his wrists and let him come in my mouth. I swallowed because I wanted him to know nothing about him will ever disgust me. I didn't know the right words but he got the message. He said, "Thank you, baby." I am pretty sure I gave him his first blow job because he was kind of a zombie for a couple days after that and he started treating me even nicer, which I did not think was possible. Once in a while I pick a fight with Jason Miller about the annoying things he does (tickling me, pouring his can soda into a glass, reminding me to do my homework like a freak, watching CNN for too long when I'm visiting which is at all). I do this because my mother told me it's not healthy for a couple to never argue. By her thinking, she and my dad are the healthiest couple in the world. Jason Miller and I don't stay mad at each other for long. He asks, "Why are you picking a fight?" and I say, "Why are you letting me?" and he says, "Good question," and generally that's the end of that.

22.

My first kiss was with a man not a boy. I was really little and he was really big and he had no business doing what he did to me. I can't really talk about it but most days I feel I wasn't ever a virgin and once this man started fucking me, he didn't stop. He told me what he liked and how he liked it. He said I belonged to him and that he was the only man who was ever going to matter, so at night I checked out. I'd turn my lights off and close my eyes and start thinking about everywhere in the world I wanted to be, which was anywhere but there. By the time he came to me, I wasn't anywhere near my body. I was in beautiful places, mostly Paris or out at the overlook or in a hidden tunnel below the subway system in the city. Junior high started and boys noticed me because I had boobs and they were great. My second kiss was with a redhead named Thomas and all we did was kiss behind the baseball diamond at school but he told his friends we did a whole lot more and that's how I lost track of how many boys I kissed. I hope Jason Miller is my last even though it's not cool to say that sort of thing.

23.

I got into three colleges, including one in the same city as Jason Miller, and that's totally where I am going. My mom was pretty happy because she actually spoke more than one sentence to me about it. My dad said, "Why bother?" but he's an asshole who's mad I'm leaving home. He knows I'm not ever coming back. When I told Jason Miller, he said he was so proud of me. That was the first time anyone said something like that to me. The next time I saw him, he was real quiet, kind of acting strange. I asked him what was wrong and he said, "When you go off to school you're going to meet all kinds of hot guys. I know what I look like. You can do better." He said, "You're too young to settle down and maybe I am too but I know what I want." It kind of broke my heart that he would think that. I pretended to get a little mad, and said something about how he must think very little of me and he started stuttering, trying to explain himself but then I sat on his lap and kissed him. I said, "I couldn't possibly do better because you're the best man I know." I said, "I think you're beautiful." I said, "I know what I want and we

both know I'm not at all young." I kissed all over his face and I looked at him right in the eye so he would know I was telling the truth.

24.

I asked Jason Miller to my prom. He dropped hints for like five weeks as if I would take anyone else. My mom got real excited and we went to the mall. I hadn't been there since that stupid thing with Manny. I told her to park on the other side of the lot. I don't know why. Before we got out of the car my mom turned to me, lightly touched my shoulder. She said, "Are you sure about this Jason Miller? He's an odd-looking young man and you're such a pretty girl." Heat rose through my face. "I like the way he looks," I muttered and then I clammed up. We went to a nice store, the kind that smells like perfume and new clothes and rich people. I tried to give her the silent treatment but my mom was so nice, smiling so much she hardly looked like my mom. She held dresses in front of me and had me pull my hair up. She said I should show my neck more. If she knew how many hickeys I've gotten in high school, she probably wouldn't suggest that. The dress we finally picked was gorgeous and so expensive. I didn't think a piece of clothing could cost so much but my mom told me not to worry, said she has her own money my dad doesn't know anything about. She made me think someday she might have a life that has nothing to do with him. I would like to think we both want that for ourselves. When Jason Miller came to pick me up, he wore a dark gray tuxedo with a pink tie to match my dress, no cheesy tails, no silly top hat, just a classic, well-cut suit. He brought me a corsage of pink roses. His hands shook as he fastened the corsage to my wrist. I wanted to keep it forever. While my mom took pictures, Jason Miller kept staring at me, kind of like a creep if I'm being totally honest, looking at me like he had never seen a girl in a nice dress before. I loved it. We drove to prom in his dad's car, a black Lexus. Even my dad was impressed, whistled as we walked to the car, and Jason Miller opened my door. He shouted, "You kids have fun." It's the nicest thing he's ever said to my boyfriend. A couple weeks ago Jason Miller said he wanted to a rent a limo but I told him only assholes take a limo to prom. He got super red. Real quick I said, "Not that you're an asshole, but you could use the money for something way better." We danced all night even though normally Jason Miller hates dancing. He didn't even complain. He totally lied about being a bad dancer. He was all over the floor like a wild man and I was right there with him. I know the girls I go to school with were jealous as hell. Those bitches never expected me to be the one who ended up with an awesome college boyfriend who can dance his ass off. Kylie Green went so far as to tell Jason Miller to keep his arms and legs to himself when she and her boyfriend were dancing too close to us. I told her to fuck off and me and Jason Miller just danced harder. Sometimes we drank from his flask, not enough to get trashed, enough to pretend we weren't in a high school gym in a dead-end town. When we left, he carried my shoes because my feet were killing me and draped his jacket over my shoulders.

25.

After prom, Jason Miller drove me to the overlook. We lay on the hood of his car, staring up at the sky, listening to Bob Marley in our bare feet. I asked if he wanted to have sex because that's what you're supposed to do on prom night. He didn't go to his own prom so I thought it would be a nice thing to do for him, a way of thanking him for treating me nice. He said, "I always want to have sex with you, but you're not ready." Why does he think he knows me better than I know myself? I smacked his stomach pretty hard and walked away, not far. I wanted to figure out why he makes me so happy and so mad at the same time. I couldn't do that thinking when his leg was hooked over mine and he was singing Bob Marley and making my skin feel tingly and sharp. The air was perfect, foggy and wet, cool. He called after me but I didn't answer. I hid behind a tree because I knew he'd come looking or at least I hoped he would. After a few minutes I heard footsteps and started to get nervous. All kinds of people go to the overlook. I worried maybe it was a serial killer. The teenage slut always gets it on prom night. When I saw his tall, lanky body about to move on by, I reached out and grabbed his arm and pulled him against me. I could still hear the Bob Marley and the beeping of an open car door. "Why'd you run off?" he asked. I shook him a little. "You make me feel like you don't want me, and if you don't want me I'm not sure what I'm supposed to be for you." I just blurted it out without even thinking, something I would never normally admit to a guy. I tried to take it back, said, "Forget I said that." Jason Miller told me to close my eyes and even though that makes me nervous I did. A few seconds later, he said, "Open your eyes." He was holding a long jewelry box and my heart started pounding so hard. I couldn't breathe, didn't need to. Jason Miller said, "I found something better to spend my money on." He looked so handsome and happy and I wanted to believe I had something to do with that. As I opened the box, I said, "What the fuck did you do, Jason Miller?" Inside sat a beautiful necklace, a silver chain with a diamond pendant in the shape of three intertwined circles. I pulled my hair up and turned around. His breath fell on my bare shoulders as he fastened the necklace. I moved to turn back around but he wouldn't let me. He rubbed my shoulders softly and leaned in real close and started whispering. Between words, he kissed my neck. He said he wants my heart not my body and that he'll know I'm ready when I don't shake or look scared after he touches me. He said other things I can't tell you. I pressed my forehead against the tree and felt the weight of the most beautiful thing I've ever owned hanging from my neck and the weight of his words, and the foggy, wet air holding us together. He said he likes how I always say both of his names. I said, "I like keeping your name in my mouth as long as possible."

26.

I've always wanted to stay at the Walker Hotel in the city. I don't remember telling Jason Miller how much I loved that hotel but somehow he knew. When I was younger I imagined what it would be like to sleep in a huge, soft bed, ordering room service, watching movies. After graduation (he came and even sat with my parents), Jason Miller took me to the hotel and when we checked in he gave me his last name, said we only needed one key, and pressed the small plastic card into my palm, let me lead the way with one hand on my back, the other carrying a bag with our clothes and toothbrushes and deodorant and such. I was nervous sliding the key into the door even though I've been alone in bedrooms with lots of boys. The room was cold but exactly how I imagined, with beautiful antique furniture and a big bed covered with lots of pillows. I was burning for Jason Miller, how he made me wait, how he knew I wanted and maybe needed to wait, how he always let me know he wanted me even though we were waiting. He set the suitcase near the dresser and stood with his hands in his pockets. It was my turn to take the lead so I pulled him to the bed and I asked, "What do you want?" biting my lower lip and closing my eyes because this time I really didn't want him to push me away. He slid my shirt off over my head and kissed my collarbone and between my breasts. He said, "I want you in any way I can have you." I wrapped myself around those words and I wrapped myself around him and he didn't fuck me. The word *fuck* is way too ugly for what he did to me, but it was the first time I ever felt anything worth feeling with a boy or a man. Later, Jason Miller sat with his back against the headboard and I sat between his legs, playing with his feet, which I pulled up into my lap. He kissed the back of my neck and my shoulders over and over, his lips soft and wet, his breath warm. I'm pretty sure it was his first time for sex too because the look in his eyes was something. My eyes, I am sure, looked the same. It was kind of like my first time too, that's what I told him. I like that maybe Jason Miller is always going to be only mine.

A version of this story originally appeared in Prairie Schooner.

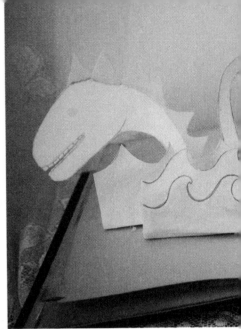

A in Rookieland

Curiouser and curiouser.
By Chrissie

A collaboration with Angel Dorr, Elvia Carreon, and David Girvan.
Thanks to Ariana for modeling and Amanda Ochoa for assisting.
Clothing provided by Amanda White and Moksha.

MAY 2013: Attention

Hey guys!

I am in the midst of writing a junior theme and it's sucking all the life out of me, so for this month's letter I am once again gonna plagiarize from the email I sent to our staff when it was time for their pitches:

May's theme is attention. Fame, what you choose to pay attention to/give importance to/spend time on/spend mental energy on/David Foster Wallace's commencement speech, doing sex stuff for attention, wanting attention, when a cry for help is dismissed as an act of attention whoring, when you realize there's so much you're not paying attention to (be it ~smelling the roses~ or how fucked up the world is), when paying attention to how fucked up the world is exhausts you but you know it's necessary, attention disorders, attention in social media/how people like market their social lives and personal interests (I am guilty of this whether I believe I am marketing or just being like, "Oh I like this thing let's Insta it"), people who give up lives full of attention to pursue something more fulfilling or to be a hermit.

Random inspiration: *The Last Days of Disco*, Chloë Sevigny, Grace Jones, Andy Warhol, Edie Sedgwick (but also how the "tortured glamorous skinny white girl" ideal is kind of messed up), the Chelsea Hotel, selfies, Beyoncé's "Countdown" video, André Leon Talley, Diana Vreeland, Debbie Harry/Blondie, Janelle Monáe, child stars, Divine, the early days of *Interview* magazine, Patti Smith + Robert Mapplethorpe, Keith Haring, candid photography/party photography, club kids.

As you can see, this will be a month of HARD-HITTING JOURNALISM about SELFIES. And here is a playlist I made of songs about wanting little signals from yer crush.

Gimme a Little Sign

1. Gimme a Little Sign - Brenton Wood
2. I'm Gonna Make You Love Me - The Supremes and the Temptations
3. How Long Do I Have to Wait for You? - Sharon Jones and the Dap-Kings
4. Say You Love Me - Fleetwood Mac
5. Ask - The Smiths
6. Don't You Want Me - The Human League
7. Call Me - Blondie
8. Send Me a Postcard - The Shocking Blue
9. Sparks Fly - Taylor Swift
10. Tell Me So - Seapony
11. Tonight? - Marine Girls
12. Behind That Locked Door - George Harrison
13. Flowers in Your Hair - John Williams
14. Let Me In - Hunx
15. Cactus - Pixies
16. Anthems for a Seventeen-Year-Old Girl - Broken Social Scene
17. Come and Find Me - Josh Ritter
18. Don't Be Shy - Cat Stevens
19. Give Me a Smile - Sibylle Baier

Anaheed and I worked really hard to come up with one last pun for this letter, but we are both zonked out. I hope none of you are also dealing with standardized tests and end-of-the-year research papers at this time. If you are, stay strong! Drink water! Resist the urge to bubble in your test form in the outline of a penis!

LOVE,
TOVI

Nobody's Perfect

It took me a long time to realize that included me.
By Rachael. Playlist lettering by Lisa Maione.

When I was younger, I could go hungry at a restaurant because I was scared to give the cashier my order, and then be onstage in my weekly drama class a few hours later, strutting my stuff with my performing-arts pals. My hand would often be the first to shoot up in the classroom, but I once burst into tears when I had to read an essay of mine aloud. I baffled my parents and my friends—the drama kids couldn't figure out why I turned into a wallflower offstage, and everyone else in my life didn't know what to make of me when I *wasn't* acting shy.

Simply put, I was TERRIFIED of negative attention. I'd rather freeze up and not do anything than say the wrong thing and be criticized for it. At the same time, I was hungry for praise, and I structured my life around getting a lot of it. I was good in school, so I spoke up in class and took every extracurricular that I had room for. Teachers loved me, I won academic awards left and right. Drama allowed me to express myself without having to come up with my own words, and as long as I worked really hard to please the director, I couldn't go wrong—at least not until I left school. My community-theater dreams were shattered by three failed auditions, and after that I stuck to classes and clubs, where I was always guaranteed parts.

My anxiety didn't end in the classroom. I'm a naturally shy person, and I used to want all my interactions to go perfectly, so I practically wrote them out in advance, always terrified that the other person would go off-script and force me to think on my feet. If I was ordering food, for example, I'd expect the waitress to ask what I wanted, I'd tell her, then she would leave. If she unexpectedly asked me what toppings or sides I wanted with my burger, I was rattled and took WAY too long to decide. Or worse, she might be chatty and ask a completely unrelated question about my day, and now my whole narrative was off and I wouldn't know how to answer. *Do I just say "good" or do I give a full rundown, and then how do I segue back to my order, and oh no, I'm taking too long to answer and I look like an idiot, WHY DOES THIS HAVE TO HAPPEN TO ME?* Even the prospect of feeling awkward counted as negative attention, which made me more awkward, because now I was this creepy quiet girl who would turn to stone when asked to do ordinary things like order a hamburger.

I can't tell you how many times my parents cajoled me into doing something I didn't want to do, like cash a check at the bank, and then I'd make a tiny little mistake, like writing down my routing number instead of my account number, and I'd stutter a little bit but pretend to laugh it off even though I was dying inside because I'd made a stupid mistake and now that teller was thinking that I was a dumb teenager who didn't know how banking works. I'd get outside and yell at my parents, "DID YOU SEE WHAT HAPPENED? You made me do this and it all went wrong and don't you feel terrible?" And they'd just shake their heads, wondering where they went wrong raising me.

In those cases, my social anxiety was extreme and noticeable, but I think the more damaging stress I dealt with is something that many, many people experience: I was working so hard to be perfect that I took any sort of reprimand or critique or social misstep as a judgment on my character.

As you can imagine, school was a minefield. When I was six or seven, I once got caught climbing a tree on the playground, and I'll never forget how sick I felt after my teacher yelled at me to get down. It was like I'd done something very, very wrong and it could never be rectified. I couldn't understand why all my friends, who'd also gotten scolded, were able to happily play somewhere else—it took me all day to get over it.

In high school, I wanted to get good marks on all my assignments, because being an honors student earned me the praise I desired, but also because when I didn't live up to my high standards, I'd be crushed. Math was my weak point, and the few Cs that made it onto my report cards stood out as black marks that would forever paint me as a failure. Even constructive criticism could shake me up, like the note I once got on a creative writing assignment to come up with a "punchier ending." The teacher loved the piece, but the ending was mediocre, and now that I was aware of it, I felt terrible for turning in that piece of crap.

That same sick feeling I got as a kid after climbing that tree was triggered any time I did something wrong, like accidentally hurt someone's feelings or make a mistake at work. A gentle reprimand—"you did this incorrectly, please fix it, and don't do it again"—sounded to me like someone screaming at me. I once forgot to return a book I'd borrowed from school before summer break, and I'm not exaggerating at all when I say it took me about EIGHT YEARS to be able to hear the name Nancy Drew without feeling shame. I was certain that the teacher who lost it harbored a grudge against me, so I hid the book in my room and spent the next decade or so fighting random spikes of anxiety whenever I thought about it.

After high school, criticism becomes even more common, while praise is harder to come by (get ready). College professors don't get excited just because you understand the coursework, and your manager at the big-box store you're working at on weekends probably won't even notice you unless you screw up. It was a big change, and it forced me to make an important adjustment: I had to start looking to *myself* for encouragement. Was this essay/poster/poem something I could be proud of? Did I do the best I could? Did I have fun doing it? I started doing photography as a hobby, just so I could look at all my pretty pictures, and I spent ridiculous amounts of time on projects that had no purpose except for the fun of creating them, like the time I spontaneously decided to make wall art out of old sticky notes. And I discovered that feeling proud of yourself for working hard feels just as good as praise from another person.

Learning to deal with criticism, on the other hand, was much harder. My constant fear of failure was starting to interfere with my schoolwork, because I'd procrastinate to stave off the possibility of not excelling, and then I'd turn in less-than-stellar work anyway because I didn't give myself enough time to complete it. So my freshman year

of college, I made the big decision to see a school counselor. And, man, I wish I'd done it a lot earlier.

One of the very first things my counselor did was ship me off to a doctor for anti-anxiety medication. Once I was on the right cocktail of pills, I felt like a new person. Suddenly, talking was a little less scary, and the shame of failure was much more fleeting. (Not everyone who has anxiety needs drugs to cope, but if you feel it's interfering with everyday life, I do recommend at least talking to your doctor.) I also started talk therapy, and my counselor really helped change my outlook on the world. In some cases, I just needed practice. She'd give me assignments to do things I found terrifying, like asking for a job application at a local fast-food restaurant, and I slowly gained more confidence in my ability to handle these kinds of interactions. Most of my fears of rejection were in my head—no one ever told me, "Wow, you really effed up that conversation!"

I also talked about other things that were bothering me, and I got some clarity. Everyday schoolwork just wasn't important enough for me to feel so stressed about, and furthermore, it was OK to fail. I took this message in, and when I started to crash and burn in college biology, I didn't force myself to stick it out. I accepted that biology and I were just never going to get along, and I dropped the course. A year earlier I would have berated myself for weeks for "quitting," but now I felt only relief.

A year or two after I graduated from high school, I had a conversation with my old algebra teacher. I said something about being bad at math, and he told me that I was never bad at math—my other classes just came so easily to me that I didn't know what it was like to struggle to learn something. He pointed out that many of my classmates celebrated when they got a C.

My perspective had been so skewed that I'd assumed that I had really embarrassed myself by not being the best, and that others thought less of me as a result.

I realize now that no one is thinking as hard about me as I am. That teacher on the playground was just worried I'd fall, and she probably forgot about the incident in five minutes, while I'm still thinking about it 15 years later. My creative writing teacher just wanted to help me improve my story. Waitresses and bank tellers have dealt with literally thousands of small mistakes and awkward moments over the years.

Earlier today, I made a rather large mistake at my day job, resulting in my having to send a correction email to several thousand people. It was really, really embarrassing. But instead of retreating in panic and begging my boss not to fire me, I calmly apologized and then wrote a self-deprecating Facebook post so that *everyone* had an opportunity to laugh at me. It felt a lot better than mentally beating myself up.

On the flip side, with the understanding that my failures were not permanent came the knowledge that most of my accomplishments have been similarly fleeting. My academic awards have given me absolutely nothing apart from a few moments of pride, and fodder for scholarship applications. Most of the compliments I got from my drama teacher are just fuzzy memories today.

I'm not saying that any of my hard work was worthless. Being a good student served me well, but not because my teachers loved me. Working hard in school gave me skills and opportunities that have helped me move forward in life. It's important to work hard and nurture ambition, but for the right reasons—not to escape criticism, but because it makes you happy. It's better to learn from your mistakes than to not make them at all. ✧

1. Brat Girl — Bratmobile

8. Notes and Chords Mean Nothing to Me — Redd Kross

9. Main Street Brat — The Zeros

10. Bratty B — Best Coast

11. I Don't Care — The Ramones

12. Art Star — Yeah Yeah Yeahs

13. Young Blood — Thee Headcoatees

Two months' worth of funtimes. By María Fernanda.

A bunch of celebrations clustered together this spring: Within two months there were two music festivals, my friend Momo's birthday party, and a farewell party for me before I moved to Mexico City. This is a diary of all that fun.

DIY Stenciling

Make your own one-of-a-kind T-shirts, patches, sweatshirts, et cetera.
By Marlena. Playlist lettering by Lisa Maione.

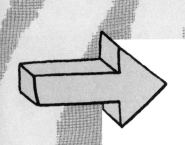

Today we're gonna to do some T-shirt stenciling! Stenciling is a cheaper, less messy, and somewhat easier alternative to screen-printing. The results aren't as detailed-looking or slick, but I actually like the lo-fi, handmade look of a stenciled tee. (You can stencil just about anything, but I mainly stick with T-shirts…I need to branch out.)

All you need is:
- An image-editing program like GIMP, Photoshop, Illustrator, or Paint
- Freezer paper (more on that later)
- An X-ACTO knife
- A T-shirt or something else that you want to stencil (I'm using a piece of scrap fabric to make a patch).
- Fabric paint
- A small paintbrush
- A sponge brush

How to do it:

1. First, pick an image that you want to put on your T-shirt(s). The images that work best are very simple, without a lot of detail or shade, and black-and-white—like the picture of Debbie Harry that I'm using here. If the picture you want to use is in color, you'll need to convert it to black-and-white before moving on to the next step. I use GIMP, a free program you can download at gimp.org, but you can use any app you want—just adjust these instructions accordingly!

2. In GIMP, click on the Image tab and find Mode in the drop-down menu. Choose that, and you'll get a second drop-down box with an option called Indexed—pick that.

3. Yet another pop-up box should appear—from that menu choose the option that says "Use black and white (1-bit) palette," then click Convert.

Just like that, your image is now stencil-able!

4. Since you're going to cut this image out of a sheet of paper, you need to make sure that the "negative space" areas are all connected—in this case, the white parts of the image. In GIMP you can use the eraser tool to create little bridges, or lines, between unconnected islands of negative space. In the image above, you can see that Debbie's lips and the whites of her eyes

need to be connected to their nearest white sections, like this:

Otherwise, your final print might end up looking pretty scary.

5. Print out your design. You can use regular printer paper, but I don't recommend it—in my experience the paint bleeds all over the place unless you use a magical product called FREEZER PAPER. It comes in rolls that are usually by the tinfoil at the grocery story. It's about $5 for a huge roll, and it's the absolute best for stencil making. Freezer paper has two sides: a regular paper side that you can print your design on, and a glossy side that you can fuse to your fabric with a hot iron—that will prevent any horrible paint-bleeding that might blur the lines of your image.

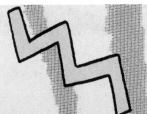

6. Now you're gonna cut out your stencil. This isn't hard to do at all, but it can be a bit tedious! Put on some good music or a podcast or something. Using your X-ACTO, cut out and remove the black areas of your design (unless you're printing on a dark background, in which case reverse these directions) and pop them out. Be sure to keep those bridges connecting the white parts intact—the last thing you want to do is cut through them.

7. Place your stencil on your T-shirt/fabric scrap/whatever and run an iron (on low heat) over the whole thing. This will stick the shiny plastic side of the freezer paper to the fabric to prevent the paint from bleeding out.

8. Using your sponge brush, *press* your paint into the open areas of the stencil—don't like *glob* it on and push it around, or else you might push the paint into places it shouldn't go (like under places the paper is covering). Leave everything alone to dry for a while.

9. When the paint is dry, check and see if you'll need to add another coat (sometimes one doesn't do the job). Wait until all coats are dry before moving on to step 10.

10. Peel the stencil off.

11. Use your small paintbrush to fill in the blank lines where you made those little bridges in step 4.

12. And there you have it! One hand-stenciled Debbie Harry patch. Don't be discouraged if your first few attempts at stenciling aren't perfect; you're bound to have little mess-ups here and there. Those just add more charm! That's what I tell myself anyway. ☆

Concentration Jams
By the Rookie staff

1. Hyper lips — Com Truise
2. Strawberries — Jam City
3. Theme from Jurassic Park — John Williams
4. Wild — Beach House
5. Electioneering — Radiohead
6. Cherry Bomb — The Runaways
7. Summer Goth — Wavves
8. Jackhammer — Skinny Puppy
9. Work is Never Over (Harder Better Faster Stronger Remix) — Diplo
10. Reflection — Ravi Shankar
11. Summoning — Adam Hurst
12. Surph — Rustie
13. Abglanz — Pantha du Prince
14. The Swings of Central Park — Alexandre Desplat
15. Fineshrine — Purity Ring
16. C'mere — Interpol

Literally the Best Thing Ever: Daily Affirmations

For when you need to remind yourself how awesome you are.

By Pixie. Playlist lettering by Lisa Maione.

I was 18 the first time a therapist tried to get me to embrace the idea of daily affirmations. I was dealing with depression, anxiety, and an eating disorder, and the only thing I told myself regularly was that I was pretty much the most terrible, disgusting person on earth. Daily affirmations, the therapist told me, were little sayings I could use to combat the default negativity that was always running through my mind. "It sounds dumb," she said, "but it works." She gave me a little box of cards, each with a happy image (sunshine, a heart, a smiling face) and a saying such as "I am a good person" or "I deserve recovery" or "I am lovable and capable of sharing love with others." I rifled through them on my bed, rolling my eyes at each card and feeling as if I'd been transported to the "Esteemsters" episode of *Daria* or one of those old Stuart Smalley sketches from *Saturday Night Live*, where now-senator Al Franken would parody the entire idea of daily affirmations with his signature catchphrase, "I'm good enough, I'm smart enough, and doggone it, people like me!" In short, I felt like an idiot. This, I decided, was not for me. For years after that, any time someone so much as mentioned daily affirmations, I mentally changed the channel.

During those years I kept up my typical routine of doing the difficult work that recovery and treatment entail, and then retreating home, looking in the mirror, and thinking, *You're a piece of crap.* It was so automatic, so natural, that I didn't even recognize that I was essentially undoing hours of hard work by allowing these reflexive thoughts to take control, as they'd always done. When I began to relapse this

year, I didn't even notice (my husband had to tell me) because these feelings had become so normal.

While struggling through outpatient treatment last month, I came to rely on repeated spins of Fiona Apple's *The Idler Wheel…* for comfort and catharsis, and I went back and read the interviews she'd given after its release. I felt like I could hear the darker and lighter parts of myself in her songs, and I wanted to know how she felt when she was writing them. I came across a *New York Times* article from last May, and something she said in it stuck with me: "What fires together wires together. If you keep on having these negative thoughts or being angry all the time, then that area of your brain is going to get stronger." I realized that I'd never opened a pathway in my brain for positive thoughts to flow through. (This, by the way, is the basic concept behind dialectical behavioral therapy, which encourages patients to be mindful of their thoughts and feelings and to try to find a balance between being rational and being emotional. It is the therapeutic approach I have found most helpful in my own treatment.) *But how would one do that?* I wondered. Oh. Right. That's why people kept pushing the whole daily-affirmations thing on me. I decided to *try* it, at least.

This was not easy—self-encouragement was a totally foreign concept to me. I was going to need all the help I could get. So I dug out the stupid cards, which had been stuffed in the back of my closet for posterity, and read one aloud.

"I am a good person."

I stood in front of the mirror and watched my mouth make those words and listened

to my voice push them out into the air. I said it again.

"I am a good person."

I felt so stupid and corny and ridiculous, but I said it again.

"I am a good person."

And then I started bawling. Not because I'd miraculously come to see my own inherent virtue as a human being, but because saying these words, feeling how strange they felt in my mouth, and watching my face struggle to look like I believed them—that's when I realized what I'd been up to all that time. I never understood why I couldn't make recovery work, why I never seemed to feel better. The fact that I could barely get out the most basic positive message showed me how negative my inner voice really was, how cruel I'd been to myself on a regular basis. It was shocking to consider that maybe there was something good in me, something worth saving, and that maybe all my brain needed was a little encouragement from the healthy side of me, as opposed to a constant stream of bullying from my illness.

When your brain is constantly telling you you're worthless, ugly, stupid, unlovable, evil, horrible, mean, disgusting, etc., you start to believe it, even when it isn't true. Taking a second to say, "Wait a minute, I'm not worthless," may sound foolish (watch out—there's that inner bully undermining you), but it actually brings you back to a state of control over your own thoughts, and the more you repeat it, the quieter that mean voice in your head becomes. Eventually, the positive thoughts are the ones that come naturally, and you can spot the negative ones creeping in

Looking Good, Feeling Gorgeous
By Pixie

1. Looking Good, Feeling Gorgeous - RuPaul
2. Lip Gloss - Lil Mama   3. Get Me Bodied - Beyoncé
4. I Love It - Icona Pop feat. Charli XCX
5. Do Somethin' - Britney Spears   6. C'mon - Ke$ha
7. I'm the Best - Nicki Minaj   8. Hair - Lady Gaga
9. Nails Done - Amanda Lepore
   feat. Cazwell and Roxy Cottontail
       10. Meeting in the Ladies Room - Klymaxx
11. Wings - Little Mix
   12. Queen of the Night - Whitney Houston
       13. Look at Me - Geri Halliwell

from a mile away and tell them to beat it before they even get close.

If this sounds awful and ineffective to you, I understand. I am as cynical as they come, and my first instinct with anything of this nature is to roll my eyes and run away as fast as possible. But rolling my eyes and running away didn't solve any of my major problems, which were (and still are) caused by a mix of tiny things, including antagonistic thoughts, self-loathing, obsessive-compulsive behavior, depression, and feeling like I didn't deserve help.

These days I use daily affirmations as needed: In dark times I try to keep an affirmation book or a stack of cards around when I need a little support, and I've also developed little sayings of my own. (My favorite is actually from my favorite movie, *What About Bob?*: "I feel good, I feel great, I feel wonderful." Not only does it work, but the thought of Bill Murray saying it just makes me laugh so hard that everything is better.) If you don't want to buy affirmation books or cards, it's super easy to make your own, just by writing down a bunch of positive thoughts and quotes on scraps of paper and sticking them into a jar and

pulling one out when you need one. Here are some examples:

I am beautiful.
I am loved and love others.
I am trying my best.
JUST BE BEYONCÉ.

Maybe this is all way too Cornball City for your liking. It definitely does feel that way for a while, but trust me, you get used to it, and then it's like a tiny meditation, a self-esteem boost, a little shot of empowerment that helps make the world seem better. But if you're not ready for that, or if you know yourself and are confident that that kind of self-cheerleading will *never* be your jam, you can tackle daily affirmations by keeping a journal and listing five things you've done or noticed during the day, including even the simplest stuff, which you may be surprised to notice adds up to a deeper appreciation of the universe around you and your place in it. For example:

1. Got out of bed
2. Laughed really hard at a dumb movie

3. Drank a delicious glass of lemonade
4. Hung out with my dog
5. Noticed how warm the sun felt on my skin

Sounds kind of basic, right? But when you do it often enough, you become more aware of how beautiful tiny moments in your life can be, which helps to make the bigger, more overwhelming stuff seem a little less scary.

There are days when I hop off the daily-affirmation train and forget to show myself, and the world around me, the love and empathy we deserve. But I always seem to come back to them, because sometimes you need to love yourself before you can notice it coming from anywhere else, and if you can take two seconds to stare the mean girl in the mirror down and pay her a compliment (and not, like, "I love that skirt, where did you get it?"), you'll eventually stop feeling like a total poser and start believing the things that are coming out of your mouth. You are beautiful. You do deserve to be loved. You are good enough, you are smart enough, and doggone it, people like you. ✱

FUNHOUSE

Mirrors can play tricks on you.

Photos by Eleanor, illustration and manipulation by Hattie.

I Want It to Be Worth It: An Interview With Emma Watson

We talk to the actor about her new movie, her other movies, and why she keeps 10 (10!) journals at all times.
Interview by Tavi, illustration by Suzy.

I am one of probably four people my age who have never read any of the Harry Potter books or seen any of the movies,[1] but that seemed unimportant when I headed to Emma Watson's apartment to interview her back in January. I'd just rewatched *The Perks of Being a Wallflower* and had been reading about some of her upcoming projects, so I had a squillion questions about the work she's done since Potter ended and the work she'll do in the future.

If you haven't seen it already, *Perks* is a flawless high school movie (based on the book by Stephen Chbosky, who also wrote and directed the film) that will make you laugh and cry your eyes out in equal measure. Emma's latest movie, Sofia Coppola's *Bling Ring*, is based on a group of real teenagers who robbed celebrities' homes in Los Angeles in 2008 and 2009. I saw a screening of it in April (after this interview, unfortunately), and as soon as it was over I just wanted to rewatch it for all of eternity. Like any Sofia Coppola fan, I was psyched that Emma would be her next ingénue, but this movie is not pretty or dreamy, it's insane and funny and scary, and I couldn't believe how hard I was laughing whenever Emma did something as small as stare at her phone.

Emma also recently filmed a leading role in Darren Aronofsky's biblical epic *Noah*, due out next year. It's sure to be drastically

[1] *I have nothing against HP, I just never got around to it! I didn't expect it to be "my thing" when the first one came out (I was like seven) and then I was too intimidated to start because I was so behind. It's on my reading/watching list, though, I swear.*

different from anything we've seen her in, and I obviously can't wait.

We sat at her kitchen table while she generously indulged my curiosity and *Perks* geekdom. Her cat slinked around the chairs, her roommate introduced herself and served some banana bread they'd baked together. It felt sort of like a gals' lunch, or something that sounds less like a yogurt commercial. Emma showed me her journals and we all watched her favorite TED talk on YouTube (look up "Brené Brown: Listening to Shame"). Even though she's been interviewed thousands of times over the 12 years since the first Potter movie, nothing she said felt like a stock answer. Every word seemed carefully chosen, save for a few moments in which she let her thoughts carry her away, and then that was exciting in the way watching people think and seek and find is exciting. She also got almost as hyper as I did when we got to talking about *Pretty Wild*, and she threw her head back in laughter when she admitted to getting through final exams with the help of *The Carrie Diaries*.

My dad came by after a couple hours and we'd started saying our goodbyes when I spotted her record player. The needle rested next to Joni Mitchell's *Blue*, and I couldn't help thinking about what a turning point that album signified in Joni's career and life. Her first three records established her as a commercially successful and critically respected artist, then she decided to take a break from performing to travel and write these incredible songs where she just to-

tally lays herself bare. Those songs became *Blue*, which was a huge and instant success on basically every level. It's widely regarded as Joni's best album, and 42 years after its release it's still gaining new fans, all of us attracted not just by her mindblowing talent but also by her honesty as she sings about her deepest secrets and desires.

These days Emma Watson seems to be writing her own *Blue*. She's managed to protect her private life while using her work to reveal the kinds of vulnerabilities that feel the *most* private. It's taken for granted that starting a career and becoming famous at a young age means sacrificing the space and peace necessary to learn about yourself or the rest of the world, but Emma has made time for both.

She also made time for me, and us, and this interview, and for that I thank her.

TAVI I have watched *Pretty Wild*, the reality show about the real-life Bling Ring, so many times. I'm obsessed with Alexis Neiers, the girl you play in the movie. Have you heard from her about the film or anything?

EMMA WATSON No, I haven't. To be fair to Alexis, [my character] is like three steps removed from who she might be in real life. A lot of the material in the movie was based on an article [in *Vanity Fair*] which was based on a reality show, which we all know isn't real life. I wasn't trying to impersonate her—she just inspired the character. I watched *Pretty Wild* so many times to try and get her into my brain, though. It gave me *anxiety*. How do you watch it?

I think I have to pretend that it isn't real. If you think about it too much it's depressing. You have to shut your brain off and be like, "They're not real people!"

But they *are*! Sofia filmed it in such a non-judgmental way, though—she never tells the audience how they should feel about these characters, which I think might be quite unsettling for people who want to be told, "We should hate these people." She made it so true to life, it almost feels like a documentary.

My final is tomorrow, so I've been living like a hermit. The only thing I have been watching—such a guilty pleasure, it's the perfect study break 'cause you just don't have to concentrate too hard—is *The Carrie Diaries*. Have you been watching it?

No!

[*Laughs*] So embarrassing to admit that! A 23-year-old that's fully been watching *The Carrie Diaries*.

Not even.

Yep. No, it's absolutely true. That's been my study break.

What was it like working with Sofia Coppola?

It was a real dream of mine. I came to the part in a very roundabout way: I told my agent how much I loved Sofia's work, and she's like, "You should meet with her producer and [unofficial] casting director, Fred Roos," and I did, and we got on really well, and that led to meeting Sofia, and she told me she was working on a project with young people in it. I read the script for *The Bling Ring* and I just got obsessed. For Sofia Coppola to be making a film which is a meditation on film and celebrity culture and what that all means, how it impacts society, and the psyches of young women in particular—I was like, "OK, I *have* to be in your movie. I really, really, really want to

be in your movie." For my audition I went out and bought hoop earrings and this crazy hat like the one Alexis wears when she goes to see her lawyer [on the show], and I put on tons of bronzer and a fake tan—I just went full-out, and had the best time doing it. 'Cause it's really the first time I've gotten to play someone who's a real character, someone just so different from me.

Sofia is incredibly smart, but she doesn't try too hard. She's very, very careful about the casting process, because when we get to the set she just wants to give everyone the space to do their own work. That attitude is so conducive to making a really interesting film, because she's completely prepared to switch around the scene that we're doing on a whim. She'll be like, "You know what, guys? The light looks really beautiful in the room next door, so let's just not do this scene today, we'll do this [other] scene instead." And everyone just moves next door. As an actress working with her, you have to be prepared for anything, because she likes capturing organic things, transcendent moments, changes in the wind and sun—which is awesome because you feel like you're really part of creating something beautiful, but also very unnerving for me because I'm used to being inside a studio at Harry Potter and being incredibly controlled and sticking to a schedule. So it was fun—it felt very freeing.

I've read that the process of filming *The Perks of Being a Wallflower* was also quite different from the usual rigid studio schedule.

Yeah, we shot it in six weeks. I'd never worked such long hours or so hard in my life, but it was also obviously the most fun. We did a lot of night shoots, and [after shooting] you have so much adrenaline running through your system, it takes a few hours for you to wind down even though it's like four in the morning. So oftentimes we would sit in the parking lot and—it sounds so cheesy—just watch the sun come up. When you make a movie on location, where you have to go and live somewhere outside your comfort zone, you have to create your own family, and you get so much closer than when you're making a movie

somewhere where everyone can stay in their own homes. And you're all trying to create something, and through that creative process you make this bond that you wouldn't really have under any other circumstances.

I got to work with Logan [Lerman], who plays Charlie, again in the last movie I did, *Noah*. He plays my brother, and it was great because we already had that chemistry; we didn't really have to push for it. It was intimidating stepping onto that set, because [the movie] is Russell Crowe and Darren Aronofsky and Jennifer Connelly, so to have Logan there was just immensely comforting.

My understanding is that you read the script for *Perks* and called your agent and said you wanted to do it, and you found out that it had been sitting on a shelf for a while because no one wanted to make it. Why did you think it was so important for this movie to exist in the world?

Well, I'd been reading scripts for two years before *Perks* came along, and nothing had really resonated with me in the same way. It was just on my brain, it was on my mind, I couldn't stop thinking about it. It didn't even occur to me that it wouldn't be made, because Logan was already attached, and I'd met with Stephen [Chbosky] and it was like he'd been waiting 12 years, really, to make this film. Then I got a call saying that no one wanted to back it financially. So it took more than phone calls: I actually flew out to L.A. and met with all the different studio heads and basically pitched the movie, which was crazy—I'd never done anything like that before in my life. [The story] just really spoke to my teenage experience and my friends' teenage experiences. I felt like I'd watched too much *Gossip Girl* and was just dying to see something that spoke to the kinds of issues that I'd encountered as a young woman. It felt unique, and like someone had really written it from the heart.

I wonder what parts of the script resonated for you, despite the fact that you were clearly working on other things that were unique in terms of teenage experience. Not to sound accusatory! Because there

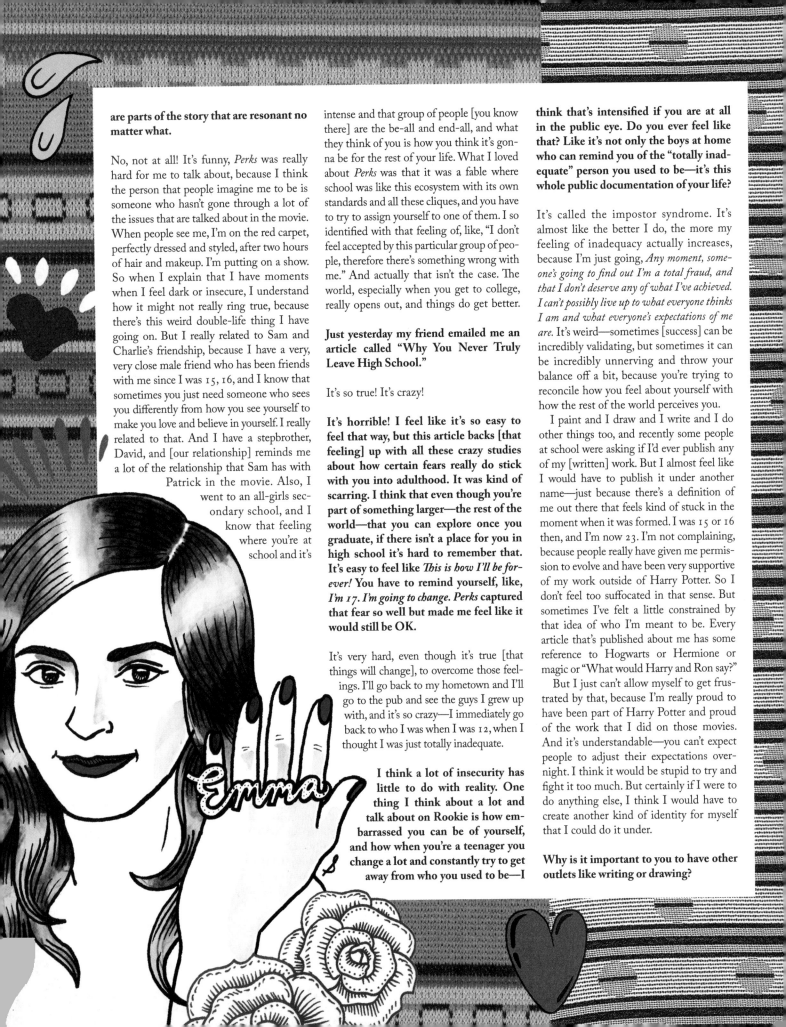

are parts of the story that are resonant no matter what.

No, not at all! It's funny, *Perks* was really hard for me to talk about, because I think the person that people imagine me to be is someone who hasn't gone through a lot of the issues that are talked about in the movie. When people see me, I'm on the red carpet, perfectly dressed and styled, after two hours of hair and makeup. I'm putting on a show. So when I explain that I have moments when I feel dark or insecure, I understand how it might not really ring true, because there's this weird double-life thing I have going on. But I really related to Sam and Charlie's friendship, because I have a very, very close male friend who has been friends with me since I was 15, 16, and I know that sometimes you just need someone who sees you differently from how you see yourself to make you love and believe in yourself. I really related to that. And I have a stepbrother, David, and [our relationship] reminds me a lot of the relationship that Sam has with Patrick in the movie. Also, I went to an all-girls secondary school, and I know that feeling where you're at school and it's

intense and that group of people [you know there] are the be-all and end-all, and what they think of you is how you think it's gonna be for the rest of your life. What I loved about *Perks* was that it was a fable where school was like this ecosystem with its own standards and all these cliques, and you have to try to assign yourself to one of them. I so identified with that feeling of, like, "I don't feel accepted by this particular group of people, therefore there's something wrong with me." And actually that isn't the case. The world, especially when you get to college, really opens out, and things do get better.

Just yesterday my friend emailed me an article called "Why You Never Truly Leave High School."

It's so true! It's crazy!

It's horrible! I feel like it's so easy to feel that way, but this article backs [that feeling] up with all these crazy studies about how certain fears really do stick with you into adulthood. It was kind of scarring. I think that even though you're part of something larger—the rest of the world—that you can explore once you graduate, if there isn't a place for you in high school it's hard to remember that. It's easy to feel like *This is how I'll be forever!* You have to remind yourself, like, *I'm 17. I'm going to change. Perks* captured that fear so well but made me feel like it would still be OK.

It's very hard, even though it's true [that things will change], to overcome those feelings. I'll go back to my hometown and I'll go to the pub and see the guys I grew up with, and it's so crazy—I immediately go back to who I was when I was 12, when I thought I was just totally inadequate.

I think a lot of insecurity has little to do with reality. One thing I think about a lot and talk about on Rookie is how embarrassed you can be of yourself, and how when you're a teenager you change a lot and constantly try to get away from who you used to be—I

think that's intensified if you are at all in the public eye. Do you ever feel like that? Like it's not only the boys at home who can remind you of the "totally inadequate" person you used to be—it's this whole public documentation of your life?

It's called the impostor syndrome. It's almost like the better I do, the more my feeling of inadequacy actually increases, because I'm just going, *Any moment, someone's going to find out I'm a total fraud, and that I don't deserve any of what I've achieved. I can't possibly live up to what everyone thinks I am and what everyone's expectations of me are.* It's weird—sometimes [success] can be incredibly validating, but sometimes it can be incredibly unnerving and throw your balance off a bit, because you're trying to reconcile how you feel about yourself with how the rest of the world perceives you.

I paint and I draw and I write and I do other things too, and recently some people at school were asking if I'd ever publish any of my [written] work. But I almost feel like I would have to publish it under another name—just because there's a definition of me out there that feels kind of stuck in the moment when it was formed. I was 15 or 16 then, and I'm now 23. I'm not complaining, because people really have given me permission to evolve and have been very supportive of my work outside of Harry Potter. So I don't feel too suffocated in that sense. But sometimes I've felt a little constrained by that idea of who I'm meant to be. Every article that's published about me has some reference to Hogwarts or Hermione or magic or "What would Harry and Ron say?"

But I just can't allow myself to get frustrated by that, because I'm really proud to have been part of Harry Potter and proud of the work that I did on those movies. And it's understandable—you can't expect people to adjust their expectations overnight. I think it would be stupid to try and fight it too much. But certainly if I were to do anything else, I think I would have to create another kind of identity for myself that I could do it under.

Why is it important to you to have other outlets like writing or drawing?

Emma

I don't know what it is. I've always kept and collected *things*, and I've always been interested in the idea of diaries. I must have 10 different personal diaries: I keep a dream diary, I keep a yoga diary, I keep diaries on people that I've met and things that they've said to me, advice that they've given me. I keep an acting journal. I keep collage books. They've given me a place where I can try to figure myself out, because those kinds of ideas feel too personal to put out into the public or even discuss with anyone else. It allows me to get things out of my head and work them out in a way that feels safe, which is really helpful. I can kind of play around with things.

That's been a big part of what school has meant to me. I got famous very young, and [college] gave me a safe zone where I could figure things out without people projecting onto me their ideas of what they wanted me to be, or thought I *should* be.

Journaling is nice because no matter how hard something is to go through, you at least *made* something out of it, which is really satisfying.

Also, I think your thoughts are so much less frightening when they're tangible, when you can see them on a page in front of you. And it's less narcissistic and egotistical than releasing your own autobiography, which would be my worst nightmare. [*Laughs*] Maybe one day I would write some things out, but not for a while. Not for a while.

Though even when it is a private thing and there are no judgments, a blank page is still so intimidating. It makes me scared to even start.

I had an art teacher who said that there is nothing scarier than a blank canvas. Before he gave us our canvases he'd scribble or splash paint on them so that we didn't have to work off this intimidating white space. I think there's something to be said for that.

Richard Burton's diaries came out [in December], and Elizabeth Taylor used to go through them and would write things in them—so he obviously wrote his diaries with the idea that people would read them,

that they would be public. My diaries are very much written as if no one would ever read them. I have, actually… [*She gets up and goes to another room, and returns with a stack of books and journals.*] This is what college does to you. You're terrified of reading a book without a pen in your hand, because time is so much of the essence that the first time you read something, if you have an idea, you have to write it down, because there's gonna be no time for you to read it again. So all of my books look like this. [*Leafs through a book—every page is filled with notes and marginalia.*] This is a really nice book that my dad got me in Venice. Everyone I've ever met who said anything interesting, everything is in here. Just so I remember these things.

Oh my god! You are so smart to keep all this!

Thank you! [*Turning pages*] So, I have Helena Bonham Carter, and this is Karl Lagerfeld—this is when he shot me for *Crash* magazine and I went to his studio in Paris. His studio is covered in books. He gave me two books which he illustrated, and he suggested that I should do that one day. He said so many funny things. This is Tim Burton. This is one of my acting teachers from RADA [the Royal Academy of Dramatic Art]…Jean Shrimpton…this is David Yates. Rupert [Grint] has a page. [*Laughs*] James Franco has a page. My mother has a page. I just get terrified I'll forget things! [*Finding a card in the stack of books*] Oh, this is so cool—this is from the president!

No!

[*Laughs*] Yeah! That's their dog! Isn't that insane?

Totally! Is acting like journaling for you, like you're figuring yourself out through a role?

Absolutely. But it's actually through the characters who are the least like me that I figure out the most about myself. Playing Nicki in *The Bling Ring* gave me such

insight into myself—parts of me that I'm uncomfortable with, or that I don't like. I realized through playing her that I can be so judgmental in a way that I wish I wasn't. And I found things that I had in common with her, which was difficult as well.

The fact that you experience that feeling of insecurity that we talked about before, no matter how successful you may seem to be—that probably helped you show us the insecurity in Sam [in the movie]. Like, there's this thing Jodie Foster wrote last year where she said that as an actor you're supposed to expose your vulnerabilities and the parts of yourself that you don't like… I'm sorry, I just did my least favorite interview thing, where someone just says something instead of asking a question.

No, no! It's so much nicer when it's a conversation. If you just do the whole question/answer thing I end up repeating myself so much. When the other person offers new angles on things, you can hopefully say something new. But yeah, it's funny: The day that I shot the scene where I had my first kiss with Logan, I just wasn't feeling good—I was feeling really tired at that point, and that was my most important scene in the movie. I remember begging Stephen, "*Please* could we do it another day, I just don't feel like I can do it today." And he did this really cool thing where he drew a line outside my trailer and was like, "When you step over that line, that's when you have to let go of everything, let go of you—you have to just go and be present as Sam, and leave everything else that you're worrying about behind."

Stephen has been such a great mentor to me. He was actually here last night, helping me with my homework. He came over and I made him dinner, and he helped me figure out what I was gonna write my thesis on. He's just the best. He's someone who walked into my life and just *got* me. I remember when I first met him—he came to my hotel, and within 20 minutes he had insights about me that I don't even know if my family has. That was what made me believe that I could play Sam. Because I get worried sometimes—I get crazy. After Harry Potter I didn't feel very confident in myself as an

actor. It's lucky that I've improved that now, but back then I needed someone to believe in me, and Stephen really did.

I read *Perks* in eighth grade, and I was so relieved that the movie would be in his hands. It feels like something that should have come out in the '90s and been misunderstood, and later become some kind of cult thing—it's heartening that it's so embraced. It's partially about the parts of yourself you don't like, so the fact that everyone seems to relate to it is really comforting.

It's funny, I was talking to Steve last night about *Girls*, and he was like, "Why do people make such a big deal about it?" I think it just came about at a moment when young women are bombarded by images of perfection which no human being can really achieve, and then Lena Dunham comes along and she's on TV and she's like this perfectly imperfect human being, and so are all of the other characters. I think that's why it's just caught on like wildfire.

My friend texted me during the Golden Globes and was like, "It's so weird to see someone I feel I could be friends with accepting an award—someone who talks and laughs and smiles like normal people I know."

I think her and Adele were like the two breaths of fresh air in the whole thing.

They were so honest about just being really excited.

Yeah, but not in like a…[*she smiles, tears up, and breathes heavily, beauty-pageant-style*] but in a really genuine way. I think Lena and Adele can kind of establish themselves as that [genuine] person from the beginning, whereas it would be very difficult for more-established actors, or anyone who's been on that stage a few times, who's been running the circuit for a while, to step out of that kind of rigid thing that they've been doing, which they now feel they have to *keep* doing—they can't break face, in a way.

Yeah, it would be weird if Julianne Moore was suddenly like, "I'm keeping it real, guys!" It's perfectly natural for her to be dignified the way she is.

That's something that I struggle with all the time, is how do you act natural when you're on a red carpet and there are people screaming at you from this way and that and you feel so watched and observed? It is an unnatural situation, so it's very difficult to find a way to be authentic. I find that to a certain degree my body just shuts down. It's sensory overload—your body goes into a kind of defense mode. People try to have conversations with me when I step off a red carpet, and I can't—I kind of just go numb and my brain stops functioning. So it's difficult to find a way to be real, because it's such an unreal situation. But hats off to [Lena and Adele], they really killed it.

Then there's the fear of being too "Look, I'm being sincere!"

Oh my god, completely. Sometimes I hear myself in interviews and I feel like I'm in that skit from *Extras* where one actor is taking the piss out of celebrities who are like, "I'm so normal! Look at me being really normal, doing all of this normal stuff!" You can take it to a point where it's like, "Well, yeah, my life is kind of weird and I can't pretend that I live exactly like everyone else," because it's an extraordinary set of circumstances to be under, so you try to find that middle ground. But yeah—sometimes I hear myself back and I'm like, "This just sounds like bullshit." [*Laughs*] Do you ever do interviews?

We put out a book, so I did some stuff to tell people about it. Normally we get on a plane and go somewhere and I remember how to talk in sound bites, but once this person came to our home, and it was just too close. I had just come home from school and we did it in my house right away, but I was just…

I can completely relate to that. I remember when I was young, getting ready to go to a *Lord of the Rings* premiere, and literally

getting changed in my school's toilet. It's just really surreal and odd. You feel quite vulnerable.

I was talking to a friend about it, but I stopped myself because it's such a silly thing to complain about. [Another friend] told me it's all relative.

It is all relative. In order to stay sane you have to give yourself permission to talk about these feelings and put them out there, because it's so unhealthy for you to feel like there isn't space for you to consider what you're going through. It's such a necessary part of the human condition. I completely agree [that it feels silly]—I feel the same way—but you just have to find the people who understand that you're a human being. There's maybe two or three people I can do that with.

Right, and though it's not a terrible problem, it's hard to relate to, and that does emphasize how it can be—

Isolating.

Yeah. Exactly.

Similar to you, I used to try to hide what I was doing, and I would end up in these awkward positions where I would have to go and do something [for work] but I would say I was doing something else. I would try to hide that I had a car picking me up—I would ask them to park around the corner so that people would think I was walking. All of these elaborate kinds of schemes to pretend I was like everyone else. I've gotten to a point now where, like, for example: I'm doing this class at NYU, and sometimes a driver comes to pick me up in case there are paparazzi outside, or there are people who have come to wait for me [to come out], and I just get straight into the car so I feel safe. And yeah, if the kids come out and see a black SUV and they go, "Oh, Emma Watson's getting into a car"—you just hope that people will understand.

I know you're going back to Brown this fall, after taking a couple of years off for

work. **What made you decide on that school?**

A few different things. I really like the fact that it has a very open curriculum, that there aren't any requirements. Really, I've kind of been in charge of my own education since I started out on Potter when I was 9 or 10, and I liked that I could design my own major if I wanted to, and I could take independent studies if I wanted to on subjects that weren't necessarily in the curriculum. I did an independent study on the psychology and philosophy of how and why we fall in love, which was awesome. [*Laughs*]

Whoa! Do you know why? Can you tell me?

[*Laughs*] We'd need like six hours! Opportunities like that, and the idea of classes being pass/fail, make it sound as if you don't have to work as hard, but it actually gives you the freedom to try out things that you wouldn't be able to do if you had to get a certain GPA on your transcript. It lets you take classes that you wouldn't otherwise. And it attracts a certain type of student: [someone] very independent who wants to take responsibility and control of what they're learning. That really appealed to me as well.

What is a dream project for you? Not just film, necessarily.

Well, there's different things you get out of different types of projects, and you can't expect to get everything in one bundle. *Perks* was really special because I made friends that I'll probably have for life. With *The Bling Ring*, through learning about the character I learned more about myself. On *Noah*, I ended up doing months' worth of research on one scene for the movie. And I got to work with Darren [Aronofsky], who really pushed me to be a better actress. In terms of my next project, I really want to do a romantic comedy. I've been looking for the perfect script. I'm getting to the point where I'm like, "I just need to write the damn thing myself," because it's so hard to find some-

thing that's original and really funny. But I'd love to do something like that, just because the last two or three movies I did were kind of heavy.

I'm a real director chaser. I really want to work with Danny Boyle or Ang Lee, I'd love to work with Lynne Ramsay, I'd love to work with Tom Hooper, David Fincher—I have this endless list. I'll do whatever as long as I can be part of someone else's creative vision, someone who isn't just creating something as a piece of entertainment, but is genuinely creating a piece of art. Though it's nice if it's commercially successful at the same time. [*Laughs*] I'm big on directors, more than I am about working with particular actors.

Do you think that's something you'd ever do yourself?

Maybe. I would definitely be interested. I'm obsessed with being very thorough and very in control and very researched, and so I would only do it if I felt like I had enough knowledge. I'd like to produce as well, so we'll see.

I was reading an interview with Lena Dunham by Miranda July in *Interview* magazine, and they were saying that it's easier now to work in different mediums and have your body of work be more about your point of view than about honing a particular craft. I guess acting requires a kind of permission from others, and just thinking about your journals, I think it's great that you have a strong point of view and that you can work in various mediums that let you express it in different ways, and I look forward to seeing all that you do. Aaah! I always feel silly complimenting people who are older than me because it feels condescending!

No, I don't see it that way at all! That's a really nice thing to hear. For me it's about knowing that what I have to say, I really believe in. I'm not gonna put anything out there just for the sake of it. I'm trying to find a really confident artistic voice before I put myself out there, because it's so easy for people to squash you. I want to make

sure that what I make is something I really have the goods to back up.

I think that is what is so special about you and about Lena, is that you're very young people who already have a very established point of view—you have a strong set of values that you can translate into different art forms. I guess my figuring out who I am and what those values are has become quite diluted, because I've just been working so much and been so tied up in being so many other identities that it doesn't feel as concrete or established yet as I would like it to be. I'm still not quite sure what my message is, what I'm trying to communicate [through my work].

Those other identities have taught you things as well.

Yeah, they have. It's interesting, because people say things to me like, "It's really cool that you don't go out and get drunk all the time and go to clubs," and I'm just like, I mean, I appreciate that, but I'm kind of an introverted kind of person just by nature, it's not like a conscious choice that I'm making necessarily. It's genuinely who I am. Have you read *Quiet* by Susan Cain?

No!

It discusses how extroverts in our society are bigged up so much, and if you're anything other than an extrovert you're made to think there's something wrong with you. That's like the story of my life. Coming to realize that about myself was very empowering, because I had felt like *Oh my god, there must be something wrong with me because I don't want to go out and do what all my friends want to do.* Anyway, I just went off on a tangent…

I think we were talking about putting out something you really believe in.

I just feel so uncomfortable with being a Google News article, really with being in the media in any way, that if I have to be in the public eye, I want it to be for something that was worth it. I'm just taking my time over it. It's building, it's got some layers. It's getting there. ☆

JUST KIDS

Because summer belongs to us. By Allyssa.

Thanks to Augusta, Chelsie, Shriya, Annabella, Jake, and Richard for modeling.
Leather jackets from Cote-Armour.

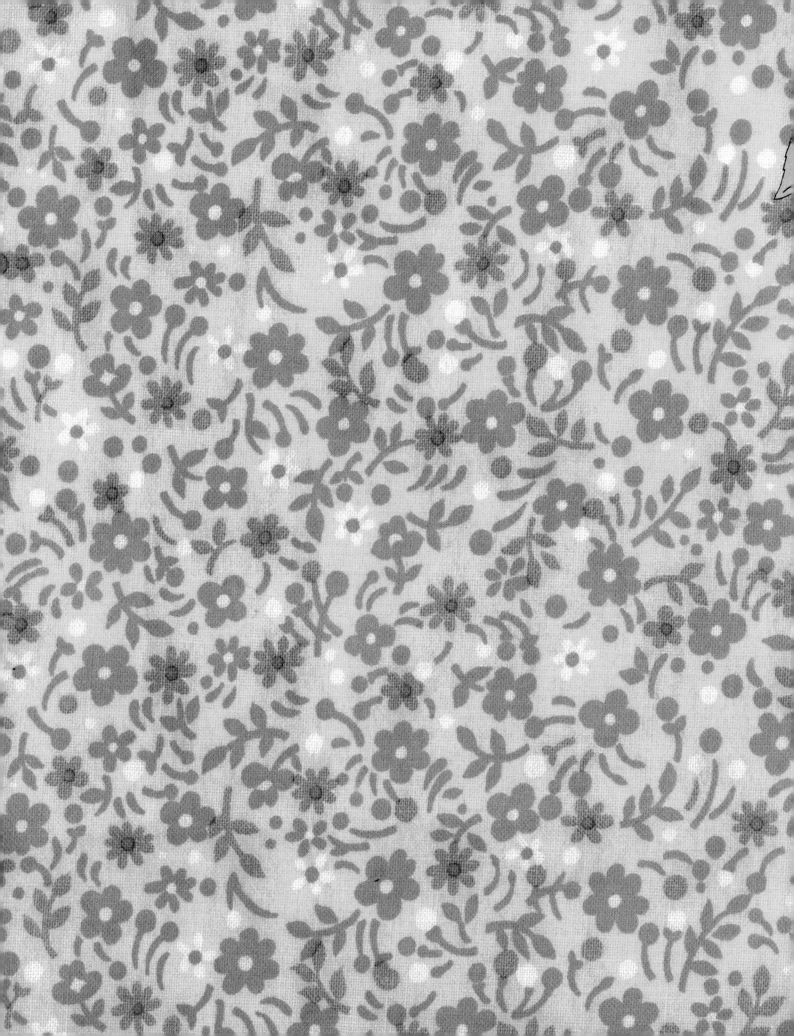

There you have it, Rookie's second year. Here's all the stuff that didn't fit in any month, and some extras you can't find online.

Just Wondering

Second opinions on your LIFE.

How do I get over an unrequited crush? I'd hate to be pining for eternity. —T.

In kindergarten I loved a boy named CAR who held my hand on the way to lunch even though there was often dried-up nose snot on it, and I thought we were in love. I told my mom that I was going to drive a car with CAR when I grew up and she was like, "What are you talking about?" and only later did I learn that he only held my hand because our whole class was required to walk in a double line, hand in hand, to the lunchroom, and Car was assigned to walk with me because our last names were both at the end of the alphabet. When I realized he didn't love me, I gouged my stuffed Minnie Mouse's eyes out and used her as a butt pillow for weeks.

In fourth grade I loved a boy named Daniel Moon, and he made fun of my crooked teeth and told me my voice was squeaky like a mouse and he "went out" with this bossy girl who gave him "Korean massages" which were just really hard slaps to his back, and three years later, on my way home from middle school, I saw him standing in front of a Toyota dealership, waiting to get on the

same bus I was on, and for months I waited for him to kneel by my feet and say, "Jenny! Be my girlfriend! I love you!" but he never acknowledged me once! I threw my Ouija board in the garbage because it had promised me that Daniel Moon would be my first kiss and also—um—my husband.

In ninth grade I was obsessed with this boy in my computer class because he told my friend Carine that I was "a really intelligent girl," and when I saw him holding hands with another girl, I thought, WAIT, WHAT ABOUT ME, THE REALLY INTELLIGENT GIRL?

In 10th grade I was in love with my friend's older brother, and for years I honestly thought that we would build a cabin in the woods together and start a family and live like creative recluses in love. That fantasy cost me many, many nights of flinging myself on my bed and crying and writing really awful poems about the depths of my despair because the one I loved did not love me back.

Each time, I swore that THIS was the boy for me, that I had found *the one* and there could be no other! Ever! But guess what? THERE ARE OTHERS. There are *so*

many others. And every time I thought that I would never recover but would just keep pining away forever—every single time—it always always ended, I always always got up, and I always ALWAYS recovered and moved on. You have to know it and you *have to* believe it.

I bet deep down inside, your rational, logical, sensible self knows that you're not going to pine for this person forever. But how do you get yourself to *believe* it? Ask yourself what you like about your crush. Why do you want to be with her or him? Do you really think you would be compatible with each other? Unrequited crushes thrive on fantasy and shrivel up and die when confronted with reality.

A few months ago, I was crushing on this dude that I barely knew. We spent less than a week getting to know each other, and I was *crazy* about him. When I realized he had a girlfriend and probably wasn't going to move across the country to start a life with me and learn to speak fluent Mandarin so that we could raise our future babies bilingually, I had to start the painful process of bringing myself back down to reality. Because, you see, in my mind, he was the perfect boyfriend, but in reality, I hardly knew him. In my fantasy, we shared everything in common, but in reality, I sometimes didn't laugh at his jokes and occasionally had cruel thoughts about his taste in books. In my fantasy, he was the best listener in the world, but he actually kind of just didn't have that much to say. I fantasized that he was the finest booty around, but the truth was that he was kind of vain and obsessed with working out. And yeah, I spent a couple of weeks drowning in my own misery and dramatically leaning against trees every time I stepped outside because it feels good to act out when things aren't so good, but then I made myself lie down on my bed, take some deep breaths, and just really think about my crush and whether I *really* thought he was the guy for me or if I just *wanted* him to be that. And anyway, how could he be the guy for me if he didn't think I was the hottest, smartest, funniest, most interesting babe in the entire galaxy-universe-space of the world? Tell me that, T., and ask yourself that about your own unrequited crush.

The next thing you need to do is TREAT YO SELF to some space. Absence may make the heart grow fonder in the case of two people who are already in a relationship, but in the case of unrequited love, trust me when I say that distance will make your heart grow stronger. If you want to stop thinking about your crush, you will need to take a break from communicating with them. This means de-friend or block them on Facebook so you don't have to see where they've checked in or what their friends are writing on their wall. When I was in the throes of my own unrequited romance, I would guiltily browse my crush's Facebook page looking for clues: *Is the girl he had his arm around in that one photo his girlfriend? How come I haven't seen any photos of her lately? Does this mean he's dumped her ass in preparation to pursue ME? How come she wrote on his wall but he didn't "like" her post? Does this mean they're fighting and maybe by this time next year they'll be broken up, and hmmn, I better make sure I'm single when that happens.* This kind of ass-backwards sleuthing comes with a lot of anxiety, and it only prolongs the agony because you're gathering fuel to keep the fantasy version of your crush warm

when what you need to be doing is icing it out of your life. Don't indulge in what could be, because you are NOT waiting around for this dude or dudette.

If your crush is in your phone, then you need to (at least temporarily) delete them. Don't text or call them, and don't respond to their texts and calls. If you feel like that's harsh or like you owe them a reason, just say, "Look, it hurts me to talk to you, so I need to take a break." If your crush is a good person, they'll understand, and if they aren't—well, all the more reason for you to take your leave from them.

Finally, flirt like the confident, cute, shy, sassy, irreverent, badass babe you are. Flirt with people you think are cute and flirt with people you're on the fence about and flirt with people who have a great sense of humor and, most important, flirt with people who flirt back with you. Flirt with boys and/or girls who make you feel interesting and confident and comfortable. Just flirt and feel good about being able to have fun with people who maybe won't be your next great love, but at the very least can provide you with your next fun, flirtatious exchange, and isn't that a million clean butts better than the next disappointing, sad exchange with your unrequited crush?

All of this stuff will seem obvious one day when you've chased the fantasy of your unrequited crush out of your head and replaced it with the reality of this brilliant, unstoppable, perfectly flawed world! One day you will see your former unrequited crush and realize that you feel NOTHING for them, and you might even wonder how you managed to get so worked up over *that person*… then you'll turn the corner and you'll see just how many cute, adorable, funny, interesting, creative humans there are out there. And guess what else? The best ones are the ones who crush back. —Jenny

I have a lot of noticeable (but old!) self-harm scars on my arms, and this fall, I'm going to be a nanny for a family with young children. How can I cover up my scars or explain them without getting fired from my first job? I don't want the parents to think I'm a bad influence/going to kill myself, because I'm not. So far, the best explanation I can come

up with is that I got bitten by a shark, and I don't think that is going to work. —Gracey

First of all, good for you for stopping the habit of self-harm. I know from experience how hard that is, and you should feel proud of yourself. I also know from experience how it feels to live with those scars. I've gotten to the point where I feel comfortable going sleeveless and dealing with any questions that may arise, but it definitely took a while for me to get there. Because self-harm can be such a secretive habit, I advise against lying about it. Plus, working up a big story about shark bites (or anything) can be anxiety-inducing. You are going to be an awesome nanny and a GOOD influence, but if you start your job with a lie, it might reflect poorly on you.

I can totally understand not wanting to sit down and explain everything to your new employers right away. Concerns about the job aside, it's personal! So I'd suggest keeping the scars covered in the beginning. Because I hate getting a lot of sun, I wear long sleeves year-round—and I don't melt in the summer because I stock up on tissue-thin almost-sheer cardigans, which you can find SUPER CHEAP (like seven dollars) at DNACoutureLA.com.

But you might get sick of wearing long sleeves at some point, or you might need to take the kids to the pool or something. Hopefully, after a couple of weeks, you will feel more comfortable with the family, and when they do see your scars, things will go one of three ways. One, they won't even say anything. They'll see that you are awesome with their kids, assume your story is personal, and leave it at that. Option two: If you feel safe enough to broach the subject yourself, or if the parents see your scars and react with concern, tell an abridged version of your story. Share whatever you feel comfortable sharing, and end with how much stronger and happier you are now. That will actually demonstrate what an awesome role model you are—you got through something hard and faced it head-on. The third option is that they notice, they say something, and you don't feel comfortable telling the truth. At this point, a little white lie may be in order, but keep it simple. Say something like "Oh, I had an accident, long story, but I'm fine now." The truth is, everybody has issues, and you are entitled to privacy. The people you work for should understand that.

Though I'm comfortable with my scars, I understand that you may want to try to minimize or get rid of them, and you do have options. If you want to go the natural route, try rose-hip oil, neem oil, or vitamin E cream. A lot of people recommend the product Mederma Advanced Scar Gel, which markets itself as the number-one doctor-recommended brand for scar treatment. Finally, you could consider laser treatments, but this is pricey, and you absolutely have to talk to a doctor or dermatologist about it.

Congrats on your nanny job, and I hope this helps. —Stephanie

I masturbate, and I suspect many of my friends do too. Is there any socially acceptable way to ask them if they do? Or is that something you just don't ask someone, ever? —C.

I guarantee that most if not all of your friends are masturbating, and the ones that aren't are thinking and wondering about it. I'm a great believer in broaching a topic like this naturally, straightforwardly, and lightheartedly—because I also guarantee that your friends would love to talk about masturbation in a safe, frank, nonjudgmental context. I'd suggest bringing it up not as a question per se—"Do you or don't you"—but putting it out there in the course of a relevant conversation, e.g.: "But don't you guys find that the best orgasms are the ones you have when you masturbate? Or is that just me?" You could also springboard the discussion off outside information, like: "Did you see that post on Rookie about masturbation and how great it is to know how to make yourself come so you can show your partner how to do it…?" You may have to help the conversation along a bit, so be prepared to take the lead to begin with, but the more you open up about it in a casual but matter-of-fact way, the more your friends are likely to—especially as it'll be a riveting conversation: Making female orgasms happen is generally a less straightforward process than making guys come, so women tend to masturbate in many more varied and fascinating ways. I wish women talked to one another about masturbation more often—apart from anything else, it's potentially an opportunity to cross-reference different ideas and approaches you can each take away and go try out at home. :) —Cindy

How do I deal with older people who try to invalidate my work and my achievements because I'm young and a girl? I'm an artist, and pretty much every exhibition I've been in has ended in tears because some middle-aged man (always a middle-aged man!) has told me I have no right to be there because of my age and gender. —Bethany

Congratulations on all the awesome stuff you're doing, and I'm sorry some turds are getting in the way of your feeling proud of yourself. Unfortunately, sometimes older people seem to feel like something is being taken away from them when somebody younger than them is successful. Sometimes guys feel threatened when a girl is successful. These feelings inevitably interfere with how they go about judging a successful young female person and her work. Maybe invalidating her achievements makes it easier for them to deal with how unsatisfied they are with their own success, career, art, etc. So, first know that their reactions have very little to do with you or the quality or meaning or effort behind your work. These dudes are just plain projecting, because that's always easier and less scary than looking in a mirror.

When you are RIGHT THERE DEALING WITH THEM IN PERSON, you could kill 'em with kindness: Smile and nod and don't let them see that you're bothered by what they're saying. You could just roll your eyes and move on. Or you can engage in an actual conversation with them and try to make them see the ridiculousness of what they're saying—that gender and age are reason to exclude someone from a community they've earned their place in. In all honesty, I don't think they deserve your time or energy or the little buzz they might get from getting you caught in a conversa-

tion. But I also think that if they make you angry, you have every right to express that if you want to. Do what feels right in the moment (unless you're compelled to, like, start punching them). Whatever makes it easier for you to avoid letting their sexist, sad remarks get to you so you can continue being creative and happy—that is the right thing to do.

If their words creep into your mind later, they might start to get you down. Don't feel defeated if this happens—you are a person with feelings, and anyone would be bugged by such immaturity disguised as "constructive criticism." But don't feel guilty once you're able to not give a shit about them, either, because you are not responsible for their happiness or success. You are just responsible for making art you love to make, if that is indeed what you plan on doing right now. And you can't do that if you feel suffocated by insecure naysayers. You *have* to ignore them. You're already aware, it sounds like, that these guys' reasons as to why you shouldn't have an exhibition are stupid as hell and have nothing to do with your art, yeah? Remind yourself of this! As often as you need to in order to keep creating!

Normally when something won't stop bugging me, I force myself to think about it and figure out why I'm upset and, if it's something I did wrong, how to fix it. But there's a difference between getting to the bottom of an issue that needs to be worked out, and letting yourself go down the wormhole of negative thought that opens up when you start to wonder if these jerks are right. BLOCK THAT SHIT OUT. KEEP MOVIN'. Keep creating. That's the point of all this anyway, isn't it? Your work is not for them, so what do they care? And if it's not for them, what do you care what they think? Just block their voices out the next time you think about it, and the time after that, and the time after that, and eventually it'll be such a long time since it's had a big presence in your brain that it might even be too tiny for you to ever think about at all.

And the next time you're working, you will be doing so in spite of someone who tried to hold you back, and that is awesome. —Tavi

There's this boy a couple grades younger than me who I talk to a little, and he's really cool, and I want to be his friend. He has a girlfriend, and I seriously don't have any romantic feelings towards him. My question is, how can you befriend a boy without making him think you have a crush on him? —Mary, 17

First off, kudos to you for understanding the difference between liking someone as a friend and liking them romantically. Some people don't figure that out for years! You can like someone who would normally be in your dating pool and even find them attractive without wanting to fall in love with them. This kind of platonic love and affection can be a beautiful thing, and it only gets better as you get older.

It shouldn't be a big deal that you want to become friends with this guy without any romantic intentions. It's totally normal and even common for a guy and a girl to be friends with each other without any concerns of ulterior romantic motives. But, as you clearly are aware, it can get weird sometimes.

My first piece of advice is to be honest with him. It takes a little bit of vulnerability, which is not always easy, but I find that being blunt and complimentary often works: "I like your ____ [taste in music, art style, podcast] and wanna be friends, and this is not me trying to date you." Boom, simple as that. If that's too forward for you, just

chat him up, and when you do, mention whatever your current relationship status is—seeing someone, interested in someone, not dating—just to make him aware that you're not fishing for his affections. Other than that, befriend him the same way you'd befriend any other dude or lady: Hang out, exchange stories, laugh together, do dumb things together. I've found showing my guy friends what I consider my least sexually alluring traits—burping, ranting about reality shows, sweating—reinforces the notion that this relationship will stay unsexy. Paradoxically, however, *forcing* a feeling of platonicness just makes the other person think you're interested in them. Imagine some guy talking you up every day and repeating over and over again that he doesn't find you attractive at all, or inviting you to do stuff but always with the tagline "I mean, just as friends. NOT AS A DATE," or shrinking in horror from any casual physical contact. You'd think he was protesting too much. Don't work to make your friendship seem super platonic, just let it be platonic. I'm guessing you don't constantly announce to your female friends that you don't want to make out with them, and that you sometimes lean on them or hug them or sit close together—if you act differently with this guy, it's gonna feel weird to both of you.

You mentioned that he has a girlfriend, and whether or not you want to address that situation is up to you. You shouldn't have to, but if you like, make an effort to be friendly with her. It just confirms that you're not into him romantically, and hell, if you like a guy's taste in a bunch of things, it may mean you'll like his girlfriend too! (Note: You are not required to be friends with both members of a couple.) Just keep it nice and easy like you do with your gal pals, and enjoy your new buddy! —Emily G.

I cheated. It was the most horrible thing I've ever done, and I hate myself for it. There are

reasons why I did it, including having a long-distance relationship, and my feeling disconnected from…everything. But I know none of these are excuses. Nothing makes it OK, because it was selfish and it was CHEATING. My boyfriend is working on forgiving me, but how do I forgive myself? I hate me. I feel like I don't even deserve to get sympathy for feeling so depressed. Help me! —J.

Let me sit you down for a moment, J. Almost every woman, at various times in her life, will experience moments when she is cheated on, and moments when she is the cheater. I have been around the block and back, and my take on this subject is that things happen in life that you just don't expect, and they usually reveal deeper problems you may not want to look at—but that you probably should. I don't want to justify your actions, but you've owned up to what you did. That is important and huge. You also obviously feel bad about it. Maybe *too* bad—it sounds like you're really beating yourself up over this, and that's not doing yourself or your boyfriend any favors. Instead of all this needless self-flagellation, try looking at the deeper problems going on in your life. You feel disconnected—why? Is it possible you cheated to sabotage a good relationship? Do you do that kind of thing to yourself a lot? What do you get out of it? Or maybe you didn't want to admit that your current relationship isn't working, so you cheated to create a more obvious issue to deal with. And what about the person you cheated with? How do they feel about it? How do you feel about them? These are all questions I think you need to answer for yourself. Are you in therapy? It's not a bad idea to talk to someone about this, besides your boyfriend—though talking openly about it with him is obviously really important and might even make your relationship stronger from here on out. Or maybe you will realize that you are not happy, and you made this "mistake" to open an exit door for yourself. J., self-hatred is a beast that you need to tackle down to the ground. Please don't beat yourself up anymore. You recognize that what you did was wrong. You are paying the price. Now forgive yourself, then find out why you did it. —Karen Elson

How do you deal with loving things that happen to be at least a little bit misogynistic? I've been getting really into rap music—it has great energy and makes me happy, and also has deep moments that let me brood and think about the meaning of life. But, as you already know, a lot of rap music is really problematic—it can be sexist and homophobic, and a lot of it endorses violence and crime. How do I reconcile my genuine love for this art form with my feminism and my general everybody-loves-everybody vibe? —K.T., Cape Town, South Africa

Oh, K.T. This is one of the fundamental and defining questions of my entire life. It sucks when you're on the dance floor, having a good time shaking it to some crazy beat like "Pop That," and then all of a sudden Lil Wayne comes on and tells you to suck his wiener for pieces from his corny-ass T-shirt line and you're like…NAH. And your whole dance-floor flow is interrupted by a lyric that isn't even clever. But! That song is fun to jump around to. What the hell is going on?! One of the things about misogyny in (American) hip-hop is that, as it goes with all art, it's a microcosm of the misogyny that goes on in society. And it's not confined to rap music: You can easily find misogynistic undertones (and overtones!) in rock, pop, country, dance, R&B. Even Taylor Swift has some lyrics that I find to be a product of the larger culture of misogyny. ("She's better known for the things that she does on the mattress"? Come on, dude!) The fact is, there is no art form that is completely devoid of problematic elements, and there never will be, unless and until we are living in a perfectly harmonious utopia where everyone is treated equally and everyone has access to the same basic necessities and we all high-five one another while walking down the street. So yeah, not to be a downer but: never. If you refuse to consume any art or culture that isn't 100 percent perfectly in line with your morals and your politics,

you will not get to watch, read, listen to, or dance to *anything* ever again. Given those choices, I'll shake my head at Lil Wayne and continue dancing.

However! I'm not saying we have to just accept things the way they are. You will never be able to unhear some of the vilest stuff, and what's worse is that most of the misogyny in rap songs is directed at women of color, for whom misogyny is compounded by racism (not just in America). Loving rap music as you do, and I do, doesn't mean making excuses for misogynistic lyrics or torturing logic and common sense to argue that they're actually *lampooning* or *subverting* misogyny somehow. If you love something, you want it to be better, right? Hold your favorite artists accountable for what they say on their records.

Meanwhile, you don't have to feel guilty or "wrong" for loving rap music. Just because you enjoy a song that is gross towards women doesn't make you a bad feminist, or self-hating. You're just part of a long continuum of complicated art appreciation that feminists (including the entire movement of hip-hop feminism) have been dealing with ever since Roxanne Shanté recorded a diss track in response to UTFO's misogynistic song "Roxanne, Roxanne" in 1984, at the age of 14. Women before us were thinking about this stuff, and those after us will continue to do the tough work and the confrontational twerk.

I recommend reading the original bible of hip-hop feminism, *When Chickenheads Come Home to Roost* by Joan Morgan. She wrote it in the 1990s, when she was in her 20s and grappling with these exact same questions, and it's a really good entry point for sorting out your feelings. (Also, Joan Morgan is the best.) And beyond that there's a whole world of strong women rappers with feminist attitudes (and lyrics to match) that can help balance out the ick of having just listened to a bunch of strip-club anthems. (I for one will never feel as good listening to the grody yet clever lines of, say, Dipset as I do listening to "You Can't Play With My Yo-Yo.") A good resource is FemaleRappers.tumblr.com, which not only posts current people like Azealia Banks, Angel Haze, and Dominique Young Unique, but also goes deep into the archives of Trina, Lil' Kim, Eve, and them. Good luck, K.T., and stay strong! And remember, a good response to the question "What you twerkin' with?" is "My fist." Pop *that*. —Julianne ☺

Best BFF Forever

An interview with Mindy Kaling. By Lena Dunham.

I was a fan of Mindy Kaling's long before I was a friend of Mindy Kaling's, and the most wonderful surprise is that the experiences are remarkably similar. Mindy's work (from *Matt and Ben*, the fringe play that got her noticed in 2003; to her nearly decade-long run as *The Office*'s resident clothes whore, Kelly Kapoor; to her best-selling book of essays; to her pièce de résistance, *The Mindy Project*) is notable for its wit, openness, and ladylike ferocity. Ditto Mindy. I started picking her brain on our first date (at her favorite Ethiopian restaurant, where she taught me how to order and told me I had small bones—a first!) and continue to do so today in email chains where we get to complain to each other about the day-to-day realities of running a TV show. So this interview is just a more formal version of what I want to do to Mindy Kaling every day: quiz her, quote her, learn from her.

LENA: **Let's start light: What would you like your legacy to be? For example, I hope to have made it easier to be oneself in this hardscrabble world and to have rescued at least 15 animals from certain death. I'd also like to be known as "prolific, iconoclastic, and winsome."**

MINDY: "She threw the most amazing parties and she had the most gorgeous and cheerful husband. Gay teenagers would dress up as her for Halloween. She seemed to have read every book, yet no one ever saw her reading. She had the appetite of an Olympic swimmer and the physique of an Olympic figure skater. She dressed like Chloë Sevigny and could fuck for hours…"

I could write those for another 10 pages. Truthfully, I guess I would like to be remembered as a great writer and a kind person. I wouldn't mind if an expensive bag were named after me, like Jane Birkin.

What makes you laugh harder than anything else on earth? I am guessing it's nothing toilet related. **I am the worst about toilet humor—I hate it, and I feel that the day I embrace it will be the day that I no longer have anything positive to offer the world.**

I love when people fall out of frame unexpectedly. I also love accents. Borat saying "my wife," you know, that kind of thing.

How would you describe your fashion style? Please answer in the form of the first paragraph of an *InStyle* profile that, while not 100 percent accurate, embodies the things you strive for in your wardrobe and your beauty regimen. For example: "Lena Dunham sits down at a café table in the sixth arrondissement. She brushes her bangs aside, revealing reddened, teary eyes. 'I'm sorry—I just passed Jim Morrison's grave and was overcome with emotion,' she says. She is 15 minutes late but too focused on her canvas satchel of antique books to care…"

"When Mindy Kaling arrived to the Chateau Marmont 30 minutes late, she apologized profusely and began dabbing ice water on a badly skinned knee. 'I thought I hit an old woman in the Loehmann's parking lot,' she said, a flush of perspiration on her cheeks and forehead. 'Turned out it was a sack of trash with a shawl draped on it. Got so mad at it that I kicked it, and this happened.' She gestured to her knee.

"Miss Kaling ushered in a scent that was a curious mix of cardamom, citrus, and Old Spice Pure Sport. Without looking at the menu, she ordered a Moscow Mule and the steak and fries with five mini bottles of Tabasco sauce. Her shirt was Ikat print, and her harem pants were tribal print. She had neon pink high-tops she promptly took off. 'You don't mind, do you? It's a hell of a lot of shoe for a summer's day,' she purred. I did mind. I minded a lot."

What do you think is the power of TV, and why do you love it?

The serialized nature of TV breeds anticipation, and anticipation breeds a kind of loyalty and excitement in viewers that I love. I watched *The X-Files* every week when I was a teenager and I was as devoted to it as I was to a boy I had a crush on. Watching it was one of the coziest hours of life. When Conan started at *Late Night*, I loved him like he was a movie star—but unlike with a movie star, I was rewarded with him every night of the week! Movies can't do that. Being on TV builds a relationship with the viewer, and I feel really lucky to have that.

What would you say is the hardest part about being a boss? I'd say it's that there's no convenient time to take naps and the constant sense that you are neglecting something or someone.

I want to be part of the gang. I don't want to be the gang leader who has to stay on gang schedule and pay gang taxes. I have to do that stuff now. Sometimes I just want to shoot my machine gun in the air, you know?

Do you ever get embarrassed to point out gender bias? I always apologize and say something dumb and sassy like "Not to be the girl who cried misogyny, but no one would ever say that to Larry David!" Somehow I feel the need to point out that I know I'm doing it, and that I may sound humorless, and that I wish I could be free and easy like Cameron Diaz at a hockey game.

I totally understand this. I don't get embarrassed, though—I get nervous. Because journalists don't like to be told that their questions are sexist. Every so often I read insane things like "Who is the next Lucille

Ball?" and they list all these red-haired actresses. As though the essence of Lucille Ball's talent was derived from the color of her hair.

More than half the questions I am asked are about the politics of the way I look. What it feels like to be not skinny/dark-skinned/a minority/not conventionally pretty/female/etc. It's not very interesting to me, but I know it's interesting to people reading an interview. Sometimes I get jealous of white male showrunners when 90 percent of their questions are about characters, story structure, creative inspiration, or, hell, even the business of getting a show on the air. Because as a result the interview of me reads like I'm interested only in talking about my outward appearance and the politics of being a minority and how I fit into Hollywood, blah blah blah. I want to shout, "Those were the only questions they asked!"

I find being young and female has its real workplace advantages, too (old men want to open up to you, people worry that you're cold). Have you found any?

I don't know how young I'm considered now (I'm 33) [*Lena: That is yooooung. I met a 98-year-old the other day!*], but when Greg [Daniels, executive producer of *The Mindy Project*] hired me at 24, I do think it was nice for both of us to be around someone with a completely different set of experiences. I was an overtly feminine child of immigrants with a big chip on my shoulder, and he was a gentle, thoughtful, gracious father of three. I think we learned from each other in cool ways.

I'm tactile and affectionate, and that is part of how I am on set with the actors, the crew, and the writers. I think it helps that I'm a woman, because I'm not sure how it would be construed if I were, say, a tall, older, physically imposing white man.

And I'm a feminist who wants to work with other feminists. I would wager that only a masochist sexist would want to work at a show with an opinionated female lead and showrunner. So I work with people who love women. That's a nice thing.

Do you get guilty? If so, what makes you feel guiltiest? I personally hate doing things I know are bad for my body, canceling plans on children, and speaking to my sister in a condescending way just because she's an undergraduate.

I feel so guilty when I upset my father or let him down. My dad is like the dad from *The Road*. He knows every highway in this country and what every building is made out of. He would do anything for me, and has done everything for me. Now I'm tearing up just writing this.

I also feel bad when I keep my writing staff late at work, even if it's for a good reason. Though I guess not that bad, because we stay late a lot.

I often feel guilty pointing out behavior in other women that I don't support. Like somehow, the moment I was pulled from my mother's severed stomach, a pen was placed in my tiny balled fist and I signed a binding document that says "I got all your backs, ladies." And the thing is, I do support women, but part of that is being clear about what behaviors aren't helping the bigger cause [of feminism].

I too feel guilty when I don't have knee-jerk unconditional love for all the decisions or all the art made by every woman I see. But that's OK. I think most educated and empathetic women probably feel the same way. Like, I don't like comedy shows where women play cutesy instruments as part of their comedy routine. But I don't like it when guys do that, either.

Who are your role models? Besides you, I would list my mother, Gilda Radner, Georgia O'Keeffe, Nora Ephron, Jane Campion, Jane Goodall, and Joan Rivers (plus Eloise and Pippi Longstocking).

You are. I love what a good writer you are, and I marvel at how much the camera loves you. I'm learning so much from younger people. A pet peeve of mine is when artists are asked who they love and they don't name anyone younger than them. They only give props to, like, super-old people or to dead ones like Dorothy Parker and Charlie Chaplin.

I love Tina Fey, Vince Gilligan, Jonathan Franzen. B.J. Novak continually inspires me. Lorne Michaels is so stylish and has perfect taste. I strive to be as balls-out funny as Danny McBride, though who could emulate that, really? Nora Ephron, not only as a writer and director, but also as a hostess, a wit, a New Yorker. These are artists I want to copy and impress.

As an overall person? I would say that my mother is the single biggest role model in my life, but that term doesn't seem to encompass enough when I use it about her. She was the love of my life.

Can you tell the readers of Rookie what inspires you about other women? I love seeing women stand up for things they believe in, teach their daughters how to do the same, prepare meals out of whatever they have in their fridges, wear helmets when they ride their bikes, call BS when they see it, and accept that feminism comes in a lotta different forms.

I love women who are bosses and who don't constantly worry about what their employees think of them. I love women who don't ask, "Is that OK?" after everything they say. I love when women are courageous in the face of unthinkable circumstances, like my mother when she was diagnosed with stage IV pancreatic cancer. Or like Gabrielle Giffords writing editorials for the *New York Times* about the cowardice of Congress regarding gun laws and using phrases like "mark my words" like she is Clint Eastwood. How many women say stuff like that? I love mothers who teach their children that listening is often better than talking. I love obedient daughters who absorb everything—being perceptive can be more important than being expressive. I love women who love sex and realize that sexual experience doesn't have to be the source of their art. I love women who love sex and can write about it in thoughtful, creative ways that don't exploit them, as many other people will use sex to exploit them. I love women who know how to wear menswear. ♛

Dear Rookies

Mindy Kaling and Judy Blume wanted to have a word with you.

Dear teenagers,

I think about you all the time. Sometimes with anger—because, let's face it, you tend to be very loud and inappropriately expressive on the subway—but more often with affection, because I know how hard this time is for you, and you are cute and don't know what the hell you are doing, like yearlings whose legs are still wobbly.

I'm 33, so I'm right at that adult crossroads where my attitude towards teens can go one of two ways:

1. I become one of those old cranks who think everyone younger than them is an entitled, bratty wuss with a lot of outlandish tech toys.

2. I become one of those simpering adults who are like, "I know what you're going through—it's *so hard* to be a youngster," and I put my hand on your shoulder and you're like, "What are you, my guidance counselor? Get off me."

To figure out which of these two competing outcomes I'm destined for, I thought I would make a case for each of them, Debate Club–style.

PATH NUMBER ONE: BEING A TEENAGER IS WAY EASIER NOW

You all have phones that your parents can't hop on. My dad used to get on our landline at home and interrupt phone calls with my friends by saying, "Is this really something you can't talk about tomorrow at school?" And I would want to die.

You have access to your heroes. When I was 15 I used to cry myself to sleep with how much I was in love with Dana Carvey and how I would never, ever get to meet or talk to him. Now, Dana Carvey would be on Twitter and I could send him Vines all

day of me doing the Church Lady and we'd probably be collaborating on a pilot.

Your bodies develop so much faster now. Thanks to genetic modification and hormone injections, the meat that's around now is basically making you all into Marvel Comics mutants. You get your periods at what, like eight? You have double-D boobs at nine? How cool is that? I started menstruating in ninth grade. I spent all of eighth grade faking that I had my period, down to sticking Kotex in my underwear in case anyone needed proof.

Computers. You can do your homework on your computer and bring your computer to school *and it's not even that heavy in your backpack.* When I was growing up, there was only one kid whose dad was rumored to own a laptop computer, and everyone thought that meant he was a pedophile. As a teen, I was forced to handwrite essays. In *cursive,* guys. Do you even know what cursive is? It's this pretentious, fancy handwriting so annoying it makes you want to curse. Actually, do you even know what *handwriting* is?

PATH NUMBER TWO: BEING A TEENAGER NOW IS BULLSHIT

You cannot escape your teenage years. I was disgusting as a teenager. My hair was greasy, I smelled weird, I wore stretchy boot-cut jeans two sizes too small, and I had terrible cystic acne that frequently gave me whiteheads. *Whiteheads on brown skin.* I was a monster. But according to the internet, I never really existed until I was 22. I am so lucky.

Everyone has to be everything. I was a pretty good student and had a couple of decent extracurricular activities, but I was by no means the best in my class, or even near the top. But I was still accepted into an Ivy League college. Now it feels like you

need to be a straight-A student, speak an obscure language, and also have spent a year living with brown bears or something to get into college. In the '90s you just had to be a pretty good kid and do OK on a standardized test.

You have to manage all your online personas. I would die if I were 15 and had to fill out a Facebook profile PLUS a Twitter bio PLUS update an Instagram to make myself appear cool and beguiling. And that's all on top of doing homework and chores and stuff. Also, I am a perfectionist and have an obsessive personality—and it was like 10 times worse when I was a teenager—so I basically would have never completed high school if social media had existed.

Live TV is basically gone. When I was a kid you would go home and everyone would be watching the same episode of *The X-Files* or *Friends* and the next day in school you'd all gab about how scared you were or how much you wanted to lose your virginity to David Schwimmer. Now no one watches any scripted television the actual time it's on, and it doesn't matter anyway because TV's basically all singing competitions.

I guess it is harder now. I don't envy you guys. Don't put anything you do on YouTube until you are 21.

Love, Mindy

Hi, Rookie readers.

I'm writing a novel right now that's set in the 1950s, a decade I know well because that's when I was a teenager. When my adorable husband tells me it's a historical novel I pretend to bash him over the head. You guys are farther removed from that decade than I was from the Roaring Twenties—you know, *The Great Gatsby*, and all those flapper dresses and beads.

I thought I hated the '50s. So boring. So bland. Every family pretending to be happy. But out of nowhere I got this idea for a book and it wouldn't let me go. I liked creative challenges as a teenager, and I guess I haven't changed that much because this one is a real challenge.

Speaking of changes, I can't believe how much *hasn't* changed since then. People stuff, relationship stuff—love and loss and friends and school and families. That's what I like to write about. OK, so we didn't have cellphones or computers and we didn't get our info online. We called our jeans *dungarees*, a high heel was three inches, and our favorite lipstick was *Pixie Pink*. (I know!) We slow-danced the night away unless we were doing the Lindy Hop, which was fun but left us sweaty and wondering if our deodorant was still working.

We worried about invasions from outer space and from the Communists. There were movies about werewolves and zombies, but they were too scary for me. Good girls didn't go all the way (but three of the top girls in my class were pregnant at graduation).

I stuffed my double-A bra and lied about getting my period. In sixth grade I pricked my finger to get enough blood to smear on a pad, then wore the pad to school to prove to my friends that I, too, had my period. When I actually got *it* I was 14, and it was spring of eighth grade. I was so anxious to be like everyone else—too anxious. I kept all my interesting thoughts and ideas to myself. I pretty much kept everything to myself and pretended to always be happy. Welcome to the '50s!

Mistakes weren't as public then. One of my mother's main concerns was with how other people saw us. *What will the neighbors think?* I can't imagine what my mother would think of Google. Personally, I have a love/hate relationship with Google. Love it for research and info, hate it for what it can do to an individual, especially someone young. A story gets out and you're cooked. You should be able to make mistakes. We all do—there's no way to grow up without making them. We should be able to admit our mistakes, learn from them, and move on. But if it's a public mistake it will follow you forever, thanks to Google. And that doesn't seem fair. A friend of mine from a political family told her kids, "Don't do anything you wouldn't want to read about in tomorrow's paper." That's pretty good advice.

I hope you have enough time to think and to dream, and to enjoy your lives. Sometimes it seems to me you're all so programmed there's no time left to just *be*. So have some fun! (The kind that won't wind up on the internet.)

Love, Judy

From Grimes's Sketchbook

Claire Boucher aka Grimes makes some of our favorite music.
Her illustrations are killer, too.

Dear Diary

Regular peeks into the lives of five teenage girls.

DYLAN

July 18, 2012

Going to an all-girls high school made me anything but enthusiastic about warm and fuzzy gatherings of females. There were a lot of "opportunities for sisterhood" that left me consistently uncomfortable and full of angst. I just couldn't relate to the "let's have a slumber party and braid each other's hair!" vibe that dominated my school, both in the classroom and in the cliques outside of it. Every year we had to go to these camping retreats designed to make everyone communally spill their guts in a ritual of forced sentimentality concerning WOMANHOOD and COMMUNITY. The whole thing left me apathetic about being a girl, embarrassed about being a teenager, and fundamentally uncomfortable with myself, despite having many very feminine and very adolescent interests. If this mushy version of community defined what it was like to have lots of teens or lots of girls in one place, I wasn't buying it. I couldn't think of anything less cool or less sincere than obligatory female bonding. Don't tell me what I'm supposed to love! I'll hug you if I feel like it!

Then last weekend I went to the San Francisco Rookie meetup, and I was exposed to a whole new set of vibes that eradicated all traces of cynicism in my JADED, JADED 19-year-old heart about gaggles of teen girls getting together and eating ice cream and hugging. OK, the way I phrased that is sending me back into my apathy zone again…but seeing the community manifest itself in Dolores Park, which is where I normally go to drink on weekends and pretend I'm cool, defied my negative associations regarding large gatherings of women being awesome and in love with one another. It can be real, it can

be cool, and I can get into it. Really into it. I was, like, *really* intensely into it.

I also finally had the chance to assault the Road Trip crew with the hugs I've been saving for the past 10 months as I've gotten to know them in our Rookie Office in the Sky (the internet—they are not ghosts). I was pleasantly surprised by how weird they are. This magazine is made by total FREAKS. And I love them. My adolescence is on its deathbed, y'all, and I am glad that before I get to the crippling age of 20, I've gotten to feel how awesome it all was, and is, and forever will be. Thanks for not sucking, everyone, I like you, and I hope to see you next week in L.A.!

August 22

Anywhere you grow up will disappoint you in some way. Seattle was often frustrating for me, because, DUH, I spent my adolescence here—*every*thing was frustrating. But I turn 20 on Friday, and I don't have room for teen angst anymore. While there are plenty of things that can never be adulted out of me, I recently decided it was time for me to retire my Seattle angst. The minute I stopped resenting it, I fell all the way in love with my hometown.

I'm there now, going through old stuff because my mom is moving in with her boyfriend on Saturday. This is the weekend when everything comes to an end, pretty much. I'm looking at it all laid out in front of me. All of my memories are mine, though, and I still get to keep them forever.

No one else has these:

I'm 16. Growing up on Capitol Hill means that my second-grade soccer games were played at the park across the block from the clubs where I go see my friends' bands now. "Posse on Broadway" name-drops my cross-streets. That mindblowing mural of a

pterodactyl eating a Metro bus on the side of the bookstore on Broadway and John hasn't been torn down for the light-rail station yet because it's only 2008! Growing up on Capitol Hill means that everything is around me all the time and I try my best to absorb all of it and I owe my life as I know it to this place.

◆ ◆ ◆

I'm 12. There's this group of six boys that are the current loved-or-hated band of the city. Of course, I LOVE THEM. Love makes me a Myspace fangirl, and I go to every one of their all-ages shows. So far, that's seven or so. They put up with—even encourage—my tweenage enthusiasm, and now I'm not just a fan, but a li'l baby-size friend. Yeah, we're totallllly friendz.

◆ ◆ ◆

Now I'm 15. They eventually put me in their liner notes *and* their Myspace Top 8, which is the pinnacle of my life on the internet!! They also introduce me to a whole new sphere of the city, the one where the music is, and that changes everything. I don't suspect that they realize their impact on me. Thank you, guys.

◆ ◆ ◆

I'm 14. I finally get to sell my handmade hair accessories at the most delightful store in the world. I start bonding with the owner, and she becomes my creative mentor and life coach as her store becomes my second home. She's taking me backstage at the Gorge to meet my favorite band for my 15th birthday; she dresses me up and lets me walk in her legendary fashion shows; she allows me to hang at her shop every afternoon like she's my babysitter, but she calls me her *intern*, and I learn about how to run a business and plan a grand fête as I try on '50s prom dresses under the watchful eye of my pink-haired guru. Her cat, Vincent, is the closest thing I have to a boyfriend.

♦ ♦ ♦

I'm 15. The afternoons not spent at the shop are spent at the record store on 15th Avenue with my best friend, who is a grade above me at my high school. We met at that record store three years ago. We buy our vinyl and occupy the organicfairtradesustainablelocalsolarpoweredsoyflavored coffee shop across the street to complain about our high school and scheme about our upcoming, more exciting social life, which consists of going to a show every single weekend because there's nothing I've ever liked to do more, and I now have an ideal partner in crime.

♦ ♦ ♦

I'm 18. My prom is inside the Space Needle, so.

♦ ♦ ♦

I'm 15. Weezer has been my favorite band since I was 12. I loathe anything they did after 1997, but I love the first two albums so much that I'm certified obsessed. Message-board obsessed. They're playing a secret show at the all-ages venue I work and basically live at, and today is the day I will tell the guitarist Brian Bell that he was my junior-high crush. I will tell him this with a bite of burrito in my mouth, and I will never regret it because it will be the most surreal moment of all time.

♦ ♦ ♦

I'm 12. My K–8 offers a Friday night ski bus for middle-schoolers, which means I get to spend three winters of my life snowboarding weekly with all of my friends. Everything happens on ski bus: makeouts, breakups, concussions, Red Bull overdoses. This might be the most fun I will ever have.

♦ ♦ ♦

I'm 19. Ski bus totally might still be the most fun I've ever had.

♦ ♦ ♦

I'm 12, or 16, or 20 or 50 or 90. I spend all rare moments of Seattle sun on the shores of Lake Washington, where on a clear day the mountain is out and it will literally melt anyone into a puddle. Lots of life happens there: It's where I take my friends for drunk swims off the dock on summer nights, where I have opened many a bottle of wine with my bare hands because I'm a teenage animal. It's where I've spent every hot day of the year at Madison Beach since I was five years old. It's where my mom and I take my dog for rehabilitating swims after the life-threatening knee surgery he got when he was seven. It gives me so much, and it is my favorite.

♦ ♦ ♦

Nothing was perfect and everything was what it was supposed to be. I got to be a teenager in a beautiful place. Now, I thank everything.

September 5
Well, it's over.

It's been a year since I started telling you everything about my life on a weekly basis for this here magazine for teen girls. Crazy! This year just so happened to be my last as a teenager, and just like my PERISHING YOUTH, this column has an expiration date. It's time for me to graduate from the Teen Girl Diary Zone and get old already.

This was the year when I finally got to live out my childhood dreams, such as living in a music venue, wreaking havoc in Los Angeles, throwing shows in my backyard, and actually enjoying school. I won my dream apartment and crushed on a dude or two and realized that since I live with my friends and my friends are always over, my life is actually a constant slumber party. Cross those off the list.

It did get real real, though, when things like theft and violence and money con

cerns started pushing through the security blanket of being young and protected from such worries. But it's OK, because this harshness is inevitable—it's part of the contract for becoming an adult. Good times are optional, and it's on us to find them.

I liked sharing all of those ups and downs with you each Wednesday. Thank you for being cool and nonjudgmental enough for me to put sometimes intense, sometimes embarrassing, sometimes stupid stuff here. And thank you for bearing witness to my first year of thinking, *This is my life, and finally, it's working.* It wouldn't have been as special without you. ♥

BRITNEY

October 3, 2012
My 13th birthday has come and gone, but I still don't quite feel like a teenager, and I don't know when I will. I realized this the other day in gym class, while about half of the kids in my grade were waiting to get measured as part of our annual fitness test.

The gym was filled with sweaty eighth-graders running around and making noise. Two of my best friends were bored; someone got the idea to steal my socks. This led to our running around with one another's socks and notebooks, screaming, "FIGHT CLUB!" every few minutes. Eventually we collapsed on the floor, laughing and trying to catch our breath. That's when I saw a couple of other girls—girls I have known since sixth grade—watching us, shaking their heads. "There's a time and a place for being immature," one of them said. "And now is not the time."

My playmates and I laughed it off, but I was left worrying that it was true—were we too old to act immature in gym class? Were my sock-flinging and tickling days over? Would I henceforth be forced to sit around with a fake smile plastered on my face, nodding politely at the "mature" conversation topics of my peers—high school admissions tests, One Direction videos, etc.?

I keep telling myself that being a teenager—being a human in general—is about having fun when you want to. But that's hard to do when everyone around me seems to be growing up so fast.

November 7

Last week I was planning on showing some of my friends a story that I wrote. When I took it out, though, I had a sudden thought: *What if I'm not the great writer that I thought I was? What if everyone laughs at me? This is stupid. I hate my writing.* I shoved it back into the depths of my binder and refused to let anyone see it. My friends protested, saying they liked my writing, but I decided that they must've thought I was fishing for compliments and couldn't be honest about how terrible I really was.

The same thing happened when my best friend recently told me that I was pretty. I refused to believe her; I protested so violently that she ended the conversation altogether, and now we're not talking. I never believe people when they compliment me. What's wrong with me? Why can't I just take in what they're saying and be happy about it? Sometimes compliments make me feel *worse*.

I can remember a time when compliments made me feel good. Since then, though, I've gotten a good share of insults, too, and those felt much more weighty. They got into my head, and eventually made any praise I received feel different—and suspect. Insults can be very persuasive that way. Now if someone tries to flatter me, I instantly shut them down. I don't believe them.

I wish I could stop being like this—it's wrecking my friendships, my self-esteem, my personality, my life.

December 26

It all started with a book.

A few days ago I checked a copy of *Feminism: Opposing Viewpoints* out from the school library. Then I made the mistake of putting the book down on my desk while I was in science class. And thus began an all-out war.

First the classmate who was sitting across from me picked up the book, took a look, and said, "Feminism? Why do we need feminism? It's useless. Women can wear pants and vote now. That's enough for me." She proceeded to flip through the book and point out how stupid it was. A boy sitting next to me said, "You're right, we don't need feminism. Women belong in the kitchen."

I tried to remain calm. I explained that we still need feminism because women and men still aren't seen as equal in our society. They shot a few misogynistic slurs my way, the worst of which was *feminazi*.

The period ended right after that insult was flung, but apparently word got around. Every class I went to, I was greeted by people yelling, "FEMINAZI!" Then some genius made up the nickname Adolf Britler, and people started standing up and saying, "Heil Britler!" when I walked into the room. I know I should have told a teacher, but I feel like the adults at my school wouldn't think I had a strong enough case to charge anyone with bullying.

Instead, I just tried to ignore everything. I tried to ignore it when a friend said that yes, I pretty much was a feminazi, so what was wrong with people calling me one? I tried to ignore it when another friend said that the name Adolf Britler was funny and that I should loosen up. I tried to ignore it when I walked into math class and a bunch of people stood up and yelled, "HEIL BRITLER!" while making a Nazi salute.

But that last incident broke me. I couldn't ignore it anymore. I had so much anger built up, so many urges I had squelched to throw something and scream and run out of school and never stop running. I shouted, "WHAT IS WRONG WITH YOU? STOP IT! I HATE ALL OF YOU!" It wasn't the best comeback, but I wasn't exactly thinking clearly. I slid down in my seat and started to cry.

A girl sitting next to me turned around to face the saluters and said, "What's wrong with you? You made her cry!" They all sat down, murmuring softly to one another. Then the girl who had picked up my book in the first place (who also turned out to be the one who made up "Adolf Britler") leaned over to me and whispered, "I'm so sorry, Britney."

Luckily we had a test that day, so no one had to talk for the rest of class. I'm still glad I checked out that book, though. It's nice to have evidence that outside of my school there are people who care about the things I care about. Maybe I'll meet them someday.

May 1, 2013

1. Denial

I reread the message from Zoey's* sister every day, trying to unscramble the words. It can't be right—my friend Zoey can't be dead. I feel like some sick joke has been played on me. In fact, every day since it happened, I've woken up and hoped I'd get a message saying that none of this was real, and that all of my tears were for nothing. I have never wished so much for something to be untrue before. I still can't think the words *she's dead* and actually believe them. I won't let myself, because I might really lose it if I do. I just want to cling to the thought that this will all sort itself out and we will be back talking to each other in French next week and laughing about life.

2. Anger

Why is she dead? Almost everyone that I've formed a close connection with—even if I don't know them personally—is gone. People keep telling me that I couldn't have done anything, and I know that they're right, but a part of me refuses to believe it. Talking doesn't help much either. One friend of mine noticed that I wasn't myself today and asked about it, and I spilled everything as we walked from math class to homeroom, but that was the only truly natural conversation that I have had so far that didn't make me either (a) tear up or (b) hate myself even more. The two most infuriating things that people have told me are "she's in a better place now" and "she was so young."

3. Bargaining

What if I had talked to her more in these past couple of weeks? What if I'd elaborated on the fact that I thought—and continue to think—that she was an amazing friend and person, and that she helped me through so much? WHAT IF?

4. Depression

I wake up thinking about it and go to sleep thinking about it. There is no escape. Any happiness that I feel is temporary. I feel lost all the time. I want to talk to people, but if

---

* Name has been changed.

I do, I feel sick—physically. At least when I'm alone I can cry freely or do whatever I feel like doing (which is usually more crying). The only person I would be completely content talking to right now is Zoey.

5. Acceptance
No. I wish.

What do I wish? I feel like it's time to move on, even though some part of me wants to remain in the past. I need to believe, for the sake of my own health, that there is no way that I could have stopped her. I can't hold on to this for the rest of my life. I've been wearing my grief like a coat, too weighed down to go back to just being me, the person who likes to write and read and say stupid things to my friends.

I fear that "moving on" means forgetting Zoey. I fear that not moving on means forgetting everything else, especially myself.

NAOMI

June 13, 2012
When I am reading my old diary entries, or looking at photos of a younger me, I can never get my head around it that that was ME. I was there, I wrote that. Those thoughts came from the same mind that is writing this now. I have to think very hard to even remember what this time last year was actually like. I wish I could bridge the gap between the past me and me now, because I feel oddly detached from myself. I look back and think, *Whoa, how did I get here?*

Sometimes I am able to have an odd perspective: I realize that one day I will look back at this time and at everything that feels so intense to me now, and it will all feel just as remote as my old diaries do today. I will look at a picture that will sum up a whole year or more of how I used to dress, how I wore my hair. The news that infiltrates my life every evening—the fighting in Syria, the Leveson media inquiry, the European economy in absolute turmoil—will be just points on a timeline, no more significant than any other event over the decades. And although at 18 I feel incredibly old and reasonably wise, I know that one day I will see how young and naïve I really am.

The further away you get from something, the harder it is to remember, and that's good, in a way. Especially if you don't want a bad experience hanging over you. But I wish I could hold all my experiences at once. I wish I could hold my whole life so far in the palm of my hand and feel it as it really was.

September 19
I am trying to think of things that have happened to me in the last week that might actually be interesting to other people. But the thing is, I feel so NORMAL. Going back to an actual school and managing my anxiety have made me feel slightly BORING. And of course, NORMAL and BORING are horrible things that I do not want to be. But going to school and overcoming anxiety—those are things I am sure I wanted.

My old therapist warned me about this phenomenon that occurs when you are recovering from something such as anxiety or depression, where it feels like you are losing, or have already lost, a part of yourself. It feels like you've lost a limb, or a chunk of your personality. It is a horrible horrible trick. I've felt pangs of it once or twice recently. A "who am I now?" feeling. What actually makes up who I am? Isn't so much of me made of trying to overcome something that has been in my way—self-doubt, panic attacks, low moods, tons and tons of anxiety? It's been such a long process, from my lowest point to now—why would I ever want to throw all that work away? Doesn't that struggle define me?

Though I've felt ashamed or embarrassed about much of what I've experienced, not being NORMAL has at least been something to differentiate me from everybody else. *Now* what differentiates me? Today I seriously looked at university for the first time and found a course and a uni that I would actually like to go to. *Just like everybody else.*

It's a weird feeling. How do you people cope?

October 31
I had nerves like blunt pins in my chest, neck, and mouth. Because I was "going out" to a new place. Out in the world—at night. It had been a long time since I'd stepped out into darkness, and there was no telling what I would find there.

I made my bed, turned off the lights, kissed Dad goodbye, and hauled my overnight bag to the car, then my mum gave me a lift to my friend Kate's* house. The whole way I was chewing gum nervously, holding tension in my jaw.

As soon as I got there I dyed my hair purple. I hadn't planned to, but suddenly I found myself leaning over her bath with mulberry water dripping from my head. I felt infused with magic—with spontaneity and mischief and everything I haven't let myself enjoy for the past few years. My hair felt like a barometer for the rest of my night.

Kate and I called a taxi and waited outside. Through the car's steamy windows I could decipher only pinpricks of light. By the time we got to our destination, the whole world was shrouded in a thick mist, like we were held inside our own special sphere. Our world was adorned: cocktails, disco lights spraying circles over the dance floor, the lights reflected in people's eyes, Kate's and my freshly dyed hair—all were jewel coloured. I danced and got lost. Only occasionally would I realise where I actually was, and *how* I was.

A boy was there: Donald from my college ("high school" to you Americans). He lives nearby. I had told him he had to come out so he could walk me to my grandparents' house, where I was spending the night. We left the party just before midnight. The streets were majestically quiet. The yellowing streetlights illuminated the thick patches of mist, making the whole scene look like a film set. It was impossible for our voices not to be too loud. Donald is really cool, and I felt safe.

When we got to my grandparents' house—all three storeys of it—he seemed impressed. I didn't want to go inside just yet. We both knew of a certain bench on the street, and we sat on it for a little while. Apart from the occasional passing car lights, the world felt empty except for us two. I could have talked to him all night.

---

*All names have been changed.

But I said, "I am so tired." He said, "Do you want me to walk you to your door?"

Lying in an unfamiliar bed, I couldn't sleep, despite feeling heavy tiredness through every limb. My eyes would close, but my brain was on fire, still excited and, on reflection, glad to be alive.

I didn't feel like a fraud at any point in the evening. My fun wasn't faked. I was me—but a new me I hadn't met yet. That was the most exciting part. In the early hours of the morning, I felt precious—but strong like a stone.

December 26
My perception of men has changed very swiftly in the space of a few months. Whereas I used to be all "people are people," now I very distinctly separate men from women. In my eyes, men are the Other.

I don't like this. It does not correlate with my feminist principles or my belief in complete equality among all genders. I hate it when I catch myself referring to "boys" or "men" as a single entity, lumping them all into the same pile of clichés and stereotypes. It just doesn't feel right.

But recently I've started to discern a dividing line, delineated by the slight brush of an arse in a pub, or the groan at a brief mention of male privilege in a classroom. And all the touching—so much touching. My body is a battleground, an object disconnected from my personhood. It just has another waist for an arm to be placed around, another "front" (as a teacher called my boobs) to make a joke about. This same body has been touched this year in private, in a way that hasn't made me uncomfortable at all. So I have been thinking a lot about the differences between the wanted touch, the unwanted touch, and the touches in the grey area in between.

I have also recently experienced what feels like a gender divide in terms of honesty in romantic relations. People are always saying that "men are all the same," and I have never believed that. But when I think about the guys I've known lately, that old cliché is starting to gather some force. And then I think about how much I hate it when people say the same thing about women. I know we're not all the same.

A bright note is that while 2012 has cast doubt on my opinions about relationships with boys, it has only strengthened my friendships with women and girls. I feel so inspired by the women I know, who have held me up when I've felt as thin as cardboard (possibly because of certain guys). These women didn't have to listen to me rant and rave, to be patient with me, to let me make my own mistakes and try to give advice, but they did. And when they tell me I am beautiful, I believe it deep down, because I know that they understand the true meaning of beauty. And when they tell me I am a good enough person, I believe it, because they are too.

January 23, 2013
I am trying to build up the nerve to write about something, but part of me feels scared and part of me feels stupid. Part of me feels like a child with too many feelings.

But let me not lie or hide anymore. I have wasted too much thinking on this particular incident—but less and less each day, like an unwinding clock that must eventually come to a stop. I wasn't thinking even about him; I was thinking about me. I was thinking about my part in this game, and how playing it changed parts of me that I had thought immutable.

Part of what lured me into the game was that it was the first time this had properly happened to me—*this* being connecting in that way with another human being (or so I thought). I felt warm inside, full, floating. It wasn't really him, it was the experience that was enamouring. Now that all feels like a complete illusion, but back then it felt intensely real. That was in October. By November I was lost.

He was only one person among billions, but still, kissing him seemed incredibly important. Eventually he said he didn't want to "mess [me] around" because I was "too nice for that"—like he thought I was some fragile little bird that couldn't fend for itself. A number of things he said made me angry, but that was the biggest one.

I hung on to my feelings for him a lot longer than I wanted to. They had somehow become deeply embedded in such a short time. I think it is possibly one of the worst feelings to care about someone more than they care about you. It doesn't help when they are dishonest. It makes you feel weak and helpless.

That already feels like a long time ago. Now it's just a blot on the setting sun of last year. I'm not sure if I learned anything from it, but part of me feels like it knows something new.

April 24
Some days certain societal expectations/conventions get to be too much for me, and I have the urge to retreat, but I feel torn. I'm expected to go out and have "fun" all the time, to have a boyfriend, to have girlfriends, to be popular, to be clever, to know everything, to be interesting, to get good grades but not be a smartass, to look pretty, to wear nice clothes, to be happy, to be nice to everyone, to not get angry, to not have feelings, to not cry (but not be heartless either). To be independent, self-sufficient, stoic; to keep it together on my own, and not rely on others. To not get tired, to have good posture, to be fit and healthy, to eat enough but not too much, to exercise, to hold my alcohol, to know my future, to not get scared. To have a clean bedroom, to live a clean life but not be a goody-goody, to be fun and easygoing but not kiss too many strangers, to not be a prude or a virgin, but not be a slut either. To not be annoying or irritating, not like anybody too much, not be a hassle of a friend, not an attention-seeker, don't be needy, don't be too nice but be careful not to be selfish. To be tough, to not show weakness or naïveté or ignorance, to have an opinion but not too *much* of an opinion, to speak up but always know my place.

It's this and more every single day, and it's exacerbated by people I know and people I meet who neither acknowledge nor even try to comprehend the massive pressure placed on women in this world and the connection between that and women's rights or (whisper the word) feminism. People who don't get why I might want to live in a society where these pressures don't have the power to make me, my friends, and other teenage girls feel intensely bad about ourselves.

A discussion in my politics class this week added a whole new bundle of demands to the list: Don't go to therapy (it doesn't work), don't take medication (you'll just build up a reliance), don't like Sylvia Plath (she is a "narcissistic bitch"), don't argue that Sylvia Plath wasn't a narcissistic bitch (it was "just an opinion"), don't have any constructive discussions, but rather just throw your stubborn opinions at one another.

I'm a young woman living in a country that has normalised the sexualisation and objectification of women to such an extent that the biggest-selling tabloid newspaper features a topless female model on the third page of every issue, but what some people seem to find far more objectionable is the idea of a woman pointing a mirror at herself, staring at her own reflection, and exploring more than her appearance. Sylvia Plath wrote about her psyche, her pains, and her pleasures. She wrote about the limited roles in life available to her as a woman in the 1950s and early '60s, and how those constraints drove her to despair, depression, and self-destruction. Even if her writing is not exactly to your taste, surely you can appreciate what an achievement *The Bell Jar* was, and you must be able to see, if not enjoy, Plath's astonishing talent? But apparently some people find nothing to admire in a person who, in the midst of a culture that constantly told her that her value was as a wife and a mother and nothing more, became well-known and earned the respect of a male-dominated literary scene by writing about her private life, thoughts, and emotions—no, that just makes her a "narcissistic bitch."

My politics class is full of strongly opinionated boys, and it is hard to make my voice heard over theirs. It's also tough to keep my passion and anger down, to force my words into coherence, in any debate or argument that means something to me. There was a study last fall that concluded that women speak less when surrounded by men. I've noticed this tendency in myself, in class, at social occasions, and with family and friends. I will keep trying, though. I don't care how small I feel, how worn down, how doubtful—I will continue to express my thoughts, feelings,

and opinions, because I don't know who I would be otherwise. Maybe this also makes me a "narcissistic bitch." Well then, I'm in good company.

May 1
My first week of being 19 was pretty average. I noticed I'm doing things that a part of me feels 19-year-olds shouldn't do: going for walks without a destination, looking for little things like a blossom forming, the church spire, a spot on the horizon. Do adults always have somewhere to go, somewhere to be? In the garden, gliding through the air on a swing I've had since childhood, I stopped and thought, *Can a 19-year-old do this?*

With each year and each new number, I'm still kind of waiting for life to start, expecting to get prettier, to gain intelligence, to become my "best self." But this imagined zenith where everything comes together must not be the most important part of life, otherwise why do books always focus on the confusion and pain it takes to get there instead of the bliss and relative boredom of being content? At least with a book you know there is an ending, a certain number of pages left before the story can continue only in your head. (Does happiness continue until the end of the protagonist's life?) I can't see where my final page is, but I often feel as if I am scrambling to get there, to find out how it all turns out.

I am slowly trying to come to terms with not knowing. Looking back to the beginning of this academic year, I can see that I knew nothing. Well, I knew about staying at home, the Smiths, feminism, the latest news, and studying for exams—but that's really it. I've grown a lot. I think I finally feel on top of things. I am intensely looking forward to going to university in the fall, and I frequently imagine myself there. I make up stories in my head for Future Me: what my bedroom will look like, what meals I'll cook, what clothes I'll wear, what music I'll listen to, and the people I'll meet.

Imagination is addictive. We haven't had a proper hot day yet this year, so I keep visualising lying in the sun, pure heat on my bare skin. In bed at night, I can almost

feel it. I feel powerful when my recollection is that vivid. Whatever happens from now on, I'll always have that.

KATHERINE

June 6, 2012
Graduation felt like it lasted a year, but it was really only three hours. Four if you count the hour before the service when all of the seniors got ready in the back rooms of the megachurch where the service was held. I seemed to be one of a rare few who liked the graduation caps. They're kind of swim-cap chic, and you can put things on top of them. Totes fab. Totes cute.

Everyone mulled around and talked about how fast it had all gone by and took pictures with one another. I just watched. They all seemed either sad or relieved, but I don't think I could really feel anything. I'd spent so much of the year feeling frustrated with my school that in my mind I had already graduated. I had closed the door, and this was the final click of the lock.

As each person gets their diploma, the headmaster always reads out three to four descriptions that the teachers brew up for the occasion. The best were the cheesy ones, like "FIND HIM AT THE GOLF COURSE" or "STILL WATERS RUN DEEP." When my turn came, my first adjective was *indie*, which made me kind of screw up my face and be super confused for the rest of forever. Like, what does that mean? Am I a music label, one that makes very little money but has a good reputation in the blogosphere?

After graduation, the whole grade took a boat cruise. We were finally able to dance to explicit music in a school setting, and everyone smoked cigars and pipes with the teachers. I was giddily laughing as I lit my cigar next to the dean of students. He told me to get a grip, which made me laugh even harder. I spent the rest of the ride at the front of the boat, looking out on the water and embracing my lonerism while secretly betting with myself about how many people would come up and talk to me. I talked to one of my classmates about Harry Styles, Christopher Owens, and RuPaul for forever. Another kid told me that he was just glad that we were finally in "the real world" and that all of the kids in our grade suddenly seemed *so real*. YA KNOW? Because everyone in high school is imaginary until the minute you smoke a cigar and sing along to "Crazy Rap" and you magically become flesh and blood.

I've spent the last few days alone in my room, wasting my time reading every blog and article on the internet. I'm watching too much TV, eating incredible amounts of candy, not getting any sun, and writing more in my diary than I have all year. Most of it is speculation on whether the people I've built up in my mind as my friends are actually my friends, whether it's my fault that I'm a loner, and how I can maybe change that. I don't want to sit around and think about how the girl I call my best friend has only once invited me to do anything with her in the past four years or how every time I invite anyone new to anything, they stand me up. I've moved on from caring what they think of me. Which is good, because those friendships were never really right. Which is bad, because now I'm at a point where I need people to talk to. To hang out with.

I bought two tickets to a Justin Bieber concert next year. I unironically and unconditionally love his music. I just about pee my pants every time I think about it. Hopefully, by next year, I will have someone to go to that concert with.

August 1
Wednesday night, I hung out with my grandmother. We were both about to change our scenes. She was about to return home from rehab (she had a hip replacement a few weeks ago), and I was flying to Los Angeles the next morning to hang out with the Rookies. "Are you ready?" she asked me. I said I wasn't.

When I got home, I stared at everything I had laid out on my floor to bring. I do this whenever I'm about to travel: stare zombie-style at all of my clothes and crap and prepare myself for the trip. I ran everything over in my mind. My flights, the order of the Rookie events, the people I would see. Since this trip would be my graduation present from my grandmother

and uncle, they put me in the W Hotel in Hollywood. Also, since my parents were being so loving and caring (obnoxiously overprotective), they wanted to make sure I had a chaperone of sorts—someone over 18 who would look after me, keep me in line. They acquiesced to the trip as soon as I'd found someone of age willing to perform that duty. WHO WAS DYLAN OMG OMG OMG. So thank you, parents, for being frustratingly untrusting, because Dylan is so fly.

The W Hotel is the funniest thing ever. It's the kind of place Tom Haverford would dream about all of the time. Ninety percent of the women there wore these dresses that were like HERE'S MY BODY, and all of the dudes looked like wannabe CEOs. The spy holes on the doors were bedazzled, there was a gourmet-dog-food menu, and the walls of the elevators were covered in some sort of sparkly faux snakeskin. Basically, everything sparkled. It was a million degrees removed from the world I'm used to. Are there people who are actually used to this kind of thing? People who feel like this is where they belong and this is what they deserve?

When I got to the hotel, I met up with Dylan and her friends, and we immediately hit the ROOFTOP POOL like the SUPERSTARS we are. The pool was more hilarity, because the music was all *unst unst unst* and *boop da doop*. People wore bikini thongs and drank crazy-expensive cocktails. Dylan and I attempted to lay out on floaties in the pool. Dylan succeeded. I failed. Luxury is hard, yo.

We went to go see Mindy Kaling do a Q&A at the Rookie event that night. I got to meet all the Rookies for the first time. It felt very unreal as it was happening. Afterward, a bunch of us hung out at a diner. Dylan, her friend, and I returned to the hotel and danced in our room all night. We called the front desk and ordered these white bathrobes. At one point, we ran through the halls, pulling the Do Not Disturb tickets out of every door and throwing them on the ground, laughing maniacally. It's my new favorite game.

We drove around L.A. the next day and ended up hanging out in Los Feliz.

We listened to awesome people read at the Rookie event Friday night and got to read ourselves. We jammed out at a King Tuff concert that was SO RAD, then we had a sleepover in our hotel with a bunch o' Rookies. We ate junk food and stayed up telling first-kiss stories. I felt weird for a little bit because I didn't have one, but it's not even that big of a deal. All the same, could someone just make out with me already? Like, I brush my teeth, I swear.

Friday night, when everyone else went to sleep, I stayed awake. I never wanted to close my eyes. I kept on replaying everything that had happened to me in L.A. I just kept on thinking, *I love this, I love this, I love this*. I replayed again and again all of us trying to go up to the rooftop pool after it had closed for what looked like a private party. Dressed in bathrobes, we sneakily took the freight elevator up to the top floor, opened the door to the pool, and were met by an angry security guard barking, "Seven intruders, SEVEN INTRUDERS" into his walkie-talkie. We hightailed it back to the elevator, dying of laughter.

I stayed up thinking about everyone who had read at the Rookie story hour, as well as everyone's first-kiss stories. I think the fact that we had talked so much that night was what kept me up. I was in love with everyone's stories and energy—the world felt like it was a place filled with people who were creative and thoughtful and had great capacities to love.

Everything felt important, because Rookie has been so important to me. As I was slowly losing my friends at home, I was given *all of this*. This community of people with stories that make me feel like everything is bursting with meaning. It's like being inside of a Kay Ryan poem.

Right now I'm in San Francisco with my aunt and uncle and my new cousin. I'm exhausted, but I still don't want to go to sleep. I want to be back in L.A., listening to stories. Falling in love with everyone and wishing that I would never have to go home.

There's this part in Stephen Fry's autobiography where he talks about the first boy he ever fell in love with when he was younger. After seeing this kid, he went back to his dorm and took out a piece of paper. On it, he wrote, "I love Matthew Osborne." He thought for a moment, realized that wasn't all he felt, and wrote underneath, "Everything is different."

This is how I feel now, except it isn't about a boy or anything. It's about these people and this city. I wish this was everyone and here was everywhere. Does that make sense?

It's like this: I love Rookie and L.A. and stories and writing and meeting people. I love almost getting in trouble at a stupid sparkly hotel and dancing at shows. I love staying up all night because I love all of these things, and I love wondering and hoping that everybody feels this way too.

I love all of this.

Everything is different.

January 23, 2013

HEYYY SQUIRRELS! HEY LADIEEESSS!!!! WAZZZUUUUUUUUUUUUPPPPP???????? Was your week totally wicked? Have you listened to Carly Rae Jepsen's *Kiss* in its entirety? Were you wearing a sequined fedora, a tutu, or anything covered in glitter last Friday night? Because if you were, there's a chance that you were with me—at the Justin Bieber concert. (!!!!!!!!!!!!!!!!!!!!!!!!!!)

I had been looking forward to this momentous occasion for a week. I listened to JB's music nonstop every day and made out with my poster right before my brother and I left for the show. JK. But I did give it a little peck on my way out the door.

When we got there, there were SO MANY PEOPLE. Apprehensive-looking parents clutched their daughters' hands as they made their way through the crowd, an ocean of tweenagers wearing anything with Justin Bieber's face on it. Shout-out to all the ladies in the crowd wearing all purple (Justin's favorite color, OBV).

This concert was somuchfun. Carly Rae Jepsen opened, and I died when she sang "This Kiss" and "Your Heart Is a Muscle." These two girls got to go up and dance with her while she sang "Call Me Maybe," and I got to seethe with jealousy. THEN, when I felt I could wait no longer, Justin came on stage. He didn't really come on stage. He flew.

You guys, it was ridiculous. He descended in this harness attached to a giant pair of metal wings. The two girls sitting next to us, apparently veteran Bieber concertgoers, had warned us that everyone would lose their shit when he came out, but I was still unprepared for the craziness that is thousands of kids simultaneously expressing their sexual desire for Justin Bieber. They screamed, they jumped up and down, they shouted lyrics at the top of their lungs. Every time he showed a sliver of stomach, they screamed even louder. I have nothing valuable to say about what Bieber is to young people that Kitty Pryde has not already said, but I can tell you that it was fun/hilarious/my favorite thing that I have ever been lucky enough to see.

Also important was that after Bieber sang "Boyfriend" he placed one finger in front of his mouth and shushed the entire crowd. This took a minute, but when all was silent, he lowered his hand and asked us, "Who wants to be my baby?" And then everyone basically fainted.

I'm going to be riding a Bieber-induced high for weeks.

February 20

I just watched the *Girls* episode from last week—"One Man's Trash"—and it was super super good as always, and in the middle of the episode, I had a breakthrough.

In the episode, Hannah (the lead character, played by Lena Dunham) has sex with this dude she just met, and he tells her she's beautiful, and she's like, "You really think so?" and he's like, "Don't you?" and she goes, "I do, it's just not always the feedback that I've been given." That last line was the one that jolted me. It was insta-empowering.

I have made no secret in this diary about my love for Samantha Jones, who is a kind of role model to me in terms of doing whatever the hell you want without worrying about what anyone else thinks. She's also the only main character on *Sex and the City* who doesn't do this annoying thing where if someone says they're sexy or beautiful they have to be all, "Who, ME, sexy??!" As if these women aren't just constantly walking up to any cute man they

see and winning them over in under a minute. They're attractive, (usually) confident women with whom half of *SATC*'s version of New York wants to have sex. Their reactions remind me of how I usually respond to any compliment, even if I actually think I look fancy as hell/hawt/adorable that day. What Hannah did by admitting that she thinks of herself as beautiful was, as Phoebe put it later in our Super Not So Secret Rookie Staff Group on Facebook, "such an affront to being coy and self-deprecating."

A few years ago I was working as a camp counselor at an all-girls summer camp. On the penultimate night of camp, all the counselors decided to go skinny-dipping. So we all walked down to the lake and stripped down and jumped in. Fun. Neat. Great.

But then this one girl, my best friend at the camp, looked at my boobs and laughed. She started making fun of them and then everyone else laughed at them too. One girl said they looked "like lopsided meringues."

I laughed along with them. Then, when everyone else had moved on, I got out of the lake, picked up my towel, walked back to my cabin, and went to bed. I didn't talk to anyone the next day except when I needed to.

For a while, I thought it was good that they had told me that I had two hideous meringue sprouts attached to my chest. I thought that I must have been stupid before and that they caught me before I had a chance to develop an unwarranted sense of confidence.

The thing is, I think my boobs look really fucking awesome. Like lopsided meringues. And I recently let my armpit hair go wild because I wanted to see what it looked like. And it looks awesome with my meringue boobs. Around where I live, in the South, pit hair is not considered a "cool" way to look, but the instant I got my first sprouts of hair I was like DAMN THIS LOOKS GOOD. I know that not everyone sees it that way. So when I'm around other people I still feel less than spectacular. But when I'm alone, I feel like a fucking queen.

Although the feedback about my face or body has not been historically stellar, I don't have to pretend I don't think I'm hot shit because of it. I don't need other people to agree with me. I can feel that way all by myself. Maybe in a month or two or more, I can feel that way all the time.

March 20

I want to toss my virginity like a salad: quickly, casually, tastefully. And soon. Because it's about to get really muggy in the South. That's not a euphemism. Well, but maybe it is.

Virginity is not that big of a deal. I used to think that the difference between people who had and hadn't had sex was the way Esther Greenwood described it in *The Bell Jar*—that people who had done it had something in their eyes that marked them as separate—but I know now that this isn't true. I know because there was this couple in high school who lorded the fact that they were having sex over everyone as if they knew so much more about it, or as if everyone who hadn't had sex thought they were doing something crazy and terrible. In reality I just thought it was healthy and normal, and nothing in their eyes signified a difference. There was no image of the other person suspended in their pupils.

Sex is not the only thing that's been on my mind. The most important things to me right now are as follows: (1) getting accepted into one of the colleges I applied to so that I can transfer, (2) RuPaul, (3) Carrie Bradshaw's happiness and fulfillment, and (4) getting over high school.

But I'm ready, you know, to "lose my innocence." Also, it's ridiculous that losing your virginity is referred to as a *loss of innocence*. Why do we have such negative terminology for something that is, like, totally not bad at all?

I'm going to keep on praying to Samantha Jones and making eyes at all the cute boys.

April 3

I know that saying "I can't wait for summer" is stating the obvious. I'm like the person who climbs the stairs and says, "I guess this is my exercise for the day"—something I hear/gag at too many times each day as I climb the stairs in my dorm. But honestly, I can't wait for summer. The only interesting thing that's happening in my classes right now is that I suspect one

of my professors has the horn for a student. Their interactions are providing me with what my class discussions and slow social life don't currently offer me: something interesting. Otherwise, school is a total drag. Here are the main reasons why:

1. My speech professor recently told me that since so many of my speeches have centered on RuPaul, I can't mention him anymore during presentations. He wants me to branch out more in my topics AS IF RuPaul isn't one of the most important humans ever!!! What's this professor's damage!?

2. I've been taking cues from Samantha Jones and flirting with everyone, and I'm discovering that all my top cuties are real evangelical, which is a problem because it means that we have incompatible beliefs, and I don't approve of foisting religion on others. When I asked one dude what he does for fun he started talking about Campus Crusade for Christ. When I told him I'm not a believer, he tried to persuade me to consider faith as an option and to come to a Wednesday meeting. These boys like talking about their "callings," but I feel like they're the type of dudes who'll grow up to say things like "My wife is always right, *hyuck hyuck hyuck*. When she asks me if she looks fat in her jeans, I always say no, *hyuck hyuck hyuck*. Men aren't worthy of women, *hyuck hyuck hyuck*." Then these same men often turn out to be super bad at genuinely loving the women they say are omnipotent and omniscient. This spring and summer are not likely to yield any cute Satan-loving boys, but the fall might, provided I am admitted to one of my transfer schools. (Thinking about that makes me nearly poop my pants in fear, which will maybe repel all the preachy boys.)

3. I had a minor breakdown this week after taking my first puff of weed. I was convinced that I had somehow burned my throat and would have to ingest food and liquid through a tube for the rest of my life. I cried, walked rapidly all around our yard and house (to cool my throat off with a gentle breeze), and met any of my brother's attempts to help me with hostility. Fifteen

minutes later, after accepting a glass of milk and a cigarette, I apologized profusely and tearily. This prompted my brother to tell me, "You're like a virus that enters someone's body and is like, 'Hi, uhh, sorry for being here, but I'm about to make you sick.'" Then he goes, "But it's fine. There are cool viruses." My insecurity levels are out of control, and I need to work on not apologizing for my existence to everyone I talk to. However, I can't progress with my personality until I get out of a place that gives me perma-bitchface, and until I rid myself of my anxiety over transferring and the fact that I feel stupid every day for coming here in the first place. ALSO, in order to get better at interacting with humans, you have to interact with humans, and I'm not doing too much of that currently.

You know that feeling you get when you're sort of expecting a text from someone and you keep looking at your phone while you wait? That's how I'm going to feel until the moment I hear back from the schools I applied to—that should be in the middle of May. Where is Carrie Bradshaw when you need her to rub your belly and tell you everything will be all right? (Answer: shopping! *Women*, am I right? *Hyuck hyuck hyuck*.)

April 24

Saturday afternoon I got a text from my dad saying that I got a letter from one of the colleges I applied to. He asked if I wanted him to open it right then and there. After an internal debate that lasted longer than it would have taken me to drive over to the house, read the letter, steal some potato chips, and drive back, I said yes, then stared at my phone for an excruciatingly long five minutes. He finally texted me back: I had been accepted. I was so excited that I took a celebratory nap (suspense wears me out), then offered to buy my brother dinner. Later that night I brought some food to my parents' house and told my brother the news. He screamed, ran around, and then tackled me.

The college I'm at now is a short drive from the house I grew up in. It feels more like an extra year of high school than like a whole new adventure or whatever college is supposed to be. It's a conservative and vaguely Christian school; talking about anything the slightest bit risqué, even if it's just sexual euphemisms in a poem, is frowned upon by faculty and students alike. And even though I was raised in the South, I'm having a hard time relating to most of these people, because all conversation and behavior down here is ruled by an obligation to be *polite* above anything else. Also, the school I go to now doesn't allow me to participate in a lot of the extracurricular activities I'm interested in; the new one does. I'm ready to be a real human who interacts with other humans outside of class again. But the thing I'm looking forward to most of all is not having to act like I've seen *The Matrix*.

All the freshmen at my school had to watch *The Matrix* in this class you're required to take your first semester, but I missed the second half of the movie in order to sleep in. Since then I've willingly lied about having seen it to SO MANY of my instructors and peers. Basically everyone I talk to wants to talk about, or at least reference in some way, *The Matrix*. Teachers regularly bring it up in class discussions. I know it's a popular movie, but, like, there are other movies.

Anyway, I get to transfer this fall, and if I discover that everything around me is an illusion created by robots that took over the world and I have to spend the rest of my life playing video games in a spaceship (that's as far as I got in the movie), I'm going to scream.

RUBY B.

June 6, 2012
I do NOT want to go to my current school next year. I don't want to be with these people. There are four or five, perhaps, that I like. I can't even really call all of them friends. That's because they aren't. We are just mutually tolerant.

Everyone knows about my mom dying, so everyone keeps feeling sorry for me and tiptoeing around like I'm about to explode. I have nothing in common with anyone, and I feel like that will never change unless we move, which my dad says we might.

I am not extremely unpopular at school or anything. I was nominated to give the graduation speech this year (as if middle school counts) by my peers. I just feel like an outsider who happens to be somewhat liked.

People act uncomfortable around me. I don't blame them. They feel bad for me. I wish they wouldn't. Then again, I wish someone would stop pretending nothing happened. I want someone to talk to. I can't trust or relate to anyone here. I need to go.

September 19
I babysit a little girl named Saigon. She is three, has a pixie haircut, and is really great. I usually find kids her age annoying and hard to deal with, but I love Saigon. She is a lot of fun.

When I go over, she pretends not to notice me for a few minutes and then demands that we go up to her room RIGHT THIS SECOND because the sick baby animals NEED us! It always begins with sick animals. Saigon is the doctor and I am her assistant. Soon she forgets about her animals and climbs into the large trunk in the middle of the room, shutting the top. I tell her that it's dangerous and cover the top with a blanket instead. She sits there silently, very still, for a few minutes before bursting out with a new idea for a game. We are now two queens who rule over Closetopia.

Queen Saigon yanks open the closet door and goes inside. When I was three I was far too afraid of the dark to do something like that. In fact, I'm still a little hesitant when Saigon ushers me inside.

"So, is this Closetopia?" I ask.

"No. Now this is where the Queens hide when bad people look for them."

"Bad people?"

"Witches."

She tells me to be quiet so the witches don't hear us, and to hold her hand so she'll know I'm still there in the dark.

Out of nowhere, Saigon bursts through the closet door. I follow her, blinking at the light. "We have to be witches now! They know where we are!" she says. Digging through the mounds of toys and clothes and stuffed animals, Saigon eventually finds what she is looking for. She puts a

witch hat on her head and a pink tutu on mine. Now we are evil witches.

We brew up a potion in the backyard made of juice from the fridge and twigs from the ground. Then Saigon throws an imaginary person inside it. She runs upstairs to her trunk and throws a blanket over herself.

Five minutes later she comes out as a giant, smashing villages with her giant feet, scaring even the witches. She goes back to her trunk and comes out a bride. Into the trunk again, now a superhero. She pulls out an issue of *People* from a drawer and asks me to read to her. She sits on my lap in her cape and witch hat.

I read her a story about a celebrity wedding.

"Your mommy was a princess, right?" she asks me. She doesn't wait for an answer. "I wish she wasn't killed by the witches. Then she could marry your daddy again and live happily ever after, right?" I don't say anything, and for a moment neither does she. "Can I watch *Dora* now?"

October 3
I haven't really written about this in my diary entries yet, but it's a big part of my life, so I thought I'd finally share it instead of randomly bringing it up in passing: I have depression, anxiety, and (according to medical-history papers I found in my kitchen) "eating disorder not otherwise specified." I have a therapist whom I talk to about the first two things, and I've been to an eating disorder clinic a couple of times. I've been depressed for so long that I often wonder if maybe it's just my personality and there's nothing that can be done about it—I'm just a cynical, sad person. But when I see old pictures of myself and think back to a *really* long time ago, I realize that I used to be mostly happy. Now the most I hope for is an occasional happy day amid a sea of days where it's actually hard for me to get out of bed.

I was going to write about this earlier. I wrote a diary entry back in May about how stressed and angry I was about my life in general. I emailed it to Anaheed to edit, and a day or two later I had to ask her not to, because I found out my mom had passed away. She had left our house a few days earlier. I thought she would come back. Sometimes she would get really upset and have to leave for a while, but she always came back.

Since my mom died, I've worried constantly about everything. I have had dreams about my little brother going missing almost every night for months. Sometimes I save him. Sometimes I don't, and then I can't function for the rest of the day. People get mad at me for acting unfriendly and antisocial.

I often stay up until 1 AM, putting off my homework because I'm so scared of dealing with thoughts of failure. When I try to sit down and accomplish something, it's so overwhelming that I physically cannot bring myself to do it. It's not laziness. I really, really try, but I end up sitting at my desk for three hours staring at a textbook, too afraid of not absorbing the material to even read it.

If I hear my name, I jump. I pace around, I bite my nails constantly. Nothing makes me more upset than being talked down to or scolded, even about the tiniest things—it feels like affirmation that I've always done everything wrong. It's really hard for me to take criticism—not because of my ego, but because I can't communicate that I'm already trying as hard as I can.

I didn't even know what anxiety was until recently. My therapist asked me to consider some medication for my depression and anxiety. When I talked to my dad about it, he said no without missing a beat. He was worried about the side effects, and how difficult medications like that are to get off of.

I never thought I would have an eating disorder, and in fact I don't think what I have now is serious enough to be considered a "real" one. I'm at a weight that is considered "healthy" by doctors. But something made me get yelled at for years about my eating habits by my parents, and something made my therapist refer me to an ED clinic. I'm not ashamed of it or anything, but I don't have much else to say about it. Food is just one more thing to get stressed about for me, one more thing to get yelled at for, one more thing to make me want to never see anyone again. I don't

have a good relationship with it. That's really all there is to it.

My week was uneventful but I felt I needed to say this. This isn't a sympathy-seeking entry or anything. My feelings and thought processes affect me and everything I do, and I figure if I'm telling you about my life every week, I may as well include this stuff, too.

February 5, 2013
The boy and I were sitting in his basement and listening to the Smiths when I got about six thousand phone calls to come home. I asked for a ride please from his mother.

We got in the back of the minivan. It was getting kind of dark, and I needed to be home soon to babysit my little brother while my granddad took my sister to dance practice. The car came to a halt.

"Bye," he said. No. I liked hanging out with him. I didn't want to say bye.

"No, come out, I want to tell you something."

"Walk her to the door," said his mother. She thrives on politeness.

As we approached the door, my grandfather and my sister emerged from it.

"Bye," he said again.

"Wait a second," I said.

We watched Bumpa and Celia get into the car and drive off.

"Wait," I said again, and I kissed him. And then he tried to kiss me and missed and tried again.

We hugged for a minute. I said, "I really like you," and so did he. Our arms unhinged and he said "thank you" or something.

I went inside to call my friends. Most of them seemed surprised that I could kiss someone without having a panic attack or prediscussing hygiene. A few said, "Ugh, now I'm going to be the last one to have a first kiss."

He called me and we talked about nothing for a long time. I think he's going to ask me out. I like him a lot.

March 20
A big X slashed into the door. Everything is ripped. Everything is destroyed. Nobody is home, so I can play my music really loud without fear of getting in trouble.

Sometimes I think for sure that I am going crazy, and I love it more than I should. I feel out of control. I'm sassy and obnoxious. There is nothing inside me, I have nothing to lose. On these days I have learned that I have no choice but to accept and embrace the emptiness. It's very refreshing to write all over your arms with lipstick and sing at the top of your lungs and break everything in reach and ignore everyone and not give a fuck.

But when I'm not spinning out of control and laughing madly to myself, I am carrying around something else, someone who sits on my back and whispers about how I am the *worst thing that has ever happened* and how everything in my life is awful and nothing is really worth living for. The darkness inside me convinces me that the world is a bad place, and nothing means anything. I feel this overwhelming anger. Meds don't seem to drive it away. Maybe it's just who I am. Maybe I am an angry person naturally, and no matter what happens, I will always be angry with myself and the world and everything I know.

Right now I'm having one of those empty moments where I go for a several-hours-long "walk," but really I am just sitting on the sidewalk behind Staples, staring into space and trying to remember what my favorite song is. It is all mechanical. It is a world without time, where there is no past to remember and no future to consider. Happiness is becoming less and less frequent. I don't remember what it feels like.

April 3
"You can wear your own clothes," says the doctor, "and your roommate will share a closet with you." I nod, still somewhat numb from hours before. Where is my mind? "You'll also have to remove your shoelaces and any other strings or belts on your clothes."

My unlaced Doc Martens flap under my leather pants. I drag my feet a little because it is hard to walk. The doctor swipes a card over a panel by the door—nobody without one can get in or out. Every door, every window, every room is locked.

The hospital walls are pale blue and yellow. There are many armchairs that look comfortable but are in fact rough and filled with air instead of fluff. It's like sitting on a burlap balloon. I see other people my age and suddenly become very aware of my eyeliner smudged all over my face, my ridiculous un-laced boots, and my baggy leather pants that I put on this morning because I forgot I hate pants. I realize that I don't care at all.

One girl looks familiar. She gives a little wave and I return it. The day is going by so fast and yet so slow, so I don't remember whether I know her or not. Is she my friend? Does she go to my school? She looks bored.

I am shown my room, which contains two plain beds with pale vomit-green quilts and plastic pillows, and one small desk nailed to the wall. The closet is locked and the window has a layer of glass over the blinds. "So we don't hang ourselves from them," a boy tells me later. There are no books or pencils or stuffed animals or pictures. There is no way to tell if someone has lived or is living in this room. I do not like not knowing things.

The girl I know waves me over. "I wouldn't expect you to be in this kind of hospital," she says, sounding bored as ever.

"Me neither. About you, I mean." I have no idea how I know this girl.

"That girl there? She's pregnant but she tried to OD anyway. That boy stabbed his twin brother."

"Oh," I say, not really hearing her. I'm in such a daze that I can't be fazed.

"That girl there? She's been here for 27 days." The day I leave, she'll have hit 40. Soon I will find out she has nowhere to go.

"That one with the red shirt just has anger issues or some shit."

"Oh, OK. Are you guys friends?"

"As good of friends as anyone could be in a place like this," she says with a bitter laugh. "So, no, but we don't hate each other or anything."

◆ ◆ ◆

On the first day, I learn the rules. No touching anyone, ever, not to brush lint off them or high-five or ANYTHING, but ESPE-CIALLY no hugging. No stuffed animals in common areas. If you're a smoker, you don't

get the patch, so watch out for the irritable kids on withdrawal. You get watched in the shower. No using a pen. No having a pen. Don't disobey the staff. Don't try to open any doors. No leaving. (Where would you go? There are only three rooms.) Eat your food. No shoelaces. No hanging yourself with the cord on the phone. No throwing things at people, especially tables and chairs. No eating things that aren't food.

We do "check-in." The staff describes it as when we all say how our day is going and introduce ourselves to new patients. A fellow patient describes it to me as "We all go around in a circle and say what's wrong with us and what we did today." I don't remember most of the names. I just hear severe OCD, anger management problems, self-harm, homicidal tendencies, PTSD from being raped, drug problems, suicide attempt. The list goes in a circle. Most of them look bored and tired, like they've been here far too long. I realize that one girl has not felt the air outside of these three rooms for almost a month. No open windows, no open doors, no going outside.

◆ ◆ ◆

First night. Roommates with night terrors = being woken up by screaming every five minutes, so that idea I had to get some sleep isn't really panning out. Besides, there is a man sitting on a chair 10 feet from me, and all the lights are on. That's how you have to sleep if they think you are a danger to yourself or others. I ask him to turn off one light. I ask to be moved. I asked for a female staff member. But here in the hospital they have better things to worry about, like making sure nobody gets stabbed or something, so my pleas are in vain. I protest by stripping my bed, throwing my mattress onto the floor, and standing on the wooden bed frame, staring the watchman in the eyes for hours on end until his shift is over. The next one arrives and I say nothing, I just stare.

This act of silent protest is literally not worth losing sleep over, I discover the next morning as I'm struggling to stay awake at breakfast. It's my first morning at the hospital. I get a slice of burnt bread and a

plastic spoon to spread a hunk of butter on it (no knives allowed). I am starving and I devour it, promising myself I'll try to make the most of this experience. I almost tore my family apart. I owe it to them to get better.

A bulimic boy of about 12 is super-vised in the bathroom after breakfast. He comes back and throws up right there in the lunchroom. Right before being hurried away by a team of nurses, the boy takes a moment to give one of the staff members a hard, menacing look that feels like a dare.

◆ ◆ ◆

"What are you here for?" I ask a girl who earlier refused to tell me her name. Her eyes are very round and give her a perma-nently surprised expression.

"Homicidal thoughts, self-harm, killing small animals. You?"

I pause to take that in, then mumble an answer.

"Oh, so just the usual," she says. "Tons of kids here are just like you. There are only a handful of me here in the nonaggressive unit. I'm a sociopath."

"Are you really?" I say.

"Yeah. I've always wanted to kill, even when I was a kid, so I must be."

"Do you care about things? About peo-ple?" I ask her.

She looks thoughtful for a minute, counting off something on her fingers. "No, not really. I don't."

◆ ◆ ◆

A few days pass. The girl I know, the bulimic boy, and the self-proclaimed so-ciopath have all been discharged by now, and there's "a new batch of psychos," I hear another patient say under her breath. When one of the new kids arrives it's clear he's just been crying. He's wearing hospital clothes, which is what they give the kids who come directly from a regular medical hospital. Isn't bloody or obviously drugged up or anything, so people whisper about what on earth he was doing in a regular hospital.

"I tried to jump off a bridge."

I am silent and look down. The boy is

about my age and when he says this I can hear the shame in his voice—not for trying, but for failing.

"I tried," he continues. "It didn't work. The police found me standing up there and grabbed me when my back was turned."

"Why do you hate life so much?" asks a staff member. For some reason, this question fills me with rage. She obviously doesn't know what she's talking about.

"I don't hate life," the boy says through his teeth. "I hate *mine*. The purpose of life is to be happy. I am not, so I have no purpose."

"Actually, the purpose of life is to reproduce," says another kid, probably thinking she's clever.

"Well, I can't do that either," he says. "I'm trans."

There's a silence, and then a pregnant girl who can't be older than 14 says, "What is trans?"

♦ ♦ ♦

I talk to my therapist and my psychiatrist and my doctor and my social worker. I tell them how I'm doing, and since I've been here (and therefore not at school) for a week, I can honestly report that I'm doing well. I haven't tried anything they'd worry about and I've been sleeping well. I've eaten at every meal and talked in group therapy. I've called my friends.

I talk to Mancala about Zach the Boyfriend all the time. He talks to me about his ex who he's still in love with. Mancala is the boy who tried to jump off a bridge. I call him that because that's the game we play together—we like it because it is mindless, so we can talk without being written up for suspicious behavior. He has on pink pajama pants, the only clothes his family would give him. "They think that if I wear pink I'll be a girl somehow. It'll give me an epiphany or something."

"I'm sorry," I say.

"It's OK. My name's legally changed and I've started testosterone, so maybe when I look more the part they'll understand." I hope he's right. Mancala is a good person and it's horrible to see good people in bad situations.

♦ ♦ ♦

"Hi, Zach," I say brightly on the phone every day. Zach the Boyfriend is my most frequent call. I take up the one patient phone for about an hour once or twice an afternoon to talk to him, and it's a relief to speak to someone without worrying what notes they're taking on you, or whether they think you're crazy. He already knows that I am and he seems pretty OK with it.

Some people make it all about them, treating my hospitalization like an act of betrayal against them personally, asking why I don't call more, they need me to call more. Making me feel guilty for focusing on myself during my treatment. But others pass the phone around the room and say hello and act normal and say they miss me and they are glad I'm OK. We will see each other soon; it was really good to talk to you, I miss you, I don't know how you are surviving in there without music; we wish we could visit you. Oh, and by the way, so-and-so broke up with so-and-so!

I know I have a strong support system back home. I change my medication to something that will hopefully work for me (and I try one that goes very wrong). My dad visits me every day and once he brings my siblings.

I look out the window and long for fresh air. I hope I can check out the radio for my room later tonight because I heard it's '90s week on 95.5. I haven't listened to music in a week and a half. The numbness in my head seems to have cleared and is replaced by homesickness, which I think is a good sign.

I care about things.

I wear sweatpants and Skechers. I feel slovenly. I can't wait to go back to eyeliner and hair conditioner and skirts.

♦ ♦ ♦

It's finally my last day. It was postponed, but now it's day 13 and I can finally leave this place. I can go back to fresh air and my friends and food that wasn't frozen several times. I can drink something that isn't milk. I can take my meds in the morning without waiting in a humiliating line and

having to open my mouth for the nurse to check that I'm not hiding anything.

I say goodbye to Mancala.

"Don't hug him," a staff member who says "fustrated" instead of "frustrated" warns.

I give a final goodbye to the group and walk out the doors with my dad and the escort who has the power to open doors. I feel new air that I haven't felt in two weeks. The world is so bright. I am going to the partial program from 8 to 2 tomorrow, and I'm going to be getting more help. I don't mind. I can't wait to go home.

May 22

I wake up at 6 AM to my two alarm clocks and a phone call, like every morning, and then wake up again at 6:45, also like every morning. I wouldn't wake up at all if Dad weren't yelling from downstairs. I finally roll out of bed. I remember, like I do every morning, that being awake entails seeing people and doing things. My stomach drops.

I try to get dressed and do my makeup in the 15 minutes before the bus comes. All my clothes are black and I can barely see with sleepy eyes, so I fumble around and put on whatever I grab first, which ends up being my leather skirt and a T-shirt. I hate wearing T-shirts.

I trudge to the bathroom, halfheartedly dab some powder on my face, and swipe a blob of black over each eye. I push everything on the counter into my bag so I can do a better job once I get to school. My bag is dull camo green. It is heavy, which is funny because I don't use any of the stuff I haul around in it.

I don't want to hate things. I don't want to be a walking stereotype like Janis Ian, who exists only to embody melodramatic teenage angst, represented through knotted black hair, torn-up clothes, and too much makeup. But I *am* a walking stereotype. I've accepted it.

The bus arrives. I get on. I fake a cheery "good morning" to the driver like I do every morning, because she bought me a hat once and remembers my name. I see people staring at me because they know the bus won't move until I sit down. My heart races because for a second, so many eyes are watching my every move. I almost trip as

I speed-walk to the back, where the empty seats are. It's always the same people in the empty backseats. One boy is in my history class. I don't know the rest. One of them cries silently every morning in the last seat.

I try to listen to Arcade Fire. I put on *Funeral*, my favorite album. I hate it. I hate music in the morning. I put my headphones away and stare out the window. It looks humid somehow. It might be the gray sky, which I associate with heat since living in China. In China it was air pollution. Today, here, it is overcast. It is ominous almost-rain, like a pimple that hasn't broken the surface yet and is just a raised bump, not even red.

I get off the bus. "Thank you, have a good day!" I take out my list notebook. I flip through the pages for the next blank one. I pull a pen out of my pocket. *People I Need to Avoid Today.* Four people. I draw out my route to all my classes and find out where it will overlap theirs. The schedule is all jumbled today because of standardized tests, so the morning is completely full of seeing people I can't see. I can't go into school.

My black velvet jacket is almost knee-length, terrible quality, and ripped up. It weighs down my shoulders as I walk away from the school. I hear a few people calling out "witch" faintly in the background, but it doesn't bother me. It used to, but I'd pretend not to care. Now I really don't. I'm a nihilist. I barely hear other people. Their opinions are irrelevant.

I walk past the kids smoking pot behind the tennis courts. They say hi and I just nod, because I don't smoke and I don't feel like talking. Besides, there's not much to talk about. I trudge away, my hair falling in a sheet around my head. I'm so tired. Every part of me is exhausted. I'm mentally tired out of my mind. I walk deeper into the woods behind the courts until I can't see any houses.

I turn on my phone and put *OK Computer* on repeat. I lay my backpack on a soft-looking area of dirt. I lie on my side, facing my phone, bag under my head like a sack of rocks. I hope nobody comes by. They'll think I'm trying to look poetic or romantic or dramatic or something. I just want to be alone.

I fall asleep. I dream the same dream I always do, where I need to scream but I can't, or at least not loudly enough. My throat is buzzing, but I can't use my lungs. I grow dizzier with every attempted yell.

I wake up. The buzzing was my phone. I ignore it and try to go back to sleep, where even nightmares are nice because they are in the moment, and when scary things happen you don't have to think.

I look at pictures of people I miss. Why do I do that? It's so fucking stupid. I hate myself when I do that.

I'm not tired at all. I try to fall asleep again but can only succeed for a few minutes.

At lunchtime I walk back to school, looking a mess and not caring in the least. I'm too exhausted to care. I want to see my friends. I live for them almost completely and can give up a few minutes of my nice little solitude for them.

I check my phone. My dad got a call saying I never showed up to school. I feel too exhausted to panic. I panic anyway. *He's going to call the police. He's going to put me back in the hospital.*

A teacher finds me in the lunchroom.

"Ruby, looks like this is for you." My friends have grown used to watching me be escorted away.

"Oh, shit." I say a goodbye as I'm led to the office.

I want to be in the woods again. I want to be alone and asleep.

May 29

A year ago I could not hug people. I could not hold hands with anyone. The idea of kissing someone almost gave me a panic attack. I hated all physical human contact. I still do sometimes, but in recent months, I've started to mind it less and less. It turns out that exposure to some very touchy friends is the best therapy. It's all hugs and cuddling with them.

I spent most of Saturday with Sam, and then with all my friends at his house. At some point we walked into town and got food. Sam, Ben, and I got lost in the woods. We watched *Mystery Men* in Sam's basement. Ben sat on my lap texting his girlfriend, and everyone else was in a heap. Eventually the others left and Sam piled onto Ben and me, and we all cuddled together for hours. One of us said "I love you guys" every minute or so.

Two of my best friends and darkness and warmth. Snuggling, I realized, is one of the most heartwarming human instincts. It is not overrated. A void was being filled that I didn't know existed. Sure, I got affection from my parents, but friends are different. You rarely get a chance to express how much you all mean to one another.

Ben's phone chirped and he said goodbye. Sam and I didn't move as we listened to his feet ascending the hollow wooden stairs up to the kitchen. The basement was quiet and black except for the colored lights of the *Mystery Men* title screen, which illuminated our faces with blues and purples. My head was on Sam's chest, and I could hear his heartbeat and feel him breathing. I twitched occasionally, which I always do when I think too much about staying still. I thought about how I didn't want to leave, how I wanted to stay like this forever, but 11 PM was my curfew. "I have to go," I said, and didn't. Ten minutes passed. I finally summoned the willpower to go home.

I am happy.

I leave and my phone buzzes. It's Sam, with a line from the e.e. cummings poem, "a connotation of infinity":

a connotation of infinity
sharpens the temporal splendor of this night

I know exactly what he means. ❦

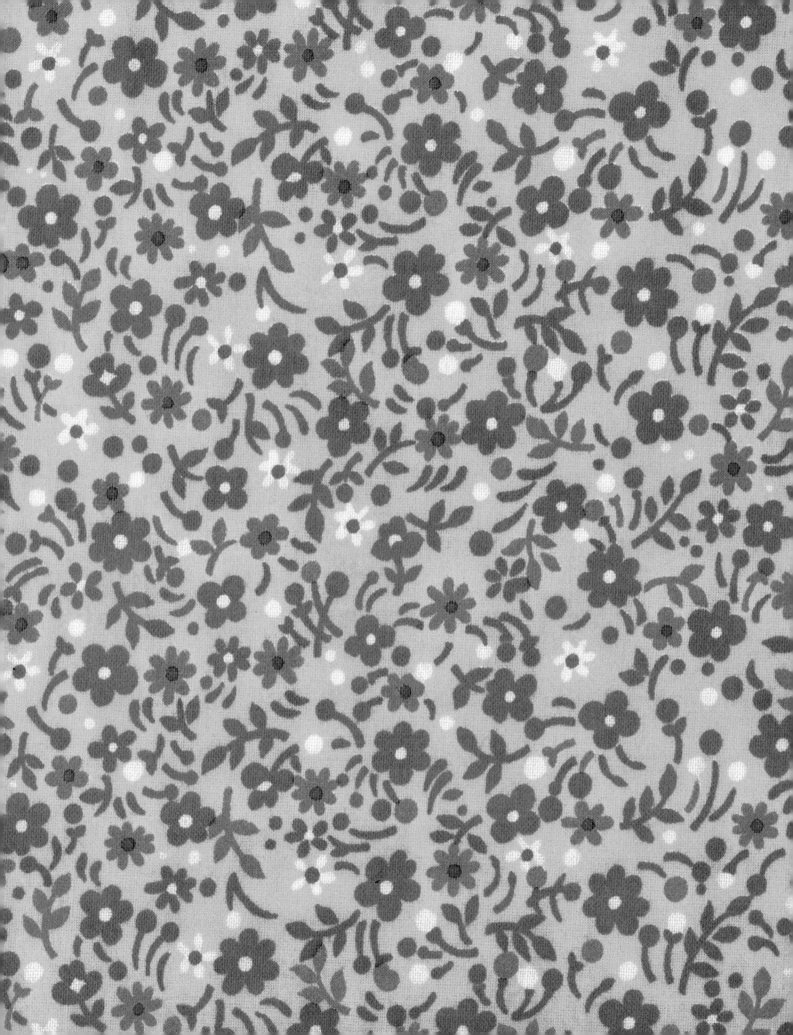

THE BEST OF
ROOKIE
IN PRINT!

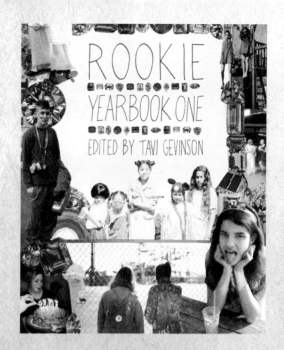

COLLECT ALL THREE BOOKS
FEATURING:

★LORDE★KELIS★
★SKY FERREIRA★
★EMMA WATSON★
★CLARESSA SHIELDS★
★SHAILENE WOODLEY★
★AMANDLA STENBERG★
★NEIL DEGRASSE TYSON★
★ZOOEY DESCHANEL★
★DAVID SEDARIS★
★MINDY KALING★
★LENA DUNHAM★
★MORRISSEY★
★GRIMES★

AND MORE!

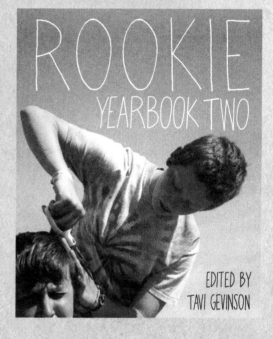

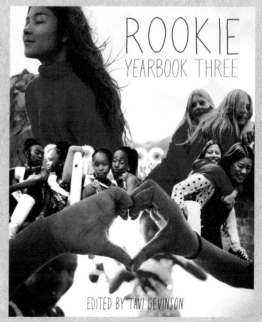

Rookie
You help make me
the badass B
I always wanted to
be. You Rule.
Always have faith.
Never give up!
Love
Katy ♥

to
ROOKIE -
Wow! I can't believe its
been a whole year!
HAGS GRRRL
Love always,
Allison C.

Dear Rookie,
Let's make out.
Love,
Arrow de Wilde

Dear Rookie Mag,
You're such a great bff.
It's been *SO FUN* getting to know
you this year, so glad we got to
sit next to each other in choir - ALTOS ROCK 4EVA!
Hope you have an AWESOME SUMMER!
♥
p.s. sorry i spilled
soup on your back!!